SCOTLAND:
THE MAKING AND UNMAKING OF THE NATION
c.1100–1707

The Uni

SCOTLAND:
THE MAKING AND
UNMAKING OF
THE NATION
c.1100–1707

VOLUME 2:
EARLY MODERN SCOTLAND: C.1500–1707

Edited by

Bob Harris and Alan R. MacDonald

DUNDEE UNIVERSITY PRESS

in association with

THE OPEN UNIVERSITY IN SCOTLAND

First published in Great Britain in 2007 by
Dundee University Press

University of Dundee
Dundee DD1 4HN

www.dundee.ac.uk/dup

ISBN 10: 1 84586 028 4
ISBN 13: 978 1 84586 028 8

British Library Cataloguing-in-Publication Data
A catalogue record for this book is available on request from the British Library

Typeset by Hewer Text UK Ltd, Edinburgh
Printed and bound in Great Britain by
CPI Antony Rowe, Chippenham and Eastbourne

Contents

Preface

This volume and the series of which it is a part represent the completion of project which began in the mid 1990s to facilitate the study of Scottish History in Scotland and beyond. A milestone was reached in 1998 with the launch of a module in Modern Scottish History – Modern Scottish History: 1707 to the Present. This module, and the five volumes which accompany it, have won consistently high praise from the students who have taken it, as well as strong commendation from many professional academics. Appropriately perhaps, with the project's completion in 2007, the 300th anniversary of the parliamentary union with England, anyone who wishes to will be able to study Scottish history from c.1100 to present day by distance learning.

In 1998, the editors said that it was a particularly appropriate moment to bring Scottish history to a new and wider readership and audience. This reflected, in the first place, the outcome of the 1997 Referendum, but also the evident depth of contemporary interest, expressed in a large variety of ways, in the Scottish past. It is no less true today. Indeed, if anything, the need and desirability of doing so is only greater with the first flush of post-devolution excitement over and the place of Scottish history in universities and schools not necessarily any stronger than it was a few years ago. And while popular history books are being written and published, and from 2003 *History Scotland* has been available on new agents' shelves, long established myths and preconceptions about the Scottish past still exert a very firm grip on general opinion and even on those who really should know better. Scottish history and Scotland deserve better than this.

These volumes aim to present recent academic research to a wider readership. As such they should be of interest to anyone with an interest in knowing about the Scottish past as well as the essential historical background to many present-day concerns and issues. They also provide a way for readers to develop their own skills as students of history, focusing on issues relating to the use (and abuse) of primary sources and the conceptual questions and challenges raised by specific topics. While we have left out some of the overtly pedagogical material which was included in the Modern Scottish History volumes, there is still plenty of discussion on sources and methods for interested readers to follow up.

The potential scope of these volumes is enormous, and this despite the fact that the sources and scholarship for the medieval and early modern periods are considerably less abundant than for the modern one. Any decision we might have taken about how to present the history of periods as long as *c.*1100–*c.*1500 and *c.*1500–1707 would have involved some awkward compromises. The first two volumes, comprising new essays by expert authors, start with a number of broadly chronological chapters, furnishing readers with a basic narrative. These chapters are followed by a range of more thematic ones. All the chapters are designed to offer a reasonably comprehensive introduction to recent work and, as importantly, a context or contexts for further reading and investigation. You will find there is some overlap between the chronological and thematic chapters, which offers scope for comparison between authors and for looking again at topics and themes from alternative perspectives. Some themes span the two volumes – for example, the Highland-Lowland divide, urbanisation, Scottish identity, Anglo-Scottish relations – so they can be traced over the 'long durée' and across conventional period divisions. There are no separate chapters on gender. Rather this theme has been deliberately blended in with other themes and topics. Some will not find this to their taste, but the aim is to present an inclusive, broad vision of the Scottish past, not one which segregates particular experiences. We have also chosen to include greater coverage of areas of cultural history than in the modern volumes. In part, this reflects recent trends in the writing of history – the so-called 'cultural turn' in historical studies – but also the wealth of scholarship which exists on such topics. It may also reflect something of an emancipation of scholars from the primacy of documentary sources, but then this no new thing for medievalists. Throughout both volumes a key theme which emerges, in terms of how we study the Scottish past, and also the patterns and meanings present in that past, is the importance of Scottish relationships and involvement in a broader European past. Let's hope the anniversary of the Union does not mask or detract from this theme, and the great strides which have been made in recent decades to recover this dimension to the Scottish past. The third and fourth volumes contain selected readings to accompany the topic/theme volumes, and should prove a great resource for those wishing to explore further a particular subject. The fifth volume is a collection of primary sources for the history of Scotland from c.1100 to 1707 designed to accompany the other volumes. It makes accessible documents of both local and national importance, quite a few of which have been specially transcribed for this volume. All students of history should want to read primary sources for the uniquely rich insight they furnish into the past. We also hope that they may encourage some readers to make their own forays into local archives.

This book represents a further product of the University of Dundee-Open University collaboration to offer modules in Scottish history to distance learning students. The modules are offered at honours level for undergraduates. However, all the volumes are designed to be used, singly or as a series, by anyone with an interest in Scottish history. Our hope is that they will inspire and deepen enthusiasm for the investigation of the Scottish past, perhaps even encouraging some to examine aspects of their own community history based on themes covered in the volumes.

From the outset, this project has depended on the efforts and enthusiasm of many people, and there are several major debts to acknowledge. Financial support for the development of these volumes was provided initially from the strategic fund of the Faculty of Arts and Social Sciences at the University of Dundee under the guidance of then dean, Professor Huw Jones. His successor, Professor Chris Whatley, has been a constant supporter, and has contributed his expertise to these volumes, as well as being an editor and contributor to the Modern Scottish History volumes. The Strathmartine Trust generously provided further vital financial support to facilitate the production of these volumes. Within the Open University, invaluable supporting roles have been played by Peter Syme, Director of the Open University in Scotland, and Ian Donnachie, Reader in History at the Open University. It is the shared commitment of individuals in both institutions, stimulated by the success and quality of the Modern Scottish History course, which has driven forward the continued development of the project. John Tuckwell, who published the Modern Scottish History volumes, and who commissioned the present volumes, has been a sage and encouraging adviser to the editorial team. The authors produced their contributions to agreed formats and, for the most part, to agreed deadlines. While they are responsible for what they have written, they have also been supported by other members of the writing team and our editors. Particular thanks are also due to Mrs Johanne Phillips, the secretary and administrator of the Modern Scottish History course, to her successor Elizabeth Bryant, and to Mrs Helen Carmichael and Mrs Sara Reid, secretaries in the Department of History, University of Dundee, for their administrative support. Thanks are also due to Jen Petrie who typed many of the texts for inclusion in the articles and documents volumes.

USING THIS BOOK

The chapters in volumes 1 and 2 include lists of books and articles for further reading. These lists are intended simply as guides to those who wish to follow up issues and topics covered in the volumes. They are not intended as obligatory further reading.

Series Editors

Contributors

Alison Cathcart, Lecturer, Department of History, University of Strathclyde, specialises in the history of the *Gàidhealtachd* and its relations with the rest of Scotland, Britain and Ireland in the early modern period. She has published a number of articles and the monograph *Kinship and Clientage: Highland Clanship 1451–1609* (2006).

E. Patricia Dennison, Director, Centre for Scottish Urban History, University of Edinburgh, has research interests in the history and conservation of Scottish towns. She has published widely on these areas, notably the Scottish Burgh Surveys funded by Historic Scotland.

Theo van Heijnsbergen, Lecturer, Department of Scottish Literature in the School of English at the University of Glasgow. His research and publications focus on early modern Scottish literature and culture, including *Literature, Letters and the Canonical in Early Modern Scotland* (2002), co-edited with Nicola Royan.

Charles McKean, Professor of the History of Scottish Architecture, Department of History, University of Dundee and Fellow of the Royal Society of Edinburgh, has published widely on Scottish architectural history. His twenty-two books include *Fight Blight* (1977), *The Scottish Thirties* (1987), *Edinburgh – Portrait of a City* (1992), *The Making of the Museum of Scotland* (2000), *The Scottish Château* (2001), and *Battle for the North* (2006).

Duncan Macmillan, Professor Emeritus, University of Edinburgh, art critic, former gallery director. His book *Scottish Art 1460–1990* was Scottish Book of the Year in 1990, and was updated and reissued in 2000 as *Scottish Art 1460–2000*. He is also the author of many other books and articles and is art critic for *The Scotsman*.

Maureen M. Meikle, Senior Lecturer in History, School of Arts, Design, Media and Culture, University of Sunderland, specialises in early modern social and political history. Her published works include *A British frontier? Landed Society in the Eastern Anglo–Scottish Borders 1540–1603* (2003) and *The Scottish People, 1490–1625* (2007).

Steve Murdoch, Reader, School of History, University of St Andrews. His major publications include *Network North: Scottish Kin, Commercial and Covert Associations in Northern Europe 1603–1746* (2006) and *Britain, Denmark-Norway and the House of Stuart 1603–1660: A Diplomatic and Military Analysis* (2003). He has also written a number of articles and edited collections of essays on Scotland's European links in the early modern period.

Derek J. Patrick, Research Fellow, Department of History, University of Dundee, specialises in parliamentary history. He has published 'Unconventional Procedure: Scottish Electoral Politics after the Revolution', in K.M. Brown and A.J. Mann (eds), *The History of the Scottish Parliament Vol. 2, Parliament and Politics in Scotland, 1567–1707* (2005), and, with Chris Whatley, *The Scots and the Union* (2006).

John Purser, Research Fellow and Gaelic Music Course Director at Sabhal Mòr Ostaig, the Gaelic college on Skye. He is best known for his award-winning book and radio series, *Scotland's Music*. A new series of fifty programmes is in preparation for BBC Radio Scotland and a revised and extended version of the book will be published in 2007. He is also a composer, playwright and poet and has published and lectured extensively on Scottish music world-wide.

Margaret H. B. Sanderson, former Head of Publications and Education, National Achives of Scotland, has published extensively on early modern Scotland, including *Cardinal of Scotland: David Beaton c.1494–1546* (1986) and *A Kindly Place? Living in Sixteenth-Century Scotland* (2002).

David Stevenson, Professor Emeritus, University of St Andrews, has written widely on early modern Scottish history. Notable publications include *The Scottish Revolution 1637–1644* (1973), *Revolution and Counter-Revolution in Scotland, 1644–1651* (1977) and *Scotland's Last Royal Wedding: the marriage of James VI and Anne of Denmark* (1997).

Margo Todd, Walter H. Annenberg Professor of British History, University of Pennsylvania, specialises in early modern British history and in the culture of Protestantism in Britain and early America. Her books include *Christian Humanism and the Puritan Social Order* (1987) and most recently the award-winning *The Culture of Protestantism in Early Modern Scotland* (2002).

Christopher A. Whatley, Professor of Scottish History, Vice-Principal and Head of the College of Arts and Social Sciences, University of Dundee and a Fellow of the Royal Society of Edinburgh. He has published numerous articles and books on early modern Scotland, his most recent publication being *The Scots and the Union* (2006).

Jenny Wormald, former fellow in Modern History, St Hilda's College, Oxford, specialises in late medieval and early modern Scottish political history. Her published works include *Lords and Men in Scotland* (1985), *Mary Queen of Scots: A Study in Failure* (1988) and *Court, Kirk and Community: Scotland 1470–1625* (1992).

Illustrations

CHAPTER ONE

Flodden to the Marian Civil War: 1513–1573

Maureen M. Meikle

In the period between the Battle of Flodden in 1513 and the end of the Marian Civil War in 1573 Scotland was dramatically transformed, from a Catholic to a Protestant country, from an ally of France to a friend of England. European dynastic politics propelled Scotland into a position of almost unprecedented international significance. The weakness of the Tudor line meant that, throughout their lives, James V and Mary, queen of Scots, were potential successors to the English throne through their descent from Margaret, sister of Henry VIII and wife of James IV. France, England, the Holy Roman Empire and Rome itself sought to influence this small, poor country at the edge of Europe. Internal factionalism and international rivalries came together as European powers, particularly France and England, built support for their causes within Scotland. The Reformation (see chapter 7) added a new complexity to political life, as religious affiliations played an increasingly important role in domestic and foreign policy. Another feature of Scottish politics, which provided significant continuities with the previous centuries, was the uncertainty and instability created by royal minorities, which took up forty of the sixty years covered by this chapter. Rule by an adult monarch was the exception rather than the norm, and James V and Mary faced significant challenges to the reassertion of the power of the crown.

THE MINORITY OF JAMES V

On the death of James IV at Flodden the crown passed to his 16-month-old son, who succeeded as James V. His mother, Margaret Tudor, became governor of Scotland and summoned the privy council to proclaim the new king, who was speedily crowned at Stirling Castle. With the sudden loss of so many senior nobles (twelve earls and fourteen lords were killed at Flodden) there was little opposition to Margaret's assumption of power. An estimated 10,000 foot soldiers also fell, leaving many widows and their families destitute. Edinburgh built its Flodden Wall in case of further English attacks, but too few were left to defend the burgh; Scotland was fortunate that the English were too busy with continental warfare to press home the advantage. There was also a serious shortage of labour to sow and harvest crops and look after livestock. It would be many years before Scotland recovered from Flodden.

Some surviving noblemen were suspicious of Margaret, for she was Henry VIII's sister. They therefore invited John, duke of Albany, nephew of James III, to return from France. Albany tactically delayed his response while Louis XII of France made peace with England and married Henry VIII's younger sister, Mary. Factions were coalescing in Scotland: Albany's champions, the chancellor James Beaton, archbishop of Glasgow, the chamberlain Alexander, third Lord Home, and James Hamilton, earl of Arran (a grandson of James II) opposed the Anglophile Douglases, led by Archibald, sixth earl of Angus, and his younger brother Sir George Douglas of Pittendriech. Queen Margaret sided with the Douglases, marrying Angus on 14 August 1514. She could be governor only while she was a widow, so was deposed by the privy council in December 1514.

Angus then provocatively attacked Chancellor Beaton at Perth and took the great seal from him, as whoever held it had symbolic power over the realm. Margaret appealed to Henry VIII for help, but events in France intervened with the death of Louis XII on 1 January 1515. Louis' successor, Francis I, distrusted Henry VIII and renewed the French alliance with Scotland in 1517 in the Treaty of Rouen. This stipulated that if England should make war against France, Scotland would come to her aid, and *vice versa*. Albany arrived at Dumbarton on 18 May 1515, with the French ambassador Anthony d'Arces, sieur de Labastie. Margaret at first refused to hand over James V and his brother Alexander, duke of Ross, to their new guardians, but eventually had to surrender them and Stirling Castle as Albany's support was stronger than hers.

The Douglases fled and Lord Home helped Margaret to escape, foiling Albany's plans to keep her under house arrest. She crossed the border at Coldstream and was escorted to Harbottle Castle in Northumberland, where she gave birth to Lady Margaret Douglas on 7 October 1515. It was an inauspicious start for the future countess of Lennox and mother of Lord Darnley. She and her mother were now totally dependent upon Henry VIII. The queen was so ill after the birth that her attendants feared to tell her that the duke of Ross had died.

Albany's grip on power was shaken by rebellions in the Lowlands and western *Gàidhealtachd*, but, before the rebels could gather their forces, Albany acted decisively against the most prominent rebel, the earl of Arran, and Angus was forced to desert Margaret in 1516 to preserve his influence in Scotland. Lord Home continued to intrigue with England, blaming Albany and de Labastie for maltreating his mother (she had been incarcerated in Dunbar Castle for six weeks for helping Queen Margaret escape). Albany's solution was to charge Home and his brother Mr William Home with treason and to have them both executed.

With his power over Scotland apparently secured, Albany returned to France in 1517, leaving government under a broad-based commission of regency, consisting of the archbishops of Glasgow and St Andrews, the earls of Angus, Arran, Argyll and Huntly and former ambassador de Labastie. As security, Albany took the eldest sons of the nobility with him to promote good government in Scotland. However, the kinsmen of the Homes still bore a grudge; they took revenge by capturing and beheading de Labastie. Albany was outraged but the earl of Arran, who was third in line to the throne behind Albany, saw his chance to assume power. He arrested Sir George Douglas (Angus's brother) and quickly pardoned the Homes. Arran's

Hamiltons were old rivals of the Douglases and in 1520 this culminated in an Edinburgh street battle known as 'Cleanse the Causeway', when seventy-two were killed, including Arran's brother Sir Patrick Hamilton. The Douglases then ousted the Hamiltons from their seat of power at Edinburgh. Clear political factions had now emerged, with the pro-English Douglases against the pro-French Hamiltons.

Albany reluctantly returned in November 1521 because of English attacks in the Borders, backed by the earl of Angus. Albany set about removing the Douglases from the offices that they had seized; Gavin Douglas, for example, was removed from the bishopric of Dunkeld. Albany now had the unexpected support of the queen, who was trying to divorce Angus and had changed sides to regain a role in government. Tension between Scotland and England returned in the summer of 1522 when Henry VIII declared war on Francis I, invading France twice during 1522–3. Henry was now in alliance with the powerful Holy Roman Emperor, Charles V. Albany appeared unperturbed by this as he was more conscious of the Scots' promise to aid France whilst under English attack. In June five hundred French soldiers arrived and Albany led an expedition towards the English West March during July. This was little short of disastrous as Queen Margaret betrayed Albany's plans to the English border warden, Lord Dacre. Albany was forced into a humiliating truce and had to travel to France to seek more aid from Francis I. He returned with 4,000 French soldiers, 500 horses and munitions to defend the frontier. But it was too late in the season to launch a major attack upon England. Instead, he sanctioned an unsuccessful raid on Wark on Tweed. Queen Margaret had returned to the pro-English camp and she helped broker Anglo-Scottish peace.

In collusion with Arran, Margaret now brought about a *coup d'état* that ousted Albany and his allies. Albany left for France whilst the 12-year-old James V was invested with the symbols of sovereignty on 26 July 1524. Parliament granted the keeping of James V to the queen; Henry VIII was so delighted that he made his nephew a knight of the Garter. Henry even tried unsuccessfully to arrange the marriage of James to his daughter Mary. Albany retained a claim to the throne and the defeat and capture of Francis I at the battle of Pavia, in February 1525, created a good deal of sympathy for France. The French ambassador sent to Scotland in June 1525 reminded the Scots that the Auld Alliance was still intact.

Arran and Margaret were in power until February 1525, when Angus returned and was appointed to the council. His power quickly grew and he sought control of the king. Parliament attempted to achieve reconciliation by giving custody of James to Margaret and control of government to Angus, but he refused to hand the king over. What followed was the most miserable time in the young king's life: Angus ruthlessly exploited James for his own benefit and that of his political allies. Queen Margaret and Arran switched their allegiance to France to oppose Angus and Margaret was remarried for a second time in March 1526 to Henry Stewart, later Lord Methven.

Abortive attempts were made to rescue James V in 1526, resulting in the murder of Andrew Ker of Cessford and the earl of Lennox. The power of the Douglases peaked in 1527 when Angus was chancellor, his uncle Archibald Douglas treasurer, his brother Sir George master of the household, James Douglas of Drumlanrig master of the wine cellar and James Douglas of Parkhead master of the larder. By 1528 the Douglases also dominated the privy council. In the absence of other nobles, many offices of state were given to able men of lesser rank, such as Adam Otterburn the lord advocate, James Colville of East Wemyss the comptroller and Sir Thomas Erskine of Haltoun the secretary. Thus began the participation of lairds in high office, a trend which continued throughout the sixteenth century.

It was the boldness of the 16-year-old king that overturned the Douglas monopoly. He escaped from their clutches in May 1528 and made for Stirling Castle. This stronghold was still held by his mother and stepfather, despite Angus's efforts to drive them out. The king's freedom precipitated Angus's downfall and flight into England.

THE PERSONAL RULE OF JAMES V, 1528–42

The adult James V had an uneasy relationship with his uncle Henry VIII for, like his father, he was caught between the Auld Alliance and the Auld Enemy. However, thanks to Angus's intervention, a five-year Anglo-Scottish peace treaty was signed on 14 December 1528. This was followed by a Scottish alliance with the Holy Roman Empire, but only after Francis I of France and Emperor Charles V had made peace in 1529. By the early 1530s the Anglo-Scottish truce became fragile as James continued to negotiate with France, England and the Empire. None of them wanted to provoke a war but James's position in the English succession made alliance with Scotland, particularly a marriage alliance, a prize worth pursuing. Charles V made him a member of the Order of the Golden Fleece in 1532, but this antagonised Francis I and threatened the Auld Alliance. To confound matters further, James almost went to war with England during 1532–3, prompted by a lack of redress for border misdemeanours and favour shown to Angus by English border officials. Scotland and England accused each other of breaking the peace. Two-way border raiding escalated and James raised his army during the winter of 1532–3. Full-scale war would not have been welcome and Henry VIII backed down. A new Anglo-Scottish peace was brokered by Francis I and a treaty signed in 1534.

Scotland, England and France may have been at peace, but both Henry and Francis wanted James to marry their daughters. For James, Henry VIII's breach with the Catholic church in 1534 proved an insurmountable obstacle to an English marriage alliance. He also declined offers from the Emperor, Denmark and Hungary. In 1531 he settled for the French royal bride promised in the Treaty of Rouen, but Princess Madeleine's ill-health led to postponements. In September 1536 James and his entourage finally left for France to solemnize the marriage. The contracts included a 100,000-crown (225,000 livres) dowry and the Auld Alliance was renewed. James and Madeleine were married at Notre Dame de Paris on 1 January 1537 to nationwide celebration. They sailed back to Scotland with her magnificent trousseau of lavish cloth, tapestries and jewels. Queen Madeleine's beauty and manners were praised by the Scots, but within months joy turned to sorrow: Madeleine's health deteriorated and she died on 7 July 1537. As soon as the official period of mourning was over, ambassadors were again despatched to France, leading to the proxy marriage of James to Mary of Guise-Lorraine, daughter of the duke of Guise and widow of the duke of Longueville. The duke of Guise gave James a dowry of 150,000 livres and Mary landed in Fife in June 1538 to a great welcome. Successive French marriages could have strained Anglo-Scottish relations to breaking point, but tensions were reduced with the birth of a son to Henry VIII in November 1537, which lessened the threat of a Franco-Scottish claim to the English throne.

Domestically, James had a mixed record. In 1528, royal finances were in disarray owing to the mismanagement of Albany and Queen Margaret. James IV had enjoyed annual revenue of around £45,000 Scots by 1513, yet by 1526 this had been reduced to £13,000. James was financially prudent and succeeded in raising the income from the crown estate to £24,000 by 1532. It continued to rise, reaching a peak of £37,630 in 1541. This was fortunate, as royal expenditure was always increasing with diplomatic missions, judicial expeditions, wars, a household of 300 to 350 and two successive queen consorts to pay for. Although feuing crown lands continued to be profitable, James readily exploited the immense wealth of the Catholic Church. He was allowed to place five of his nine illegitimate sons in charge of substantial abbeys and priories whilst they were only minors. This may have netted the king an extra income of as much as £40,000 a year, and his annual income may have approached an impressive £100,000 from 1539 to 1542. When he died, his coffers contained £26,000 in cash. He could well afford to spend money on arms, the navy and royal buildings to the benefit of monarch and nation.

James had some success in governing his elite, although several nobles were aggrieved by policies directed against them, particularly the earl of Angus, Lord and Lady Glamis and Sir James Hamilton of Finnart. James initially tried to reward the anti-Douglas faction by bestowing patronage upon them from the forfeited estates of Angus and his kinsmen. That James was able to spend a prolonged period in France in 1536–7, leaving Scotland in the hands of a commission of vice-regents, suggests firm confidence in the stability of his realm. This impression is reinforced by James's act of revocation in 1537, a traditional revenue-raising exercise by Scottish monarchs upon reaching the age of twenty-five. All land grants made since his succession had to be re-registered for a suitable fee. The nobility hated these costly and cumbersome measures and some feared that James had designs on their estates. To undertake such a move, James must have known that his grip on power was secure.

James's determination to rule with a firm hand was demonstrated after his return from France, when he sanctioned action against John, master of Forbes, and Dame Janet Douglas, Lady Glamis. Forbes was involved in a power struggle in the northeast with the earl of Huntly, who accused him of treason. He stood trial in July 1537 and was found guilty of plotting the king's death. Cameron hypothesised that Huntly may have 'manufactured the evidence' against Forbes and 'rigged the jury to obtain a guilty verdict' (Cameron 1998, 164). Lady Glamis's greatest misfortune was to be born a Douglas. She had married John, sixth Lord Glamis, but was a widow in 1528 when she was summoned before parliament on charges that she had assisted her outlawed brother, the earl of Angus, and his followers. She was also accused of poisoning her husband, but the trial collapsed and she married Archibald Campbell of Skipness, uncle of Scotland's chief justiciar, the earl of Argyll. This should have protected Lady Glamis, but in July 1537 she was convicted for conspiring to poison the king and was burned to death. Her estates were forfeited but mercy was shown towards her son, the seventh Lord Glamis, who had his execution commuted to a prison sentence on account of his youth. This shameful episode in Scottish history tarnishes the king's image but does demonstrate that adult Stewart monarchs could be 'men of terrifying power' (Wormald 1991, 14).

James's next victim was Sir James Hamilton of Finnart, a skilled politician, architect and influential courtier. He was a royal favourite, who had perhaps risen too far, too fast. He was beheaded in August 1540 for conspiring to kill James. There are several theories about Finnart's downfall (McKean 1993). Perhaps it was due to the misfiring of a new weapon of his own devising at Linlithgow, whereupon the king and his company had to run for cover. James V would have known that a malfunctioning cannon had killed his great-grandfather James II in 1460. Finnart was also associated with the maligned Douglases and had made an enemy of his ward James Hamilton, earl of Arran.

By 1540 European events again came to dominate Scottish affairs. The Catholic League of France and the Empire was under threat and James accepted an invitation to meet Henry VIII at York. He did so without consulting his full privy council, which subsequently advised him not to attend, so James informed his uncle that he could not meet him without the consent of Francis I. Councillors feared that Henry would detain the heirless James and force him to sever ties with France. Most historians agree that James was wise not to attend, but the snub certainly soured Anglo-Scottish relations. This was compounded by the break-up of the Catholic League. In a situation horribly reminiscent of western Europe in 1511–13, Protestant England allied with the Catholic Holy Roman Empire against Catholic France in 1542, demonstrating that the new factor of religious division did not need to dictate alliances.

Anglo-Scottish war seemed inevitable and Henry VIII was prepared, having already rallied his northern English forces in 1541. James V was far from prepared. He faced renewed division among his nobility, an inefficient army and an unreliable ally in France. Just as had happened in 1513, France let Scotland down. The final showdown came at Solway Moss on 24 November, when a seemingly cunning Scottish raid turned into a humiliating rout. The Scots found themselves trapped between the River Esk and a bog, nullifying their numerical advantage. Few were killed, but many were taken prisoner.

The birth of a daughter, Princess Mary, at Linlithgow on 8 December 1542 left James in despair of ever having a son to succeed him. Two legitimate sons, James and Arthur, were dead and James himself died on 14 December, possibly from cholera (Cameron 1998, 325). He had failed to smooth the factionalism of his court, yet he had managed to prevent a single faction from dominating for long. He had, after all, put down Douglases and Hamiltons alike, but pro-English and pro-French lobbies were poised to destabilise the country once more during the minority of Mary.

THE MINORITY OF MARY, QUEEN OF SCOTS, 1542–61

The earl of Arran and Cardinal David Beaton, archbishop of St Andrews, emerged as leading candidates for the governorship of Scotland. As before, it was the Scottish elite's inclination towards a French or English alliance which came to dominate policy. Arran favoured an English alliance and religious reform, whereas Beaton led the pro-French and Catholic faction. Mary of Guise distrusted Arran, but could not intervene as she was still recovering from the birth of her baby. Most leading nobles wavered, but Arran (as heir presumptive) was named governor and promptly issued an arrest warrant for Beaton. The apparent triumph of the pro-English party led to the 1543 Anglo-Scots treaties of Greenwich, which formed a military alliance and agreed to the marriage of the infant Queen Mary to the young Prince Edward of England. To allay Scots fears of English imperial ambitions, clauses were inserted guaranteeing that Scotland's laws and liberties would be preserved and that, should Edward die without issue from the marriage, Mary was free to return to Scotland.

Henry VIII failed to ratify the treaties within the agreed time limit and an act of English piracy led the Scottish parliament to renounce them in December 1543. Arran now abandoned England and the Reformation and joined the growing pro-French faction. Guardians were appointed to protect Mary and, inauspiciously, she was crowned on the anniversary of Flodden, 9 September 1543. The pro-French Arran, Lennox and Argyll took part in the ceremony, but those like Angus who remained inclined to England boycotted the event. Noble alliances were never firm though, and Lennox swapped sides soon afterwards, securing the backing of Henry VIII for a bid to become governor of Scotland. Henry was happy to exploit divisions in Scotland as a means to extend his sway over the whole of the British Isles. As diplomacy failed after the Scots' denunciation of the Treaties of Greenwich, Henry turned to military intervention.

The subsequent war, now known as the 'Rough Wooing', involved invasions by the earl of Hertford in 1544 and 1545, and the devastation of much of southern Scotland. The Scots were taken by surprise and Haddington, Leith and Dunbar to the south of the Forth and Kinghorn, Pittenweem and Burntisland in Fife were badly damaged. Religious houses at Newbattle, Musselburgh and Haddington were also sacked. The Scots had little foreign aid, while the English army was reinforced with mercenaries from Ireland, Spain and other parts of Europe. To make things worse, some Scottish borderers assisted Hertford in 1544. They were probably 'assured Scots', who had been bribed and intimidated into siding with Henry VIII (Merriman 1968; Donaldson 1983, ch. 2). France also offered pensions to Scots willing to adhere to the Auld Alliance. In the *Gàidhealtachd*, raiders who attacked Arran, Bute and Dunoon were following chiefs who had opportunistically sworn allegiance to

Henry VIII. The claimant to the Lordship of the Isles, Donald Dubh MacDonald, had 4,000 followers and was in receipt of an English pension, but his death in 1545 put paid to this particular Henrician ploy to destabilise Scotland (see chapter 6).

A Scottish victory at Ancrum Moor in February 1545 was a reminder that French money was as good as English for gaining the borderers' allegiance. However, this humiliation of the English and the late intervention of some French forces provoked a second major offensive under Hertford, which devastated much of the Merse and Teviotdale. The English use of Spanish mercenaries led to vicious fighting and the wealthy monasteries of Dryburgh, Jedburgh, Kelso and Melrose were attacked. English invasions failed to deliver the office of governor to Lennox and their savagery caused elite Scots to question their allegiance to England. Even the staunchly pro-English earl of Angus turned against Henry VIII after his ancestral tombs at Melrose Abbey had been desecrated by English forces.

The role of religion in the conflict, both internal and international, was highlighted in May 1546 when Cardinal Beaton was murdered by a group of Protestant Fife lairds. The rebels took control of St Andrews Castle, obtaining the nickname 'Castilians', whilst the earl of Lennox seized Dumbarton. Governor Arran recaptured Dumbarton, but failed to oust the Castilians, who held out for a year. Both England and France intervened, with French forces taking the castle in July 1547; many of those captured were imprisoned, some becoming French galley slaves, including the young John Knox. Lennox was forfeited and fled to England where he remained in exile for twenty years.

By the time of his death early in 1547, Henry VIII's military campaign in Scotland had failed to secure the marriage of Edward and Mary. Hertford, now Protector Somerset, maintained the English claim, returning in September 1547 with land and sea power. The Scots mustered one of the largest armies ever seen in Scotland but in the Battle of Pinkie (on 'Black Saturday', 10 September 1547) they were heavily defeated by a two-pronged attack on land and sea. It would be the last major Anglo-Scottish battle until 1650. The Scots lost around 6,000 men, with another 2,000 taken prisoner. England probably lost only between 500 and 600 men.

The English hold over Scotland was strengthened with the establishment of twenty-two garrisons from Broughty in the north to Dumfries in the south, an occupation which would not be paralleled until the Cromwellian conquest of Scotland in the 1650s (see chapter 3). With the notable exception of Marcus Merriman, few historians have given Henry VIII's Scottish policy during the 1540s the attention it deserves, preferring to concentrate instead on Anglo-French relations (Merriman 2000). Considering that these English campaigns in Scotland cost more than £1,000,000 sterling, this is a serious oversight.

Scotland was now an Anglo-French battleground and the infant Mary, queen of Scots, was sent to Inchmahome Priory, on the Lake of Mentieth, to prevent her being kidnapped by the English. French aid to Scotland was underpinned by a novel agenda. Instead of just giving military assistance in the true spirit of the Auld Alliance, France aimed to trump England by securing control of Scotland through a marriage. During a Franco-Scottish assault on the English garrison at Haddington in

1548, a treaty was signed agreeing that, in return for French help against England, Mary would marry the heir to the French throne, the Dauphin François, when she came of age. She left Scotland for France soon afterwards and, although Scotland's laws and liberties were guaranteed, many would have found this sudden capitulation to France hard to swallow.

Arran's acceptance of French intervention was fortunate for the Hamiltons: his half-brother John became archbishop of St Andrews and Arran himself acquired the lucrative French duchy of Châtelherault in 1549. The French soldiers that arrived in 1548 ultimately proved as unpopular as the English occupying forces in the 1540s. Nevertheless, these men were well-trained and also brought lucrative custom to Scotland's merchants and craftsmen. They helped to take back all the occupied fortifications; by the summer of 1550 the English had been driven out of Scotland and for that the Scots were grateful.

Mary of Guise now felt that Scotland was secure enough to allow her to visit France. She was accompanied by nobles who had remained loyal to Scotland (and France) during the 1540s, as well as some of the pro-English elite, whom she hoped to impress. Gordon Donaldson portrayed this as a 'brain-washing expedition', a propaganda campaign to woo pro-English Scots like Cassillis, Glencairn and Maxwell with French hospitality and pensions (Donaldson 1965, 80). Pamela Ritchie suggests less political motives, including those of a mother who wished to see her daughter (Ritchie 2002, 62–5). Many Scots nobles received substantial rewards from Henry II and Scotland, for once, was at peace with England, France and the Empire.

Whilst Arran enjoyed his French-assisted governorship, Mary of Guise bided her time. The death of Protestant Edward VI of England in 1553 and the succession of his Catholic half-sister Mary weakened England's influence in Scotland, for a significant aspect of it had focused on giving succour to Scottish Protestants. Arran could be sidelined because he would be much less inclined to turn to England under a Catholic monarch. In December 1553, Mary, queen of Scots, entered her twelfth year, making her old enough, as far as the French were concerned, to name her own regent. Arran was therefore replaced with Mary of Guise and this was endorsed by both the Parlement de Paris and the Scottish parliament. Everyone expected favours from the new regent, but it was impossible to reconcile the divergent interests. Mary had a strong personality and, like her predecessor, Margaret Tudor, she concerned herself with domestic and international problems. Mary corresponded with France and with Mary Tudor and the wardens of the Anglo-Scottish marches to keep the peace. At first she adeptly balanced the demands of the growing numbers of Protestants and their detractors. She even tried to win Protestants to the French cause but Scottish coffers were too impoverished to do this, for she had inherited a deficit of £30,000. This financial shortfall led to unpopular demands for taxation for which Mary was unable to secure parliamentary approval.

Noble opposition to taxes, combined with dearth, inflation, attacks on French influence and on Catholicism, proved difficult to handle, yet Mary sought to maintain order and conciliate those who challenged her authority. When she turned to France for support, the response was to hasten the marriage of Queen Mary to the Dauphin. True to her balanced approach to politics, Mary sent both Protestant and Catholic commissioners to France to agree the marriage contract and raised a £15,000 tax to pay for the embassy. They reaffirmed the Auld Alliance and offered François the crown matrimonial, but there was a dark side to this commission. Secret negotiations that would have astounded most Scots were concluded. The first clause bequeathed Scotland and Mary's claim to the English throne to the king of France if she died childless. The king of France would also have possession of Scotland and all its revenues until 1,000,000 gold crowns were reimbursed for Mary's education and the defence of her realm. Lastly, there was a catch-all clause that undermined Scottish sovereignty: Mary was to overrule the Scottish parliament's authority in order to grant the kings of France their rights. This was French imperialism, not the Auld Alliance. That half the commissioners died before returning to Scotland raises further suspicion regarding French motives. France wanted to use Scotland to conquer England by dynastic union rather than war. The marriage of Mary to François was celebrated at Notre Dame de Paris on 24 April 1558. The pageantry, masques and games that followed lasted for days. A French marriage would have appeared traditional to many Scots, but the secret betrayal of their sovereignty was unpardonable. As previous peace treaties had shown, Scottish sovereignty was not negotiable.

The last two years of Mary of Guise's regency were turbulent. She relied upon the nobility and France to maintain her position, but her days as regent were numbered as events in France and England again affected Scottish policy. The death of Henry II of France led to the succession of François and Mary. Henry had already declared Mary to be queen of England and Ireland after the death of Mary Tudor in November 1558. François and Mary had thus quartered the arms of England, Scotland and France on all their plate and furniture. The treaty of Cateau-Cambrésis, in April 1559 brought an end to decades of war between France and the Habsburgs of Spain and the Empire. Since England was also a party to the treaty, it did not recognise the Franco-Scottish claim to the English throne, although François signed it as king of Scotland, England and Ireland.

The death of Mary Tudor and the accession of her Protestant half-sister Elizabeth dealt a severe blow to Mary of Guise. Once more, Scottish Protestants could turn to England and Mary turned on them, no longer needing their support to secure her daughter's marriage. In the spring of 1559 a war broke out between her forces and the Protestant 'Lords of the Congregation'. Perth, Dundee, Stirling, Linlithgow and Edinburgh were the main flashpoints. The Congregation occupied Edinburgh but French reinforcements were sent to Mary's aid. They occupied and fortified Leith, and drove the Congregation from the capital. The Hamiltons sought to exploit the situation by warning of a French takeover. Mary hit back with a proclamation reassuring the Scots that she would not trouble her peaceable and obedient subjects and would uphold the laws of the land. Châtelherault emerged as leader of the Congregation and his forces reoccupied Edinburgh in the autumn of 1559. They declared that Mary had forfeited the regency, but again they faltered due to lack of foreign support and the French pushed them back. The Reformers turned to Elizabeth, who, persuaded of the danger from France, signed the Treaty of Berwick with the Congregation in February 1560, agreeing to send forces to expel the French. Significantly, the treaty made no mention of religion, but did promise to preserve Scottish sovereignty, a significant concession from the daughter of Henry VIII.

When English ships were sighted, French reinforcements were rushed to Leith and Inchkeith in the Forth. When news that an English army, consisting of 8,000 horse and foot, was at Berwick reached Mary she retreated into Edinburgh Castle. Suffering from an incurable illness, she died on 11 June 1560. The turbulence of the times meant that Mary could not even be buried beside her husband at Holyrood. Instead, her coffin was transported to Leith and sent to France for burial at St Peter's Abbey in Rheims, where her sister was abbess.

The power of Mary's Guise relations was waning in France and Catherine de Medici, regent for François and Mary, needed her troops to return to fight heresy there. So, on 6 July 1560, English and French envoys agreed to remove their forces from Scotland. The Treaty of Edinburgh, and the fighting that preceded it, ended French dominance of Scotland. The military assistance of the Auld Alliance would never return, but strong social, economic and cultural links remained. Critically, the treaty included French recognition of Elizabeth as queen of England, thus undermining the claims of Mary and her husband François II. Just when the status of the Anglo-Franco-Scottish triangle appeared settled, ill fortune intervened once more: François II died in December 1560. This was truly an *annus horribilis* for Mary, who had lost her mother and husband in the same year. Her plight only worsened when Catherine de Medici made it clear that her widowed daughter-in-law was no longer welcome in France.

The Treaty of Edinburgh was followed by the 'Reformation parliament' of August 1560, which altered the nation's politics, religion and culture. The Reformers, however, did not have long to bask in their victory: Mary's impending return could overthrow the Lords of the Congregation, overturn the Reformation and restore the power of the monarchy. Everything was still to play for in the complex and evolving world of mid-sixteenth-century Scottish politics.

THE PERSONAL RULE OF MARY, 1561–67

Mary's personal rule, lasting less than six years, has been the subject of more debate than that of any other Scottish monarch. Some consider her a 'failure' as a ruler (Wormald 1988), while to others her policies enjoyed 'conspicuous success' (Donaldson 1965, 113). Historians have even been accused of 'double standards' in their assessments, judging her differently because of her sex and unfairly comparing her with her successors rather than her predecessors or contemporaries (Lynch 1987, 9–23). The wealth of writing on Mary has itself been the subject of a number of essays and even books (Donaldson 1974, ch. 8; Lee 1985). The judgement of Mary offered here lies towards the negative end of the spectrum of opinion.

Mary returned to Scotland on 19 August 1561. When her French galley sailed into

Leith, she was warmly welcomed by the crowd, but not by the Protestant leader John Knox, who saw her return as a portent of gloom. Most people ignored Knox and partied for a week in celebration of their young queen's homecoming. It would have taken a monarch of considerable political skill to manage both the warring factions and the religious situation within Scotland at this time. The factions consisted of the earl of Huntly's pro-French Catholics on one wing and Châtelherault's pro-English Protestants on the other. In the middle were the quasi-neutral Lord James Stewart (the queen's half-brother) and William Maitland of Lethington. Mary tried to be neutral at first: she was young and politically inexperienced, but in matters of religion she was less than pragmatic in her public defence of Catholicism, which led to open friction between the queen and Protestant leaders. It was perhaps as well that during 1561–5 Mary made progresses that took her from the Lowlands to Whithorn Priory in the south-west to Inveraray in the *Gàidhealtachd* and Dingwall in the north. She would have welcomed the break from Protestant haranguing and she used these occasions to socialise with powerful local magnates as well as to enforce royal authority and domestic justice.

During 1561–4 Mary demonstrated caution in her personal affairs and government. In 1562 she gave Lord James Stewart a magnificent wedding, and also took on the rebellious Gordons at the Battle of Corrichie in October 1562, subsequently using forfeiture and execution to quell them in spite of their Catholicism. This action, along with financial concessions to the Reformed church, pleased the Reformers and led to reasonable harmony amongst the nobility. Lord James was rewarded for leading the queen's forces by being created earl of Moray in 1563. Mary's marital status was, however, the source of plots to abduct her and marry her into one faction or another. One tragic suitor, Lord James Hamilton, was declared insane when he tried to abduct Mary in 1562. This checked the power of the Hamiltons, but Mary, like her father, also had European suitors. If she had resisted these advances as did her diplomatically skilled cousin, Elizabeth, she might have avoided civil war. Realistically, though, they were two very different women with separate dynastic ambitions. Elizabeth knew that marriage would diminish her power, whereas Mary believed that marriage would bolster her claim to Elizabeth's throne.

Mary's foreign policy was mostly directed towards keeping peaceable relations with England. A meeting between Mary and Elizabeth was mooted in 1562, but never materialised. Mary turned to England, rather than Europe, for her second husband, her cousin Henry Stewart, Lord Darnley, son of the exiled earl of Lennox. Although Elizabeth sanctioned the Lennox Stewarts' return to Scotland, she soon had a change of heart: Darnley also had a claim to the English throne through his grandmother Queen Margaret Tudor. Mary had to assure Elizabeth that the match would uphold Elizabeth's right to the English throne, protect the rights of England and avoid leagues with nations which wanted to harm England's religion. The catch was that these promises were conditional upon Elizabeth naming Mary as her heir. Elizabeth refused to comply and kept meddling in Scottish politics.

Mary and Darnley married on 26 July 1565 at Holyrood, but the marriage was controversial and Darnley proved a highly unsuitable consort. The only good thing to come out of it was their child, the future James VI. Mary refused to grant Darnley the crown matrimonial, giving him the title of Prince Henry, duke of Albany, instead. This compromise was sanctioned by the privy council, but many nobles were unhappy about having to acknowledge an earl's son as 'Prince' Henry and plotted to destabilise Mary's government. Moray and others would have led a rebellion against Mary but they failed to raise sufficient support. Mary's concessions to the Reformed church, although not generous, were enough to keep many Protestants loyal. Royal forces mustered to challenge Moray's men, resulting in the so-called 'Chaseabout' uprising of August and September 1565, an inconclusive cat-and-mouse game between Edinburgh and Dumfriesshire. The rebels fled to England and domestic politics calmed down, but the power of the crown had been undermined.

The nobility's challenge to Mary continued with the murder of David Riccio, her personal secretary, in March 1566. This sordid murder was masterminded by a jealous Darnley and led by the Protestant lords, Morton, Lindsay and Ruthven. That Mary did not lose the child she was carrying as result of this terrifying incident is miraculous. She fled to Dunbar to rally her loyal nobility and divided the opposition by selectively pardoning those involved in the Chaseabout rebellion. With a strong army at her back, Mary returned to Edinburgh to summon Morton, Lindsay, Ruthven and their co-conspirators to justice. They too fled to England and Mary was left increasingly isolated.

The well-known tragedies that Mary experienced during the twelve months following Riccio's murder exposed her political incompetence. Problems emerged with the birth of Prince James in June 1566, after which she become infatuated with the earl of Bothwell. The birth of a male heir to the throne was much celebrated but it also opened up the old problem of a male heir who could be manipulated by discontented nobles. James was, after all, a potential king of Scotland and England. His baptism at Stirling in December 1566 was a magnificent occasion, but within weeks of what seemed a high point of Mary's reign, Darnley was murdered at Kirk o' Field in February 1567. This heinous crime was reported throughout Europe; Darnley, for all his inherent faults, was a royal father and consort to a queen. The conspirators against him undoubtedly included the earls of Moray and Morton, as well as Maitland of Lethington. The main suspect was James Hepburn, earl of Bothwell, who was protected by his proximity to the queen. She was not above suspicion herself. Bothwell's royal ambitions led him to plot the death of the chief obstacle to his plans, despite the fact that Darnley would probably have died of syphilis anyway. Mary had pardoned Riccio's murderers in December, perhaps knowing that they might become embroiled in a conspiracy against her husband. It was just as well that Prince James was placed in the keeping of the earl of Mar at Stirling in March 1567, well away from a regime about to collapse.

After Bothwell obtained a divorce in May 1567, Mary unwisely married for the third time at Holyrood by Protestant rite. Bothwell was created duke of Orkney and Shetland but, unlike previous royal weddings, few of the nobility attended and festivities were limited. The use of these rites was hypocritical for a staunchly Catholic queen who had triumphed in having James baptised by Catholic rite at Stirling Castle the previous December. It is virtually impossible to retrieve Mary's honour from her marriage to the chief suspect in Darnley's murder, but she tried to reassure Catherine de Medici and her uncle, the cardinal of Lorraine, that Bothwell's lineage, loyalty and royal service on the Borders made him suitable. Mary added that the Scots would not have tolerated a foreign husband, but Catherine de Medici was still outraged by the murder of Darnley and Mary's inability to defend her innocence. Her decision to marry so soon after Darnley's murder even led the pope to break off communications with her in July 1567. This ruined the diplomatic channels Mary had built up with Pius IV, Pius V and the Vatican. It could also have cost her the support of other Catholic powers. Furthermore, the marriage turned sour very quickly as Bothwell turned out to be a ruthless and altogether wicked husband.

As far as the opposition of the nobility was concerned, Mary's dalliance with Bothwell was her final undoing. Any sense of good government left in her was gone. In September 1568 the earl of Morton handed to the privy council the infamous 'casket letters' between Mary and Bothwell that revealed her innermost thoughts during 1566–7. They cannot all have been forgeries and they made Mary appear a weak Francophile queen who had squandered her inheritance. Damaging civil war was the inevitable result of her poor judgement, but Mary still had some support. At Carberry, near Musselburgh, on 15 June 1567, the queen's supporters faced mightier opposition. The cowardly Bothwell conveniently escaped, leaving his wife to face a humiliating surrender. A crestfallen Mary reached Edinburgh dishevelled and in tears. She was then imprisoned in Lochleven Castle, in what would be the start of many years of captivity. Her misery was further compounded by a miscarriage, before she was forced to abdicate on 24 July in favour of her one-year-old son James. The opposition lost no time in crowning her successor at Stirling on 29 July 1567, as James VI, king of Scots.

THE EARLY YEARS OF JAMES VI, 1567–73

Mary's forced abdication returned Scotland and the Stewart dynasty to its historic pattern of unsettled royal minorities. The first regent to be appointed was James, earl of Moray. A parliament in December ratified Mary's abdication, James's coronation and Moray's regency, but this did not ensure stability. Mary escaped from Lochleven Castle in May 1568 to rally her supporters. She headed south-west, seeking the support of the Hamiltons. Many of those who had opposed her at Carberry now changed sides, proving that her cause was far from lost at this stage. Amongst the most notable of these men was Sir William Kirkcaldy of Grange, to whom Mary had surrendered at Carberry, and who would continue to support her cause for the rest of his life. At Langside near Glasgow on 13 May 1568 a superior queen's army was defeated by those who fought in the name of James VI and Mary opted to flee to England, hoping for assistance from Elizabeth. Mary would remain a dilemma to both Scottish and English administrations until her death in 1587. The greatest tragedy in this was not her English incarceration and execution, but her enforced separation from her only son James, destined to grow up 'alone, without father or mother, brother or sister'. France, embroiled in its own Wars of Religion, took no part in these events and Scotland descended into civil war. This was further complicated by the 1569–70 Northern Rebellion by English Catholics who sought the restoration of Mary. It was crushed within months and an English army under the earl of Sussex came into Scotland to attack the strongholds where fleeing rebels had been sheltered. It was a horrifying reminder of the brutality of the 1540s.

Four regents governed Scotland during James's minority: the earls of Moray (1567–70), Lennox (1570–1), Mar (1571–2) and Morton (1572–8). Only Mar died in his bed. Of the others, Moray and Lennox were murdered and Morton was executed. These disruptive regencies demonstrate the turbulence of the early years of James VI's minority. Factionalism was rife and the administration was constantly unstable. Moray gave firm backing to the Reformed church but was unable to make much headway in the civil war. He was murdered by a member of one of the leading Marian families, James Hamilton of Bothwellhaugh, at Linlithgow in January 1570. Moray's regency proved that he was ambitious, but, as Gordon Donaldson noted, he lacked 'political acumen, for his manoeuvres had often involved miscalculation and failure, and his rare successes owed at least as much to favourable circumstances as to his own unaided designs' (Donaldson 1965, 163).

Moray's successor, Matthew Stewart, fourth earl of Lennox, was Darnley's father and therefore the king's grandfather. So the Stewarts still held the reins of power, but they had as many enemies as friends. Lennox's rise, with the backing of England, particularly antagonised the Hamiltons, while those who had been involved in Darnley's murder were targeted for revenge. Lennox sent his forces against Huntly, Argyll and the Hamiltons and even scored a notable victory when Dumbarton fell to the king's men in April 1571. However, Edinburgh Castle and parts of the burgh nearby were still held for the queen by Kirkcaldy of Grange and Maitland of Lethington. Neither side was able to gain the upper hand and rival parliaments met once more: in August 1570, the king's men held a parliament at Edinburgh, while Mary's supporters met at Linlithgow. In the following year, when Lennox held a parliament in the king's name in May 1571 in the Canongate, it was followed by a queen's parliament in Edinburgh in June. It was hard for government to function in this context and both sides claimed legitimacy for their officers of state. Ordinary Scots who had any interest in local and national government must have been perplexed by these events. In the summer of 1571, Sir Thomas Ker of Ferniehirst was elected provost of Edinburgh by the queen's men but was promptly forfeited by the king's men meeting in a convention of estates at Stirling. Ferniehirst joined the attack upon this gathering by the queen's men, during which Regent Lennox was fatally shot on 4 September.

John Erskine, earl of Mar, then took over the regency. As the guardian of James VI, Mar held an important office and was more politically neutral than his predecessors. Yet, in spite of the disarray of the queen's men, he could not end the civil war that was still raging in central Scotland. He died in October 1572 and was succeeded by James Douglas, fourth earl of Morton, who was already effectively the leader of the king's men. As chancellor and great admiral of Scotland he was pre-eminent among the nobles of the king's party. He had a fearsome and thoroughly deserved reputation for ruthlessness and he would remain in power for the next eight years.

To foreign observers, Scotland in 1572 looked in a parlous state and rumours of plots to kidnap the young king only added to this negative impression. It was gradually becoming clear, however, that the king's men were gaining the upper hand in the civil war and, by early 1573, only Edinburgh Castle remained in the hands of the queen's men. Morton turned to Elizabeth for help and in April 1573 English guns and their gunners arrived at Leith. By 17 May 1573 they were firing on the castle and after twelve days of bombardment the castle surrendered. English expeditionary forces left Scotland and Morton's rise to power was complete.

CONCLUSION

In 1573, Scotland found itself in a position which was in some ways remarkably similar to that of 1513, but in other ways very different. A child was on the throne, rival factions continued to destabilise politics and government, and the power of the crown seemed weak. Yet fear of English invasion, which had featured so strongly after Flodden, was gone. The Reformation crisis of 1559–60 had marked a profound shift in Scotland's position in Europe and, most significantly, in its relationship with its southern neighbour. Elizabeth's regime had dropped England's old claims to overlordship of Scotland, and in doing so had achieved something that had eluded generations of English monarchs: a friendly northern neighbour. England had helped to secure the Scottish Reformation in 1560 and the triumph of the supporters of James VI in 1573. These were strategic moves rather than hostile interventions. Underpinning these interventions was a desire on the part of the Elizabethan regime to create a Protestant Britain, and an awareness that a Scottish monarch would probably succeed to the English throne. Centuries of Anglo-Scottish war had come to an end.

REFERENCES

Donaldson, G. 1965 *Scotland: James V–VII*. Edinburgh.
Donaldson, G. 1983 *All the Queen's Men: power and politics in Mary Stewart's Scotland*. London.
Lee, M. 1985 'The Daughter of Debate: Mary Queen of Scots after 400 years', in *Scottish Historical Review*, 185, 70–9.
Lynch, M. (ed) 1987 *Mary Stewart: Queen in Three Kingdoms*. Oxford.
McKean, C. 1993 'Hamilton of Finnart', *History Today*, January, 42–7.
Merriman, M. 1968 'The Assured Scots: Scottish collaborators with England during the Rough Wooing, 1543–50', *Scottish Historical Review*, 47, 10–35.

Wormald, J. (ed) 1991 *Scotland Revisited*. London.
Wormald, J. 1988 *Mary Queen of Scots. A study in failure*. London.

FURTHER READING

Brown, K.M. 2004 'The Reformation Parliament', in Brown, K.M. and Tanner, R.J. (eds), *The History of the Scottish Parliament, vol. 1: Parliament and Politics in Scotland, 1235–1560*. Edinburgh.

Cameron, J. 1998 *James V. The Personal Rule 1528–1542*. East Linton.

Emond, K. 2005 'The Parliament of 1525', in Brown and Tanner (eds), *The History of the Scottish Parliament*, 160–78.

Fraser, A. 1985 *Mary Queen of Scots*. London.

Lynch, M. 1991 *Scotland: A New History*. London.

Meikle, M.M. 2007 *The Scottish People, 1490–1625*. Edinburgh.

Merriman M. 2000 *The Rough Wooings: Mary Queen of Scots 1542–1551*. East Linton.

Ritchie, P.E. 2002 *Mary of Guise in Scotland, 1548–1560: A Political Career*. East Linton.

Ritchie, P.E. 2005 'Marie de Guise and the Three Estates, 1554–1558', in Brown & Tanner (eds), *Parliament and Politics in Scotland*, 179–202.

Wormald, J. 1981 *Court, Kirk and Community. Scotland 1470–1625*. London.

CHAPTER TWO

The Reign of James VI: 1573–1625

Jenny Wormald

The reign of James VI was one of the most dramatic and pivotal in Scottish history. The king succeeded at the age of one in 1567 at a time of crisis, thanks to the scandal created by his mother Mary, queen of Scots, and her enforced abdication; and Scotland was plunged into the civil war between king's men and queen's men which was not resolved until 1573. Interwoven with the political crisis was the new and traumatic religious problem as the Reformed church struggled to establish its polity and its authority over the realm. Then, in 1603, came the Union of the Crowns, when James succeeded the childless Elizabeth and began his triple monarchy as king of Scotland, England and Ireland. This promised to resolve the long struggle to bring England and Scotland together, that dream of imperialist medieval English kings, Edward I and III, and more recently of Henry VIII and Protector Somerset in the 1540s (Williamson 1983, 34–58). But it did not happen in the way they envisaged it, with Scotland becoming a vassal state of the English crown; rather, the new 'British' king had to find a way of ruling his territories as equal and independent entities.

THE MINORITY OF JAMES VI

Personal monarchy is not well served when the king is a child. No regent has the aura of kingship. Nor does it help the king, or minority governments ruling in his name, when the authority of the crown is undermined by the antics of his predecessor. Scotland had one saving grace: long experience of minorities, with which every reign since 1406 had begun. But no other minority had opened with civil war and none, save that of Mary (1542–61), had been so beset with religious and political problems, with their inevitable impact on international as well as national affairs.

After 1573 the kaleidoscopic events and changes of regents calmed down somewhat, under the tough regime of James Douglas, earl of Morton and regent from 1572. So, to an extent, did the affairs of the church, with the Concordat of Leith of 1572, which formally restored bishops, and the Act of Conformity of 1573, which finally deprived Catholic benefice-holders, transferring the revenues to clergy of the Reformed church. Yet 1574 saw the return from Geneva of that greatest of ecclesiastical firebrands, Andrew Melville, who would become a presbyterian figurehead and afflict King James in the years of his adult rule with his greatest headache. Tough though Morton was, his rule was hardly popular, given his predilection for favouring his friends and adherents, and his enthusiasm for

England. Remote in Stirling Castle, the young king was growing up and developing the passion for scholarship which would remain with him for life, despite the savagery of his tutor, George Buchanan. In 1578, he was abruptly pitchforked into the political world by the *coup d'état* headed by the earls of Argyll and Atholl, who patched up their own disputes to bring Morton down – to the fury of Elizabeth. James, then in his twelfth year, announced, with characteristic insouciance and confidence, that he was old enough to take on himself the governance of the realm, and in 1579 moved from Stirling to make a ceremonial entry into Edinburgh. Reality was somewhat different. Morton never regained the regency, but he recovered power and held it until he was finally destroyed in 1581, executed for his part in the Darnley murder fifteen years earlier. It was a trumped-up charge which symbolises the instability of Scottish political life since the mid-1560s. James did begin to take a more active role in government, and 1581 saw another piece of symbolism, the passing of the first of his acts of revocation. Such acts, which had come into being in the reign of James II, revoked grants made during the king's minority and over which he had had no control and thus marked his assertion of majority rule.

James was by no means, however, a free agent after 1581. In 1579 his cousin Esmé Stuart arrived from France to enjoy the king's favour, becoming earl and then duke of Lennox in 1580 and 1581. The extent to which he influenced the king may well have been exaggerated; accounts of James sent to Elizabeth in 1581 – 'that false Scots urchin', she called him – certainly indicate that at fifteen James very much had a mind of his own. But the pro-French and Catholic Lennox was inevitably an object of hatred, and in 1582 he lost power when the Ruthven Raiders (William Ruthven, earl of Gowrie, and other presbyterian nobles) kidnapped the king, holding him until his escape in 1583; in 1584, Gowrie paid with his life. When, in 1583, James announced his intention to be a 'universal king', above faction, he was making a far more definite statement about his kingship than his act of revocation of 1581. At that point, and in messy circumstances, a messy minority came to an end.

PERSONAL RULE

How does a king establish control after a minority? An obvious answer in James's case was that those who dominated the minority, Morton, Esmé Stuart and Gowrie, were dead. More generally, the history of Scottish royal minorities suggested that, although individual magnates might temporarily benefit, the aristocracy as a whole preferred adult royal rule; royal patronage and favour were a considerably better bet than chancy advancement under regents. Faction-ridden as the Scottish aristocracy might be, they were no more faction-ridden than other contemporary aristocracies; the traditional idea that the Scottish magnates were a particularly ungovernable crew is a myth (Lee 1959, ch.1; Donaldson 1965, 216–17). It was perfectly possible for an able king to make good the boast of being 'universal' and James moved fast to demonstrate the prestige and strength of his kingship. In 1584 Gowrie was executed and parliament, with Mary, queen of Scots, clearly in mind, legislated against any calumnies made against the king, his parents and progenitors. The works of George

Buchanan, exponent of contractual kingship and very definite calumniator of his mother Mary, were banned; and for good measure the authority of the three estates of parliament was firmly asserted. Ironically, it was in this year that James himself complained about forty years of government by women, children and avaricious regents since the death of James V, anticipating his undutiful comment in *Basilikon Doron* on Mary as a double curse to the realm, a female who became queen when a baby. And in 1585 he firmly rejected the idea that Mary might return to rule jointly with him, a solution first mooted in 1581 and deeply appealing to Elizabeth. It was the best of all worlds: an authoritative parliament underwrote the authority and dignity of monarchy, while King James made clear to both Elizabeth and Mary that he, and he alone, was ruler of Scotland.

The underwriting of royal authority might be worth no more than the paper it was written on, however. The real question is how far the king could cope with the legacy of scandal, minority, and the deep ecclesiastical divisions which had rent his kingdom for twenty-five years before he began his personal rule, and with relations with England. After 1567, the old enemy had become a friend as two Protestant countries drew together, but traditional mutual suspicion died hard. Moreover, although the question of the English succession gave a particular twist to Anglo-Scottish relations, they did not totally predominate over relations with other kingdoms. Much of the prestige of Stewart kingship had lain in its success in making its mark in Europe. For King James, therefore, restoration of royal authority involved recreating that prestige.

FOREIGN RELATIONS

Fortunately for James VI, the scandal of his mother was firmly located in England, as it had been since 1568. It was the unfortunate Elizabeth who had to cope with Mary, who, after her involvement in the rising of the northern earls in 1569 and the Ridolfi Plot of 1571, had been quiescent throughout the 1570s. In the 1580s, she was once again plotting against Elizabeth, beginning in 1582 – the year of the assassination of William of Orange – with the 'Enterprise', a plot involving Francis Throckmorton and the Spanish ambassador. English fears exploded. While James's parliament of 1584 legislated against calumny of his mother, Elizabeth's pushed through a Bond of Association, allowing the killing of anyone who was the subject of a plot designed to dethrone her. Undeterred, Mary carried on to her final disaster, the government-infiltrated Babington Plot of 1586. Despite Elizabeth's efforts to avoid the inevitable – and it is worth commenting on the fact that Elizabeth strenuously tried to protect the life of the woman who would cheerfully have had her murdered – Mary was tried, found guilty and executed on 7 February 1587. This was the only time she came back to haunt James, who had to walk a tightrope: protesting against his mother's death while making sure that no-one actually reacted against it, despite Francis earl of Bothwell's sword-rattling and the calls for revenge in parliament. Mercifully, the tears were crocodile ones, and in the following year James capitalised on Elizabeth's embarrassment at having executed a queen. He remained neutral when the Armada threat loomed, netting £5,000 from Elizabeth, whose fears in this instance outweighed her parsimony. The problem of Mary was over. Apart from James's dutiful gesture when he constructed glorious tombs for both her and Elizabeth after his accession to the English throne, she was little thought of in the seventeenth century, beginning to emerge only in the eighteenth as a figure of legend and romance – and that hardly bothered King James.

The resolution of the Marian problem sits uneasily with the old idea that James inherited his mother's obsession with the English throne, being more concerned with an English future than a Scottish present, and therefore taking care to please Elizabeth. Instead, the payment in 1588 – the second of a series of virtually annual payments between 1586 and 1603 – symbolises Elizabeth's efforts to ensure Scottish co-operation (Goodare 2000, 110–25). The 1586 payment of £4,000 was part of the negotiations for an alliance between England and Scotland: the 'Amity'. James received £1,000 less than he asked for and his request for horses was rejected, although that for deer was not turned down. But his insouciance in asking for deer and horses in the negotiations for an alliance for the defence of religion and mutual assistance against foreign invasion speaks for itself; so does Elizabeth's promise to uphold any right or title due to him, even if it stopped short of explicit recognition of him as her heir. From an early stage in his personal rule, relationships between Elizabeth and James were visibly different from those between Elizabeth and Mary; increasingly infuriated as he might get as Elizabeth lived on and on, James, unlike his mother, had the wit to realise that it would not be primarily her *diktat* which would determine what happened after her death. Hence he rejected her attempts to act as wise mother to an inexperienced king, arousing her to bursts of hysterical fury, as when, in 1592, he refused to follow her counsel over his rebellious northern Catholic earls, while ruminating about the advantages and disadvantages of friendship with Spain.

It made much more sense to James to follow the foreign policy of his predecessors, carving out for himself that role in Europe which would ensure his reputation at home. It was the natural instinct of the Scottish monarchy and now had the added advantage of enabling him to negotiate with those who might well intervene in the English succession on Elizabeth's death, notably France and Spain. Indeed, despite howls from the church, trade with France continued, and was opened up with Spain. In the 1580s, neither could provide an answer to James's marriage plans, for naturally he sought a Protestant bride. The obvious choice, therefore, was to look to Scandinavia, where Scotland had long-standing diplomatic and economic links. In 1589, James married Anna, younger daughter of Frederick II of Denmark, turning down the Protestant Henry of Navarre's sister Catherine, because that would have brought a less generous dowry and dragged him into expensive support for Henry's efforts to gain the French throne. Once again the Scottish king pursued his own policy and the English queen obliged: £6,000 was forthcoming in 1589 to help with his marital costs.

The 1590s saw more focused attention on the future. In 1595–6, John ('Pourie') Ogilvy was sent to Madrid and Rome to intimate that James supported the Catholic faith, and would do so in England, although unable to do so openly; in a typical piece of Jacobean financial cynicism, he further suggested to the papacy that a pension would help. Naturally this was not forthcoming, but as an effort to persuade Spain not to promote the Infanta Isabella as Elizabeth's successor it seems to have worked. The embassy may look premature, given that Elizabeth lived until 1603, but that is hindsight; in view of her age, she might have died at any time. It was the belief that James might indeed bring his Scottish and English kingdoms back to Rome, which lingered until after 1603, that helped to persuade the Infanta to remain neutral. By the late 1590s, the king was beginning to make contact with leading English politicians, first Robert earl of Essex and, after his downfall in 1601, Robert Cecil, maintaining the 'Secret Correspondence' with Cecil and Henry earl of Northumberland for the last two years of Elizabeth's life (Akrigg 1984, 178–205). Once again, it was not the English queen whom James regarded as the most relevant player.

DOMESTIC POLITICS: THE 'STATE'

In foreign affairs, James had, from a very early date, reasserted the independence of the Scottish monarchy in European politics; this was no bit-player hanging on to the coat-tails of the English succession. At home, the same confidence is detectable, but the outcome perhaps more confusing. The nature of the Scottish kingdom is an intractable problem, partly because of the ubiquitous difficulties of internal politics but also because of the political developments which have raised the question of how we define that kingdom. Historians have a predilection for thinking of concepts, be they feudalism, absolutism, or whatever. The sixteenth century sees the rise of the nation state, which then becomes complicated by the idea of the absolutist state. The idea of the state is not, of course, new in the sixteenth century. It goes back to Aristotle, who at least knew exactly what he meant by the term, and it has been seized upon by scholars of subsequent ages, early-medieval, late-medieval, early-modern, though too often used as a given rather than a word which can be clearly explained. Jacobean Scotland certainly witnessed profound and rapid changes. The question is how we can best characterize them (Goodare 1999, 1–107).

The king himself poses the first problem: how did he see his kingship? He told us, in 1598–9, in his two works on kingship, *The Trew Law of Free Monarchies* and *Basilikon Doron*, the first a tract on kingship by divine right, the second a manual of kingship for his son and heir Henry. But the message is conflicting. *The Trew Law* sets out clearly the theory of divine right: kings are ordained by God and answerable only to God; no earthly institution can restrain kings – kings, for example, made laws before parliaments came into being; tyrants must be endured, for they are imposed by God, and God alone will punish them (a point which James took very seriously; this was not a tract advocating untrammelled power). *Basilikon Doron* is set in the framework of divine-right monarchy, but it is a much more practical handbook, advising his son on his dealings with the various estates in his kingdom (ecclesiastics, nobles, burgesses), on his choice of a wife, on the making of war or peace and on his leisure pursuits.

These works were written in Scotland and reflect James's experience of Scottish kingship. Yet they are not wholly accurate guides to his way of ruling Scotland, and the circumstances in which they were written indicates why. A new and threatening level of resistance theory was developed by Calvinists in the 1550s during the reign of Mary Tudor and then in the 1570s after the killing of French Calvinists in the Massacre of St Bartholomew's Day. It asserted the duty to assassinate tyrants, the right of the lesser magistracy to contain them, and the contractual nature of kingship. The reaction to this was a forcible re-statement of the conservative theory of divine right: the powers that be are ordained by God. Two leading Scotsmen, John Knox and George Buchanan, were notable exponents of resistance theory; another Scot, James the scholar king, strenuously advanced divine right. That was in the *Trew Law*. *Basilikon Doron* reflects another side of James, the counsellor king, the father instructing his son.

His kingship had more in common with the more pragmatic message of *Basilikon Doron*. Indeed, James was in many ways more conservative than some of his leading politicians and advisers. In his attitude to control of the localities, for example, he stuck to traditional methods, the justice ayres and, in 1587, the General Band, by which clan chiefs and lords in the Highlands and Borders were made responsible for the good behaviour of their followers and tenants. The Band itself was an extensive version of the Scottish practice of bonding, whereby lords and their men offered mutual protection and service, or men of equal rank agreed to mutual support. Normally made for local purposes, such bonds had been taken over into the religious sphere in the 1550s and 1560s, when Protestant nobles, the Lords of the Congregation, used them to swear to act together to advance the true religion (Wormald 1985). These bonds had emerged in the fifteenth century, and still flourished in the late sixteenth, and the king seems to have seen the advantages in them. Indeed, he saw the advantages in the aristocracy. At any time, the great men of the realm – any realm – posed problems for kings: they were necessary because of their power but potentially dangerous precisely because of that power. It is unnecessary to return to that old chestnut, the 'overmighty aristocracy', of whom Scotland is supposed to have had its fair share, to recognise that. To an extent, the Tudor monarchy – and in the seventeenth century the French one – found an answer in seeking to bind the aristocracy more firmly to their courts: Louis XIV's Versailles is the example *par excellence*. By contrast, despite the occasional aristocratic conspiracy – the northern earls and Bothwell in the 1590s, the Ruthvens in the mysterious Gowrie conspiracy of 1600 – James was more relaxed with his great men. Aristocratic conspiracies were hardly confined to his reign or his kingdom. As he said in *Basilikon Doron*, nobles were the 'armes and executors of your laws', in the localities. In 1595, for example, the death of the earl of Atholl saw James greatly concerned about who would control Perthshire, more concerned than with the death of his powerful chancellor John Maitland of Thirlestane. The appointment of a new chancellor exercised the 'factioners' at court but it was four years before a replacement was nominated. In central government, the magnates retained a notable presence, as officers of state and on the privy council. The king himself ruled as a personal monarch, much as his predecessors had done. It is difficult to see here any notable shift towards a 'state'.

Where the impetus for change in Jacobean government, the beginnings of a change in balance between centre and locality, came from lies more in changing attitudes within the political nation. These were not entirely novel in the late sixteenth century for they can be traced back at least to the reign of James V. The impetus came from the Renaissance and the Reformation. From the fifteenth century, literacy – hitherto the preserve of clerics – had been spreading among aristocrats and lairds. By the sixteenth, the assumption that literate skills and a humanist education were no longer to be despised by the laity, but to be sought, was becoming widespread (Mason 2005, 114–16, 141–2; Lynch 1991, 238). Humanist scholars offered the laity a new view of themselves; an essential part of nobility was to serve and counsel the prince, and where better to do that than the court, in council, on royal embassies? The process was enhanced by the Reformation. The great prince-bishops, massively involved in government and secular politics, became a thing of the past. The Reformed church put its emphasis on its clergy fulfilling their obligations to the spiritual welfare of the kingdom, and set its face against their involvement in secular affairs. Mary's secretary William Maitland of Lethington and his younger brother John Maitland of Thirlestane, James's secretary and chancellor (Lee 1959), are notable examples of those lairds who sought advancement in royal service.

The influence of men such as these showed itself particularly strongly in the law. Justice may have been the king's justice, but in practice it was peripatetic, local and sometimes private. Only in the reign of James IV did Scotland get its first central court – the session – for civil business. Not until 1674 was a central court established for criminal matters; before that, the office of justice-general had been hereditary in the family of the Campbells, earls of Argyll. Moreover, the justice of the bloodfeud was flourishing, based on the principle of compensating victims of crime or their kin, and presided over by heads of kin and lords. There was a lot to be said for local and private justice. It worked precisely because it was local – on the spot, rather than remote in the capital – and because lords did enforce it. But, as the laity became educated in the law, and a thriving legal profession grew up in Edinburgh, so expectations of the law changed. Laymen took over the college of justice, established by James V in 1532 on the basis of the older court of session, with its judges equally divided between clerics and laymen and with a clerical president. Rules for procedure were introduced and by the late sixteenth century the judges were demanding ever-increasing standards of legal expertise, for themselves and for the advocates who practised in the court, while setting themselves against royal interference in the composition of the college. Old habits died very hard. Senators of the college such as Sir Patrick Waus of Barnbarroch were heavily lobbied by heads of kin and lords to find in favour of their kinsmen. And only in 1584 did the king's advocate begin to take over families' hitherto unchallenged right to initiate criminal actions. But in the Lowlands at least, the justice of the feud was dying by the early seventeenth century, helped on by the acts of 1598 and 1600, inspired more by the lawyers than the crown. In this area at least, as the amateur gave way to the professional, as local justice gave way to central, it is perhaps legitimate to think in terms of an embryonic state (Donaldson 1976, 1–19. Lynch 1991, 247–8).

The other huge shift was taxation. Unlike its European counterparts, the Scottish nobility was not tax exempt, although, unlike its English counterpart, it was taxed very lightly. That changed after 1581, when taxation became regular, not for extraordinary reasons such as war (the traditional justification) but to support an impoverished and spendthrift crown. This can be understood as part of a move towards a 'state', for regular taxation alters the relationship between centre and localities. In Scotland, because of the absence of taxation and regular warfare, and because of minorities, the localities had enjoyed an unusually high level of autonomy. Regular taxation meant increased bureaucracy and a growth in intervention in the localities. It also altered the business of parliament (Goodare 1989, 23–52).

Already, however, the nature of parliament had changed dramatically, with the Reformation parliament of 1560, when over a hundred very interested lairds turned up. Nothing like this had been seen before (Brown 2004, 203–31). What now happened was that control of parliamentary membership became urgent, and in 1587 the shire election act was passed: by introducing elections, the government hoped to impose some order on those who wanted to attend. But with religion very much now in the parliamentary arena, and with taxation added to that, not only membership but also business needed a new level of attention. And in the 1590s the king saw that it got it, with legislation such as that of 1594, which laid down that four members of each estate should meet twenty days before parliament to sift out frivolous material; only the king was exempt from this rule. Moreover, strenuous attempts were made to control the parliamentary drafting committee, the committee of the articles. Parliamentary tensions would increase after 1603 when the king went to London and it may be that the efforts at control in the 1590s were to an extent looking ahead to the future of absentee kingship. But they were also intended to cope with new and very present tensions.

Scottish government when James went south in 1603 was therefore very different from the Scottish government James took over in the early 1580s, in personnel, aspirations and nature. This section has offered secular reasons for that but the establishment of the Reformed church also had an enormous impact, and to that we can now turn.

ECCLESIASTICAL POLITICS: THE KING AND THE CHURCH

How did monarchs cope with the religious divisions which beset every kingdom in western Europe during the course of the Reformation? The answer is, with profound difficulty. With the exception of Philip II's Spain, where heresy was virtually eradicated, they had to live with the conflicting presence of the orthodox and the heretics, the definition depending on the religious disposition of the monarch. Charles V's wars with the Lutherans in Germany, Mary Tudor's notorious burning of Protestants, the Wars of Religion in late sixteenth-century France, Elizabeth's onslaught on Catholics in the last two decades of her reign – horrible deaths for priests, ruthlessly savage fines for laymen – all testify to the earthly hell which the search for new paths to heaven could create. Monarchs struggled to control these new problems; official religion in England changed dramatically under each of the four Tudor monarchs from Henry VIII to Elizabeth, and continued to shift, though less dramatically, under the four successive Stuart kings before 1688.

But what happened if there was no monarch to control the Reformation movement and to seek to direct it? Uniquely, this was the case in Scotland. The Calvinist church put down its roots after 1560 under the Catholic Mary, itself an astonishing occurrence. After her brief reign it had almost another two decades to establish itself with only sporadic and ineffectual intervention by secular authority. The doctrine of the separation of the two powers, church and state, which first surfaced in Scotland in the writings of an early reformer, Henry Balnaves, in 1548, could hardly be challenged (Kirk 1980, 22–53). By the early 1580s, when James VI was beginning to assert his authority, the church, under the leading influence of Andrew Melville and his followers, was setting its face against episcopacy and towards presbyterianism; theirs was not the only voice in the church, but it was the dominant one. The result was a curious one. In terms of blood spilt, Scotland was very restrained indeed; the usual circumstances which led to violence – the king and his church against the heretics – simply did not happen. Instead, the battle was between the king and the church, or at least the powerful presbyterian wing of it; and it was an intellectual rather than a physical battle, in which royal authority was under greater potential threat than anywhere else in Europe. Dangerous resistance theories which advocated contractual kingship were in fact the last resort, the cry of despair. But that associate of the French Huguenots who advanced these theories, George Buchanan, was pushing the same line in a very different situation: Scotland before the 1580s, with its discredited monarchy and minority government. It was an intolerable position for the crown, even if a happy one for the church. And it was therefore in ecclesiastical affairs, far more then secular ones, that James VI had his greatest struggle for ascendancy.

There are significant milestones along the route to achieve it: the Black Acts of 1584, which affirmed the authority of bishops, denounced presbyteries, and stated the king's supremacy over ecclesiastical as well as secular matters; the Golden Act of 1592, which re-asserted the Melvillian vision, making presbyteries legal; the spectacular and famous row between James and Andrew Melville in September 1596, when Melville took the king by his sleeve, calling him 'God's silly vassal', and told him that in the church, it was Christ who was king and James only a member; the Melvillian-inspired riot in Edinburgh in December 1596, a move which was trumped by the king when Edinburgh gave way to his threat to move his government away from the capital; the appointment of three parliamentary bishops in 1600, and thus the emergence of the episcopate after eight years in abeyance, which would lead, in 1610, to the restoration of diocesan episcopacy. These milestones give the impression of violent swings in the fortunes of the contenders for ecclesiastical authority, and there is something in this. But the battle lines were less clear-cut than has been supposed. James was certainly not trying to replace the presbyteries and other courts of the church with an episcopal church on English lines, with himself as supreme governor. Indeed, his enthusiasm for bishops was distinctly less strong than used to be thought (MacDonald 1998, 37). Despite the Black Acts, he made no effort to fill bishoprics between 1585 and 1600, and it is hard to believe that, had the restoration of episcopacy been central to his policy, he would have stopped at a mere three parliamentary bishops. He was in basic agreement with the general assembly that there should be a clerical estate in parliament. The difference lay in the fact that the assembly wanted those parliamentarians to be ministers but the king wanted them to be bishops. Yet there is no reason to doubt his reassurance in 1598 that 'I minde not . . . to bring in Papistical or Anglican bishopping' (the first use of 'Anglican' to describe the English church).

This was not the only occasion on which king and assembly had much in common. Earlier, they had been in agreement in opposition to the vitriolic attack of Richard Bancroft, bishop of London, on Scottish presbyterians in a sermon in 1589. Indeed, that unity produced, in the 1590 general assembly, the remarkable spectacle of the king 'praising God, that he was borne . . . to suche a place as to be king in suche a kirk, the sincerest kirk in the world', upon which 'the Assembly so rejoiced, that there was nothing but loud praising of God, and praying for the king for quarter of an houre'. James and the church were equally united in the desire for an educated and properly-paid ministry in a way which left Elizabeth and her church lagging behind, a desire which brought him, as James I, into conflict with Archbishop Whitgift of Canterbury and Bishop Bancroft very early in his English reign. Even that most glorious achievement, the King James Bible of 1611, had its origin not in the Hampton Court Conference of 1605, but in the king's proposition to the Assembly of 1601 for a new translation of the Bible.

This is not to downplay the real tensions between king and presbyterians, fought out with their own vitriol and bitter invective, the king on the whole investing his with rather more wit than his ministerial opponents. None of Elizabeth's churchmen would have dared to address her as ministers addressed James. The 1590 Assembly itself referred to the church's power to bind kings in chains; five years earlier, the minister Robert Gibson had compared James to the persecuting King Jeroboam. And the situation was not helped by Elizabeth, herself paranoid about English puritans, and yet willing to allow the hardline Scottish ones to preach openly in London (Wormald 1995, 171–91). But to an extent it is possible to see this as a development, if in an extreme form, of a tradition rooted in Scottish secular politics: more open, more hard-hitting comment than English kings, with their cultivation of the cult of flattery, had to endure. Scottish political rhetoric was more free than English from the idea of evil counsellors; no such rhetoric, with its attempts to conceal royal failure, was employed in the case of Scottish kings who came to grief. Moreover, the evidence for James's dealings with the church is undoubtedly skewed by the fact that it is the presbyterian writers David Calderwood and John Row whose accounts of these dealings reigned supreme, being hardly dented by the more anodyne writing of John Spottiswoode, archbishop of St Andrews. There was indeed a battle, but it was not one between a king who wanted bishops and no presbyteries, and a church which wanted presbyteries and no bishops. No more than in secular affairs was James VI simply James I in waiting.

THE UNION OF 1603

The union of 1603 was a long-awaited event, not least because Elizabeth lasted for an unconscionably long time. North of the border there was enthusiastic anticipation; south of it misgiving and dread. The Scots knew who Elizabeth's rightful successor was. The English hoped that they did; but until James actually inherited her throne, they lived with the spectre of invasion from France or Spain, or the nightmare of internal claimants and a return to dynastic civil war, recreating the horrors of the Wars of the Roses, which the Tudors, that spectacularly unsuccessful dynasty, had done so much to foster. Moreover, the Scots had no doubt that that important European creature, a Scottish king, was fully worthy to sit on the English throne. The English, whose imperialist policy towards Scotland since the late thirteenth century had been a failure, and whose defeat in the Hundred Years' War had further reduced their international standing, naturally regarded a Scottish king as an inferior being. Leading English politicians had learned how to behave to kings, and never more so than under Elizabeth, so they concealed their view, deluging the new king with praise and flattery such as he had never experienced in Scotland. They had to, out of sheer self-interest, for the king was the greatest source of patronage. James's peaceful accession came as a huge relief and, initially, the omens looked good. The voices of the small fry in the southern English counties who in the summer of 1603 spoke against the accession of a foreign king, challenging its validity, were drowned out by the roars of acclamation which greeted James as he travelled from Edinburgh to London. Crowds poured out to greet him; a loyal Yorkshire farmer had the arms of Scotland and England painted over his mantelpiece; English and Scottish poets extolled union; and the Great North Road was jammed by the rush of Elizabethan courtiers and officials to get to the new king and fix their interests, while Robert Cecil, dominant Elizabethan politician, forced to stay in London, did his best in a flood of correspondence in which he portrayed himself as the king's most loyal and greatest servant. It was a veneer.

Like any veneer, it had some substance, but it was thin. Within weeks of the union, the dreaded subject of equal opportunities reared its head; should James's Scottish household officials be paid as much as his English ones? James was so quickly disabused of his over-optimistic hope that Anglo-Scottish familiarity at court would produce liking that, from May 1603, his bedchamber, that political inner sanctum with its priceless benefit of access to the king, was staffed exclusively by Scots (Cuddy 1987, 173–225). Despite the British imagery of the triumphal arches erected for his ceremonial entry into London in 1604, the House of Commons, terrified of losing the name England, decisively rejected his demand to be styled King of Great Britain. In 1605, therefore, he assumed the title by proclamation, thus challenging his English parliament, and showing a level of arbitrary behaviour which his pre-1603 Scottish subjects would hardly have recognised. In 1606 he followed this up with a proclamation which introduced the union flag for shipping. In 1607 the English parliament killed any hope of a union which went beyond the purely personal. James's hope of 'one king, one law, one people' would be no more than 'one king', just as his other desire, 'a union of hearts and minds', foundered amidst the relentless Anglo-Scottish brawling – at court, in the streets of London, at horse races – which was still virulent in 1616. Meanwhile, by 1607, his Scottish parliament and privy council were showing distinct unease about royal neglect and fear of being reduced to a province, while Scottish pamphlets on union, mainly designed, like their English counterparts, to survey ways of making union work by drawing on the examples of contemporary European unions, began to state the belief that the king would not forget his ancient and native kingdom (Galloway 1986; Galloway and Levack 1985). The experience of union was such that, while some of the pre-1603 English fears had been allayed, others had been reinforced, while for the Scots doubts had replaced enthusiasm. Union was not a blessing; and the king's position, while enhanced, was deeply unenviable.

COMPOSITE MONARCHY, 1603–25

James's dual monarchy lasted as long as his personal rule in Scotland. This chapter gives it less space, intentionally; for inevitably James's style of kingship changed. The question is how it changed and with what consequences, and that can be assessed only by getting away from the old idea that James sprang into life in 1603, and by giving thorough consideration to the way in which he governed as king of Scots. Older generations of English and American historians, such as S.R. Gardiner, Wallace Notestein and D.H. Willson, thought it axiomatic that James could not succeed as king of England, because that task required skills far beyond the capabilities of a king from Scotland. The most such historians might allow was that surviving the overmighty Scottish aristocracy was to his credit. In this, they were following the lead given by Nicholas Fuller, MP, who in the English parliament of 1610 said that it was the duty of the commons to tell the king of England what by the laws of England he could do. If few were so outspoken as to make such an amazing claim, there was much grumbling about a Scottish king who must be restrained from favouring the Scots, letting them get their grubby and grasping hands on English offices, English trade, English money. In 1609 Cecil looked wistfully back to Elizabeth, who had listened to few counsellors, of whom he was the chief, whereas James listened to many. It did not help that after 1603 James drew on the theory of divine-right monarchy, as set out in his *Trew Law of Free Monarchies*, in a way he had not done before 1603, and kept the House of Commons constantly on the jump, sometimes talking unexceptionally about king-in-parliament as the legislator, sometimes indicating that the king was the legislator and it was of his choice and goodness to use parliaments. That, and his use of proclamations, gave rise to the belief that the road to the English Civil War of the 1640s began in 1603, with the accession of the first of the two arbitrary and tyrannical Stuart kings, a belief not challenged until 1965 (Elton 1965, 325–47).

The problem in Scotland was rather different. James VI's reputation did not sink as low as that of James I. Not only was there his reign before 1603 to draw on, but it could be argued that absentee kingship in Scotland was less of a problem than elsewhere, simply because of the long experience of *de facto* absentee kingship, during repeated royal minorities. Moreover, with the exception of the pre-eminent politician of the early years of union, George Hume, earl of Dunbar, who died in 1611, those with whom he had worked before 1603 lived on until the end of his reign. Absentee kingship was therefore sustained by and mitigated through mutual personal knowledge. It was also sustained by correspondence. James's claim to the English parliament in 1607, that 'here I sit and govern Scotland with the pen, which my ancestors could not do by the sword' has been over-quoted and often misunderstood. He was addressing a very sceptical English audience, and trying to persuade it that the Scots, whom the English regarded as only a little less barbaric than the Irish, were, whatever the past, now governable and civilized. James's words were PR, not a strictly historical comment – in lamentable modern parlance, a spin. But they had this much truth: the king having in 1603 set up an efficient postal service between Edinburgh and London, letters flowed between him and his Scottish councillors. And it is notable that these letters, between men who knew one another, were much more discussion documents than those arbitrary letters sent by Charles I to Scots that he did not bother to know (Lee 1980).

Another way of coping with absentee kingship was to ennoble those lairds who had risen in his service; this was the way to advancement in post-union Scotland. Of James's twenty-seven creations of earldoms, there were five in 1580–1 (before he was fully in control), four in 1599–1600, and eighteen between 1605 and 1624. Moreover, the post–1603 earldoms, unlike those before, markedly favoured the king's servants. Whether this was the creation of a *noblesse de robe* is a debating point, as is the question of how far the 'old' nobility were re-thinking their role and seeing themselves as servants of the 'state'. Both are entirely possible. What is certain is that King James, far from fearing the aristocracy, saw that his absentee government should be maintained through them. In the new circumstances after 1603, the traditional reward for service in the localities was also conferred upon those who served in central government for an absentee king. It is worth pointing out, in assessing James's attitude, that Elizabeth's great secretary William Cecil died as Lord Burghley while his son Robert's service to King James brought him the earldom of Salisbury.

There is, however, a vast difference between minority and absentee kingship. The very fact that the king's need for the aristocracy had changed had an undoubted effect on its nature and aspirations. The court, the nerve-centre of political life and, crucially, of informal politics, had gone for good, as had that other arena for informal politics, the hunting-field. The king was not only absentee but part-time, embroiled now in the government of England. Present in England, he was certainly frustrated by being unable to take a personal part in council and parliament there; in the latter, he could only operate through set speeches. Absent from Scotland, he could no longer be the presence in council and parliament which he had been there before 1603. For different reasons, therefore, but with the same result he began to show a more arbitrary face to his Scottish subjects as well as to his English ones. He became king of Scotland instead of king of Scots; that identification with the people rather than the kingdom, which the Scottish monarchy had maintained long after it had gone in England and in France, was now broken. He was no longer, for the Scots, 'our soverane lord'; he was now 'his sacred majesty'. In his efforts to control parliament, he began to make unacceptable demands. In 1609 he attempted to nominate the committee of the articles, although that was successfully resisted. And in 1617 when, during his return to Scotland, he sat with that committee in parliament, he was forced to concede that it would never include more than eight officers of state. But the 1621 parliament, in which the burning issues were a new form of taxation (on interest payments) and, even more contentious, the five articles of Perth (see below), witnessed a level of manipulation never before experienced (Goodare 1995, 29–51). The election of the committee of the articles was a political fix and even before they met at 8 a.m. for their daily deliberations, the king's manager, Thomas Hamilton, earl of Melrose, was up at 6 a.m. lobbying. Proxy voting was allowed and two English peers were given Scottish titles in order to be able to vote. The king won the vote on the five articles. But the combination of votes against and abstentions was greater than the total of votes in favour.

It is difficult to know how far the move towards this more arbitrary style was forced on James because of the circumstances of absentee kingship, and how far it was one which he himself willingly adopted, helped on, no doubt, by the cocoon of flattery in which he was wrapped in England. No doubt it was a combination of both. With his Scottish feet still firmly on the English ground in the first years of his dual monarchy he did recognise the dangers of flattery. He had complained to his English parliament in 1604 that in Scotland he was heard as counsellor as well as king, whereas in England there was only 'curiosity' to find fault with his propositions. But in 1607, in his last battle with parliament over the union issue, the grounds for complaint had shifted; his English counsellors, he said, had misled him over the question of opposition to his proposals, so that he had gone in so deep that he could not in honour draw back. But in time, no doubt, he came to find English style more soothing than Scottish; even in his 1604 complaint he had described his Scots as 'men not of the best temper'. Yet had it only been a question of secular affairs, that crucial mitigating factor – that he was a very known quantity in Scotland – might have seen him through. The trouble was of course that it was not.

ECCLESIASTICAL POLITICS AFTER 1603

Separating secular and ecclesiastical politics may be a matter of convenience, but it is also potentially misleading. The fact that in the 1621 parliament taxation and the five articles of Perth were presented as a single package symbolizes the extent to which both were inextricably intertwined. And if in 1617 James was genuine in his salmon-like wish to return to his native kingdom, it could hardly be ignored that his insistence that this time he really was coming to Scotland, in the teeth of strenuous opposition in England, was because of his intention to introduce the five articles, which included restoring the celebration of Christmas and Easter, kneeling at communion, and private baptism and private communion for the sick. It is also a measure of his awareness that this time he would have a real fight on his hands that he determined to wage it in person, rather than by edict from London – although, as with his English advisers in 1607, he could complain that his Scottish ones did not warn him of the extent of hostility to the articles until too late.

It is now much better understood that before 1603 it was not simply a matter of episcopal king against presbyterian ministers; and revisionary work on the Hampton Court conference has shown that in 1604 James was not lining up with his English bishops against English puritans (Collinson 1983, 27–51). Indeed, English puritans appeared positively mild compared to Scottish presbyterians, and certainly had an easier time of it in James's church than in Elizabeth's. For James was not, in ecclesiastical affairs, a hard-liner, determined to impose his views on his subjects; even the Catholics found life more tolerable, despite the notorious – and in part anti-Scottish – Gunpowder Plot of 1605. As late as 1612, when he claimed supremacy over the church, he did so in a notably restrained way. And in 1616–18 he spearheaded a successful effort to increase clerical stipends. Yet his support for the Arminian Richard Montagu's *New Gagge for an Old Goose* has raised the question of whether by the end of his reign he still held by the Calvinist doctrines of his youth and much of his adult life. The break in the pattern comes with the five articles, with their accompanying and highly offensive idea of putting statues and an organ into the chapel royal at Holyrood and introducing a new liturgy – proposals which were not carried through. The gentler face of the English church seemed to have seduced the Scottish king.

Well, perhaps, but again we have to look beyond the railings of the presbyterian writers. Kneeling at communion, which did smack of Anglicanism, or, even worse, popery, was certainly an outrage. But the 'Anglican' James never attempted to turn the Scottish bishops, dressed in the plain black gowns of the ministry and working alongside the courts of the church, into English-style bishops, as Charles I would do. Private baptism and communion could be seen as a charitable leavening of the church's denial of spiritual consolation for the sick and the dying. The article on Christmas and Easter called only for preaching on these days, something which fell distinctly short of the celebration of Christmas which continued in Perth and Aberdeen (Todd 2002, 183–9). Not all Scots enjoyed the experience of being made to be godly, and that was surely in the mind of a king whose own lifestyle had never been noted for austere piety.

In Anglo-Scottish terms, the argument has been advanced that what he was aiming at was not wholesale conformity, which he could not have achieved, but 'congruity' (Morrill 1990, 1–30; 1994, 209–37); and certainly this would have minimised the problem of royal schizophrenia in British ecclesiastical affairs. But more recently it has been convincingly pointed out that his religious policy should not just be seen as a parallel to his Anglo-Scottish secular pursuits, but rather set in the context of his European ecumenical vision (Patterson 1997; MacDonald 2005, 885–903). That vision failed, as it was bound to do, in both the European and the British context. What was left, at the end of James's British rule, was a riven, uneasy and distracted church in Scotland. It was not a good omen for the future.

CONCLUSION

One of the early signs of unease in Scotland about the effects of union was the demand in 1604 that the Scots should be kept informed about foreign policy and given copies of treaties.

It was because of his foreign policy – peace with the arch-enemy Spain in 1604, refusal to fight for his Calvinist son-in-law Frederick Elector Palatine when he was attacked by the Holy Roman Emperor in 1620, his attempt to avert the Thirty Years' War through marrying his son Charles to the Spanish Infanta – that James's kingship of England would end in failure (Redworth 2003). In this, Scotland was indeed left on the sidelines. In Scotland, questions about the success of his kingship turn on domestic affairs: were absentee kingship and, even more, his ecclesiastical policy, bound to bring him to failure? Indeed, while English historians no longer see the origins of the English constitutional revolution and civil war of the 1640s in James's reign, is it possible that the origins of the Scottish constitutional revolution and civil war of the 1630s, which began the chain of events, can be located in his Scottish rule? There are grounds for suggesting this. James's rule from England did put huge strains on Scottish government, and even more the Scottish church. Yet the answer must surely be no. For twenty-two years a Scottish king of proven ability in Scotland held together the ramshackle, messy and highly problematic union; and his legacy was a commitment to union which would endure even when, after Charles I's execution in 1649, Cromwell and the English republican government would willingly have broken it, leaving the Scots to have a Stuart king for themselves in the person of Charles II. That was a remarkable achievement. At the time, Scotsmen, like their English counterparts, were well aware of the profound difference between James VI and I and Charles I. Whatever mistakes James had made were violently compounded by his infinitely less able son; and in the 1630s it was churchmen as well as laymen who, experiencing that son, looked back to the days of 'blessed king James'.

REFERENCES

Akrigg, G.V.P. 1984 *Letters of King James VI and I*. Berkeley.

Brown, K.M. 2004 'The Reformation Parliament' in Brown, K.M. and Tanner, R.J. (eds), *The History of the Scottish Parliament, vol. 1: Parliament and Politics in Scotland, 1235–1560*. Edinburgh.

Collinson, P. 1983 'The Jacobean Religious Settlement: The Hampton Court Conference', in Tomlinson, H. (ed), *Before the English Civil War: Essays on Early Stuart Politics and Government*, London, 27–51.

Cuddy, N. 1987 'The revival of the entourage: the Bedchamber of James I, 1603–1625', in Starkey, D. (ed), *The English Court from the Wars of the Roses to the Civil War*, London, 173–225.

Donaldson, G. 1965 *Scotland: James V–VII*. Edinburgh.

Donaldson, G. 1976 'The Legal Profession in Scottish Society in the sixteenth and seventeenth centuries', *Juridical Review*, new series 21, 1–19.

Elton, G.R. 1965 'A High Road to Civil War?' in Carter, C.H. (ed), *From the Renaissance to the Counter Reformation: Essays in Honour of Garrett Mattingly*. New York.

Galloway, B.R. and Levack, B.P. (eds) 1985 *The Jacobean Union: six tracts of 1604*. Edinburgh.

Galloway, B.R. 1986 *The Union of England and Scotland, 1603–1608*. Edinburgh.

Goodare, J. 1989 'Parliamentary taxation in Scotland, 1560–1603', *Scottish Historical Review* 68, 23–52.

Goodare, J. 1995 'The parliament of 1621', *Historical Journal* 38, 29–51.

Goodare, J. 1999 *State and Society in Early Modern Scotland*. Oxford.

Goodare, J. 2000 'James VI's English Subsidy', in J. Goodare and M. Lynch (eds), *The Reign of James VI*. East Linton, 110–25.

Kirk, J. 1980 ' "The Polities of the Best Reformed Kirks": Scottish achievements and English aspirations in church government after the Reformation', *Scottish Historical Review* 59, 22–53.

Lee, M. 1959 *John Maitland of Thirlestane and the Foundation of the Stewart Despotism in Scotland*. Princeton.

Lee, M. 1980 *Government by Pen: Scotland under James VI and I*. Urbana.

Lynch, M. 1991 *Scotland: A New History*. London.

MacDonald, A.R. 1998 *The Jacobean Kirk, 1567–1625: Sovereignty, Polity and Liturgy*. Aldershot.

MacDonald, A.R. 2005 'James VI and I, the Church of Scotland, and British ecclesiastical convergence', *Historical Journal* 48, 885–903.

Mason, R.A. 2005 'Renaissance and Reformation: The Sixteenth Century', in Wormald, J. (ed), *Scotland: A History*. Oxford.

Patterson, W.B. 1997 *King James VI and I and the Reunion of Christendom*. Cambridge.

Redworth, G. 2003 *The Prince and the Infanta: The Cultural Politics of the Spanish Match*. New Haven.

Todd, M. 2002 *The Culture of Protestantism in Early Modern Scotland*. New Haven.

Williamson, A.H. 1983 'Scotland, Antichrist and the invention of Britain', in J. Dwyer, R.A. Mason and A. Murdoch (eds), *New Perspectives on the Politics and Culture of Early Modern Scotland*, Edinburgh, 34–58.

Wormald, J. 1985 *Lords and Men in Scotland: Bonds of Manrent 1442–1603*. Edinburgh.

Wormald, J. 1995 'Ecclesiastical vitriol: the kirk, the puritans and the future king of England', in Guy, J. (ed), *The Reign of Elizabeth I: Court and Culture in the Last Decade*, Cambridge, 171–91.

FURTHER READING

Brown, K.M. 1989 *Bloodfeud in Scotland, 1573–1625*. Edinburgh.

Brown, K.M. 1992 *Kingdom or Province? Scotland and the Regal Union, 1603–1715*. London.

Brown, K.M. 2000 *Noble Society in Scotland: Wealth, Family and Culture, from Reformation to Revolution*. Edinburgh.

Croft, P. 2003 *King James*. Basingstoke.

Donaldson, G. 1942 'The attitude of Whitgift and Bancroft to the Scottish church', *Transactions of the Royal Historical Society* 4th series, 24, 95–115.

Goodare, J. 2004 *The Government of Scotland 1560–1625*. Oxford.

Goodare, J. and Lynch, M. (eds) 2000 *The Reign of James VI*. East Linton.

Kirk, J. 1989 *Patterns of Reform*. Edinburgh.

Lee, M. 1990 *Great Britain's Solomon: James VI and I in His Three Kingdoms*. Urbana.

Lee, M. 2003 *The 'Inevitable' Union and other essays on Early Modern Scotland*. East Linton.

Levack, B.P. 1987 *The Formation of the British State: England, Scotland and the Union, 1603–1707*. Oxford.

Mason, R.A. 1998 *Kingship and the Commonweal: Political Thought in Renaissance and Reformation Scotland*. East Linton.

Morrill, J. 1990 'The National Covenant in its British context', in Morrill, J. (ed), *The Scottish National Covenant in its British context*, Edinburgh, 1–30.

Morrill, J. 1994 'A British Patriarchy? Ecclesiastical imperialism under the early Stuarts', in Fletcher, A. and Roberts, P. (eds), *Religion, culture and society in early modern Britain: essays in honour of Patrick Collinson*, Cambridge, 209–37.

Mullan, D.G. 1986 *Episcopacy in Scotland: the History of an Idea, 1560–1638*. Edinburgh.

Mullan, D.G. 2000 *Scottish Puritanism, 1590–1638*. Oxford.

Murdoch, S. 2003 *Britain, Denmark-Norway and the House of Stuart, 1603–1660*. East Linton.

Smith, A.G.R. (ed) 1973 *The Reign of James VI and I*. London.

Williamson, A.H. 1979 *Scottish National Consciousness in the Age of James VI*. Edinburgh

Wormald, J. 1983 'James VI and I: Two Kings or One', *History* 68, 187–209.

Wormald, J. 2005 'O Brave New World? The Union of England and Scotland in 1603', in Smout, T.C. (ed), *Anglo-Scottish Relations from 1603–1900*, Oxford, 13–35.

CHAPTER THREE

Charles I, the Covenants and Cromwell: 1625–1660

David Stevenson

In the years covered by this chapter, Scotland experienced a revolution in the original sense of the word – a complete turn in the wheel of fortune. Absolute monarchy was followed by the collapse of royal power, years of war, conquest, republican rule, and finally a return to absolute monarchy. But the turn did not take Scotland back to where she had started, for the wheel had moved on. Post-Restoration monarchy and society were to be notably different from their predecessors. This succession of political upheavals imposes a basically chronological approach to the period.

ABSOLUTISM TRIUMPHANT? THE YEARS OF PEACE, 1625–37

That the reign of Charles I culminated in complete disaster, with civil wars in all three of his kingdoms, his own execution and the abolition of monarchy, is undeniable. With the benefit of hindsight it is obvious that the king's policies and style of kingship played the prime role in bringing about catastrophe. It is therefore tempting to study the early years of Charles's reign largely as a matter of finding the causes that were to lead to failure. The period 1625 to 1637 has indeed been described as 'the road to revolution' (Lee 1985). Other modern studies basically agree on this (Donald 1990; Macinnes 1991).

But this assumption is worth questioning. The events which began in Scotland in 1637 came as a complete surprise, not just to the king himself but to the vast majority of his subjects. If Charles had assessed his reign in Scotland early in 1637 he would have had justification for regarding it as a success story. He was implementing many reforming policies. True, he had faced strong opposition, but he seemed to be overcoming it. His claim to absolute power as a sovereign, appointed by God to rule, was being successfully asserted. An over-powerful nobility had been put in its place. Religious reforms, following on those made by his father, had been pushed faster and further than James would have dared – or even wanted. There had been grumbling and protest, but no organised opposition on any scale. His visit to Scotland in 1633 for his coronation had been (in his eyes at least) a triumphal one. Parliament had done all he demanded of it. Though it is true that resentment had been visible, obedience had been given. Royal power had reached a new peak. Undoubtedly, Charles was complacent (and had the arrogance that almost inevitably followed from believing he was God's direct agent), but he had some reason to be. Looked at in a wider European context, the three kingdoms of the British monarchy seemed among the most fortunate and best ruled. They remained at peace (apart from brief and limited conflicts with France and Spain in the later 1620s) while much of Europe was locked in the vast and bloody religio-dynastic conflict that was to become known as the Thirty Years War (1618–48). Britain seemed a haven of stability. Yet, as 1637 was to prove, Charles's absolutism was fragile, a house of cards that collapsed with remarkable speed.

Key to the king's early successes as well as his ultimate failure was his rigid personality, as displayed in his attitude to his own position. He being absolute, the role of his subjects was simply to do as they were told. That some disliked his policies was irritating but irrelevant. They should obey, and if he ruled with proper firmness they would obey. Even some of his officials were deeply unhappy at his policies but he retained them in office so long as they obeyed. In this extremely simplified vision of the relations of king and subjects, there was very little room for manoeuvre, compromise, or taking account of what might be expedient or politic. When dissenting views, however loyally expressed, were put before Charles, his reaction was to complain about sedition and challenges to royal authority. He was a king for whom almost everything was a matter of principle.

When Charles came to the throne in 1625 there were two main areas in which he was determined to act – finance and religion. That urgent and sweeping action was needed in the first place was obvious. The Scottish crown was running ever deeper into debt, so income had to be increased. In the case of religion, the need for action of the type and on the scale Charles took rested on his strongly-held personal beliefs. Acting as he did was his duty to God. In both areas Charles was certain to meet strong opposition. If more of Scotland's gross domestic product went to the king, less would be retained by his subjects. In religion, Charles's rigid beliefs on church government and worship conflicted with the equally rigid beliefs of many of his subjects. Today to say someone is innovative is usually a compliment. Unfortunately, Charles was an outstandingly innovative king who lived in a tradition-based society in which innovation was nearly always regarded as obnoxious.

The traditional annual revenues of the crown totalled about £200,000 Scots. This was less than the incomes of some of the king's greatest English and Irish subjects. By contrast, annual expenditure in the mid 1630s on pensions, fees to officials, the household, and interest payments on royal debt alone was about £335,000. The debt itself approached £1,000,000 (Stevenson 1974).

One approach to the problem of an under-resourced crown was to increase taxation. This rose extremely fast: in the decade after 1610, the total of land tax granted to the king had been £507,000; in the 1630s it was £4,000,000 (Brown 1989, 73–4). The amount that was actually paid was much lower, as collection was highly inefficient. Nonetheless, the rate at which tax demands were rising aroused resentment and fears for the future among the merchants and landowners who paid it – and among tenants, who feared rent rises would be imposed so that their landlords could pay higher taxes. Big rises in the taxation of interest payments alarmed the mercantile community (as well as the many landowners who were frequently in debt and thus paying interest on loans). Customs rates were also augmented.

Yet, until the mid 1630s, all these rises in taxation brought little benefit to the crown, through the incompetence and corruption of the financial administration, and the king's tendency (like his father) to grant hefty pensions to those he favoured. By the later 1630s there were signs, however, of a concerted attempt at greater efficiency, with the king giving power in such matters to the treasurer depute, the earl of Traquair, who was promoted to treasurer in 1636. He was a man ready to get tough with those who thwarted the king's intentions. Inevitably, this made him enemies, but he made things worse by his personal behaviour. He seemed to enjoy bullying people. By the time crisis came, Scotland was seething with resentment at increased taxation and harsh, insensitive administration.

Increased taxation, however, was only part of the king's strategy for reforming royal finance. He wanted a fundamental change that would permanently endow the crown with enough capital resources (land) to enable it to rely largely on 'ordinary revenues' derived from it. The result would be less dependence on taxation and the removal of the need for calling parliaments. The crown and the church would both benefit, for the church lacked the resources necessary to implement Charles's plans for it.

From the king's point of view such a redistribution of property from lay land-owners to crown and church was fully justified, as it would represent the correction of a structural imbalance that had been growing for generations. Over the previous century, the scale of the transfer of land to lay landowners had been vast, as the great wealth of the pre-Reformation church had been looted, and a weak crown had sanctioned this as well as alienating its own lands. Thirty-nine new lordships had been erected from former church lands, greatly boosting the size of the titled nobility, which totalled 102 in 1637 (Brown 2000, 9–10). Many other titled and non-titled landowners had also benefited from the fall of the old church and the weakness of the crown. The argument that the balance of wealth in Scotland needed a major adjustment in favour of crown and church was strong. But the changes required were revolutionary and were bound to be bitterly resented.

On coming to the throne in March 1625 Charles acted fast, so as to take advantage of the traditional right of a Scottish sovereign to revoke gifts of crown property made to subjects during his minority. This right would expire when he reached the age of twenty-five in November, so he needed to move quickly. He also resolved to extend the scope of his action far beyond any previous revocation by including all grants of royal and church property since 1540.

The revocation was never fully enforced. Perhaps, indeed, Charles never meant it to be, intending it rather as a statement of principle and a demonstration of his powers, designed to encourage landowners to agree to more limited changes. If this was part of his reasoning, it was a disastrous miscalculation. Scotland's landowners, the dominant class in society, came to believe that the king was hostile to them and was no respecter of property rights. The lasting distrust that Charles induced in them was not compensated for by the limited financial gains he achieved. After years of negotiation, revocation was toned down to a fraction of what was originally threatened. A few surrenders of church property were arranged, enough to prove the king's right to enforce them. Much more widespread than outright surrenders, however, was the calling of landowners holding former church and crown property before a commission to reach settlements which involved changes in tenure and increases in payments due to the crown.

The king had of course realised that there would be opposition to the revocation, but he had expected it to be limited to the greater landlords, the tenants-in-chief who held their land directly from the crown. He had hoped to counter their opposition by presenting the act as something that would benefit landlords further down the feudal hierarchy. Many who were vassals of tenants-in-chief would become tenants-in-chief themselves, and thus be freed from the tyranny of great men. But it turned out that those offered such supposed benefits were ungrateful. They preferred long-established noble 'tyranny' to the complicated reforms of a king who, after meddling in the property rights of the great, might well put them next on his shopping-list.

If the revocation and taxation gave landowners plenty to grumble about, so did Charles's religious policies. Many might have had objections in principle to episcopacy, but the men James VI had appointed as bishops had generally been fairly modest in their ambitions and their powers had been limited. But Charles I wanted to restore full episcopacy, as in England, with bishops dominant in the church, enforcing its discipline and also playing a major role in civil affairs. The Reformation had not only brought lay landowners riches in land; it had also seen the collapse of the ecclesiastical hierarchy that had previously stood alongside their lay hierarchy and played a major role in ruling the country, providing the crown with advisers and officials. Now King Charles was determined to restore part of that hierarchy, and inevitably this seemed to greater landowners a threat to the dominance they had become used to. Pre-Reformation bishops had, moreover, mainly been men from noble families, acceptable in power, whereas the bishops of Charles I were of relatively lowly birth, and therefore much less palatable to the nobility as men with whom they would have to share power. When the king made the archbishop of St Andrews chancellor of Scotland in 1634 he was the first cleric to hold any of the great offices of state for three quarters of a century – and the chancellorship was the highest office of all. The hierarchies of church and state were being united in a way that made a bold statement about the new status of bishops, and some of the bishops appointed by Charles tended to be zealous and assertive. Eight gained seats on the privy council, where they met with lay resentment. Other challenges to the nobility were less concrete but nonetheless real. Traditionally, they were the crown's main instruments in ruling the country: they were the 'inferior magistrates' (not a derogatory term, but one distinguishing them from the king, the supreme magistrate), the king's natural advisers and companions. An absentee monarch, based hundreds of miles to the south, made these roles difficult to play – especially when the king was a man unwilling to listen to advice. What was the point of having a seat on the privy council when, under Charles, its chief function was implementing instructions sent by post? The king's 1633 visit to Scotland confirmed that he was unwilling to listen to advice or criticism even when he was on the spot. Growing bureaucracy in government led to the expansion of the numbers of administrators and lawyers, who annoyed landowners by seeming to play a more important role in government than they did, and by their willingness to help the king with his complicated reforms.

Resentment over taxation and revocation may have affected the nobility most directly, but worries about the implications of these measures were much more widespread, and led to unease in Scotland that can be labelled patriotic. The king was planning to change Scotland dramatically, in ways which seemed to diminish the country's status. Those who had seen the union of the crowns as a Scottish triumph, with a Scottish dynasty taking the English crown, found that within a generation it had a king who might be Scottish by birth, but was English in everything else. Some of his policies (as in religion) were clearly anglicising. Reducing the dominance of the greater nobility and creating a free gentry was also intended to make Scots society more like English. Charles's tendency to show impatience when told he was ignoring customary practices in administrative and legal matters caused alarm among his own officials. He was unwilling to show respect for Scottish traditions that were, to many, important to national identity. It has, it is true, been said that 'James made the union work and there was no reason it should not work just as well under Charles' (Brown 1989, 84). But in Charles Scotland had a king who might be a Stuart but was an alien. Absentee monarchy had 'removed the keystone from the edifice of government' (Sharpe 1992, 773); the country's financial and religious difficulties had been inherited from his father, and 'arguably, James had exacerbated these problems in the last decade of his reign' (Brown 2001, 241).

Opposition to religious change was partly based on aristocratic determination not to surrender church lands. It was easy for men to persuade themselves, when the time for resistance came, that their actions were based on religious principles. Some, however, had accepted King James's low-key bishops in practice, though opposed to them on principle, but were openly hostile to the new-style bishops of King Charles, especially when they actively promoted changes in worship. To most people in society the way the church was governed might be a matter for some controversy, but such matters impinged little on their daily lives. Changes in worship, by contrast, were immediately evident to all, and were seen as violations of practices that had become traditional and were regarded as sacrosanct. James VI had discovered the particular dangers of meddling with worship with the imposition of the five articles of Perth. The price he paid for them was high. Some of the more 'godly' ministers and laymen had taken to holding gatherings outside the official worship of the Church – prayer-meetings, or conventicles. These cells of defiance involved only a tiny percentage of the population, but contained men (and women) who were committed, and were taking a first, quiet step in deciding to organise themselves into groups which put their own version of obedience to God's will above that of a king who also claimed divine authority. These cells should not be seen as actively revolutionary in intention or mood. As has recently been shown (Mullan 1998), these 'godly' folk who kept in touch through conventicles and letters tended to be gloomy about the future. Recent decades had seen the areas of Europe in which Calvinism prevailed shrink dramatically in the face of the success of Catholic Counter-Reformation. The godly saw themselves as remnants of a true national church which was being destroyed. They were determined to remain loyal to their presbyterian/puritan beliefs, but were becoming reconciled to the fact that they were an isolated minority. A handful of ministers drew persecution down on themselves by openly preaching and worshipping in defiance of official policy. A number fled with their followers to Ulster, hoping to find freer conditions among the Scottish settlers there. Others planned to emigrate with their most committed supporters to New England, as many English puritans had done. In effect, they were coming close to accepting that they were a small sect in a sea of the ungodly, a position that seemed to fit in with the Calvinist notion that only a small minority was predestined for salvation.

In conflict with this, however, was another strand of belief. As in many countries that had accepted Protestantism, in Scotland the Church had come to the smug conclusion that it was better reformed than most – or even all – other churches. In the Scottish case, this perception was applied mainly through comparisons with England, and some persuaded themselves that part of the Church's mission was to bring England's church up to scratch. Instead, in matters of worship and church government Charles I intensified James's campaigns to remodel the church on English lines. Charles's insistence on elaboration of ritual in worship seemed to a great many Protestant Scots to be moving Scotland back to Roman Catholicism – a perception shared by a modern historian who has claimed that the king 'favoured theatrical devices that resulted in a ceremonial closely resembling that of Rome' (Brown 2001, 243). There could, in the eyes of most Scots, be nothing worse, for the pope was the Antichrist, and Rome the Whore of Babylon.

Organisation and confidence might be lacking among the many parish ministers who were worried by royal policy, but their potential for bringing pressure on the crown had been revealed under James VI. Their strength was to be dramatically demonstrated in and after 1637. Reformation had dissolved the old clerical structures, but there had emerged in their place a powerful new professional group: the parish ministers, usually men of fairly humble birth (the pay and status were too low to attract men from wealthy backgrounds into the Church). But the ministry had gained great influence over ordinary people, an influence that was soon to be shown in some instances to be greater than that of lay authorities – landowners, burgh councils, and even the king himself. It was awareness of the latent power of the ministry over the people that made it essential in the king's eyes to bring them under the strict control of powerful bishops and to curb their tendency towards independence of mind. After 1560, the strains between an ambitious new church, run by men from relatively low social backgrounds, and the crown and landowners had become obvious – and clashes between them at times dominated politics. The alliance of crown and landowners won, for their resources of wealth and authority vastly outweighed that of the ministers and those of their parishioners who supported them. Ministers held fairly negative opinions of great men, whose main interest in Reformation seemed to lie in looting the church of resources. If the Church was to gain resources to increase its status and preach its message more effectively, this would have to be at the expense of the nobility. The nobility's resistance to such a move made it easy for the ministry to consider them a barrier to God's work, and go on from there to see them as even more sinful than the majority of men. Wealth increased opportunities to indulge in sin.

Thus, in demanding that the nobility give up some of its ill-gotten gains, the king and the ministry were agreed in principle. But of course it was impossible for the two to make a common cause, for the king was determined to use such new resources to further his 'Catholicising' policies. In these circumstances the provision of extra resources became, for those opposed to the king, a deadly threat to the Church's purity.

The first sign of organised protest against royal policy was provoked by what must have seemed to the king his highly successful Scottish parliament of 1633. The way he had suppressed debate and made it clear that he was noting the names of those who showed any sign of opposition, as well as the policies he advanced in parliament, produced a backlash. A supplication was drawn up protesting at some of the king's actions, especially those relating to religious change, claiming that they were in breach of acts of parliament and the rights of the nobility. But the supplication had much wider constitutional implications. In suggesting that the king was breaking the law, it implied that royal power was limited by law. Significantly, the author of the supplication (William Haig) was not only a lawyer but a man who had been the king's solicitor in Scotland until a few years before. Thus another strand of growing concern at Charles's rule emerged. To noble and religious grievances were being added the disapproval of many in the powerful legal profession.

Two nobles who had emerged earlier as spokesmen for opposition to the revocation headed the group of dissidents behind the supplication: the earl of Rothes and Lord Loudoun. A few years later they were to become prominent in the leadership of the Covenanting movement, but in 1634 they decided against presenting the supplication to the king. Nonetheless, its existence was brought to the king's attention. Haig fled to safety abroad, and the best evidence found of noble involvement in the document was that Lord Balmerino had read a copy of it. He was tried and sentenced to death. The king doubtless saw this as an act which would terrify those who thought of opposing him, by showing them the fate they could expect. In time, Balmerino was pardoned, but instead of giving satisfaction as a sign that a strong king could also be a merciful one, the Balmerino affair may well have led the king's more determined opponents to the conclusion that the only sort of supplication the king would ever listen to would be one backed up by determination to resort to force if necessary. No general assemblies had met since 1618 and only one parliament since 1621: all constitutional channels for expressing grievances had been blocked.

Charles continued his religious reforms after 1633, moving into the sensitive matter of worship. On his 1633 visit to Edinburgh the king had horrified many by using English forms of worship, a clear demonstration of his plans for the Church as a whole. In 1636 appeared a Scottish Book of Canons (ecclesiastical laws), which was offensively 'anglicising' to many. It was well known that a next step, a Scottish Prayer Book, was planned, and this intensified fears for the future. When it was completed, orders were issued to make ministers agree to conform to it before they knew its contents. In the highly-charged atmosphere, this was taken to mean that the king knew that it would be unacceptable to many if they knew in advance what changes were to be made. By the time the book was published, its precise contents were irrelevant. A great many Scots had already decided that it was ungodly.

THE REVOLUTION OF THE COVENANTERS, 1637–41

The alliance that was to destroy royal power was one of nobility, Church and people. Modern commentaries tend to put the 'blame' for what, in the longer term, was to be disaster primarily on a nobility acting to protect its own interests. But the nobility, though undoubtedly the most powerful section of Scottish society, could never have brought about what happened on their own. What is remarkable about the early years of the revolution was that it was supported by strong elements in all the main groupings in Scottish society (except, of course, the bishops). The nobility led, but that was the nobility's accepted role in society, and, though many were driven by selfish motives, their claims that they had to act in the interests of protecting Scotland's liberties, traditions and religion were not entirely false. Opposition to the king was patriotic. What happened in Scotland might have strong resemblances to 'old fashioned' factional noble rebellions, but there was far more to it than that. The nobility could not have brought about the revolution that was to take place without widespread popular support arising from national and religious ideologies. The revolution's success was based on the alliance of noble (and mercantile) worldly resources and the ideology of puritan/presbyterian Calvinism. It was an alliance based on expediency rather than compatible ambitions, but enthusiasm at first hid this fatal flaw. It was Charles's genius for alienating almost every grouping of importance that drove his enemies into an unnatural alliance.

With the imposition of the Prayer Book imminent, some of those most committed to opposition decided that the time had come to act if the king was to be stopped. The first use of the Prayer Book was greeted with supposedly spontaneous opposition. In reality, this was organised by dissident ministers and godly Edinburgh citizens. Whether noble supporters were urging them on in secret is impossible to know for certain. It is often assumed, and it would be naïve to dismiss the idea. Certainly the speed with which landowners and others appeared to support the first protest suggests that they were prepared in advance; but their reaction may have been unplanned, a sign that the mood in Scotland was one of such tension that the first spark triggered a conflagration.

It was ordered that the Prayer Book be used first in Edinburgh, on 23 July 1637, so that the capital would set a good example to the rest of the country. The dissidents reversed the message. The Prayer Book was met with shouts of horror, the throwing of stools and books, and the furious withdrawal of congregations from churches. The response of the regime to this limited defiance was crucial. Perhaps if prompt and firm action had been taken, opposition could have been suppressed. But the nature of the regime was such that this was not possible. In Edinburgh the privy council, the heart of the government, was itself deeply unhappy at the king's religious policy. After the 23 July disturbances, councillors seemed more concerned to escape being blamed by the king than to impose his policies. Led by Traquair, lay councillors blamed events in Scotland on the provocative policies of the bishops. The bishops in turn blamed the lay members for lack of will. The weakness of absentee government and the centralising of power were revealed, for the council dared not act decisively without consulting the king. His reactions to the news from Edinburgh were predictable. No concessions were to be made to the dissidents, and his policies must be enforced. This blindly ignored the fact that open disobedience was spreading and there were no armed forces in Scotland to restore order. Yet month after month Charles simply repeated his orders that royal power be asserted.

Active defiance of the king fanned out from Edinburgh, and a movement begun by ordinary (if well-rehearsed) members of congregations very quickly won the support of many members of the country's elites. Moreover, the dissidents, finding widespread support in Scotland met by a refusal by their absentee king to take the situation seriously, rapidly widened their demands. What had begun as simply a plea that the Prayer Book be withdrawn grew into demands that all religious reforms since James VI's later years be cancelled. Increasingly, the dissidents, now led by members of the nobility, organised themselves into a committee structure that became a rival government, controlling much of the country. Caught between the rebels' demands and those of the king, the privy council's authority collapsed. That the highest legal official of the crown, Sir John Hope, the lord advocate soon showed open support for those defying the king revealed the hollowness of the regime's absolutist façade. Men who in the past had obeyed now showed what they thought. There were many who were soon to be called royalists in Scotland, including a number of nobles, but in many parts of the country they were powerless. Left without orders from the king, they were uncertain how to act. At all levels of society a remarkable wave of religious zeal became evident, rallying the people against innovations which were seen as bringing heresy and Catholicism to Scotland. They were driven at first as much by fear for the future as hope. Presbyterian-inclined ministers who might have reluctantly accepted the innovations were stunned at the scale of the opposition. The majority of the people, it seemed, were not ungodly after all, and (however theologically unsound) the idea that successful resistance was proving that God was on their side, and would support them instead of concentrating on punishing them for their sins, was intoxicating. A recent judgement is that they were 'opportunistically, lusting after power . . . and prostituting their religion in the embrace of an untrustworthy nobility pursuing its own goals' (Mullan 1998, 322). But the suggestion that lusting after power was a new temptation is misleading. They had always sought power but only now did it seem that they had a chance to gain it.

The culmination of the resistance to royal policy came in the National Covenant of February 1638, which was drafted by a leading minister, Alexander Henderson, and a zealous young lawyer, Archibald Johnston of Wariston. For a revolutionary declaration it can seem inappropriate, being very long and legalistic. It was a symbol, just as the Prayer Book had become, and doubtless few knew or understood it fully. The revolution the Covenant stood for was conservative and backward-looking, appealing for the restoration of a past that the king was destroying. It opens by renewing the anti-Catholic 'Negative Confession' forced on James VI in 1581. Endless anti-Catholic acts of parliament are then cited. Thus the new Covenanting movement appealed to the past for legitimacy, and defined itself as being essentially anti-Catholic. The document then explained how the Covenanters' actions were necessary to uphold the liberties of both church and nation. A free general assembly and a free parliament should be held to reach a settlement with the king. Signatories of the Covenant bound or 'covenanted' themselves to stand together in the cause, and similarly bound themselves to God. Copies were sent out around the country, and signed in most places with enthusiasm, though there are signs of compulsion when support was not readily given.

The Covenant at least persuaded Charles that he had to do more than shout repeated commands at his privy council if royal authority was to be restored in Scotland. He at last accepted that there was a need to negotiate with the Covenanters, and sent the marquis of Hamilton to Scotland as his commissioner. Hamilton (a man with no love of bishops) undertook his task with great reluctance, for though the king conceded that a general assembly might be held as part of a settlement, he insisted that this could happen only after the National Covenant was disowned. Eventually, however, he had to concede to a meeting without this, and in November 1638 an assembly was held at Glasgow, with Hamilton presiding as king's commissioner. The Covenanters were thorough in ensuring that membership was to their liking. Opponents were terrorised (many of the bishops had fled to safety in England). Powerful laymen pushed their way into presbyteries and the assembly in the guise of elders. Many more attended as 'assessors', while threatening crowds gathered to ensure the success of the cause. Hamilton soon lost control and ordered the assembly to dissolve. On its refusal, he withdrew. Left to themselves, the Covenanters indulged in an orgy of reform: the five articles of Perth, the Canons and the Prayer Book were all outlawed. Not only were the existing bishops all denounced and deposed, but the office of bishop itself was declared unlawful. Scotland was to have a church independent of the crown, presbyterian in structure.

Most were carried forward on the wave of enthusiasm, but some had fears for the future. Even among committed Covenanters there were men who were worried that they had gone too far, and there was an acceptance that civil war was now likely. Some ministers had a different worry. The independence of the Church from the crown had been proclaimed, but the ministry was in danger of succumbing to a new master – the nobility and lairds – through the Trojan Horse of the elders. Even those among the nobility who were sincere in their religious enthusiasm had other agendas. They were determined that, having got rid of the bishops who had challenged their dominance in society, they would not let an over-powerful parish ministry take their place. Yet, for the moment, Covenanting ministers were ready to hail (with a hint of surprise) the nobility as truly godly.

War as an outcome of the Covenanters' conflict with the king had long been a possibility. The radical actions of the Glasgow assembly made it likely. The opponents looked at first sight unevenly matched. Charles might have lost Scotland, but he still had (on paper) the resources of England and Ireland at his disposal – and they provided about 97.5% of the total ordinary crown revenue. But in reality the king's position was weak. Since 1629 he had ruled in England without a parliament, deciding that it was better to do without grants of taxation than endure parliament's complaints about his rule. Moreover, a great many Englishmen had considerable sympathy with the Scots, sharing many of their grievances about the king's methods of government and religious policies. Thus there was little enthusiasm in England for war with the Covenanters; and the Covenanters in their propaganda, while keen to appeal to patriotism, had stressed that this was not an anti-English patriotism, and that their grievances against the crown were shared by Englishmen (Sharpe 2002, 213–24). Trying to use Irish military resources against the Covenanters was also difficult: in the strong Scots plantation in Ulster, sympathy for the Covenanters was widespread. An army raised from among the Irish would inevitably be largely Catholic – and thus confirm fears that the king was pursuing Catholic policies.

The king began to raise forces in England in 1638, but lack of money, incompetence and the reluctance of Englishmen to fight Scots who were no threat to them were clear from the start. Things went little better in 1639 in the 'First Bishops' War'. Royal plans were grandiose, including invasion from England and Ireland by land and sea. But Charles failed to raise a strong enough army, and some of the main reasons for this echo the failure of his administration in Scotland. He sought to govern by giving orders and assuming that they would be implemented, not allowing for the fact that adequate administrative machinery was lacking (Fissel 1994). Thus the Covenanters were given time to raise an army, seize royal castles, and send forces to Aberdeen and the North-East to subdue resistance in a region in which support for the king was strong. An army was raised which, compared to that of the king in England, was well-organised and effective.

In the face of Scotland's obvious readiness to oppose invasion, the king had to back down, and a negotiated settlement was reached by the treaty of Berwick in June 1639. The rival armies disbanded, but this was clearly a truce rather than a peace, for neither king nor Covenanters would agree to make major concessions. Charles, determined on a new war, at last accepted that he needed taxation in England to finance one. But the English parliament which met in April 1640 proved a disaster. It refused to grant taxes until grievances had been settled, whereupon the king hastily dissolved it. All the 'Short Parliament' had achieved was to demonstrate that, having lost Scotland, Charles was now losing control of England. This gave the Covenanters the confidence to force a showdown. In June 1640 the Scottish parliament met, and its actions were revolutionary. Not only did it ratify the religious revolution of the Glasgow assembly, but also it carried out a constitutional revolution. It was a logical development: how could true religion be safe if the king retained absolute power? More mundanely, how could the Covenanters themselves ever feel safe from the vengeance of the king in the future unless his power was curbed? Scotland's laws and liberties had to be asserted to make this impossible.

The structure of parliament itself was radically changed. The lords of the articles, through which the king had come to control parliament, were abolished. The first estate, the bishops, was abolished (on Calvinist principles of separating church and state). At the same time, the voting power of the shire commissioners was doubled (previously, each shire elected two commissioners who shared a vote but now each commissioner was given a vote). More than ever before, parliament was to be the instrument of Scotland's landowners, who made up two of the three estates of nobles, shire commissioners and burgh commissioners. It was still nominally 'the king's parliament', but it would meet at least every three years whether he liked it or not, and parliamentary approval would be necessary for appointment of the officers of state, privy councillors and court of session judges.

Military action quickly followed. In the 'Second Bishops' War' of 1640 the Covenanters' army surged across the border, swept aside half-hearted English resistance, and occupied Newcastle and the rest of the north of England. They were then in a position to dictate their immediate terms to the king, and he agreed them in the treaty of Ripon in July. The Scottish army would remain in occupation of northern England until they were satisfied that the king would make a satisfactory settlement. Moreover, the king would pay this rebel army. This last point was obviously financially important to the Covenanters, but its significance was much wider. The Covenanters had crushingly defeated the king of Scotland, but they were well aware of being part of a three-kingdom monarchy. They could never feel safe while the king retained nearly absolute power in England. In the three years since 1637 the agenda had moved on. Original demands for the removal of a few religious innovations had widened into religious revolution, then into a Scottish constitutional revolution to protect it, and now into acceptance of the need to bring about a similar English constitutional revolution to protect everything that had been achieved. The 'Short Parliament' had shown its appetite for curbing Charles's power and, by making the king pay the Scots army, the Covenanters forced him to call another English parliament to vote taxes. What was to become the 'Long Parliament' duly met in November 1640, and the king was soon embroiled in disputes with it over grievances and demands for reform.

The Scottish crisis had been Charles's priority for over three years but, as the crisis in England grew, his perspective changed. Loss of control of a distant and small kingdom was bad, but compared to the threat of losing power in England it was a secondary matter. In 1641 he therefore accepted that he must bring an end (for the moment at least) to his conflict with the Covenanters, so that he could turn his attention to England. However, he was still determined to make the minimum of concessions, and hoped for the support of the considerable number of Covenanters who felt that the movement had gone too far in limiting royal power. He came to Scotland and parliament met, but though Charles made some compromises he resisted others with delaying tactics. Then his hand was forced by news of another catastrophic blow to his authority: in October 1641, Irish Catholics rose in rebellion, and soon controlled much of the country. Dealing with this threat became his first priority.

In the face of the Irish disaster, Charles caved in to the Covenanters, accepting their religious and constitutional revolutions in full so that he could return to London. Covenanters were appointed to the main offices of state, promotions to the nobility (and within it) of Charles's leading opponents were handed out – the dominant figure among the Covenanting politicians rose from earl to marquis of Argyll. Though the Scottish parliament was dissolved in November 1641, a number of powerful commissions were set up to work alongside the privy council (which still contained a substantial number of royalists) in running the country.

The Covenanters had triumphed, but they were still insecure. Catholic Ireland was a threat in response to which they could find common ground with the king they had just humiliated, for they agreed to send an army to Ulster to oppose the rebels. But no-one could doubt that the ultimate outcome of the struggles of the three kingdoms would depend on events in England. There the quarrel between parliament and the king deepened, and by mid 1642 civil war had begun. The last of the three-kingdom dominoes had fallen.

THE COVENANTERS AND THE BRITISH CRISIS, 1641–7

In the fighting in England in 1642–3 the royalists clearly gained the upper hand. In Scotland, which anxiously watched events, deep divisions emerged about how to react. Royalists, some of them former Covenanters, argued that the country should intervene on the king's side. He had granted them all they asked in 1641, and loyalty now meant that they must help him. Others argued for fence-sitting: it was England's war, and no business of the Scots. Yet it was clear that Scotland's future depended on England's fate. If the king crushed his English parliamentarian opponents and thus restored his power south of the border, how long would it be before he turned the resources of England against his Scottish enemies? Harsh political realism drove the Covenanters, led by Argyll, towards the conclusion that they must save the English parliamentary cause in self defence. Some reached this decision with great reluctance, but for others there was confidence, even enthusiasm. The Bishops' Wars had instilled an unrealistic belief in the country's military potential, and ideological support for intervention was strong among leading parish ministers. Originally amazed by the success of the Covenanting cause, some now excitedly believed that it showed them that the Scots were God's Chosen People who were now to be His instruments in imposing their religious ideas on England and Ireland.

Such political calculation and religious zeal combined to produce the Solemn League and Covenant (1643). Scotland would send an army of over 20,000 men into England, and the English parliament would pay it. In return, the English would enforce presbyterianism in their country and, after victory in the civil war, would reach a settlement that protected Scotland's interests by establishing links between the two parliaments. The union would become more than just a union of the crowns.

In one sense the Scots army that entered England in January 1644 served its purpose. It swung the balance in the civil war in favour of parliament by occupying the North. But it did not live up to the expectation that it would bring the war to a quick conclusion. Moreover, intervention in England provoked royalist rebellion in Scotland. The Irish reacted to Scots military intervention in Ireland by sending an expeditionary force to the Highlands, where it accepted the leadership of the earl of Montrose and was reinforced by other Scots royalists. In 1644–5 this little army of a few thousand men inflicted six successive defeats on the Covenanters. Now fighting in all three kingdoms, the Covenanters were militarily over-stretched. Only by recalling troops from England were they able to defeat Montrose and disperse his army.

The Montrose campaigns lost the Covenanters any hope of having a major part in a post-war settlement in England. Montrose's victories discredited them, and made their army in England reluctant to take the offensive. By the time he was defeated, it was clear that parliament was winning the English civil war, but it was now reluctant to give the Scots much credit for bringing this about, and was increasingly determined to renege on the religious and political promises it had made to the Scots in the Solemn League and Covenant. Disillusioned and feeling deeply betrayed, the Covenanters argued over how to react. Argument intensified when the king, fearing capture, fled and joined the Scottish army in England. His hope was that, now the Covenanters had no prospect of achieving their ambitions in alliance with the English parliament, they would support him against it. There was some sense in this, given how desperate the king's position was. Royalist sentiment was growing in Scotland, and many Covenanters were coming to think that the best way to a peace settlement in Britain which protected their interests might be to work in alliance with the king rather than in opposition to him. In the end, however, the king refused to make sufficient concessions on religion in England for the Covenanters to support him, and in January 1646 they withdrew their army from England, leaving Charles behind to fall into English parliamentarian hands.

This brought only short-term relief. To many, deserting a king who had turned to the Scots, his native people, for help was a betrayal. Complicating matters further, the English parliamentarians also found it impossible to reach any agreement with the captive king – and the proposals they made to him for a settlement were also unacceptable to Scotland. The belief that the main enemy to Scotland's interests was the English parliament grew ever stronger, especially among the nobility. It was concluded that another attempt must be made to make an alliance with the king.

COUNTER-REVOLUTION AND THE KIRK PARTY, 1647-51

At the end of 1647 a small group of Scots nobles secretly negotiated a treaty – the Engagement – with the king, and after furious debate it was pushed through the Scottish parliament by an alliance of Covenanter and royalist nobles. A new army would be sent into England to rescue the king and impose a British settlement. But it was clear that this new war would have far less support than those of 1640 and 1644. The general assembly of the Church rejected the Engagement, and thus the core alliance of landowners and ministers which had brought the Covenanters their early victories was shattered. Scotland had experienced a limited counter-revolution.

When the Engagers sought to raise a new army they met widespread resistance: men who took their lead from ministers rather than landlords sought to avoid recruitment. Nonetheless, a substantial army was raised, but it was commanded by the duke of Hamilton with monumental incompetence. It straggled into England and was shattered at Preston in August 1648 by Oliver Cromwell, now the dominant military and political figure in England. News of this defeat spurred the Kirk Party, as the Engagers' opponents were becoming known, into action. They seized power in Scotland and disowned the Engagement, but were humiliated by Cromwell insisting on marching into Scotland to ensure that enemies of the English parliament were excluded from power. As a result, when the Kirk Party's own parliament met, only a handful of nobles were allowed to sit, and many of the shire and burgh commissioners were new men, more committed to the Church than their predecessors.

In terms of British politics, Scotland was further than ever from being able to insist on a significant say in the future of Britain. But the Kirk Party had plenty to do at home. Scotland had to be changed so that no regime in future could seize power in defiance of the Church. Engagers had to be hunted down, banned from holding public office, and forced to do penance for their sins. The nobility in particular had to be humbled. A decade before, the ministry had hailed them as a true godly nobility but experience had led them to revert to old ideas about the nobles' lack of virtue. Instead, the Church put its faith in those further down the social scale. It was the people who were truly godly, so policies were introduced to protect them from oppressive landlords. But the failures of the Covenanters were not simply seen as the fault of treacherous nobles. Far more fundamentally, God, who had at first brought them success, had clearly grown angry with them and was punishing them. A priority therefore was a campaign to search out and punish sin, and a refusal to accept the services in church, state or army of those branded as ungodly. Thus, it was hoped, God's favour could be recovered.

However, before the Kirk Party regime got into its stride, the political situation was changed dramatically by the English executing Charles I and abolishing monarchy in January 1649. The Scots furiously rejected this unilateral attempt to settle the British constitutional crisis, and proclaimed the late king's son as Charles II. In this the country was united, but few doubted that it would mean war with the formidable army of Oliver Cromwell. War was delayed, however, by the fact that Cromwell made Ireland his first priority.

Isolated, the Kirk Party was forced into a policy that sought to resist an English threat by seeking alliance with the crown. Though it could never be admitted, in some ways the removal of the stubborn and devious Charles I might help. His son (born in 1630) was young and (it was hoped) impressionable, and could be moulded into a godly prince as the price for help in regaining his thrones. Negotiations with the exiled king in 1649 failed, for Charles II was reluctant to accept the strict terms demanded by the Scots, while still holding out hopes of making an alternative alliance with the Irish. But once Cromwell's conquest of Ireland had removed that option, Charles at last made concessions. Returning to Scotland in 1650, he bound himself to both the National Covenant and the Solemn League and Covenant.

The political situation in Britain in 1650 was totally different to that of 1643: for the Scots and their new king to insist on the full implementation of the Solemn League was totally unrealistic, but to the Kirk Party it was a covenant with God, and therefore not negotiable. Yet even with, at last, a Covenanted king, the Kirk Party's position was weak. The new king had to be kept as a virtual prisoner to prevent him being a rallying point for royalism, which was rising fast in influence. The Kirk Party itself began to split. The more realistic among the ministry came reluctantly to accept that, in the face of the military threat from England, some modification of the strict exclusion from power of the 'ungodly' might be necessary. Former Engagers who had repented their sins might, they suggested, be allowed to serve in the army. Those less flexible opposed this: the size of the army did not matter, it was the godliness of its members that counted. God would not be on the side of the big battalions, but of the small godly ones. What followed was a schism between the uncompromising Remonstrants and the Resolutioners, who were prepared for a degree of compromise. The regime of the godly began to fall apart amidst furious denunciations and counter-denunciations, while in the background royalist revival accelerated. Even without the external pressure of the English threat, it is hard to believe that the Kirk Party regime could have lasted for long. It had been able to come into existence only because Cromwell had crushed the Engagers, and had helped the Kirk Party to banish the sinful majority of the nobility from power. Once the nobles began recovering from defeat and demoralisation, they would be bound to demand a return to their traditional dominance of society.

Charles II landed in Scotland in June 1650. In the following month, Cromwell invaded. At first the Scots defended their country successfully, frustrating English probes at their defensive lines. They even managed to cut Cromwell off from his supply lines, and it looked as though he was trapped at Dunbar. But, under the surface, this Scots success was being undermined by elements among the ministers and their supporters, who were obsessed with their idea that the godliness of the troops mattered more than their numbers. Right up to the critical moment at Dunbar, soldiers and officers were being purged as morally unfit to fight. The zealots then added further to disaster by pressurising the commanding officers not to be content with trapping Cromwell but to leave a strong position and advance to confront him.

The result was an overwhelming disaster in the battle of Dunbar (3 September 1650). Its scale was such that it was immediately clear that Edinburgh would have to be abandoned, and the regime retreated north of the Forth. This was a death-blow to the already ailing Kirk Party. If resistance to the English was to have any hope of success, it was obvious (in worldly terms) that the services of all who were willing to fight would be needed. Royalists and Engagers flooded first into the army, and then into government. The nobility reclaimed its place in national life. After the disastrous events of the previous decade, they were eager to revert to partnership between king and parliament, and determined that the upstart ministers of the Church should be put firmly in their place.

In military terms, however, the flood of royalists into the army came too late. After the English crossed the Firth of Forth they were able to threaten to cut off the regime (which was based in Stirling) from the north. Charles II and his advisers decided on what was really a last gesture of defiance rather than a strategy that was expected to succeed, and marched their army south into England. It got as far as Worcester before Cromwell caught up with it and destroyed it (3 September 1651). After this, all that was needed was mopping-up operations. Scotland was a conquered country. One of her great national boasts had long been that she had never been conquered, this being contrasted to the slavish England, which had been subjugated by Romans, Anglo-Saxons, Vikings and Normans. Cromwell had destroyed the myth for ever.

CONQUEST AND UNION, 1651–60

The Covenanters, who had begun by hoping to force King Charles I to make limited changes in policy and methods of government, had started a process that had led to revolution in Scotland, and thus destabilised the other two British kingdoms. The Covenanters had then sought to protect their revolution by military intervention in England and Ireland, aiming at a loose federal union and the imposition of presbyterianism on all three kingdoms. As it became clear that these ambitions were impossible to achieve, the Covenanting movement had disintegrated. Some continued to hope for a settlement in alliance with the English parliament; others turned back to the crown. Eventually the English had lost patience and executed Charles I.

With monarchy abolished, the English had turned their attention to the troublesome two outlying kingdoms, and, in a stunning demonstration of military power, conquered both within three years. But the way in which the English treated their two conquests was very different. The Irish were held to merit harsh punishment, with huge land confiscations and active persecution of Catholicism. Ireland was an English dependency that had rebelled; Protestants had been massacred, and revenge was appropriate. Most Scots, on the other hand, were seen as erring brethren. Their presbyterianism had much in common with English puritanism, but their determination to impose their presbyterianism (and, latterly, their king) on England had been seen as intolerable. Nonetheless, after conquest, the English left presbyterians in Scotland free to worship and retain their structure of church government. The one general assembly that met under English rule was, it is true, forcibly dissolved, but that was because faction fighting within it was so bitter that it threatened to cause disorder. But what the Church was no longer allowed to do was impose its discipline on those who were unwilling to accept it. For the first time Scotland was to have a degree of officially-sanctioned religious toleration. It was very limited, being confined to Protestants (except episcopalians), but nonetheless it was a first small step in the long and faltering process whereby the state came to accept that it could be secure even if religious uniformity was not enforced.

For the great majority of Scots, however, toleration was not a liberty to be welcomed but something as ungodly as anything Charles had tried to impose on them. The numbers who took advantage of toleration and turned to Independency or Quakerism were tiny, but the Church could no longer punish those who refused its discipline. Clerical energy was instead directed inwards, with rival Resolutioners and Protesters re-fighting old battles over the disasters of the previous decade.

Toleration and ensuring that ministers did not meddle in political affairs were the central planks of the religious policy of the new republican Commonwealth regime. In civil affairs the emphasis was on union. The Covenanters had wanted to develop the union of the crowns into a federal union, whereby Scotland and England would have equal influence in matters of joint concern. The English, on the other hand, sought what would later become known as 'incorporating union,' whereby the wealth and populations of the two countries were taken into account. Obviously, this would mean only a handful of Scots representatives in a united parliament, but, being a conquered country, it was impossible to resist English plans. A show of consent was obtained by men fearing something worse if they resisted, and the new Commonwealth of England, Ireland and Scotland was created, with 30 Scottish (and 30 Irish) MPs joining nearly 600 English and Welsh MPs in a single parliament in London. Scots had little enthusiasm for their new constitution, but at the same time there was acceptance by some that acting as an MP or taking administrative offices in the republican government had advantages – both personal and through insuring that there was a Scottish voice in government, however small.

As in England, the ideal was civilian rule, but the reality was that the Commonwealth had been created through military power, and was dependent on it. In Scotland there was an incoherent royalist revolt based on the Highlands in 1653-4; though it failed, it was troublesome, and suppressing it emphasised that Scotland's government remained English and military. Continuing instability led to Cromwell being given the office of Lord Protector in 1653, making him a semi-monarchical figure designed to bind the Commonwealth together. But growing royalism and arguments about the constitution meant that, on the removal of his commanding presence when he died in 1658, the republic crumbled fast. Eventually, General George Monck decided that the best way forward lay in the restoration of monarchy. Of all Cromwell's generals he had the largest force at his disposal – the army of occupation in Scotland.

He resolved to march this army to London; many Scots were ready to rise in arms to support him, but this was forbidden. Monarchy was to be restored in all three kingdoms, but this would be done by the English alone. As a result, when restoration took place it was conditional in England, terms having been negotiated with the king, but in Scotland Charles II was restored unconditionally. There were very few Scots who were not in favour of restoration. Rebellion against the crown had resulted in over twenty years of disaster; now turning back to monarchy seemed the best way ahead. Yet many were worried or fearful. Most had at some time or another acted against the interests of the king or his father, even fought in arms against them. Presbyterians feared for their church. The revolutionary wheel had completed its circle, from absolute monarchy to absolute monarchy. Having risen in arms against Charles I, the Scots were now ready to grovel before Charles II.

REFERENCES

Brown, K.M. 1989 'Aristocratic Finances and the origins of the Scottish Revolution', *English Historical Review*, 104, 46–87.

Brown, K.M. 2000 *Noble Society in Scotland. Wealth, Family and Culture from Reformation to Revolution*. Edinburgh.

Brown, K.M. 2001 'Reformation to Union, 1560–1707', in Houston, R.A. and Knox, W.W. (eds), *The New Penguin History of Scotland*, London, 182–275.

Donald, P. 1990 *An Uncounselled King: Charles I and the Scottish Troubles, 1637–1641*. Cambridge.

Drummond, W. 1976 *William Drummond of Hawthornden: Poems and Prose*, ed. MacDonald, R.H. Edinburgh.

Fissel, M.C. 1994 *The Bishops' Wars. Charles I's Campaigns against Scotland*. Cambridge.

Lee, M. 1995 *The Road to Revolution, Scotland under Charles I, 1625–37*. Urbana and Chicago.

Macinnes, A.I. 1991 *Charles I and the Making of the Covenanting Movement, 1625–1641*. Edinburgh.

Mullan, D.G. 1998 *Scottish Puritanism, 1590–1638*. Oxford.

Sharpe, K. 1992 *The Personal Rule of Charles I*. New Haven.

Stevenson, D. 1974 'The King's Scottish Revenues and the Covenanters, 1625–1651', *Historical Journal*, 17, 17–41.

FURTHER READING

Brown, K.M. 1993 *Kingdom or Province? Scotland and the Regal Union, 1603–1715*. Basingstoke.

Cowan, E.J. 1977 *Montrose. For Covenant and King*. London.

Dow, F.D. 1979 *Cromwellian Scotland, 1651–1660*. Edinburgh.

Makey, W. 1979 *The Church of the Covenant, 1637–1651*. Edinburgh.

Mitchison, R. 1983 *Lordship to Patronage. Scotland 1603–1745*. London.

Morrill, J. (ed) 1990 *The Scottish National Covenant in its British Context, 1638–51*. Edinburgh.

Mullan, D.G. 1986 *Episcopy in Scotland: The History of an Idea, 1560–1638*. Edinburgh.

Nicholls, A.D. 1995 *The Jacobean Union. A Reconsideration of British Civil Policies Under the Early Stuarts*. Westport and London.

Stevenson, D. 1973 & 2003 *The Scottish Revolution, 1637–1644: The Triumph of the Covenanters*. Newton Abbot.

Stevenson, D. 1977 & 2003. *Revolution and Counter Revolution in Scotland, 1644–1651.* London.

Young, J.R. 1996 *The Scottish Parliament, 1639–1661: A Political and Constitutional Analysis.* Edinburgh.

Young, J.R. (ed) 1997 *Celtic Dimensions of the British Civil Wars.* Edinburgh.

CHAPTER FOUR

Restoration to Revolution: 1660–1690

Derek J. Patrick

In 1661 parliament rejected Covenanting innovations and republican rule, in favour of the restoration of monarchy. However, within three decades, the Restoration settlement would be overturned, James VII exiled in France and the Dutch stadtholder, William of Orange, would be king. The major contributory factor was the volatile religious situation which dominated Scottish politics from the reinstitution of episcopacy in 1662. Presbyterian dissent was a constant problem for government, but King James's Catholicism and reckless religious policy was his undoing. The Protestant prince of Orange was asked to intervene but the throne he inherited was significantly altered. Unlike in England, the Revolution settlement was explicitly contractual and adjusted the relationship between king and parliament. This chapter will explore the Restoration period, explain how and why royal authority collapsed in 1688–89 and examine the nature of the Revolution.

THE RESTORATION SETTLEMENT, CHURCH AND STATE IN SCOTLAND, 1660–66

Charles II returned from exile in the Netherlands in May 1660. The news of his arrival was well received in all corners of his kingdom. For the episcopalian churchman, Gilbert Burnet, the Restoration brought to Scotland a 'spirit of extra-vagant joy'. The proclamation of Charles as king in Edinburgh was followed by three volleys from the castle's guns, bonfires, dancing and scenes of celebration: 'the spoutes of the croce ryning and venting out [an] abundance of wyne'. The Scots had every reason to be enthusiastic: Charles's restoration promised a return to the days before religious strife, civil war and English occupation. For the Scots lords who flocked to London in the wake of the king's arrival, it was an opportunity to reclaim their traditional role in government. The fact that Charles was a Covenanted king was a cause for presbyterian optimism. His choice of Scottish ministers included several former Covenanters, raising the hope that he might endorse a presbyterian settlement. But it was not to be.

Parliament met for the first time in ten years on 1 January 1661. The king's commissioner, John, first earl of Middleton, presided over a session that restored much of the king's prerogative power. Middleton initiated the legislative programme with an oath of allegiance recognising Charles as 'Supream Governour of this Kingdome'. This was followed by acts re-establishing royal privileges that had been ceded to parliament in the 1640s. The lords of the articles – the parliamentary drafting committee – were restored, along with the king's right to appoint officers of state, privy councillors and lords of session. The estates (a byword for parliament) recognised Charles's exclusive power to summon, prorogue and dissolve parliament. Legislation prohibited people renewing their obligation to the Covenants or entering into leagues or bonds without royal permission, and determined that only the king could make war and peace and control the army.

Former Covenanters expected immunity from prosecution but there was no act of indemnity until September 1662, and even then it excluded almost 700 individuals. The uncertainty kept former dissidents in check. Charles's Restoration was an opportunity for royalists to settle old scores but there were relatively few immediate victims. The leading Covenanter, Archibald Campbell, first marquis of Argyll, was executed in May 1661 for cooperating with Cromwell; Sir Archibald Johnston of Wariston, co-author of the National Covenant, was put to death in 1663; Samuel Rutherford, one of the Covenanters' principal theorists, died in prison; and James Guthrie, a leading Protestor minister, was hanged. There was, however, no systematic attempt to exclude former Covenanters from office for Charles could not afford to alienate so many of the Scots elite.

With Charles's prerogatives restored, in March 1661 parliament granted the king a generous financial settlement of £480,000 Scots (£40,000 sterling) per annum for life, raised from customs and excise duties, and approved the act rescissory, rescinding all legislation of the Covenanting parliaments of 1640–8. It also swept away all legislative support for a presbyterian structure in the church. Church government was not settled until September, although in March parliament decreed that it was the king's right to choose the form 'most agreeable to the word of God, most suteable to monarchicall Government, and most complying with the publict peace and quyet of the Kingdome'. Charles had little sympathy for presbyterianism after his experience of it in the early 1650s and was inclined towards an episcopal settlement, for bishops offered greater control of the church (Brown 1992, 148). Episcopacy would have the added benefit of introducing a measure of conformity in all three kingdoms. Instructions were dispatched to the privy council, indicating that it was Charles's intention to restore 'government by bishops, as it was by law before the late troubles' (Harris 2005, 113). The council issued a proclamation in September approving this and parliament formally recognised the restoration of the episcopate in 1662. Charles offered bishoprics to several leading Resolutioners (moderate Covenanters of the later 1640s) in an attempt to smooth the transition, but only James Sharp accepted, being appointed archbishop of St Andrews. He had been sent to Charles in 1660 to encourage him to support a moderate presbyterian settlement; this betrayal of his former allies and the appointment of some undistinguished ministers as bishops provided an inauspicious start for the Restoration church.

As well as restoring episcopacy, parliament reinstated lay patronage: the right of landowners to appoint parish ministers. All ministers appointed since its abolition in 1649 were ordered to receive presentation from their patrons, and collation from a bishop. Almost one third refused and were 'deprived', with a particular concentration of deprivations in the South-West. In England only ten per cent of churchmen felt compelled to withdraw from the church settlement which followed the Restoration. Gordon Donaldson has argued that, despite the number forced from the church, Scotland was not essentially anti-episcopalian, pointing out that far more conformed than refused to submit (Donaldson 1994, 366). However, compliance did not necessarily denote approval of bishops.

Keith Brown has described the ecclesiastical settlement as the 'fundamental blunder' of the restored monarchy (Brown 1992, 150). The majority of the population of Lowland Scotland was presbyterian and the restoration of episcopacy caused widespread discontent. This was most obvious where ministers were deprived, with violent opposition directed at their replacements, whom Burnet uncharitably described as the 'very dregs and refuse of the North'. Hostile congregations boycotted the new clergy and attendance in some parishes declined dramatically as parishioners chose to worship with their former ministers. Despite legislation prohibiting irregular services, many deprived ministers preached to open-air 'conventicles' in order to accommodate the large numbers who withdrew from the church. The extent of nonconformity in Lowland Scotland, particularly the south-west, was a threat to the establishment and influenced much government policy before the Revolution.

The government's approach to presbyterian dissent shifted on several occasions during a period which was dominated initially by John Maitland, second earl (later first duke) of Lauderdale, who served Charles as secretary of state and commissioner to parliament. A former Covenanter, he forged a career in Charles's service, eventually exercising almost complete control over the Scottish administration and government patronage. Historians often characterise his ascendancy, and Restoration politics in general, as dominated by corruption, greed and nepotism: for example, Lauderdale's brother was appointed general of the mint and was convicted of embezzlement and perjury after Lauderdale's downfall (Donaldson 1994, 373). He was a moderate Presbyterian, favouring the accommodation of dissenters, although at first the court adopted a hard-line approach towards nonconformists.

In July 1663 parliament imposed heavy fines on individuals who withdrew from the established church. Fines were exacted by soldiers under Sir James Turner, who was charged with suppressing conventicles in the South-West. His methods were arbitrary and often severe, and military intervention became increasingly harsh due to heightened tensions during the second Anglo-Dutch War (1665–7). The government feared a presbyterian insurrection in support of the Dutch, especially as many Scottish religious exiles were resident in the Netherlands. Faced with often brutal persecution, outed ministers denounced the government and large armed conventicles became the norm (Mitchison 1983, 73).

The government's efforts failed to crush dissent but succeeded in inciting rebellion. In November 1666, 2,000 ill-equipped presbyterian rebels seized Turner in Dumfries before marching on Edinburgh, hoping for concessions from the government. This ragged army arrived on the outskirts of the capital, but was forced to retreat into the Pentland Hills. It was routed at Rullion Green on 28 November by General Thomas Dalyell of Binns – a sadistic veteran soldier who had served Tsar Alexei I with distinction. Over a hundred prisoners were brought to Edinburgh, where the lord chancellor, John Leslie, seventh earl (later first duke) of Rothes, determined 'to proceed with utmost severity'. The captives were subjected to torture to force confessions or to discover information on the revolt. Thirty-six were later executed and more were transported to Barbados (Harris 2005, 119). Forces under Dalyell were sent into the south-west to reinvigorate the government's campaign against presbyterian dissent. Besides quartering soldiers on suspected law-breakers and collecting punitive fines for nonconformity, the military made liberal use of torture and summary execution. These draconian policies did affect church attendance: 'people began to come regularly to church for fear'. Nevertheless, despite having been harried, occupied and impoverished, presbyterian dissent endured.

LAUDERDALE'S ADMINISTRATION: DEALING WITH DISSENT, 1666–79

The aftermath of the Pentland Rising saw a shift in the government's attitude to dissent. Lauderdale used it to discredit Rothes and his allies – Archbishops James Sharp and Alexander Burnet – whose handling of dissent had provoked the insurrection. Lauderdale preferred a more inclusive policy and was instrumental in Charles's offer of his first Scottish indulgence in June 1669. This allowed the privy council to reappoint more moderate outed ministers. The government hoped to accommodate moderate presbyterians and isolate the intractable nonconformists. However, only forty-two deprived ministers accepted the indulgence. All that was achieved was discontent among episcopalians. Opposition increased in October when parliament passed the Act of Supremacy, confirming the king's absolute control of the church. It was both inconsistent with presbyterian beliefs and detested by episcopalian ministers, who objected to the king being given full power over religious policy and clerical appointments. Alexander Burnet, archbishop of Glasgow, was dismissed for his vigorous protests and superseded by Robert Leighton, a prominent advocate of comprehension. Before the close of the year Lauderdale was confident enough to inform Charles that 'never King was soe absolute as you are in poor old Scotland'. This was a reasonable assessment of royal authority. Policy was shaped by Charles and his ministers; parliament's role was to implement, not question, his instructions.

Despite turning from repression to accommodation, the government continued to clamp down on dissenters who refused to accept the indulgence. Legislation required landowners to report anyone staging conventicles on their lands, made each parish responsible for the good behaviour of its inhabitants and also declared that an assault against an established church minister or his property was a capital offence. In August 1670, parliament passed the 'clanking act', increasing fines for unlicensed ministers, their congregations and the magistrates of burghs where any illegal meetings were held. Heavier penalties were also set for attending field conventicles, while any minister preaching at one would be executed. Lauderdale reluctantly complied with this to appease his critics. Nevertheless, the court remained committed to accommodation and in September 1672 Charles issued a second indulgence to bring in more deprived ministers as part of a broader British strategy which saw the king seeking nonconformist support for another Dutch war. Only eighty-nine more ministers were licensed as a result. Lauderdale's attempts at accommodation had failed.

Bishops and ministers in the established church also opposed accommodation because it undermined the Restoration settlement. Although only a handful of deposed ministers had accepted the indulgences, they felt that a presbyterian fifth column had been created within the church, while active dissent was neither suppressed nor contained. After the second Dutch War had ended (1667), the army had been largely disbanded and replaced by local militias. This, coupled with the government's more conciliatory approach, facilitated the spread of armed conventicles into the Lothians and Fife. Episcopalian ministers were subject to violent abuse, and church attendance declined again. Punitive legislation did little to deter those who remained outside the church. Faced with a barrage of criticism from his enemies in both Scotland and England, Lauderdale abandoned accommodation in favour of a return to repression. In June 1674 the privy council required landowners to act as guarantors for their tenants' peaceable behaviour and subscription of a bond agreeing to observe the 1670 act against conventicles. Magistrates were similarly responsible for the inhabitants of the royal burghs. Troops were again sent into the south-west to restore order, collect fines and establish garrisons. In August, the episcopalian hardliner Alexander Burnet was reinstalled as archbishop of Glasgow, underlining the decisive switch in policy. Landowners, now obliged to guarantee that their tenants would obey the laws against withdrawing from church, objected to being held responsible for people they could not control and with whom many sympathised. In Lanarkshire, the nobility and gentry, headed by William Douglas, third duke of Hamilton, refused to comply, as did those in several other counties. The king ordered the raising of the 'Highland Host', a militia force of some 8,000 men, which assembled at Stirling in January 1678. This militia – almost one third were actually Lowland irregulars – was dispatched to the south-west and 'let loose upon free quarter'. Although most of their worst alleged atrocities can be attributed to presbyterian propaganda, violence, intimidation and looting were widespread. However, coercion only stiffened the dissenters' resolve. Few landowners in the western shires supported government policy and as soon as the militia was withdrawn in February, armed conventicles reappeared. The coming months saw the outbreak of intermittent guerrilla warfare and another full-blown rising looked ever more likely.

In England, politics had become increasingly volatile since the revelation that the king's brother and heir to the British thrones, James, duke of York, had converted to Catholicism in 1669. This, combined with reports that Charles had conducted secret negotiations with Louis XIV, provoked hostility, which intensified with the discovery of the 'Popish Plot' to murder the king and extirpate Protestantism in the autumn of 1678. Against this background, English Whigs won a convincing general election victory in February 1679 and, with control of the House of Commons, attempted to have James excluded from the succession. As Brown has emphasised, this was as much a British as an English crisis, and events in England affected the actions of Scottish presbyterian nonconformists (Brown 1992, 160). On 3 May 1679, Archbishop James Sharp was ambushed and assassinated near St Andrews by a small group of dissenters. The murderers fled to the south-west, where, on 29 May (the king's birthday), militants framed the Rutherglen Declaration denouncing successive breaches of the Covenants since 1648. On Sunday 1 June, John Graham of Claverhouse (later Viscount Dundee), commander of a troop of horse raised to police the west, attacked a large armed conventicle at Drumclog in Lanarkshire. Graham's men, heavily outnumbered, were routed by William Cleland's well-ordered conventiclers. The rebels marched on Glasgow, raised over 8,000 men and issued a declaration which complained of the oppressions of the government, asserted loyalty to the Covenant, and concluded with a demand for a free parliament. However, the dissenters were hopelessly divided between moderate presbyterians and extreme Covenanters – known as Cameronians after the leader of one faction. Meanwhile, Charles had dispatched his illegitimate son James, duke of Monmouth, with English troops, to suppress the insurrection. The rebels assembled at Bothwell Brig on the River Clyde, where, on 22 June, they were defeated by Monmouth's army. Estimates suggest that as many as 400 were killed, while over 1,000 surrendered, were taken to Edinburgh and secured in Greyfriars churchyard. Most were released after Monmouth secured an indemnity for those who swore to live peacefully; a few were executed, some dispossessed, and another two to three hundred transported, although almost all of these drowned when their ship, bound for the West Indies, was wrecked. There were harsh reprisals in the south-west, where Claverhouse's dragoons were deployed, but no systematic repression followed the rising. Monmouth was an advocate of moderation, and on 29 June 1679 Charles issued a third indulgence relaxing the laws against house conventicles. The latest rising was also responsible for the political demise of Lauderdale, blamed for policies that had incited rebellion. He was replaced as head of the Scots administration by the king's brother, James, duke of York.

JAMES, DUKE OF YORK, PARLIAMENT AND THE SUCCESSION, 1679–85

In 1679, James was sent to Edinburgh to distance him from the English 'exclusion crisis', providing him with an opportunity to build relationships with the Scots nobility. His initially conciliatory approach pleased those who had been excluded by Lauderdale. His residence also saw a revival in court culture. James's faith did cause some concern, but there was no real interest in his exclusion. His 'impartial temper' and 'obliging manner' helped him construct a large following amongst the Scots elite. This success in establishing a loyalist interest became apparent during his second period in Scotland from October 1680 – just before the second English 'exclusion parliament'. He was appointed high commissioner to what proved a particularly agreeable Scots parliament in July 1681. His return coincided with yet another shift in royal policy. The bishops believed that the church was being undermined by indulgences and, pressed by James and the English bishops, Charles was convinced that accommodation had failed. In May 1680, the indulgences were subjected to limitations restricting the freedoms granted to nonconformist ministers and conventicles.

The court's new agenda was continued in parliament. Charles's letter to the estates emphasised his intention of maintaining the established church and underlined his expectation that parliament would assert 'His Royal Prerogative' and 'the Rights of His Crown in its Natural and Legal course of Descent'. The session began with an act ratifying all legislation since the reign of James VI in favour of Protestantism, and 'all the laws formerly made against Popery'. Next, they guaranteed James's status as Charles's successor, confirming that the crown would pass to 'the nixt Immediat and laufull heir' whose religion would not 'alter or divert the . . . descent of the Croun'. Gilbert Burnet observed that this was approved without 'one contradictory vote'. Parliament's compliance was strikingly at odds with opposition to the prospect of James's succession in the English House of Commons.

Parliament also approved the contentious Test Act, which led to a rigorous purge of Scottish office-holders. Proposed as a means of securing episcopacy, the act stated that 'all that should be capable of any office in Church or State, or of electing or being elected members of Parliament' had to prove their commitment to the church settlement. The oath was incompatible with the beliefs of many. Most objections concerned what was understood by the phrase 'Protestant Religion'. Sir James Dalrymple of Stair suggested that parliament should accept the confession of faith of 1560 as a suitable standard. This held that Christ, not the king, was supreme head of the church, contradicting the Act of Supremacy. Episcopalians and presbyterians struggled with the Test Act's inconsistencies (it appeared both to endorse and oppose royal supremacy). There were several high-profile dismissals of those who refused to take the oath, most notably Stair and Archibald Campbell, ninth earl of Argyll, who was charged with treason and sentenced to death. The two fled to the Netherlands to join a sizeable contingent of Scots émigrés. The oath also revived presbyterian dissent, which had been weakened since Bothwell Brig. The session went well for the court, but its ill-advised attack on moderate and indulged nonconformists did much to re-establish a broader-based opposition.

The revival of an active presbyterian movement saw the government intensify its campaign. In the South-West Claverhouse's men were ruthless, with many nonconformists fined or transported. The government's attitude hardened in June 1683 with the discovery of the Rye House Plot to assassinate Charles and James, which implicated Monmouth, many English Whigs and some Scots, including George Baillie of Jerviswood, later executed for his involvement. The final years of Charles's reign saw an unprecedented level of repression: imprisonment, torture, quartering, heavy fines, intimidation and summary execution were common, as martial law was imposed on the south-west. The presbyterian minister and historian Robert Wodrow referred to this as the 'Killing Times', not without justification. Perhaps a hundred people were executed between 1683 and 1685, often on charges as arbitrary as refusing the test oath or denying the royal supremacy. The government's approach to dissent in this period was brutal and unrelenting.

JAMES VII, CATHOLICISM, TOLERATION AND THE LIMITS OF ABSOLUTISM, 1685–8

James VII succeeded his brother on 6 February 1685, the English Whigs having failed to have him excluded from the succession. Although dissent in Scotland remained a problem, the crown's repressive campaign had left nonconformists demoralised. Consequently, the new king's accession went unchallenged in all of his kingdoms. Encouraged by the success he had enjoyed during his time in Edinburgh, James was keen to have the Scottish parliament meet before the English. He hoped that the Scots would be 'examplary' in their 'demonstrations of affection to our person, and compliance with our desires'. He was not disappointed. His letter to parliament made it clear that there would be no change in the style of kingship: he would maintain royal power in 'its greatest Luster'. Likewise, he gave notice that he had no intention of relaxing the prosecution of Protestant dissenters and 'wild and inhumane traitors' who endeavoured to disrupt the peace. With regard to the episcopalian establishment, he undertook to 'defend and protect your Religion as established by Law'. In its deferential reply, parliament promised to offer 'such Laws as may best secure your Majestys sacred Person, the Royall Family and Government', and to 'be so exemplarly loyal, as to raise your honour and Greatness to the utmost of our power'. Parliament approved an act for the security of the Protestant religion on 28 April, James giving an assurance that he would not 'endure nor connive at any derogation from or violation of it'. The estates continued their campaign against religious dissent with acts declaring it treason to acknowledge the Covenants, and against nonconforming preachers and those attending field conventicles, 'the Nurseries and rendezvouzes of Rebellion'. Parliament also made good its offer to secure James's government and enhance his authority, with a generous grant: the excise of 'Inland and Forraign Commodities' for life, which, with other taxes, would raise some £60,000 sterling per annum. The Excise Act, while ensuring a measure of financial independence for James, said much more about parliament's attitude to royal authority, which it recognised as 'sacred, supream, [and] absolute'. This first session of parliament had gone well: the estates had conceded that James's power was absolute, taken further stringent measures against presbyterian dissidents, offered him a generous financial package, and shown a readiness to defend his person and government. The strength of this loyalty was tested only days later, when news arrived that Argyll was *en route* for Scotland with three ships and almost three hundred men.

Since 1681, Argyll had been in exile in the Netherlands, where dissidents had contrived an invasion which, they hoped, would exploit dissatisfaction with James's

Catholicism. His landing in Scotland was intended to coincide with the arrival in England of the duke of Monmouth, the new king's illegitimate half-brother, to lead a simultaneous rising there. Monmouth's expedition had not yet set sail when Argyll arrived at Tobermory on 11 May. Argyll insisted on landing in the Highlands, where he expected to raise his clansmen, rather than the south-west, where he might have harnessed popular dissent. However, since his departure, his lands had been occupied by government forces, his supporters had been imprisoned and his authority undermined: he struggled to raise 2,500 men. He issued a declaration condemning King Charles's government and James's succession, but it did little to garner further support. He marched south but soon became convinced of the futility of his actions, attempted a retreat but was apprehended in Renfrewshire, imprisoned in Edinburgh Castle and executed on 30 June without trial (already being under sentence of death for opposing the test oath). Monmouth fared little better. He landed at Lyme Regis on 11 June, claiming to be Charles II's legitimate Protestant heir. Like Argyll, he attracted little support and his small army was crushed at Sedgemoor on 5 July. Ten days later, he too was executed.

By the end of July 1685 James was in a strong position. Rebellions in Scotland and England had been quickly overwhelmed and their leaders executed. It was this initial success, and apparent popularity, that gave James confidence to pursue the policy that dominated the remainder of his reign: full toleration for his Roman Catholic subjects. Argyll's invasion was the pretext for James's appointment of the Catholic George Douglas, first earl of Dumbarton, as commander of Scottish forces in May 1685. Following the defeat of the rebels, his Catholicising programme intensified. In June, the chancellor, James Drummond, fourth earl of Perth, converted to Catholicism, followed by his brother, John, first earl of Melfort, secretary of state since 1684. But the anticipated flood of converts failed to materialise. In November, James granted dispensations to several Catholics, allowing them to participate in local administration. This came only a month after Louis XIV had revoked the Edict of Nantes, which had guaranteed toleration for French Protestants since 1595. In England, James informed parliament that he would exempt almost ninety Catholic army officers from penal legislation. Members of both houses protested and parliament was prorogued. Dissatisfaction grew with the increasing number of Catholics employed in central and local government. James's continued promotion of his co-religionists undermined the Protestant establishment, whose support had been crucial in assuring his peaceful accession.

By late December the earl of Perth – whose conversion had been discovered in the autumn – was openly celebrating mass in Edinburgh. Such behaviour was condemned by a growing number of episcopalian churchmen, fiercely opposed to Catholicism. In the New Year, the chancellor banned the sale of anti-Catholic literature in a vain attempt to limit Protestant disaffection. Perth's zeal provoked anti-Catholic rioting in the capital. His private chapel was ransacked, along with the homes of several Edinburgh Catholics. The chancellor was instructed to be more discreet but the Protestant duke of Queensberry was reprimanded: as governor of Edinburgh Castle, it was his job to prevent disorder. The duke was dismissed and his offices conferred on Catholics: the treasury was placed in commission, with Perth at its head, and the governorship of Edinburgh Castle went to the duke of Gordon.

Having placed several Catholics in high office, James's next step was to call parliament and repeal anti-Catholic legislation. In March 1686, the privy council advised that parliament would not acquiesce unless he offered additional securities for Protestantism and relaxed the laws against moderate presbyterians. James ignored their advice: had not this parliament supported him in 1685? Parliament began on 29 April with Alexander Stewart, fifth earl of Moray, a suspected Catholic, replacing Queensberry as high commissioner. The king's letter to parliament noted that his Catholic subjects had 'given good experience of their true Loyalty and Peaceable behaviour', and were 'always assistant to the Crown in the worst of Rebellions and Usurpations'. Therefore, James asked that they 'may have the Protectione of our Lawes . . . which others of our subjects have'. In return he offered free trade with England. Most opposed removal of the civil disabilities imposed on Scotland's 2,000 Catholics. The commissioners from the royal burghs, who would have been the main beneficiaries of free trade, were described by Sir John Lauder of Fountainhall as 'the brazen wall the Papists found hardest'. It became obvious that parliament would not consent and Moray prorogued the session on 15 June. James had been unceremoniously rebuffed. In 1681 and again in 1685, the Scottish parliament had set an example for Westminster. It did so again in 1686, but not as James had hoped: it was impossible to imagine toleration succeeding in England.

The king was undeterred and began purging disloyal office-holders. The lord advocate, Sir George Mackenzie of Rosehaugh, a notable casualty, was committed to monarchical government and James's service, but not his religion. Most of those dismissed were loyal subjects, but baulked at his efforts to re-establish Catholicism. Where possible, Catholics like Gordon, Seaforth and Traquair, were chosen to fill vacancies. The changes did little to improve the Scots administration but added to the ranks of the opposition.

Parliament had rejected James's policy, so he resorted to exploiting his prerogative powers. On 21 August, he told the council that he had decided to allow Roman Catholics freedom to worship privately. The abbey church at Holyrood was converted into a Catholic chapel, which was consecrated on 30 November; a Catholic printing press and Jesuit school were also established. In February 1687, a declaration of indulgence offered additional liberties to Catholics, who were free 'not only to Exercise their Religion, but to enjoy all Offices, Benefices and others'. It also authorised moderate presbyterians to hold house conventicles. The test oath was abolished and replaced with one acknowledging the king's 'absolute Power and Authority', but the outcome was disappointing. It was grudgingly endorsed by the council, but few presbyterians were satisfied and the established church resented the erosion of its legal status. James's initial success in Scotland had depended on cooperation with the nobility and episcopate. James was now aware that relations with these natural allies were fragile, and wanted to broaden the base of his support. He pursued a similar strategy to that implemented in England, where an indulgence was issued in April. On 28 June, a second Scottish indulgence allowed everyone 'to meet and serve God after their own way, be it in private houses, chapels, or places purposely hired or built for that use'. Most presbyterians, with the exception of militant Covenanters, accepted these terms. Large numbers declared their preference for presbytery. They deserted the established church and a presbyterian church re-emerged, built its regional organisation and recovered its strength. There had been little hope of a presbyterian restoration before 1687 but, as Donaldson observed, it was again a cause with a future (Donaldson 1994, 383). James had alienated the established church, but any hopes he had of building bridges with the presbyterians, who were deeply hostile to Catholicism, were seriously misplaced.

He remained determined to have parliament endorse toleration. His heirs – his daughters, Mary and Anne – were Protestant, so anti-Catholic legislation would probably be restored on his death. If toleration was to have any chance of enduring, it needed statutory security. Parliament was overwhelmingly hostile to Catholicism, so he dissolved the estates and set about engineering a more compliant assembly. Burgh councils elected commissioners to parliament, so in September 1686 the privy council told all royal burghs 'that all [council] elections . . . be suspended untile [the] royall pleasure be known'. Shortly after suspending municipal elections, James and his ministers began to replace councils with crown nominees. James sought to pack councils with men willing to legitimise toleration and so control at least a third of votes in parliament. He implemented a similar policy in England, where he initiated significant changes in the boroughs and ordered his lord lieutenants to discover whether local office holders would support toleration. In Scotland, it is uncertain whether James's interventions would have produced a compliant parliament. He would not accept that many who were essentially loyal had no sympathy for Rome. James's increasingly provocative policies added to the unrest and suspicion in both kingdoms. Although this was the background to revolution (the freedom of parliament was a pretext for William of Orange's invasion), the catalyst was the birth of the king's son, James Francis Edward – a Catholic male heir – on 10 June 1688.

Notwithstanding a Whig smear campaign intended to cast doubt over the legitimacy of the infant prince, British Protestants faced the prospect of a Catholic dynasty: the boy would succeed to the throne before his half-sisters. This was enough to persuade seven high-ranking Englishmen to invite the Dutch stadholder, William of Orange – James's nephew and son-in-law, nemesis of Louis XIV and champion of Protestant Europe – to intervene. Like the Restoration, the Revolution of 1688–9 was determined in England. Circumstances dictated that the opening acts were played out on an English stage. William's initial declaration of 30 September 1688 dealt exclusively with England, although a Scottish manifesto appeared some days later. English considerations shaped William's decisions. Thus most historians have concluded that 1688–89 was an essentially English Revolution. In comparison, the Scots elite are characterised as reluctant participants in the revolution or at best indifferent. However, there were Scottish precedents for revolution and James's policies had left a large number of Scots aggrieved and alienated. Simmering discontent in Scotland did not take long to boil over after the invasion, while the *émigré* Scots contingent that accompanied William guaranteed that the Revolution would not be without its Scottish dimension.

THE REVOLUTION, WILLIAM OF ORANGE, THE CLAIM OF RIGHT AND CONTRACTUAL KINGSHIP, 1688–90

The prince of Orange, with around 15,000 men, landed in Devon on 5 November 1688. He maintained that his objectives were to secure the Protestant faith from Catholicism and arbitrary government, and to restore the independence of parliament (Holmes 1993, 185). Determined to resist his son-in-law's advance, James's army advanced; but their morale was low, the weather and roads were bad and the officers were unenthusiastic and mutinous. Following several high-profile defections to William (including Princess Anne), James ordered a retreat. William continued to march on London, arriving at Hungerford in Berkshire on 7 December, where he received news that James, after summoning a 'Great Council' of English peers, intended to call a free parliament 'whither all the peers, even those joined with the Prince, may freely come'. However, having received a discouraging report from his commissioners, and alarmed by the rising level of anti-Catholicism in the capital, James, whose mind turned to the fate of his father, resolved to flee (Beddard 1988, 32). Once his wife and son were bound for France, James burned the writs summoning parliament and abandoned London. On his way to board a ship that he hoped would carry him to France, he tossed the great seal of England into the Thames in a futile bid to frustrate the creation of an interim administration. Instead, his decision to flee removed the main obstacle to William's becoming king. Hitherto, William had carefully avoided any suggestion that he sought the throne. Had he openly declared an interest in the crown, he might be cast as a foreign usurper. As it was, he entered Britain as a deliverer, defending the laws and liberties of the nation, and censuring James's 'evil counsellors'.

Whatever William intended, the news that James had been apprehended while fleeing threatened to disrupt his plans. The king was returned to London, where he received an enthusiastic welcome. If this disappointed William's supporters and interrupted his progress, it did little to encourage James. He was determined to flee and his brief captivity simply delayed the inevitable. James was escorted to Rochester and, with William's knowledge, fled to France on 23 December. A few days later William called a meeting of the MPs of Charles II's reign, which concluded that 'the government of the Kingdome was extinct'. He was asked to call a convention and assume direction of the English administration until the convention met on 22 January 1689. Within weeks, William and Mary were offered the English throne, which they accepted on 13 February. William was now king of England but Scotland's revolution remained on hold.

The Dutch invasion was a signal for many Scots to descend on London. This is often cited as evidence that the Scots elite cared more for royal favour than the government of Scotland (Riley 1979, 11). In Edinburgh, John Murray, first marquis of Atholl, was left heading an impotent council. James's decision to order the Scottish regiments into England in October had presented an ideal opportunity for the 'Presbyterian and discontented party' to establish itself in the capital. The council was unable to prevent the 'rabbling' of episcopalian ministers in the south-west or to stem the rising tide of popular anti-Catholicism throughout Lowland Scotland. Students in Glasgow publicly burned effigies of the pope and the archbishops of St Andrews and Glasgow on St Andrew's Day, 30 November 1688. Similar demonstrations were staged in Edinburgh a few days later and in Aberdeen early in the New Year. Students in St Andrews wanted to follow suit but were thwarted by staff who remained loyal to James.

In December, a rumour that armed Irish Catholics had assembled in Kirkcudbright, intending to march on Edinburgh, persuaded the magistrates of Linlithgow to take defensive measures. Similarly contrived reports that Catholic insurgents planned to burn the capital were the pretext for an outbreak of anti-Catholic rioting on 10 December. The Edinburgh mob, perhaps as many as 3,000, marched on the Catholic chapel in Holyroodhouse, which was occupied by a small royal garrison. The soldiers dispersed the rabble, who returned with arms and a warrant signed by the few privy councillors still in Edinburgh, requiring the defenders to surrender. Following a brief skirmish, the mob stormed Holyrood, 'pulled down all they could find in the private Chapel, demolished all things within the Abbey Church . . . and plundered the house the Jesuits had lived in', burning the contents. Rioting continued for two or three days, fuelled in part by the ransacked wine cellars of the earls of Perth and Balcarres. The homes of a number of Catholics were looted and the trappings of their religion burned in the street. Christmas Day 1688 was marked by another bout of pope-burning after a 'solemn processione' witnessed by several thousand people. The disorder in Edinburgh was mirrored elsewhere, albeit on a smaller scale. Catholics were subjected to intimidation, violence and in some cases imprisonment. Catholicism was abhorrent to the majority of Scots, who had been alienated by James's ham-fisted efforts to establish freedom of worship for his co-religionists.

Episcopalians and presbyterians agreed on the need to secure Protestantism, which would ideally be done in a free parliament – a key objective outlined in William's declaration for Scotland. Although Protestants shared a contempt for Roman Catholicism, there were deep divisions over church government. Support for presbyterianism was strongest south of the Tay, where news that James had fled sparked attacks on conforming clergymen. Episcopalian ministers were turned out in almost every parish south of the Forth and Clyde (Drummond and Bulloch 1973, 7).

By the beginning of January 1689 over a hundred Scots nobles and gentlemen, including at least fourteen who had accompanied William from the Netherlands, were at Whitehall. Self-interest was undeniably a factor in encouraging them to take the road south but there was much more at stake. The presbyterian or Revolution interest, the largest and most influential Scots grouping in London, met regularly in the Ship Tavern in St James's Street to debate the settlement of church and state. One option which enjoyed considerable support was closer union with England as a means of securing Scotland's 'Religion and Liberty'. An address from East Lothian appealed for the kingdoms to be 'united in a more strict and inseperable Union'. Criticised for making no mention of presbyterianism, it was condemned as an episcopalian contrivance. The same could not be said of an address from Lanarkshire, urging William 'to indeavour an union of these two nations of Great Britain into one politick body as divine providence hath united us in one island and under one head'. This was considered to be the best way of securing Scotland from Catholicism and arbitrary government. However, a union would require lengthy consideration and at this stage the free parliament of William's declaration was the swiftest way to address Scotland's 'religious and civil concerns'.

William convened the London Scots on 7 January for advice on what should be done 'for Securing the Protestant Religion, And Restoring your Laws and Liberties'. Two days later an address inviting him to accept the administration of Scotland was offered to him by the duke of Hamilton. This asked William to call a convention of estates at Edinburgh on 14 March 1689. A key clause concerned how the royal burghs should choose their representatives. James's interference with burgh councils meant that, had elections gone ahead as usual with each council selecting a commissioner, most might side with King James. It was therefore decreed that the 'whole Burgesses . . . being Protestants without any other Exception or Limitation' could vote in the election. This decision guaranteed conflict between the electorate and the burgh councils, most of whom were disinclined to accept the order. In Culross two supporters of the 'illegallie elected' council assaulted the burgh clerk as he read William's proclamation for the convention of estates. When over a hundred Protestant burgesses assembled in Jedburgh to choose a commissioner, the magistrates 'threatened and menaced' anyone who protested against their handling of the election and warned that electors who voted against their candidate would have their 'heads broken'. In St Andrews some students, 'comeing with suords and battons under their gounes', were encouraged to disrupt the reading of William's declaration. Later, 'Maisters and students' attempted to dissuade burgesses from voting for candidates who supported the Revolution, threatening to boycott local merchants and tradesmen and withhold all debts – a serious threat in an impoverished burgh. In Edinburgh, over 1,000 participated in an election that lasted several days. It was contested by supporters of the council and the provost, Magnus Prince, described as 'the most obnoxious man in the corporatione', and by the presbyterian party. Similar confrontations occurred throughout Scotland and, in the majority of cases, the party of Revolution triumphed.

The burgh elections in 1689 were distinguished by unprecedented participation and controversy. This had a clear impact on the membership of the convention. Only thirteen of the sixty-five burgh commissioners had sat in James's parliament and almost 70% of those elected had never sat before. Most supported the Revolution and were sympathetic to presbyterianism. Several had experienced imprisonment, fines or exile since the Restoration. For example, the commissioner from North

Berwick, Sir Thomas Stewart of Coltness, had been suspected of assisting the rebels at Bothwell Brig, had opposed the test oath and was implicated in the Rye House Plot. He spent almost four years in the Netherlands before returning to Scotland after King James offered his indulgence in 1687. There was no innovation in the shires – the size and status of the electorate (the lairds) made it impossible to manipulate – but the outcome was much the same. Contests were common and, although several Jacobites were elected, the majority of commissioners were Revolutioners. In the shire of Haddington, the electorate returned an *émigré*, Sir Robert Sinclair of Stevenson, and Adam Cockburn of Ormiston, an implacable presbyterian and a leader of the opposition to James. The struggle for control of the convention of estates was won several weeks before it met, in the parish churches and tolbooths where the elections were staged.

The notion that the Scots were reluctant revolutionaries – a description coined by Ian Cowan – is based on the premise that the political elite were indifferent, opportunistic and slow to react (Cowan 1989; Lenman 1991). Most historians have accepted the view that most members of the convention were undecided and that letters from William and James, received on 16 March, tipped the balance for William (Ferguson 1994, 2; Cowan 1991, 164–5; Hopkins 1986, 127; Lenman 1991, 146). The conciliatory tone of the former was matched by the belligerent style of the latter. This, it is supposed, all but guaranteed the success of the Revolution in Scotland. James's ill-advised letter may have influenced a few but it was not decisive. The careful work that determined the composition of the estates guaranteed that from the outset the convention was dominated by the Revolution interest (Patrick 2005).

The most important matter before the estates in March 1689 was the future of the crown. It was in the interest of supporters of the Revolution that this should be settled quickly in favour of William. A committee was appointed to consider how best to arrive at a solution. It agreed that the throne was vacant but was divided as to why, or how authority should be transferred to William and Mary. Had James abdicated or deserted his throne and should it be settled on Mary as legitimate heir, on her husband as regent, or as part of a closer union with England? A subcommittee was chosen to draft acceptable reasons for vacancy. After some lively discussion, Sir John Dalrymple of Stair declared 'that, by doing acts contrary to law, [James VII] had forfeited [his] right to the Crown'. This was unanimously approved by the committee and by a majority of the estates. Only twelve members (including all seven bishops in attendance) opposed it. The convention declared that 'King James the Seventh being a profest papist . . . hath by the advyce of evill and wicked Councillors, Invaded the fundamentall Constitution of this Kingdome, and altered it from a legall limited monarchie to ane arbitrary Despotick power . . . Wherby He hath Forefaulted the right to the Croune and the throne is become vacant.' The notion that James had forfeited the crown was at odds with the English settlement, which suggested that he had abdicated. In Scotland, James was held to have broken an implicit contract between monarch and subjects. With this concluded, Hamilton proposed that the vacant crown should be settled on William and Mary and a suitable instrument of government prepared, determining the Scots' priorities for church and state.

The strategic aims of the Scottish Revolution were clarified by the Claim of Right, which was put to the estates on 11 April 1689. It comprised two parts: the first listed James's alleged abuses and illegal acts, and the second, closely mirroring the first, established guidelines for the future. Its key clauses stated that no Catholic could succeed to the throne of Scotland; condemned James's policies and prerogative powers; criticised his maintaining a large standing army; denounced the levying of exorbitant fines and the liberal use of torture; highlighted attempts to subvert the rights of the royal burghs; declared it illegal to raise money without the consent of parliament; established the right of subjects to petition the crown and that parliament should meet frequently with guarantees for its freedom; and concluded that episcopacy was an 'insupportable grievance'. Two days later the estates approved the Articles of Grievances, a further list of complaints that the Scots expected William to redress. The lords of the articles, the committee which Charles and James had used to manage parliament, was declared 'a great grievance to the nation', as was the 1669 Act of Supremacy. The Claim of Right revealed what Scots believed were their incontrovertible rights, re-established a solid constitutional framework and set boundaries on royal authority.

The Scottish Revolution settlement was strongly contractual, a concept with a long pedigree in Scotland. Many clauses were clearly influenced by Covenanting legislation of 1640–1, which had enhanced parliament's power at the expense of the crown. The notion that James had 'forefaulted' his throne for breaking a contract between crown and nation was implicit in the Scottish coronation oath – which he had not taken – and can be found in George Buchanan's *De Jure Regni Apud Scotos*, of 1579. This stressed that monarchs were accountable to the people and subject to the law. Similar comparisons can be made with Samuel Rutherford's *Lex Rex* of 1644, or even the 1320 'Declaration of Arbroath', which contains a clause suggestive of elective kingship. It was no coincidence that these all enjoyed renewed popularity in 1689.

That the Claim of Right was regarded as a contract was implicit in the manner of its presentation to William and Mary. The three commissioners appointed to offer them the throne – Argyll, Sir John Dalrymple of Stair and Sir James Montgomerie of Skelmorlie – were instructed to deliver the Claim of Right and Articles of Grievances before William and Mary took the coronation oath. This implied that the crown was granted conditionally. Nonetheless, it was at odds with the interpretation of William and his ministers, who considered them merely as recommendations. Consequently, his insistence on maintaining the committee of the articles, albeit in a revised form that allowed the estates to choose its members, caused a crisis that saw parliament paralysed for most of 1689–90. The committee's job was to frame legislation but it was associated with the excesses of Charles and James, who had dominated the choice of its members and used it to control parliament. For most Scots parliamentarians, a central steering committee was now unacceptable. The opposition group, 'the Club', led by Skelmorlie, demanded abolition of the articles and restoration of presbyterianism. After an eight-month adjournment, during which William's Scottish ministers offered incentives to leading members of the opposition in return for their compliance, William relented and the articles were abolished in May 1690. In the same session, William's commissioner, George, first earl of Melville, assented to an act rescinding the royal supremacy and restoring ministers deprived since the Restoration. Although the presbyterians were William's strongest Scottish supporters, he wanted to retain bishops, since they were a useful means of control. The abolition of episcopacy was the price he had to pay to secure support in Scotland. The episcopalians weakened their prospects considerably because of their firm belief in the divine right of kings and continued support for James. The bishops' unwillingness to conform and the presbyterian majority in parliament forced William's hand. On 7 June, parliament ratified the 1560 confession of faith, revived anti-Catholic legislation and re-established 'Government of the Church by Kirke sessions, presbyteries, provinciall synods and Generall assemblies'. Presbyterianism was restored, but it would be several years before it recovered sufficient strength to make significant inroads in the north.

CONCLUSION: AN UNSTABLE SETTLEMENT

The king's Scottish ministers had successfully managed parliament but had been forced to grant several concessions not of William's choosing. This highlighted a new relationship between king and parliament. The Revolution marked the end of Stuart absolutist pretensions and James's unpopular Catholicising policies. From an apparently secure foundation, the restored monarchy and the bulk of its programme collapsed spectacularly. Charles's religious reforms, persecution of presbyterian dissent and increasingly absolutist kingship caused genuine concern. James's approach to rule was essentially the same as his brother's, but his religion created a far more volatile situation. His pro-Catholic policies, interpreted by many as the first step towards restoring Catholicism in Britain, added fuel to already simmering discontent. He alienated the nobility and episcopalian church, the architects and agents of the Restoration in Scotland. When the birth of a male heir ignited opposition, few were prepared to defend James's throne. The Revolution settlement was shaped by experience, pragmatism and Covenanting ideals which justified the change of monarch and placed certain limits on kingship. William did retain the right to appoint officers of state, privy councillors and lords of session, and remained the single most important source of patronage, but his relationship with parliament was significantly altered. He could no longer rely on prerogative powers. Without the articles, he had to cooperate with the estates, particularly as his wars with France required substantial revenue. He had to employ more indirect means of control: patronage and the managerial abilities of his ministers became more important in shaping the parliamentary process. The Revolution parliament enjoyed more independence than its predecessor, and it was often difficult, if not impossible, to manage the estates. Ironically, it was this level of autonomy which regularly put Scotland at odds with English interests and contributed to a decline in Anglo-Scots relations, and a revived interest in incorporating union on both sides of the Tweed.

REFERENCES

Beddard, R. 1988 *A Kingdom Without a King, The Journal of the Provisional Government in the Revolution of 1688*. Oxford.

Brown, K.M. 1992 *Kingdom or Province? Scotland and the Regal Union 1603–1715*. London.

Cowan, I.B. 1989 'The Reluctant Revolutionaries: Scotland in 1688', in Cruickshanks, E. (ed), *By Force or By Default? The Revolution of 1688–1689*, Edinburgh, 65–81.

Cowan, I.B. 1991 'Church and State Reformed? The Revolution of 1688–1689 in Scotland', in Israel, J.I. (ed), *The Anglo-Dutch Moment: Essays on the Glorious Revolution and Its World Impact*, Cambridge, 163–84.

Donaldson, G. 1994 *Scotland James V – James VII*. Edinburgh.

Drummond, A.L. and Bulloch, J. 1973 *The Scottish Church 1688–1843*. Edinburgh.

Ferguson, W. 1994 *Scotland 1689 to the Present*. Edinburgh.

Harris, T. 2005 *Restoration, Charles II and His Kingdoms*. London.

Harris, T. 2006 *Revolution, The Great Crisis of the British Monarchy, 1685–1720*. London.

Holmes, G. 1993 *The Making of a Great Power, Late Stuart and Early Georgian Britain 1660–1722*. London.

Hopkins, P. 1986 *Glencoe and the End of the Highland War*. Edinburgh.

Lenman, B.P. 1991 'The Scottish Nobility and the Revolution of 1688–1690', in Beddard, R. (ed), *The Revolutions of 1688*, Oxford, 137–62.

Mitchison, R. 1983 *Lordship to Patronage: Scotland 1603–1745*. Edinburgh.

Paterson, R.C. 2003 *King Lauderdale, The Corruption of Power*. Edinburgh.

Patrick, D.J. 2005 'Unconventional Procedure: Scottish Electoral Politics after the Revolution', in Brown, K.M. and Mann, A.J. (eds), *The History of the Scottish Parliament, vol. 2, Parliament and Politics in Scotland, 1567–1707*, Edinburgh, 208–44.

Riley, P.W.J. 1979 *King William and the Scottish Politicians*. Edinburgh.

FURTHER READING

Buckroyd, J. 1980 *Church and State in Scotland 1660–1681*. Edinburgh.

Ferguson, W. 1977 *Scotland's Relations with England, a Survey to 1707*. Edinburgh.

Jackson, C. 2003 *Restoration Scotland, 1660–1690: Royalist Politics, Religion and Ideas*. Woodbridge.

MacIntosh, G.H. 2005 'Arise King John: Commissioner Lauderdale and Parliament in the Restoration Era', in Brown and Mann (eds), *The History of the Scottish Parliament, vol. 2*, Edinburgh, 163–83.

Mann, A.J. 2005 'James VII, King of the Articles: Political Management and Parliamentary Failure', in Brown and Mann (eds), *The History of the Scottish Parliament, vol. 2*, Edinburgh, 184–207.

Patrick, J. 1991 'A Union Broken? Restoration Politics in Scotland', in J. Wormald (ed), *Scotland Revisited*, London, 119–28.

CHAPTER FIVE

The Crisis of the Regal Union: 1690–1707

————————————— *Christopher A. Whatley*

Whereas the seventeenth century had opened optimistically – with James VI adding England, Wales and Ireland to his Scottish dominions – by its end many thoughtful Scots were deeply pessimistic. Their conviction was that, for all its promise, the regal union had in practice been seriously disadvantageous for Scotland. Monarchs who were now based in London tended to favour England's interests, even at the expense of their Scottish subjects. The tide seemed temporarily to have turned when Charles II's brother, the duke of York, was resident in Edinburgh as the king's commissioner in 1679 and again between 1680 and 1682, and when he was was crowned king in 1685. As we saw in the previous chapter, however, James lost the hearts and minds of the people – primarily over his religious policies – and was succeeded by the Protestant William, prince of Orange, and his wife Mary. Under William the Scots again felt neglected and became increasingly sour in their attitudes not only to the king, but also towards England. It was for this reason that some Scots believed that the only way of dealing with the problem of uneven treatment was to 'complete' the union, that is by creating a British legislature in which Scottish representatives would sit as of right, and thereby be in a position to articulate Scottish demands. This was the solution advocated by John Clerk of Penicuik, son of Sir John Clerk, a devout presbyterian and commissioner in the Scottish parliament for the shire of Edinburgh from 1690 until 1702. Clerk junior, commissioner for Whithorn from 1703, was a patriotic Scot but also an advocate of incorporating (parliamentary) union – a step that he felt should have been taken in 1603, thereby sparing Scotland a century of disappointment and rumbling dissatisfaction (Whatley 2006).

This chapter, however, is not about the causes of the union of 1707, although inevitably it provides the backdrop to that momentous event in Scottish and British history. Rather, its purpose is to help us to understand the 'condition' of Scotland at the turn of the eighteenth century. John Clerk's support for union was based on his assessment of Scotland's position at this point in time: his belief was that the country's situation was critical and unlikely to improve while Scotland remained politically independent (Duncan 1993, 199–200). Many of Clerk's fellow Scots shared his pessimism, but offered different solutions. If there was to be a union with England, the majority view was that such a union should be federal. This was the position taken by the much-travelled lover of large European cities, Andrew Fletcher of Saltoun – the 'Patriot' – although his analysis of the failings of Scottish society was, if anything, more critical than Clerk's (Robertson 1997).

There were other contemporaries who believed that Scotland could survive independently; they have been joined recently by a group of historians who have become convinced that the extent and significance of the country's pre-1707 Atlantic trade has been overlooked (Macinnes, Harper and Fryer 2002, 11–14). This has led to the charge that some pro-Unionists were economic defeatists who lacked faith in their countrymen's capacity to generate sufficient wealth to support a viable independent state. In addition, there are historians who have contested the notion of crisis at this point in Scotland's history. They argue instead that what was being experienced was simply a temporary downturn, or 'blip', in what was otherwise a rising trajectory of Scottish development that would culminate in the Enlightenment and the industrial revolution (see Devine 1985; Lynch 1991, 300–17). Although the focus of this re-evaluation has been the economy, supporters would also point to social and cultural evidence of a country that was advancing along lines that had parallels elsewhere in Europe (Emerson 1995). It is worth noting, though, that some historians who have looked at Scotland's cultural history in the period – including Roger Emerson, whose work has just been cited – argue that the sorts of books Scots were reading and the values they were adopting were drawing them closer to England.

Other factors too were working to bring the two countries closer together. Service in the British army is one example, especially after 1689, with William's greatly expanded military machine. Also, with political power and patronage in the British Isles now based in London, Scottish politicians looked south of the border for preferment and to advance their careers. Although divines in the Church of Scotland as well as the Church of England viewed each other with deep suspicion – fearing the other's claims for confessional ascendancy – they had a shared Protestantism, and there were Scots who regarded this as the essential bulwark against the Catholic France of Louis XIV, and the Church of Rome.

THE SEVENTEENTH CENTURY: AN ERA OF ACHIEVEMENT?

Whatever conclusion we reach about Scotland's condition and the options there were for the country as the eighteenth century opened, what is beyond doubt is that earlier generations of historians who wrote off seventeenth-century Scotland as a parochial and inward-looking backwater, engrossed by religious disputation and governed by a factionalised governing class in an ineffectual parliament, were at worst simply wrong and at best seriously misleading (for a discussion of how our understanding of the period has altered, see Stevenson 1991). Some of these features were present, but there are other elements in the story. Economic change and development can be discerned in the emergence of trade with the Americas and moves from subsistence to commercial agriculture (Devine 1994). Intellectual and cultural links were strengthened with the most advanced societies on the European mainland, notably the Low Countries, where growing numbers of Scottish lawyers and physicians were trained. Some of the finest minds and most highly-regarded scholars in Europe were nurtured in Scotland: John Napier of Merchiston, inventor of logarithms and the decimal point in the early seventeenth century, and, later in that century, James Gregory, Archibald Pitcairne and Robert Sibbald, the last two having spent time at the University of Leiden. Many Scots made their reputations overseas, as soldiers and generals, and as sailors, captains and admirals in the armed forces of the warring rulers of Denmark, Sweden and Poland, but also in France, the United Provinces and Russia, and as merchants and smaller-scale traders in Scandinavia, Poland and the Netherlands (see chapter 8). The Scottish elite – major landowners and merchants – demonstrated no lack of ambition or awareness of what was required to achieve social standing and respect: fine houses were commissioned and built, using Scottish architects such as William Bruce and James Smith, and workmen as well as craftsmen from abroad. They were filled with the finest and most fashionable imported furnishings (Whyte 1979, 114–9; Brown 2001, 230–1), including Dutch paintings, sometimes purchased in bulk from Amsterdam. And for all the difficulties of the 1690s and the years immediately thereafter, even during this 'long' decade there were positive developments, which included the passing by the parliament and privy council of a series of measures designed to support and improve agriculture and manufactures, and to bolster trade. An act of parliament in 1695 founded the Bank of Scotland, only a year after the Bank of England was established; in the same year a post office opened in Edinburgh to facilitate commercial and political communication with the south. The royal burghs also sought to turn the tide that seemed to be overwhelming them, and in Glasgow and Edinburgh the length of apprenticeships was cut and efforts were made to attract new business. The context of this was the Revolution of 1688–9, which saw what one historian has rightly called the emergence of 'economic politics' in Scotland (Saville 1999), with the state playing a considerably more active role in an era when other countries were adopting measures designed to protect and stimulate their own economies – activities which historians call mercantilism.

IDENTIFYING DIFFICULTY – AND SENSING CRISIS

Ironically, given older assumptions about the parochialism of the Scots, it was partly Scottish inquisitiveness about and interest in the wider world, and travels on the part of growing numbers of Scots into England, and particularly through Europe, that did much to reveal the country's shortcomings. Clerk, one of many Scots who attended university in the Low Countries, observed what we now call relative decline, pointing out in 1705 that once 'we had such a Proportionable share of the riches of Europe, as served us to make no Contemptible Figure, both at home and abroad', but that this was no longer the case. John Hamilton, Lord Belhaven – who would later earn a place in history for a passionate anti-Union speech delivered late in 1706 – commented ten years earlier on the distasteful sight of 'all of our neighbour nations', some of which were 'not to be compared with us some hundredth years ago', now 'raising their honour, enlarging their territories, increasing their riches and consequently their power'. What was particularly irritating was not only that England seemed to be racing ahead, but also that smaller states more similar in size to Scotland, such as Denmark, Savoy and Tuscany, were faring better. The sense that something was wrong was not confined to a few unrepresentative or hysterical gloom-mongers, but was widespread. References to economic hardship recur constantly in diaries and documents from the period, both public and private. Particularly acute, and lasting right through the period and into the final session of Scotland's pre-Union parliament, were complaints about shortages of specie (hard currency) because the value of imports was outstripping that of exports. In 1706 it was estimated that only one-sixth of the coin minted in Scotland since 1686 was still circulating in the country. Cash shortages hit the lower ranks especially severely – wage labourers in the towns, who bought food and raw materials in small quantities in weekly markets, and who had only limited access to credit. Even for those higher up the social scale, coin was the essential medium of exchange for a host of everyday transactions like travel (which involved paying for horses, horse feed, board and accommodation), and to pay for other services such as tinker work or the day labourers who cleared ditches (Whatley, 1987b).

The manifestations of a troubled society were not only economic; there was also a psychological dimension. On the national level this is seen in the concentration of anguished calls by the general assembly of the Church of Scotland for days of fasting, humiliation and prayer. These were called for nearly every year between 1699 and 1706, inspired by misery-inducing events such as dearth, poor spring weather (which threatened food shortages and even famine), ailing trade, the abandoning of the Scots' colony at Darien (see below), and even the 'stupendous wasting fire' that swept through part of central Edinburgh in 1700. Throughout early modern Europe urban fires and the devastation they caused for both rich and poor were interpreted as visitations from an angry God (Roberts 1997). The ministers of the church had no doubt about the causes of the nation's distress: the wickedness of her people and the drift from the principles of the Covenant of 1638, when the Scots had seen themselves as a chosen people, akin to the Israelites. Each additional setback, no matter how obviously to modern eyes its causes were self-evidently natural, was interpreted as further proof of the depth of Scottish sinfulness. In December 1704, when the news broke that the Bank of Scotland had closed its doors, Sir John Clerk thanked God that he had only a handful of banknotes but begged forgiveness too for the nation's 'crying sins and provocations the bitter foundations of all of our plagues & miseries'.

There are signs of heightened religious fervour in the 1690s. With presbyterianism restored in 1690, kirk sessions engaged in a round of sin-seeking apparently more intense than their episcopalian predecessors (although in many parishes north of the Tay episcopalian preachers remained in post, while some congregations forcibly resisted presbyterian intruders). The moral crusade had its counterpart in England, with the formation of societies for the reformation of manners from 1691. Such a society was formed in Edinburgh (Houston 1994, 195). Nor indeed was Scotland alone in experiencing an increase in public anxiety in the wake of the revolution of 1688–9. As religious certainties were challenged, in England too fears were articulated over the succession and the way this was embroiling the nation in

Europe-wide dynastic struggles, and the costly Nine Years War waged by King William from 1689 to 1697 (Hoppit 2000, 88–106). England, however, as a wealthier society, could better cope with adversity. England had also begun to make a substantial mark as a world-ranking commercial power, and was becoming a military force to be reckoned with. Thus in England there was little of the slight but clearly visible resurgence in accusations of witchcraft and enchanting that emerged in Scotland during the 1690s and early 1700s. This was in spite of a growing scepticism on the part of Scottish lawyers, advocates and judges about the rationality of such charges, and the disappearance from much of the rest of Europe of the conditions in which witch-hunting flourished (Levack 1987). Albeit tentatively, in several Scottish cases links can be established between deteriorating living standards, economic hardship and social distress, and a compulsion within vulnerable communities to eliminate the perceived causes of localised suffering – 'witches'. It is not altogether coincidental that the last major witch-hunt in the English-speaking world – in Renfrewshire, in south-west Scotland – took place between 1697 and 1700, coinciding with the most difficult of the famine conditions that swept much of Scotland in the second half of the decade (Wasser 2002).

THE FOUR 'DISASTERS' OF THE 1690S: CRISIS IN THE MAKING?

Traditionally, historians have identified four 'disasters', or blows, that struck Scotland in the 1690s (Smout 1963, 244–53). These were: raised tariff barriers on the part of Scotland's main trading partners; the wars with France; famine; and the loss of the country's trading colony at Darien, on the isthmus of Central America. Hitherto the tendency has been to examine these in isolation, when in fact they were inextricably linked: this leads me to believe that the term crisis is an apt one (Whatley 2005). The crisis was partly of the Scots' own making; equally, however, it was caused by a combination of natural and external man-made forces which the Scottish state proved incapable of dealing with.

Economically the Scots had made substantial progress during the seventeenth century (Smout 1963). Earlier, raw materials and foodstuffs had been the country's most important exports, but before the end of the century, linen – manufactured by thousands of part-time spinners and handloom weavers mainly in the counties of Fife, Renfrew and Perth, then the most populous in Scotland – took pole position. In Aberdeenshire the specialities were plaidings and fingrams – a coarse type of woollen cloth – made by thousands of domestic workers, and exports grew from the end of the sixteenth century. There had been marked expansion in coal mining, with some collieries rivalling their counterparts in England in terms of numbers employed and output. The allied industry of salt manufacturing – from sea water – had grown too, while a host of new enterprises had been established, including soaperies, sugar refineries, and paper and glass works (Whatley 2000, 16–47). New markets were also exploited. Scottish skippers, whose voyages had largely been confined to Scandinavia, the Baltic and the northern European ports, began to venture further afield. Ayr can probably boast the first Scottish transatlantic trading venture: in

1642 the *Rebecca* of Dublin was chartered to carry goods and servants to the Caribbean islands of Barbados, Montserrat, Nevis and St Estatius. Other ventures followed from Ayr and other west coast ports, bringing back with them tobacco and sugar, providing thereby the raw materials for new processing industries. The Scots' progress, however, was far from smooth, and received a severe check after 1660 when England's Navigation Acts prohibited non-English vessels and crews from trading with their colonies. Although the measure was designed primarily to keep out England's main commercial rivals – the Dutch – concerns that they would use Scottish vessels as cover meant that the legislation was extended to the Scots. Thereafter, Scottish merchants had to conduct business in England's colonial empire illicitly.

By its very nature, the scale of such activity is impossible to measure, but we do know that merchants in London and Bristol were outraged by Scottish merchants colluding with merchants and skippers in the north-west of England to evade high English import tariffs (Graham 2002, 102–4). That Scotland's share of the customs collected at Scottish and English ports in the immediate pre-Union years was a mere 2% of that of England (the population ratio was around 1:5) points to weaknesses in the Scottish customs system, but also to large-scale evasion. The evidence suggests that the wealth generated benefited individuals rather than the Scottish state, either nationally or locally: many royal burghs, the main trading towns, were in a wretched state, as we will see below. Nevertheless, some merchants and lairds became very rich, sometimes by milking the Scottish customs and excise duties, which were farmed out for a set rental or tack. These were not always paid. As landowners – which many merchants were – they could borrow money with relative ease (virtually everyone in Scotland who could was prepared to lend), and thus commission and furnish their great houses. A few hundred merchants and manufacturers were able to live in comfort and with style, particularly in Edinburgh, where lavish spending sustained the luxury trades and professions in far greater numbers than anywhere else (Dingwall 1994), although other places, notably Glasgow, were catching up. Significantly, despite the difficulties of the 1690s, Edinburgh's fruit market continued to thrive and there was a steep rise in luxury purchases after 1700.

So the Scots lacked nothing in entrepreneurial endeavour; indeed for centuries the country's merchants had responded quickly and aggressively to trading intelligence which revealed opportunities for windfall gains overseas. Wars, localised crop failures and dearth all opened doors through which the Scots managed to sell cargoes of their goods, such as coal and salt, fish and grain. But conditions even for illicit trade with the plantations became more difficult after 1696, when English Orders in Council tightened further the Navigation Acts. It is worth noting too that, whilst we can interpret the apparent willingness of so many Scots in the seventeenth century to travel overseas as a positive attribute (in the region of 200,000 people went over the course of the century), there was a powerful compulsive element at work too. This was largely an exodus of the poor and the desperate: the term 'merchant' captures a wide range of commercial activity and as often as not included pedlars and up to 3,000 packmen who travelled into England annually, selling their wares from door to door. The chances of returning alive or in good health from a spell of army service abroad were relatively slim – during the Thirty Years' War it was 'a one-way ticket to almost certain death' (Smout, Landsman and Devine 1994). Scottish out-migration in the seventeenth century may have been as much as a third of that of England, from a total population that was four or fives times less. Scotland's economy was strengthening, it is true, but subsistence farming still predominated and the population was vulnerable to minor economic and climatic fluctuations. For most Scots the business of maintaining the viability of their household economies made necessary a variety of income streams: sales of agricultural produce and earnings in cash or kind from what would rarely be a single or a full-time occupation, invariably on an irregular day-to-day basis. Should one source fail, individuals and families were often plunged into poverty, as was the nation, with dire consequences, when harvest failure struck, as it did periodically even before the great famine of the 1690s (Devine 1994, 3).

It was not only England that was making life more difficult for the Scots in the final decades of the seventeenth century. But the more stringent application of English economic policies was quite bad enough, as increasingly England had become the main destination for Scottish exports. With increases in tariffs on Scottish coal and salt, and in 1698 a substantial increase in duties on imported linen cloth, the value of Scottish exports to England halved from some £114,000 per annum at the end of the 1690s to around £54,000 five and six years later (Smout 1963, 255). European markets were closing too, with increased coal duties in the Spanish Netherlands and a reduction in English coal duties in 1694 combining to encourage the Dutch to take coal from Tyneside rather than the Lothians and Fife. France imposed a ban on Scottish woollens and fish, and raised tariffs on coal and some other goods in 1689. Aberdeenshire's burgeoning exports of woollens may have reached their peak as early as 1670, after which import substitution in Sweden, the loss of the Dutch plantations in Brazil, French tariffs and rising raw material prices combined to crush the export trade. By the turn of the next century only a quarter of the previous volume of plaidings was being sent abroad, and one-sixth of the fingrams (Dennison, Ditchburn and Lynch 2002, 165–8). Hardly a single Scottish commodity was spared the adverse effects of the European mercantilist mind-set, but Scotland suffered especially badly as purchasers were usually able to find substitutes – home-produced if possible. And anyway most Scottish goods were of a poor quality and little value. It was for this reason that parliament and the privy council supported a number of schemes to import skilled labour.

Although the world could survive without Scotland, Scots needed the world beyond their borders. Imports included the luxury goods already alluded to (a ruinous indulgence that was condemned by the earl of Cromartie and others) but also everyday wares, such as pots and pans and pewter goods, and even better qualities of cloth, including linen. The outcome was a growing balance of payments deficit, which became worse, as did the problem of the shortage of specie, when nervous merchants overseas sought payment in coin (Saville 1996, 39–58). War could open up trading opportunities, as happened with the Scottish salt industry in the 1620s and 1630s when Spain attempted to blockade the merchant shipping of their Dutch enemies. Starved of their supplies of 'Bay' salt from Biscay, and as salt prices soared, the Dutch turned to the Scots for this vital commodity (Whatley 1987a, 37–41). But war could also devastate trade: the Nine Years War with France, led by King William, who aimed to counter French aggression and the threat this posed to the Dutch economy, brought Scotland directly into the line of fire. As a potential entry point for the return of James VII & II, the country was now at the centre of one of Europe's great dynastic struggles, with William and his supporters standing firm for a Protestant succession. Trade routes were interrupted and French privateers wreaked havoc on Scottish merchant shipping. Hunting in packs, they raided groups of merchant vessels returning from the Baltic and picked off the largely unprotected Dutch and Scottish herring fleets around Orkney. The country's east coast was especially vulnerable. There was a lull with the peace which followed the Treaty of Ryswick in 1697, but hostilities between Britain and France resumed in 1702, with the onset of the War of the Spanish Succession. For the Scots the situation was worsened when, from the early 1690s, the English too began to seize Scottish merchantmen – to the extent that English naval vessels even made forays into the upper Forth. The Scots were suspected of harbouring Jacobites, and had offended English trading interests by promoting Scottish merchant adventurer companies – thus challenging English monopolies. The impact on the royal burghs, through which most overseas trading was conducted, was profound, and from around the country came protests about shipping losses, contracting trade and urban poverty – and, ultimately, urban decay, as town councils ran out of funds with which to maintain public buildings and harbours (Whatley 2006). Even some of the more prosperous new burghs of barony were hit too, as in the case of Bo'ness (founded in 1669), where it was complained in 1705 that two-thirds of the shipping it had had in 1698 had been taken. Glasgow claimed it lost as many as seventeen merchant ships in the year prior to 1707, fourteen as a result of enemy seizures.

In part, the problem was the Scots' inability to defend their traders at sea. The entire naval defences of Scotland in 1691 comprised two ships – both ex-merchant vessels hastily armed. Between them they were able to carry only thirty guns and 200 men; the English and Dutch navies boasted thousands of both. Recognising that the lack of naval power was a major weakness if the Scots were ever going to be able to expand their commerce overseas in an era of muscular mercantilism, parliament had backed proposals to establish an independent seaborne force. Without the protection of the merchant fleet by convoys, Lord Belhaven feared 'the utter ruin of the nation'. Yet such was the paucity of the public purse that the Scots had little option but to ask the king to lend suitable hulls from England, three of which were then fitted out at Scottish expense. Before the Union, English protection was being provided for Scots merchant shipping in the North Sea, although Dutch men of war sometimes assisted too.

Bad though things were for the Scots at sea, it could have been worse. Proportionately, Scottish merchant shipping losses were less than England's or Holland's. In 1703 over a hundred Dutch herring busses were set on fire by French raiders in the

Bressay Sound, although in this instance the Scots were losers too. Dutch fishermen had bought provisions and hand-knitted stockings in the Northern Isles and demand subsequently collapsed, depressing further the local economy and widening the pool of the poor which had been created by the famine of the 1690s (Smith 1984, 35–45). In the west of Scotland, however, the war brought certain benefits. The Clyde ports were able to supply the garrison at what from 1690 was Fort William (formerly Inverlochy) with victuals, and also to supply William's forces in Ulster. A twice-weekly dispatch boat began to operate between Portpatrick and Donaghadee. With French privateers operating from the channel ports of St Malo and Dunkirk, Scottish skippers were able to slip more easily across the Atlantic, and maintain their illicit links with the plantations (Graham 2002, 149–50). With the disruption and partial destruction of the Dutch fishing fleet, the Scots were even able to increase their sales of fish into the Baltic in the first years of the eighteenth century.

The scale of this, however, should not be exaggerated and at the end of the seventeenth century, overall, the Scottish economy was ailing. For all the promise and high hopes of the state's 'economic politics', little was achieved. Of forty-seven joint-stock companies that had been formed with state support between 1690 and 1695, only twelve appear to have been in business in 1700, and those that kept going did so only by the skin of their teeth. For all the fanfare that had greeted some of these new establishments, and the giddy promises of their projectors, in comparison to their neighbours in Ireland and England, the Scots were lagging behind. In 1695, for example, the Scottish glass industry was represented by a single glass house, whereas in England there were eighty-eight, several of which were in the north (suggesting that it was not just distance from markets that was the problem). The other new trades present similar pictures. Where time-series showing output over a number of years are available, these too point to a downturn, as with Scottish publishing: buoyant in the 1640s and 1680s, in the years following, the industry entered a trough which lasted at least until 1707 (Whatley 2006, 118). Under-development was a trap from which it was well-nigh impossible for the Scots to escape; where others were doing so, it was with money, military force and strong political leadership – none of which was in abundance in Scotland.

What evidence we have about Scotland's state finances in the years preceding the Union of 1707 suggests that the government machine was bankrupt; one of the few historians to have looked at this subject in any detail, Athol Murray, concluded that by 1707 Scotland 'was not financially viable' (Murray 1974, 34). There was a shortfall in government finances of some £14,000 sterling per annum, around 12% of total income. Revenues from customs and excise duties were simply insufficient to pay for the army and navy. Salaries of army officers and government officials were years in arrears (going back to 1688 in some cases), and unlikely to be paid, even though England bore the cost of the royal household, diplomatic representation overseas and Scottish regiments stationed outside Scotland. Economic privation and the weakly-developed revenue service in Scotland hardly helped: new taxes were fiercely resisted, especially at the ports, where customs evasion was rife. The minister of Bo'ness, John Brand, preached against such 'sinful practices', but to no avail; he wished he could find a country parish where such temptations were less in evidence and his lot would have been easier. The miniscule Scottish treasury was simply unable to support a viable, early modern state. It was partly because they had this, as well as relatively powerful centralised governments, that other states in Europe, such as England, Sweden and even Russia, where St Petersburg was under construction, had been able to advance so rapidly. But in Scotland things were getting worse: public revenue was less in 1706 than it had been in the 1650s.

The most ambitious venture ever attempted in Scotland's economic history, designed to free the country from its mercantilist prison, was the formation in 1696 of the Company of Scotland Trading to Africa and the Indies. Better known as the Darien Company – after the locality in Central America where the Scots established a trading colony – it was modelled on the great Dutch overseas companies, and brought into being by William Paterson, the Scot who had been instrumental in founding the Bank of England and who had some familiarity with the region in which Darien was located (Bannister 1968).

Lured by the prospect that Scotland might command a great commercial empire of the seas by linking the Atlantic and the Pacific, and the likelihood of exploiting vast deposits of silver and gold (which the Spaniards had been doing), Scots flocked enthusiastically – near maniacally in some cases – to invest in the company when the subscription books open in February (Douglas Jones 2001). Four years later, with virtually the unanimous blessing of the people of Lowland Scotland, the first ships set sail from Scotland bound for Darien, carrying with them the nation's hopes, much of the country's liquid capital and a cargo which included men, women and a few children, linen and other goods which it was hoped would be sold, and a sizeable quantity of Bibles. The mission was spiritual as well as material, although this was not unprecedented: Scotland's first settlement in North America, in East New Jersey in 1683, included religious refugees (Whatley 2006).

Yet within two years the Darien dream had turned to disaster. The colonists were driven out, ultimately by Spanish forces, after a brief triumph by the Scots against the same enemy at Toubacanti, under the command of Alexander Campbell of Fonab. But the seeds of failure had been sown earlier. Although £400,000 sterling (around £103 billion in today's money) was subscribed to the company, only some £153,000 was paid up, and then with difficulty. The company's ships were constructed and fitted out abroad, at great expense, while some of the capital invested was embezzled. Equipment levels were inadequate, as was provisioning, and death rates amongst the Scots were high, both on board ship and in 'Caledonia' itself, where the climate was hostile and the terrain difficult. Settlement was made more problematic by conflicts which broke out amongst the colonists' leaders and by the character failings of some of the settlers. Contrary to expectations, the Scots were far from welcome in what the Spaniards considered to be their territory – in close proximity to mines for precious metals, which were under their control, and within striking distance of their naval bases at Panama and Cartagena. Pope Innocent XII, anxious about the presence in the region of Protestant proselytisers, granted funds to counter the Scots' incursion. There were Scots, however, who preferred to ignore most of this and, with some justification, blamed English interference for the debacle. The English chartered companies had lobbied William and persuaded him to order the withdrawal from the Scottish company of London-based subscribers. Later, orders were given that the company's ships should be denied the right to take on supplies in the West Indies. As a result, despair and outrage swept Scotland. Some looked on the evacuation of Darien as a judgement of God; most, however, blamed King William and the English. Not only had wildly optimistic expectations been dashed, but thousands of individuals, from the mightiest in the land to burgh incorporations and aged widows, had lost small fortunes (Whatley 2006).

In part, the heady enthusiasm for the Darien scheme can be explained by the gloomy economic backcloth against which it was proposed. Within months of the opening of the Company of Scotland subscription books, however, it became apparent that the country faced an even greater challenge: debilitating dearth and famine. The period c.1680 to c.1730 was the coldest cycle during what has been called the Little Ice Age (Fagan 2000). Countries like Scotland, where peasant-based subsistence agriculture was still the norm, were acutely vulnerable to the effects of cold and wet weather, along with the freak conditions such as excessive heat and wind that seem to have marked this period. Indeed, the deterioration in the weather seems to have been preceded in Scotland by two factors which combined to worsen the blow when it came. The first was a long-term fall in living standards (apparently over two centuries), and a shift in dietary habits which saw a drop in meat consumption and a greater dependence on oats and oatmeal. It was these that provided most of the calories required by the majority of Scots at the end of the seventeenth century. Fortunately for Scottish consumers, there was in Scotland and throughout much of Europe in the second half of the seventeenth century something of a glut in cereal production – the weather had generally been fair and improvement was in the air – but for landlords this was less beneficial, as prices were low. The second factor concerned agricultural output. Notwithstanding the evidence for change and innovation in Scottish agriculture in the early modern period, by the 1690s Scotland may have been suffering from serious ecological degradation: specifically, low nitrogen levels brought about by centuries-long woodland decline, the leaching of the mineral content of soils and their further cultivation without adequate fertilisation. Large-scale liming and other means of redressing this imbalance lay in the future. Seventeenth-century improvements such as adding turf to the infield – the heavily cultivated lands – and paring and burning moss-lands provided only a temporary solution (Smout 1999, 211–14). The consequence was that there was little room for failure and when crop yields began to fall markedly, as they appear to have done after 1691 in some parts of eastern Scotland, and 1693 elsewhere, the situation began to be critical, much to the alarm of some contemporaries (Young 2004; Smout 1963, 246). In some years the crop yield ratio was worse than 3 : 1, meaning that returns from seed were insufficient to perform their required functions: to feed the farmer and his household; provide seed for next year's crop; and generate a surplus for sale or to pay the rent. The result was an increase in landed debts: bankruptcies amongst the landed classes rose between 1660 and 1710 (one in four estates changed hands), while estate papers from the 1690s and the years immediately following bear witness to a rise in unpaid rents. For many thousands of poverty-stricken tenants there was no alternative but to flee in search of sustenance on the road or in the burghs, where poor relief was often better organised.

The consequences of crop failure penetrated more deeply into rural society than is at first sight apparent. Owing to the difficulty of finding sufficient grain to eat during the years of scarcity, tenants on upland estates and where cattle and sheep were bred were forced to consume part of their animal stocks. As a result, sales of these fell off too, as did the quantities of butter, cheese and tallow, animal by-products that farmers had been able to sell in the towns. By the end of the century too the circumstances of tenants and sub-tenants in counties such as Perthshire and Renfrewshire had worsened as the effect of higher English tariffs on imported linens began to bite after 1698 (Young 2004). In these areas – and parts of Fife too – flax spinning and the weaving of linen had become ubiquitous and in many cases these were the occupations that earned the income with which households managed to pay their rents; as the work began to dry up, so the tenants' difficulties increased.

This is not the occasion to explore in any detail the full effects of the famine. In any case, it is only very recently that it has been studied on a nationwide scale in the depth required (Cullen 2004). Accordingly, historians' views of its severity and duration differ, some suggesting that there were really only three harsh years (1695, 1696 and 1698), although there were significant regional variations. In terms of mortality, 1697 was the worst year in Aberdeen and the North-East, but not everywhere else (Flinn 1977, 164–86; Tyson 1986). Over the famine period this region may have lost as much as 21% of its population, a level matched only in the Highlands and probably the Northern Isles, although for neither of these areas has the evidence required to quantify the loss survived: namely, mortality registers, and registers for marriages and baptisms. Sights of people starving and dying by the roadside were commonplace, however, while church records from many parts of the Lowlands contain harrowing accounts of mass burials of those who more often died as a result of disease brought on by malnutrition than by starvation. Recent research on the counties of Angus (Forfar) and Perth suggests that conditions became more difficult from 1693 and did not recover until the harvest of 1700. The population loss for Scotland appears to have been in the region of 15%, high enough, if not as severe as the famine's effects on mortality in Estonia and Finland. The figure included around 50,000 people who emigrated to Ulster from Scotland during the 1690s, many of whom were desperately poor and hungry (Cullen 2004). Dearth was acting as a spur, driving out the young, healthy and economically active, as well as women, pensioners and poor families, and also soldiers disbanded with the peace heralded by the treaty of Ryswick. This was a matter of grave concern to some who worried that Scotland would become 'the only Christian Nation in the universe' that 'suffers it self to run the hazard of being dispeopled'. Some of course went to Darien, although this channel for migration was quickly blocked; its flow had also been checked by the fact that grain shortages and resultant high prices meant that the second expedition was inadequately provisioned and many lives were lost on the voyage out (Whatley 2006).

The famine exposed cruelly the inadequacies of the Scottish state, but also exacerbated them. In 1696 alone, £100,000 sterling was spent to purchase grain from England and elsewhere. This was just about equivalent to the government's entire annual revenue, but excise revenues fell during the crisis years as the tax farmers found that, in some areas, brewing and the sale of ale were curtailed owing to the difficulty of finding grain (Cullen 2004). Efforts to raise additional income for the state were implemented in the form of three poll taxes (1693, 1695 and 1698), but all disappointed their proposers' expectations. One contemporary reckoned the cost of famine relief was £400,000 sterling – almost certainly an exaggeration – but, with doubts growing about Scotland's financial robustness, grain dealers overseas expected to be paid from the nation's dwindling reserves of coin.

Burgh councils, charities and kirk sessions also spent considerable sums to support the swelling band of the poor. While the authorities in some burghs were able to cope with the influx of rural migrants (in Edinburgh's case by opening a refugee camp in Greyfriars churchyard and in Aberdeen by providing relief for as many as 10% of the town's inhabitants), as the crisis deepened, councils were left with no alternative but to provide solely for their resident poor. The rest were excluded, cast out – as 'extraneous beggars' were from Stirling in May 1699, when the council decided that the number of vagrants was 'insupportable' – and left to fend for themselves by begging for private charity. Some historians doubt the accuracy of Andrew Fletcher of Saltoun's estimate that 200,000 people were begging from door to door by 1698, but this represented only 16% of the total population, and is less than the 20% or so who needed relief in England (Whatley 2006). As with the towns, provision on the part of the rural parishes was variable. It was only in the Lothians, possibly Perthshire and in random parishes elsewhere that the system of poor relief was effective. But growers in the Lothians and some other parts of eastern Scotland seem to have escaped the worst of the weather, so the suffering there may have been less anyway. Three quarters of the country's parishes failed to assess the landholders in their bounds and thereby bolster parish coffers; where the means of relief were inadequate, mortality levels were higher. Many landholders would have had difficulty paying, of course. In 1690 they had been subject to a swingeing increase in land tax, and landed estate rent rolls were hardly burgeoning. Some had also drawn on any surplus funds they had available to subscribe to the Company of Scotland, and prior to that the Bank of Scotland, which had managed to raise £60,000 sterling, £6,000 of which was in cash. There was a dramatic fall in church-door collections for the poor in Edinburgh as news of the retreat from Darien reached Scotland's shores, but also as a result of simple donor fatigue.

SLOW RECOVERY AND HARD CHOICES

In most places the worst was over by 1700. Stomachs began to be filled. Yet it was to be decades before the population losses were made good. State coffers had been drained dry and salary arrears and debts mounted. Money remained scarce and in 1704 the Bank of Scotland was even forced to close its doors temporarily, the event which led Sir John Clerk to invite God to 'pitie' the poor Scots while he begged forgiveness for the nation's 'crying sins'. In the country and in the towns the number of permanent paupers was higher in the first years of the eighteenth century than it had been at the start of the 1690s – double in Edinburgh for a time (Dingwall 1994, 250–71). There is little sign of recovery in the burghs: indeed, complaints about their circumstances intensified because difficulties incurred by war, trading losses and investments in the Company of Scotland had been compounded by the additional burden of supporting the poor. They had always complained about taxes, but their objections were now merited; in some places burgh government broke down because inhabitants were unwilling to accept office as councillors in case they became responsible for burgh debts. Weather conditions improved, but there were still some bad years. In Lanarkshire the harvest of 1703 was described as 'the worst . . . of any that has been yet'. It was not until the 1730s or even later that the Scottish economy was lifted from the trough into which it had descended in the 1680s.

Responses to the crisis varied. Darien in particular excited political passions, and demands were made for reparation from William and England. What became clear to the majority of thinking Scots was that the regal union was no longer tenable as it stood. Some sought greater independence; others favoured a federal arrangement with England. Less popular was the route eventually accepted by parliament: incorporating union. This involved the loss of a separate parliament and what some believed to be two thousand years of independence, although the pragmatic commissioner for Whithorn and leading authority on Scotland's economy, John Clerk, urged his countrymen to 'lay aside airy Schemes of Government, lest like the Dog in the Fable, we catch at the Shadow, and lose the Substance'. Hard choices had to be made if the Scots were to fulfil their aspirations to become a polite, commercial society, on a par with the best of the rest in Europe. But why and how the Scots settled on this is another story. What is certain, however, is that on the Scottish side at least, the crisis of the 1690s was a key element in determining that outcome.

REFERENCES

Bannister, S. 1968 (ed) *The Writings of William Paterson*. New York.

*Brown, K.M. 2001 'Reformation to Union', in Houston, R.A. and Knox, W.W. (eds.) *The New Penguin History of Scotland*, London, 182–275.

Cullen, K.J. 2004 'Famine in Scotland in the 1690s: Causes and Consequences', unpublished PhD, University of Dundee.

Dennison, E.P., Ditchburn, D. and Lynch, M. (eds), *Aberdeen Before 1800: A New History*. East Linton.

Devine, T.M. 1985 'The Union of 1707 and Scottish Development', *Scottish Economic & Social History*, 5, 23–40.

Devine, T.M. 1994 *The Transformation of Rural Scotland: Social Change and the Agrarian Economy 1660–1815*. Edinburgh.

Dingwall, H. 1994 *Late 17th Century Edinburgh: a demographic study*. Aldershot.

Douglas Jones, W. 2001 'The Bold Adventurers: A Quantitative Analysis of the Darien Subscription List (1696)', *Scottish Economic & Social History*, 21, 22–42.

Duncan, D. (ed) 1993 *History of the Union of Scotland and England by Sir John Clerk of Penicuik*. Edinburgh.

Emerson, R.L. 1995 'Scottish cultural change 1660–1707 and the Union of 1707', in Robertson, J. (ed), *A Union for Empire*, Cambridge, 121–44.

Fagan, B. 2000 *The Little Ice Age*. New York.

Flynn, M. (ed) 1977 *Scottish Population History from the 17th Century to the 1930s*. Cambridge.

*Graham, E.J. 2002 *A Maritime History of Scotland 1650–1790*. East Linton.

Hoppit, J. 2000 *A Land of Liberty? England 1689–1727*. Oxford.

Houston R.A. 1994 *Social Change in the Age of the Enlightenment: Edinburgh, 1660–1760*. Oxford.

Levack, B.P. 1987 *The Witch-Hunt in Early Modern Europe*. Harlow.

Lynch, M. 1991 *Scotland: A New History*. London.

Macinnes, A.I., Harper, M-A. and Fryer, L.G. (eds) 2002 *Scotland and the Americas, c.1650– c.1939: A Documentary Source Book*. Edinburgh.

Murray, A.L. 1974 'Administration and the Law', in Rae, T.I. (ed), *The Union of 1707: Its Impact on Scotland*, Glasgow, 30–57.

Roberts, P. 1997 'Agencies human and divine: fire in French cities, 1520–1720', in Naphy, W.G. and Roberts, P. (eds), *Fear in Early Modern Society*, Manchester, 9–27.

Robertson, J. 1997 (ed), *Andrew Fletcher: Political Works*. Cambridge.

Saville, R. 1996 *Bank of Scotland: A History, 1695–1995*. Edinburgh.

Saville, R. 1999 'Scottish modernisation prior to the industrial revolution', in Devine, T.M. and Young, J.R. (eds), *Eighteenth-Century Scotland: New Perspectives*, East Linton, 6– 23.

Smith, H.D. 1984 *Shetland Life and Trade, 1550–1914*. Edinburgh.

*Smout, T.C. 1963 *Scottish Trade on the Eve of Union 1660–1707*. Edinburgh.

Smout, T.C. 1999 'The Improvers and the Scottish Environment: Soils, Bogs and Woods', in Devine, T.M. and Young, J.R. (eds), *Eighteenth-Century Scotland: New Perspectives*. East Linton.

Smout, T.C., Landsman, N. and Devine, T.M. 1994, 'Scottish Emigration in the Seventeenth and Eighteenth Centuries', in Canny, N. (ed), *Europeans on the Move: Studies in European Migration, 1500–1800*, Oxford, 76–112.

*Stevenson, D. 1991 'Twilight before Night or Darkness before Dawn? Interpreting Seventeenth-Century Scotland', in Mitchison, R. (ed), *Why Scottish History Matters*, Edinburgh, 37–47.

Tyson, R.E. 1986 'Famine in Aberdeenshire, 1695–1699: Anatomy of a Crisis', in Stevenson, D. (ed), *From Lairds to Louns: Country and Burgh Life in Aberdeen 1600–1800*, Aberdeen, 32–52.

Wasser, M. 2002 'The western witch-hunt of 1697–1700: the last major witch-hunt in Scotland', in Goodare, J. (ed), *The Scottish Witch-hunt in Context*, East Linton, 146– 65.

Whatley, C.A. 1987 *The Scottish Salt Industry: An Economic and Social History, 1570–1850*. Aberdeen.

Whatley, C.A. 1987b 'Salt, Coal and the Union of 1707: A revision article', *Scottish Historical Review*, 66, 26–45.

Whatley, C.A. 2000 *Scottish Society, 1707–1830: beyond Jacobitism, towards Industrialisation*. Manchester.

*Whatley, C.A. 2005 'Taking Stock: Scotland at the End of the Seventeenth Century', in Smout, T.C. (ed), *Anglo-Scottish Relations from 1603 to 1900*. Oxford.

Whatley, C.A. 2006 *The Scots and the Union*. Edinburgh.

Whyte, I. 1979 *Agriculture and Society in Seventeenth-Century Scotland*. Edinburgh.

Young, M. 2004 'Rural Society in Scotland from the Restoration to the Union: Challenge and Response in the Carse of Gowrie, *c*.1660–1707', unpublished PhD, University of Dundee.

FURTHER READING

The items above marked * are recommended for further reading, along with the following.

Devine, T.M. 1999 *The Scottish Nation, 1700–2000*. London.

Mitchison, R. 2000 *The Old Poor Law in Scotland: The Experience of Poverty, 1574–1845*. Edinburgh.

Mitchison, R. 1983 *Lordship to Patronage: Scotland 1603–1745*. London.

Robertson, J. (ed), *A Union for Empire*. Cambridge

CHAPTER SIX

The Western *Gàidhealtachd*
Alison Cathcart

Much of Scottish historiography has dealt with Gaeldom separately from the political development of Lowland Scotland. Indeed, the view that a clear distinction existed between the barbaric and savage Gaels and the law-abiding, civilised inhabitants of the Lowland south and east has characterised many perceptions of Scotland, its people and its history for centuries. Gaelic culture and language existed in the western Highlands and Isles and much of northern and central Scotland, including northern Perthshire, eastern Inverness-shire and Ross. Although recent research has made some effort to redress the imbalance, the perception of a Highland–Lowland divide is long-standing, having emerged by the fifteenth century. By the following century, this characterisation of two separate societies was reinforced by the realisation that there were clear political and economic differences between the two regions. The Scottish crown had come to view the Gaels as lawless and disobedient and, throughout the sixteenth century, successive monarchs attempted to assert royal authority in the region by both coercive and conciliatory means. The effects of increased crown intervention and the interaction of local and national politics became most evident during this period. The current chapter will examine the organisation of Highland society and the main events which shaped its development during the period *c.*1500–*c.*1700, focusing on the protracted decline and disintegration of Clan Donald during the sixteenth century as a result of the forfeiture of the Lordship of the Isles in 1493, and the impact for the Highlands as a whole of the resulting Clan Donald–Clan Campbell rivalry, which emerged during the last decades of the sixteenth century and became prominent in the seventeenth. Also, it aims to provide a rounded portrayal of clan society and to explore the reasons why the region formed the bed-rock of support for the exiled Stewart dynasty after 1689.

CLAN SOCIETY

Clan society is said to have emerged in Scotland during the eleventh and twelfth centuries, a product of the interaction of the largely kin-based society of the indigenous people, the so-called 'feudal' society of the incoming population, and the bonds of obligation that existed within a localised community. Kinship, whether real, marital or fictive, remained important, although it was only one of a number of organising principles within clan society (Cathcart 2006, 59–98). Membership of a clan was not confined to those related by blood to the chief. Clan society was more fluid than traditional views would suggest and blood ties alone did not predicate membership of a particular group. In Gaeldom an individual was known by his forename, often accompanied by a nickname, for example *Donnachadh Dubh* (Black Donald), or was identified as the descendent of his father and grandfather, for example *Iain mac Dhomhnaill mhic Aonghuis* (John, son of Donald, son of Angus). An individual might also be identified by association with his territory, his place of residence, or his profession, such as *Fear na Pàirce* (The Man of Park, MacCulloch of Park in Ross) or *An Clàrsair Dall* (The Blind Harper, Roderick Morrison). For most, the final strand of identification was with the wider clan to which they belonged. Personal, local and collective identities allowed individuals to understand themselves within a range of contexts (Dawson 1998, 261).

For Gaels, their primary identity was as part of Gaelic society, whether in Ireland or Scotland, bound together by a shared language, culture and society. Much has been made of the close links between Gaelic society in Ireland and in Scotland, with some historians talking of a homogeneous, pan-Gaelic entity. But by *c.*1500 the heads of the main Highland clans were tenants-in-chief of the Scottish crown, holding land from the crown and acknowledging royal authority; and through the sixteenth and seventeenth centuries there was increased cooperation between the crown and Highland society. The crown and central government adopted a number of policies relating to the Highlands and sought to work with clan chiefs who were law-abiding. Thus clan chiefs were crucial to the success of Stewart crown policy but at the same time had a fundamental role in maintaining and preserving their own clan and estate.

The role of the chief was central in clan society and his primary obligations to the clan were to protect, provide and administer justice (Macinnes 1996, 2–3). In other words, it was the chief who was responsible for the economic, political and social welfare of the clan as a whole, ensuring solidarity between clan members who did not necessarily live in close geographic proximity to one another. He was not alone, however, in managing clan affairs and chiefs relied heavily on the principal men of the clan – the *fine* – consulting with them on issues ranging from marriages of clan members to involvement in localised feuding. To some extent the chief was accountable to them (Cathcart 2006, 60–79). The role of the *fine* in maintaining clan cohesion became increasingly important as, due to the diminishing importance of blood kinship, chiefs needed to secure the cooperation of disparate satellite clans absorbed within the main clan. They also created alliance networks with other clans, gaining political and military allies as a means of protection and assistance. The obligations these alliances involved were regarded with suspicion by the crown, which sought to ensure that royal authority was not compromised. But the crown also capitalised on the pivotal role of the chief within clan society by making chiefs responsible for the actions of their clansmen, tenants and dependants, as well as any caterans (landless or 'broken' men) inhabiting their estate.

Chiefs held their land either directly from the crown or from another landlord. By receiving written charter for clan territories, chiefs acknowledged the crown as their ultimate superior while gaining legal rights to the clan's land. In purely legal terms it was the chief who had title to the land, yet it was inhabited and worked collectively by the clan. Land was the main economic resource in the Highlands and communal farming emphasises how all members worked towards economic provision for the clan as a whole. Farming, which was predominantly pastoral, operated at a subsistence level for the majority of clan members, although chiefs benefited substantially. They collected rent and tribute, known as calp, from tenants and clansmen, using the surplus to trade with the Lowlands, England, Ireland and the Continent, while also paying for increasingly comfortable residences on their estates. Rents in kind are said to have served a significant socio-political function, evident in the lavish feasts a chief would hold to emphasise wealth, prestige and social standing (Dodgshon 1998, 88–92). Nonetheless, throughout this period rents increasingly came to be paid in cash, thus beginning the transformation of a hereditary estate into an economic resource.

As written title to land became established in the *Gàidhealtachd* many chiefs benefited, but for some this was an unwelcome development. Macinnes has argued there was a crucial distinction within Highland society between *dùthchas*, the land traditionally settled by the clan, and *oighreach*, lands which the chief held from the crown. For chiefs whose *oighreach* was not coterminous with the clan's *dùthchas*, problems arose: members of other clans on the *oighreach* might pay rent to their own chief rather than their legal landlord (Macinnes 1995, 5–6). While evidence suggests the division between *dùthchas* and *oighreach* is not always clear-cut, clan chiefs did maintain claims of customary possession on account of inheritance and continued occupancy regardless of tenurial rights. Such conflicting claims to land could often result in dispute. Although the creation of political and military allies was primarily defensive, designed to prevent outbreaks of unrest, it could contribute to the rapid escalation of minor, localised disorder into something more widespread.

For the most part, feuding was the result of a combination of political and economic factors. Minor economic disputes were expressed through tit-for-tat raids, in which livestock or grain was stolen, or lands wasted. The prevalence of caterans within the Highlands, and the maintenance of a military elite within some clans, meant that chiefs could retaliate quickly without having to rely heavily on those clansmen involved in farming. Endemic feuding, combined with the militarised character of Highland society, reinforced the perception of the region as lacking in law and order and disdainful of royal authority. This view has coloured much of subsequent historiography: clan society has been portrayed as inherently antagonistic towards the crown and as a region remote and isolated from Lowland political and economic development. As this chapter hopes to emphasise, the Highlands should not be treated as a homogeneous unit, nor should they be regarded as having little relevance to the rest of Scotland during this period.

THE EFFECTS OF THE FORFEITURE OF THE LORDSHIP OF THE ISLES

In the later middle ages, the MacDonald Lordship of the Isles had provided a political, economic, military and cultural focus in the West Highlands and the Isles

(See volume 1 chapter 5). At the zenith of their influence in the middle of the fifteenth century the MacDonalds were one of the most powerful families in Scotland, with extensive territorial holdings in the Western Isles, Kintyre, Knapdale, Lochaber, Ardnamurchan and Morvern, as well as the earldom of Ross. Successive Stewart kings relied on the Lords of the Isles to provide effective government in the west and to maintain stability in a region that lay outside the influence of royal authority. But the lordship began to disintegrate internally and John, fourth Lord of the Isles, was no longer able to provide effective government, rendering him dispensable. As a result, the MacDonald lordship was forfeited in 1493 during the final months of the minority of James IV. Once the king assumed personal control of government he embarked on a number of expeditions in the Isles to impose the authority of the crown (Nicholson 1974, 542–4; Macdougall 1989, 100–5).

Stability proved elusive as the Highlands witnessed no less than seven rebellions during the next fifty years. The first, only a year after the 1493 forfeiture, was led by Alexander of Lochalsh, who was subsequently murdered by another member of the Clan Donald, John MacIain of Ardnamurchan. In 1503 rebellion broke out once again, this time with Donald Dubh, grandson of the fourth lord, as its figurehead. It took a number of government campaigns to suppress unrest caused by this rising. However, following the defeat of the Scottish army at Flodden in 1513, the islanders sought to capitalise on weakness at the centre and two rebellions occurred in quick succession, in 1513 and 1517. A period of relative stability lasted until 1529 when Alexander MacDonald of Dunivaig and the Glens rebelled, while Donald MacDonald Gorm of Sleat on Skye headed a rising in 1539. The last major outbreak of unrest came in 1545; this, despite its devastating potential, was largely ineffectual (see below). These risings have been perceived as attempts on the part of MacDonalds and other island clans to restore the lordship but many were actually the result of inter-clan feuding or personal ambition on the part of clan chiefs. Nonetheless, this level of disorder meant that the crown was forced to take steps to pacify the region; in doing so James IV and James V adopted broadly similar policies.

In order to 'daunt the isles' James IV embarked on a number of expeditions in which he extracted submissions from the main island chiefs and garrisoned various castles. Such expressions of royal authority may have worked in the short term but they failed to make any lasting impression: once the royal fleet had returned to Edinburgh, local issues would re-surface and at times this resulted in renewed outbreaks of unrest. Thus, promising obedience to the monarch in person was very much a pragmatic gesture, exemplified by John MacDonald of Dunivaig and the Glens in 1494. After submitting to James IV, MacDonald hanged the new constable of Dunaverty Castle from the castle wall in full view of the departing king. Despite these gestures of discontent, during the early years of James IV's reign when the king made regular visits to the West Highlands and Islands, there was relative stability. However, by the turn of the sixteenth century James's attention was focussed elsewhere and he began to rely heavily on regional magnates to enforce royal authority. The Campbell earls of Argyll and the Gordon earls of Huntly received successive commissions of lieutenancy to police the western *Gàidhealtachd* through-out the rest of James's reign.

Unlike the Gordons of Huntly, who tended to execute their commissions with force, the Campbells of Argyll had a more conciliatory approach. They were Gaels whose lands lay in the south-western Highlands and their leaders, although given a peerage in 1457, were still viewed as traditional Highland chiefs in their own territory. They had co-existed peacefully beside the MacDonalds for centuries and had links with island clans through marriage alliances. James IV exploited the connections of Archibald Campbell, second earl, in order to negotiate and work with some of the clan chiefs as a means of providing better law and order immediately after the forfeiture of the Lordship of the Isles. James rewarded those who cooperated with crown policy with additional grants of land, the main beneficiary in the west being the Mackenzies of Kintail, while clans like the Grants in the central Highlands were also used by the crown to help establish good rule in a region perceived as lacking in law and order.

This same policy of cooperation with clan society was adopted by James V. He continued to parcel out former lordship lands to law-abiding clans but also, initially, relied on the Campbells. In an attempt to pacify the region after the rebellion of Alexander MacDonald of Dunivaig and the Glens in 1529, he issued a commission to Colin, third earl of Argyll. But the earl's death and MacDonald's submission saw a shift in James's attitude. He deprived Archibald Campbell, fourth earl of Argyll, of the chamberlainship of Kintyre and gave it to MacDonald. This attempt to work more closely with the island chief produced some stability but, following Donald Gorm's rebellion in 1539, James embarked on his own effort to assert royal authority in the west with a naval expedition in the summer of 1540 and the circumnavigation of his realm. Until this time, most of the risings in the Highlands were minor and, in spite of the perception of the crown, not directed against royal authority. After the death of James V, however, plans were made for a rising that could have had disastrous implications for the Scottish crown.

During Henry VIII's 'rough wooing' of Scotland in the 1540s, whereby he sought to force the Scots into accepting dynastic union with England, negotiations began between Henry and the island clans, led by the recently released Donald Dubh, imprisoned in Edinburgh since 1506. Donald Dubh's promise to restore the Lordship of the Isles drew strong support. Even though such an outcome was unlikely, branches of the Clan Donald and other island clans sought to regain lands which had been lost following the forfeiture of 1493. Henry promised the return of traditional clan lands, now in Campbell hands, along with an attractive pension for Donald, an upfront payment of cash and the military assistance of some Irish kerne. In return, these clans agreed to harry the lands of the earls of Huntly and Argyll. The distraction of the forces of both earls from fighting the English would help Henry's campaign in the Lowlands while also offering the islesmen the opportunity to take revenge on Argyll, who had benefited from the forfeiture of the MacDonalds. The islesmen, however, were unable to maintain unity, apparently arguing amongst themselves over the distribution of Henry's money. The abortive rebellion brought an end to any lofty aims of reviving the Lordship of the Isles, although the various branches of the Clan Donald continued to quarrel over lands and seniority. The 1545 rebellion highlighted Clan Donald's continuing willingness to make pragmatic political alliances in order to achieve their ends.

CIVILISATION AND COLONISATION

During the 1550s and 1560s a three-kingdom agenda continued as Archibald Campbell, fifth earl of Argyll, sought to align wider Campbell policy with a 'British' policy: the earl arranged a number of politically significant marriages between Irish lords and Highland families (Dawson 2002). With a branch of the MacDonalds (the MacDonnells) now established in the north of Ireland, cooperation and movement between Ireland and Scotland continued. Meanwhile, the political unrest caused by the Marian civil wars and the factionalism of James VI's minority spilled over into the Highlands, intensifying clan feuding and ensuring that by the time James succeeded to the throne he was keen to establish royal authority, law and order throughout the region.

There is some debate regarding James's policy towards the Highlands and the extent to which he sought to implement a coherent programme for reform. Julian Goodare asserts that as early as 1581 it is possible to determine the emergence of a 'Highland policy' (Goodare 1999, 256), although the reigns of James IV and James V would suggest such a policy was already in existence. Legislation concerning the Highlands in the parliament of 1587 is certainly a clear indication of James's decision to deal firmly with his Gaelic subjects. An act was passed to reinforce what James IV had sought to do in making clan chiefs and landlords in the Gàidhealtachd accountable for the actions of their clansmen and their tenants, as well as any broken men inhabiting their lands. This delegation of responsibility to the chiefs themselves was reinforced by extracting surety and caution, a promise of good behaviour backed up by a monetary payment included in such a pledge. But although James expressed his concern regarding the continuing maintenance of caterans in the Highlands, these efforts to resolve the issue of lawlessness in the west by following, somewhat sporadically, the policies of his predecessors met with little success.

James's desire to bring order to the Highlands was also informed by the wider debate concerning 'uncivilised' peoples. He saw his own 'barbarous' subjects as a threat not only to civil society in Scotland but also to his vision of Great Britain (Williamson 1996). What emerged was a scheme to 'plant' Lowlanders in the region in the hope that their example would transform the Gaels into law-abiding subjects of the crown. James expressed this new policy in terms of rescuing his Highland subjects from poverty and from ignorance of God's word. Thus, sending God-fearing Lowlanders into the Western Isles would not only bring about civility but also raise the standard of living and spread religious education. But behind such lofty ideals lay an economic agenda. James believed that it was the poor education and moral weakness of the savage islanders that kept living standards so low in the west because, in his eyes, the area was rich and fertile. As the crown never received its full rental returns from the region, James's Highland policy sought to increase revenue through a programme of 'civilisation'. The groundwork was prepared through an act of parliament of 1597, which stated that any Highland chief unable to produce written title to the lands he held would be liable to forfeiture, with the lands passing back into crown hands. This was followed up with another act of the same year, which allowed for the creation of three burghs in the Highlands in an attempt to incorporate the region more fully into the Scottish polity, economically as well as politically.

Following implementation of the 1597 act, and due to internal clan troubles, in 1598 James forfeited the Macleods of Lewis and subsequently gave a commission to Ludovic, duke of Lennox, and the 'gentlemen adventurers of Fife' to begin the process of plantation on Lewis for an initial period of five years. The Macleods, unwilling to relinquish land they had occupied for centuries, caused havoc for the newcomers. While some were murdered, others beat a hasty retreat back to Fife. After three successive attempts the venture ended in complete failure, although this did not signal the end for James's plans. Further schemes for plantation in the Western Isles were considered until after 1610, although only in Ireland was the idea properly implemented. But the most successful part of James VI's Highland policy came after his succession to the English throne. In 1608, the year that the third and final attempt at the plantation of Lewis ended in disaster, the king shifted the emphasis of his Highland policy from coercion to conciliation.

James sent Andrew Knox, bishop of the Isles, to negotiate with the West Highland and Island chiefs in the hope of finding some common ground. This led to the implementation in the following year of what has become known as the Statutes of Iona, although historians still debate their actual significance. Allan Macinnes has argued that the Statutes were not a straightforward attack on Gaelic culture but were intended to increase the standard of living in the west. In an effort to reduce unrest, the carrying of arms was regulated and chiefs had to reduce the size of their households. Churches were to be repaired, inns built and the consumption of wine subjected to government control in an effort to improve communications and help the spread of religious knowledge. While there were measures clearly designed to improve Gaelic society – for example, parish schools were to be erected in the west – other clauses highlight James's attitude towards Highlanders and his efforts to stamp out 'incivility'. Despite the emphasis on schooling, all chiefs were required to send their heirs to be educated in the Lowlands, where they would learn the values of Lowland society and be educated in English – a deliberate effort to eradicate Gaelic language and custom, which were perceived as symptoms of the barbarism of Highland society.

The Statutes of Iona also began the process by which clan chiefs were assimilated into Lowland society. Their implementation led to the annual appearance of many chiefs before the privy council, indicating their acquiescence in the crown's intervention in the Highlands, and increasing their familiarity with the fashions and commercial culture of the south. Nonetheless, ongoing clan warfare meant that it was necessary for the regulations to be reinforced and extended in 1616–17, which suggests that the earlier statutes had failed to fulfil their purpose. Unrest in the region continued in spite of the crown's efforts, as the Campbells exploited weaknesses within the Clan Donald to extend their territory and influence. At the same time, however, this should not suggest that lawlessness was uniform across the region. A number of clan chiefs, such as the Campbells of Argyll, had cooperated with the crown throughout the sixteenth century and were reaping the fruits of such a policy, as is evidenced by the elevation of the chief the Mackenzies of Kintail to a peerage in 1613.

POLITICS AND RELIGION IN THE WEST HIGHLANDS AND ISLES

The Clan Donald and the Clan Campbell had, until the sixteenth century, co-existed peacefully and were connected by numerous marriage alliances. The Campbell chiefs, however, had adopted a policy of cooperation with and service to the crown and were successful at balancing their role as traditional Highland chiefs in Argyll with that of crown agents, with successive chiefs becoming prominent in national politics. Although their links with the crown were resented by some branches of the Clan Donald and West Highland and Island clans, others maintained their connections with the Campbells. For example, Archibald, fourth earl of Argyll, made a marriage alliance with the Macleans of Duart, while Archibald, fifth earl, fostered Lachlan, future chief of the Macleans. In 1554 James MacDonald of Dunivaig and the Glens married Lady Agnes Campbell, a daughter of the third earl of Argyll.

Unfortunately, marriage connections could not prevent the outbreak of, or contain, unrest. In 1542 the Macleans of Duart gained legal title to the Rhinns of Islay, land which the MacDonalds of Dunivaig and the Glens had previously held and still claimed as part of their clan estate. The resulting feud had serious consequences for the Clan Donald but, despite the unrest in the region, Archibald, fifth earl of Argyll, largely remained aloof. In 1578, however, the chief of the Macleans accused the sixth earl of Argyll of encouraging the MacDonalds to attack Maclean's lands and tenants. Although attempts were made to end the feud through further marriage alliances, the complex network of marriages, bonds and personal obligations meant it was difficult to contain disorder. The MacDonalds of Dunivaig (also known as Clan Donald South after the Irish branch, the MacDonnells of the Glens, broke away in 1589) were assisted by the MacDonalds of Sleat, the Macleods of Lewis, the MacIains of Ardnamurchan and Clan Ranald, amongst others. The Macleans were supported by the Macleods of Harris, the MacNeills of Barra and other former lordship clans such as the MacKinnons and the MacQuarries. In this way, a localised dispute between the Macleans of Duart and the MacDonalds of Dunivaig escalated and, by the 1590s, unrest was widespread.

At this time, the Campbell clan was facing its own crisis on account of political rivalry between its various branches during the minority of Archibald, seventh earl of Argyll. This resulted in the murder in 1592 of John Campbell of Cawdor at the hands of his own kinsman, an event which threatened to throw the Campbell clan into disarray similar to that which beset the MacDonalds. But the seventh earl of Argyll worked to restore the cohesion of the clan. In stark contrast, the MacDonald–

Maclean feud had brought to the fore internal disputes among the Clan Donald South. The Irish branch, the MacDonnells, retained a claim to lands on Islay, while the chief of the Scottish branch, Angus MacDonald, and his son, Sir James, disagreed over how best to respond to James VI, who was seeking to come to an agreement with MacDonald regarding the Rhinns of Islay. When the negotiations failed, the king looked to the Campbells for help; they responded by exploiting the weakness caused by Clan Donald feuding. Consequently, throughout the 1590s and early seventeenth century the Campbells gained tenurial rights to Kintyre, Islay, Jura, Colonsay, Ardnamurchan and Sunart, having effectively destroyed their traditional owners, the MacIains of Ardnamurchan and the Clan Donald South. The other branches of Clan Donald now feared that they would be next. It was the unrest caused by the dispossession of Clan Donald South that led to the extension of the Statutes of Iona in 1616–17, after which there was a noticeable decrease in unrest in the west. The West Highland and Island clans saw what had happened to those who defied the crown and were unwilling to commit themselves to a similar fate.

One of the main results of increased central intervention was a furthering widening of the breach between Gaelic society in Ireland and Scotland. Scottish Gaels developed a distinctive identity, expressed through artistic, literary and linguistic means, and also through political and religious differences, which came to the fore in the seventeenth century (Dawson 1998, 265–6; McLeod 2004, 194–219). Although often regarded as negligible, the impact of the Reformed church in the Highlands in the decade after 1560 was significant, considering the size of Highland parishes (Kirk 1989, 305–33). One of the earliest and most active converts to Protestantism was Archibald Campbell, fifth earl of Argyll, and the Campbells exploited every opportunity to spread the new religion. Other clans, such as the Macleans of Duart, converted early, while the Macleods of Harris and the MacDonalds of Sleat adopted Protestantism as a result of the Statutes of Iona when new chiefs, educated in the Protestant Lowlands, returned to their estates. In contrast, other branches of the Clan Donald, such as Clanranald and the MacDonalds of Keppoch, continued to adhere to the Catholic church (McLeod 2004, 197).

The introduction of Protestantism was gradual in the century after the Reformation but, as learned Gaels were recruited to the ministry, the view that Protestantism was an alien religion imposed on Gaelic society by the Lowlands began to diminish. Counter-reformation initiatives were staged by the Jesuits in the 1610s and more consistently by the Franciscans from 1619 to 1646; this resulted in many conversions to Catholicism. But the situation remained in flux, as evidenced when Archibald, seventh earl of Argyll, converted to Catholicism, made his way to the Low Countries and joined with other exiled Catholics, before ending up in the service of the king of Spain. However, while confessionalism remained a major issue throughout Scotland, within Scottish Gaeldom religion was no indicator of political allegiance. In Ireland, Catholicism became associated with opposition to the Protestant, English colonisers, whereas in Scotland, Catholic and Protestant clans would join together on a number of occasions during the seventeenth century with shared political aims (McLeod 2004, 194–212; Dawson 1998, 265–7).

THE HIGHLAND DIMENSION OF THE CIVIL WARS, INTERREGNUM AND RESTORATION

Following the loss of their lands, the Clan Donald South relinquished all claim to their ancestral lands on Islay, whereas the MacDonnells continued to pursue their rights. The chief of the MacDonnells, Sir Randal MacDonnell, first earl of Antrim, had failed to retrieve these lands through peaceful means. On his death in 1636, his son, the second earl, also called Randal, continued his father's quest but sought to advance it by capitalising on the national situation and the weakness of the king, Charles I. Following his succession to the thrones of Scotland, England and Ireland in 1625, Charles alienated many of his Scottish subjects and by 1638 both the Scots and the king were making preparations for war. The wider discontent Charles faced throughout his three kingdoms left him in desperate need for allies and he found unexpected support within the Highlands. His former attitude towards his Gaelic subjects had been nothing short of contemptuous but political isolation drove him to listen to a proposition put forward by Antrim, who was both liked and trusted by the king, to seek assistance from an army of Irish and Scottish Gaels. In his endeavour to gain Charles's approval for the scheme, Antrim claimed that none of the Clan Donald had signed the National Covenant. Antrim's real plan, however, was to bring an army of MacDonnells to Scotland, to join with the Clan Donald, and to make war on the Campbells, thus recovering Islay and other ancestral lands.

Various reasons have been put forward to explain Highland support for Charles I. The notion that he was pursing a return to Catholicism, which the Highlanders supported, should be treated with caution. Support for the king had more to do with opposition to the Covenanting movement and to Campbell dominance than any particular affection for Charles. Although Archibald, seventh earl of Argyll, had converted to Catholicism and by the reign of Charles was living in London, his son, Archibald, Lord Lorne (later eighth earl), had gained possession of some Campbell lands in 1636 and by 1639 was one of the most powerful figures in Scotland. In contrast to his father, his sympathies lay with the Covenanters who, in preparation for war, were making military demands on clan society. As David Stevenson has argued, for the Gaels, Charles was the lesser of two evils and the army that mustered behind him was something of a mixed bag (Stevenson 2002, 64, 121–3).

Under the leadership of Alasdair MacColla of the Clan Donald South, this group of Highlanders and Irish would prove to be of fundamental significance for the royalist campaign in Scotland between 1644 and 1647. His army consisted of Catholic and episcopalian Highland clans who opposed the Covenanters and the Campbells; Catholic and episcopalian Lowlanders under George Gordon, second marquis of Huntly; Catholic Irish who fought for Clan Donald in an attempt to regain land from the Campbells; Catholic Irish who fought for religion; and others who actually fought for the king. Although MacColla commanded the Irish and Scottish Gaels, the whole army was led by a committed Protestant, James Graham, fifth earl of Montrose (created first marquis in 1644). Having signed the National Covenant in 1638, Montrose had become uneasy about the increasingly anti-royalist sentiments of the Covenanter regime. Gaining support for the royalist cause was not easy but it increased with every victory. Between August 1644 and September 1645, Montrose and MacColla fought together but went their separate ways when a conflict of interest emerged. Montrose had wanted to take the royalist cause into England, but this would have done little to further the Gaels' aim of regaining their ancestral lands. At the same time, committing to a campaign in England would have left their estates open to attack from clans who either remained neutral or supported the Covenant and the Campbells: only twenty-one out of a total of forty-seven main clans had come out in support of the king. MacColla and his army returned to the west, while Montrose struggled on, only to suffer declining fortunes and ultimate defeat.

The Highlands suffered greatly from the effects of the civil wars. Conflict depleted economic resources, while the resurgence of petty clan warfare allowed for an easy conquest by the English after the defeat of the Covenanters in 1651. The conquest was brutal and was followed by a heavy military presence. Many chiefs found this oppressive and it was in the Highlands that the only significant opposition to the Cromwellian interregnum arose, in the Glencairn rising of 1653. At the same time, however, some chiefs benefited from cooperation with the regime: after Sir Ewen Cameron of Locheil submitted to the English he had his debts cancelled and disputes over land were settled in his favour. In general terms there was a return to relative stability during the 1650s, but the Restoration in 1660 was widely welcomed. Indeed, the high degree of intervention in Gaeldom during the interregnum ensured that the return of Charles II had practically unanimous support. Clan society, displaying its conservative nature, sought a return to earlier times and the removal of a strong, centralised and interventionist government.

CLAN SUPPORT FOR THE HOUSE OF STEWART

In spite of the strength of royalist support from the *Gàidhealtachd* during the civil wars and interregnum, the reign of Charles II saw further alienation of clan chiefs and their *fine* (the clan gentry). The Restoration regime regarded the Highlands as an area of 'endemic lawlessness', while chiefs were keen to disassociate themselves from the unruly behaviour of caterans (Macinnes 1996, 126). The requirement for chiefs to appear annually before the privy council to give surety and caution for their kin, tenants and dependants resulted in a growing attraction to the commercial society of the Lowlands. Prolonged visits to Edinburgh, or even to court in London, saw chiefs spending lavishly on luxury goods and fashions, leading to mounting debts. This compounded the already dire financial state of some chiefs following periods of absence from their estates during the civil wars. The result was mortgaging of lands, even traditional clan lands, to alleviate indebtedness. The efforts of chiefs to assure government of their good behaviour bore little fruit: the Restoration regime continued to use the threat of forfeiture and eviction, as well as using Highland lawlessness as an excuse for military intervention – itself a cover for the extraction of taxation by force.

The Restoration regime was more concerned with the suppression of religious dissent. The growth of militant conventicles in the Lowlands saw government in Scotland turn to the Gaels for military assistance in bringing an end to this revived Covenanting (see chapter 4). This was counter-productive, in that it provoked the conventiclers into open rebellion and it was harder to curtail unrest amongst the now re-armed Highlanders. This reinforced the Lowland perception of Highland lawlessness, but disorder in the Highlands was also the result of the actions of Archibald, ninth earl of Argyll. The eighth earl and first marquis of Argyll was executed in 1661 and all his lands and offices forfeited for his part in the civil wars; but in 1663 his son was created ninth earl (although not marquis) of Argyll and restored to his father's estates. Heavily burdened with debts, Argyll protected himself by exploiting his position as hereditary justiciar of Argyll and the Western Isles, while fiercely pursing repayment of his loans. In doing so he expropriated the chief and *fine* of the Macleans of Duart, gaining superiority over new territories and provoking an increase in clan warfare. In 1679, James, duke of York and duke of Albany, brother of Charles II, was sent north as king's commissioner to the Scottish parliament. By the time of his arrival, the privy council admitted that it had lost control and that reliance on Argyll had undermined Highland stability.

James's two sojourns in Scotland between 1679 and 1682 saw the only period of conciliation in crown–clan relations during the Restoration era. He established the Commission for Securing the Peace of the Highlands, which made a determined effort to work with clans and chiefs alike between 1682 and 1684. Despite its brief success, its work came to an abrupt end in 1685. The duke of Monmouth, illegitimate son of Charles II, supported by the earl of Argyll, rose in arms to oppose the succession of the Catholic James as king. Large numbers of clansmen who had been victims of Argyll's repressive and acquisitive measures took the opportunity to ravage the earl's lands (during the 'Atholl Raid'), as well as the lands of Lowland Covenanters associated with the earl. The unrest was another indication of the lack of government control in the region and was used to justify further repressive measures. Argyll was captured and executed and orders were given for the execution of all those who had assisted him.

Despite oscillation between repression and conciliation, James VII and II remained popular in the Highlands. His policies of religious toleration and arbitrary rule did, however, arouse immense discontent throughout the three kingdoms. His reign came to an abrupt end in 1688–9 when William of Orange and his wife Mary were accepted as monarchs after James's flight into exile. The removal of James as king did not sit easily with many, but few came out in open rebellion. He had used the royal prerogative to bypass parliament in granting toleration to Catholics but the bulk of his support came from episcopalians. In Scotland the episcopalians were natural allies of the monarchy, which had sought to control the church through bishops. For them the Restoration signalled a return of the natural hierarchy; the traditional alliance between crown and nobility mirrored the ecclesiastical hierarchy of archbishops and bishops. Although episcopalians had become increasingly disillusioned under James and agreed that his actions had to be curtailed, this was a far cry from removing a legitimate king and replacing him with another, an act they regarded as treason and heresy. Episcopalian opposition to the Williamite regime increased after the Revolution settlement of 1690–2, which saw presbyterianism established by parliament and hundreds of episcopalian ministers forcibly removed from their parishes. While most of this opposition was vocal rather than militant, there was a small element within Scotland that sought to take a stand in support of the Stewart monarchy.

In 1689, shortly after the convention of estates deposed James VII, rebellion was raised in support of the Stewart cause by James Graham of Claverhouse, Viscount Dundee. His call to arms met with little support and, in order to increase his army, he looked towards the *Gàidhealtachd*. Debate continues over why Highland chiefs supported the first Jacobite rising. Certainly Dundee would have emphasised the opportunities for plunder that the Highlanders could exploit on such a military campaign and there is no doubt that some chiefs, like Coll MacDonald of Keppoch, participated for their own ends. Another factor was the re-emergence of anti-Campbell sentiment. The ninth earl of Argyll had been a strong supporter of William of Orange and the restoration of his son, later tenth earl, was a part of the Revolution settlement. As had been the case during the civil wars, a pro-Stewart cause was equated with an anti-Campbell one. The actions of the ninth earl of Argyll in the Highlands between 1663 and 1685 had pushed many clans towards support for James. Bruce Lenman, however, argues that the anti-Campbell stance was not the decisive factor, and points to the number of clans that had close connections to the Campbells but who sided with James. And while David Stevenson emphasises the anti-Campbell stance throughout the seventeenth century, he also acknowledges that there were other contributory factors (Lenman 1980, 44–9; Stevenson 2003, 296).

Allan Macinnes has argued that religion was a major determinant in clans' support of the first Jacobite rising, although it does not necessarily explain long-term commitment to the cause (Macinnes 1996, 180–1). The traditional view is that Jacobite support was essentially Catholic, but throughout the *Gàidhealtachd* Catholicism was very much a minority religion, with only six major clans predominantly Catholic (Macinnes 1996, 173–4). The majority of Highland clans were episcopalian and believed strongly in the divine right of kings, a hierarchical concept of social order which goes some way to explaining the strength of Highland support. The view of the king as absolute but also as a father figure is said to have resonated with, and complemented, clan society and analogies have been drawn between clanship and kingship. Just as a chief was regarded as protector and defender of his clansmen, holding land in trusteeship for his clan, the king was regarded as the protector of his people, holding Scotland in trusteeship. There was also a strong emphasis on hereditary right: the throne, like the chiefship of a clan, came through lineal descent, which underpinned justice and government. Although somewhat idealised, such sentiments were prominent in Gaelic poetry and, after 1689, support for James VII was regarded as the antidote to all the evils that had befallen Scotland (Macinnes 1996, 188; MacInnes 1971–2; ni Suaird 1999).

Highland support was vital for Viscount Dundee but, despite initial success at Killiecrankie, defeat at Dunkeld in 1689 and the containment of the rebellion in the Highlands resulted in its degeneration into local skirmishes before final defeat at Cromdale in 1690. This could have signalled the end of the Jacobite cause – certainly the fluctuating support of clan society combined with localised clan rivalry did not help matters. Just as in the civil wars of the mid-century, Highland society did not act in concert. In the civil wars, enemies of the Campbells would oppose the Covenanters, while others happily switched sides depending on royalist or Covenanter success. In the 1690s, there was significant support for James in the Highlands but some clans remained neutral and others accepted the Williamite regime.

Through his own policies, however, William ensured that support for the exiled Stewarts would remain strong in the region. He demanded that all chiefs sign an oath acknowledging him as king, although they were allowed the opportunity of explaining their position to the exiled James before officially taking the oath. The deadline was 1 January 1692. Within the administration in Edinburgh there were those, notably John Dalrymple, master of Stair, who were adamant that any clan which did not comply would be dealt with severely (Ferguson 1965, 19–26) This was the fate of the MacDonalds of Glencoe, whose chief, Alexander MacIain, through a disastrous combination of events, was unable to register his oath until 6 January. By that time the decision had been taken to make an example of this small clan, widely regarded as Catholic although actually episcopalian. Troops were sent north to extirpate the Glencoe MacDonalds: many of those who survived the massacre before dawn on 13 February later perished in the snow-covered mountains while attempting to escape. This action met with widespread condemnation throughout Scotland and England. Not only did it go against perceived notions of military honour, it also violated Highland codes of hospitality and caused outrage within Gaeldom. This resulted in increased opposition to King William, and pushed a number of neutral clans firmly into the Jacobite camp. William provided the grounds on which his Highland subjects would now consistently oppose him until his death in 1702.

CONCLUSION

The sixteenth and seventeenth centuries were a period of significant change within Scottish Gaeldom. A Scottish Gaelic identity was evident, emphasising its difference from Gaelic society in Ireland and from Lowland Scotland. Increased intervention in Highland affairs during the early sixteenth century aimed to extend royal authority in the wake of the forfeiture of the Lordship of the Isles and saw increased cooperation between some Highland clans and the crown. However, reliance on the Campbell earls of Argyll for policing and enforcing law and order in the west ensured their increasing political and territorial dominance. The acquisitiveness of the Campbells and the repressive measures adopted by various earls of Argyll perpetuated unrest in the west and contributed significantly to reinforcing Lowland prejudices regarding Highland lawlessness.

The alliance between parts of Gaeldom and the Stewart dynasty is said to have been forged during the civil wars, a result in many cases of political pragmatism rather than ideological commitment. In some cases, however, this alliance was the product of political cooperation during the sixteenth century. Confessional issues also were prominent in the Highlands after the Reformation. However, while religion played an important part in securing clan support for the exiled Stewarts after 1688–9, it was not a reliable indicator of political allegiance throughout this period. It has been argued that the civil war era saw the Highlanders thrust into the arena of national politics, but to a large extent their primary concerns were local, personal and territorial. In the last decade of the seventeenth century, the Highlands provided the bedrock of Jacobite support and it was this that brought upon the Highlands the full force of government intervention.

The requirement to appear annually before the privy council to make promises of good behaviour, initiated through the Statutes of Iona, was arguably more productive than other methods which aimed to integrate Gaelic chiefs into Lowland society. Annual sojourns in Edinburgh and at court encouraged chiefs to adopt the fashions of their Lowland counterparts, although the resulting indebtedness was exploited by the ninth earl of Argyll for his own ends, intensifying unrest in the region. Along with the financial implications of this level of debt, the re-orientation of clan chiefs and *fine* towards market opportunities created tensions within clan society as chiefs became less concerned with custom and more with commerce, even to the extent that they saw the economic potential of their traditional clan estate. The Campbells were to the fore in taking advantage of commercial opportunities, but many other chiefs began to direct their estates towards the market, through re-structuring the system of landholding, increased agricultural production or investment in industries such as coal, salt, lime or fish (Macinnes 1996, 142–8). Nonetheless, it was not until the eighteenth century that Highland estates were fully geared towards commercialism. Until then and until the defeat of Jacobitism, the Highlands were regarded as a region of political and military instability: the threat from Jacobitism was real, not least because of the international support it could attract. By the end of the seventeenth century, the Highlands featured significantly in national affairs, although, in comparison to the early sixteenth century, it was not instability in Gaeldom itself that was the issue. Rather it was the threat that the Highlands posed to British stability that was of utmost concern.

REFERENCES

Dawson, J. 1998 'The *Gàidhealtachd* and the emergence of the Scottish Highlands', in B. Bradshaw (ed), *British Consciousness and Identity: The Making of Britain, 1533–1707*, Cambridge, 259–300.
Ferguson, W. 1968 *Scotland, 1689 to the present*. Edinburgh.
Goodare, J. 1999 *State and Society in Early Modern Scotland*. Oxford.
Kirk, J. 1989 *Patterns of Reform. Continuity and Change in the Reformation Kirk*. Edinburgh.
Macdougall, N.A.T. 1989 *James IV*. Edinburgh.

Macinnes, A.I. 1996 *Clanship, Commerce and the House of Stuart, 1603–1788*. East Linton.

MacInnes, J. 1971–2 'Clan Unity and Individual Freedom', *Transactions of the Gaelic Society of Inverness*, 47, 339–73.

McLeod, W. 2004 *Divided Gaels: Gaelic Cultural Identities in Scotland and Ireland c.1200–c.1650*. Oxford.

Nicholson, R. 1974 *Scotland: the Later Middle Ages*. Edinburgh.

Stevenson, D. 2003 *Highland Warrior: Alasdair MacColla and the Civil Wars*. Edinburgh.

ni Suaird, D. 1999 'Jacobite Rhetoric and Terminology in the Political Poems of the Fernaig M.S. (1688–1693)', *Scottish Gaelic Studies*, 19, 93–140.

Williamson, A.H. 1996 'Scots, Indians and Empire: the Scottish politics of civilisation 1519–1609', *Past and Present*, 150, 46–83.

FURTHER READING

Bannerman, J.W.M. 1997 'The Lordship of the Isles: historical background', in Steer K.A. & J.W.M. Bannerman, *Late Medieval Monumental Sculpture in the West Highlands*, Edinburgh, 201–13.

Bannerman, J.W.M. 1977 'The Lordship of the Isles', in Brown, J.M. (ed), *Scottish Society in the Fifteenth Century*, London, 209–40.

Cameron, J. 1998 *James V*. East Linton.

Cathcart, A. 2006 *Kinship and Clientage: Highland Clanship 1451–1609*. Leiden.

Cathcart, A. (forthcoming) 'Symbolic figurehead or political opportunist: the rebellions of Donald Dubh', in Oram, R.D. (ed), *The Lordship of the Isles*.

Cowan, E.J. 1979 'Clanship, kinship and the Campbell acquisition of Islay', *Scottish Historical Review*, 58, 132–57.

Dawson, J. 1988 'The Fifth Earl of Argyll, Gaelic Lordship and Political Power in Sixteenth Century Scotland', *Scottish Historical Review*, 67, 1–27

Dodgshon, R.A. 1989 ' "Pretense of Blude" and "Place of Thair Duelling": the nature of Scottish Clans, 1500–1745', in Houston, R.A. & Whyte, I.D. (eds), *Scottish Society, 1500–1800*, Cambridge, 169–98.

Dodgshon, R.A. 1988 'West Highland Chiefdoms: A Study of Redistributive Exchange', in Mitchison, R. & Roebuck, P. (eds), *Economy and Society of Scotland and Ireland 1500–1939*, Edinburgh, 27–37.

Donaldson, G. 1965 *Scotland, James V–James VII*. Edinburgh.

Goodare, J. 2000 'Scottish politics in the reign of James VI', in Goodare, J. & Lynch, M. (eds), *The Reign of James VI*, East Linton, 32–54.

Goodare, J. & Lynch, M. 2000 'James VI: universal king?', in Goodare & Lynch (eds), *The Reign of James VI*, East Linton, 1–31.

Goodare, J. 1998 'The Statutes of Iona in Context', *Scottish Historical Review*, 77, 31–57.

Grant, A. 1988 'Scotland's "Celtic Fringe" in the late Middle Ages: The MacDonald Lords of the Isles and the Kingdom of Scotland', in Davies, R.R. (ed), *The British Isles, 1100–1500: Comparisons, Contrasts and Connections*, Edinburgh, 24–41.

Gregory, D. 1836, *The History of the Western Highlands and Isles of Scotland from A.D. 1493 to A.D. 1625*. Edinburgh

Hill, G. 1873 *An Historical Account of the MacDonnells of Antrim*. Belfast.

Hill, J.M. 1993 *Fire and Sword: Sorley Boy MacDonnell and the Rise of Clan Ian Mor 1538–90*. London.

Kirk, J. 1986–89 'The Kirk and the Highlands at the Reformation', *Northern Scotland*, 7, 1–22.

Lee, M. 1990 *Great Britain's Solomon: King James VI and I in his Three Kingdoms*. Urbana.

Lee, M. 1976 'James VI's government of Scotland after 1603', *Scottish Historical Review*, 55, 41–53.

Lenman, B. 1980 *The Jacobite Risings in Britain, 1689–1746*. Aberdeen.

Lenman, B. 1982 'The Scottish Episcopal Clergy and the Ideology of Jacobitism', in Cruickshanks, E. (ed), *Ideology and Conspiracy: Aspects of Jacobitism, 1689–1759*, Edinburgh, 36–48.

Lynch, M. 1991 *Scotland: a New History*. London.

Lynch, M. 2000 'James VI and the "Highland Problem"', in Goodare & Lynch (eds), *The Reign of James VI*, East Linton, 208–27.

MacCoinnich, A. 2002 ' "His spirit was given only to warre": conflict and identity in the Scottish *Gàidhealtachd* c.1580–c.1630', in Murdoch, S. & Mackillop, A. (eds), *Fighting for Identity: Scottish Military Experience c.1550–1900*, Leiden, 133–62.

Macdougall, N.A.T. 2000 'Achilles' Heel? The Earldom of Ross, the Lordship of the Isles, and the Stewart Kings, 1449–1507', in Cowan, E.J. & McDonald, R.A. (eds), *Alba: Celtic Scotland in the Medieval Era*, East Linton, 248–75.

Macinnes, A.I. 1982 'Repression and Conciliation: the Highland Dimension, 1660–1688', *Scottish Historical Review*, 55, 362–77.

Macinnes, A.I. 1991 *Charles I and the Making of the Covenanting Movement, 1625–41*. Edinburgh.

Macinnes, A.I. 1993 'Crown, clans and *fine*: the "civilizing" of Scottish Gaeldom, 1587–1603', *Northern Scotland*, 13, 31–55.

Macinnes, A.I. 1999 'Scottish Jacobitism: in search of a movement', in Devine, T.M. & Young, J.R. (eds.), *Eighteenth century Scotland: new perspectives*, East Linton, 70–89.

Macinnes, A.I. 2005 *The British Revolution, 1629–1660*. Basingstoke.

Munro, J. 1981 'The Lordship of the Isles', in Maclean, J. (ed), *The Making of the Middle Ages in the Highlands*, Inverness, 23–37.

Munro, J. & Munro, R.W. (eds.) 1986 *Acts of the Lords of the Isles*. Edinburgh.

Munro, R.W. 1981 'The Clan System – Fact or Fiction?', in Maclean, J. (ed), *The Making of the Middle Ages in the Highlands*, Inverness, 117–29.

Pittock, M. 1995 *The Myth of the Jacobite Clans*. Edinburgh.

Thomson, T. & Innes, C. (eds) 1814–1875 *Acts of the Parliaments of Scotland*, 12 vols. Edinburgh.

MacPhail, J.R.N. (ed) 1914 'History of the MacDonalds', *Highland Papers*, vol. 1. Edinburgh.

CHAPTER SEVEN

The Church and Religion
Margo Todd

During the sixteenth century, the religion of Scotland underwent a profound transformation from the Catholicism that had bound together Western Christendom for
centuries to the most radical form of Calvinist Protestantism. The religious change in
turn restructured how people lived their lives – how they celebrated seasons, regulated
their family life, settled their quarrels, and understood themselves and their relationships with rulers as well as with God. As much a political as a religious movement,
Protestantism would create deep rifts between church and king, culminating in violent
civil war between 1638 and 1651. And when political order was finally re-established
in 1660, the church would remain rent by schism between rival visions of a truly
purified church and society. This chapter will examine the interaction of politics and
religion in this period of change, with its implications for religious experience in the
parishes, in four sections: before the Reformation; the Reformation movement, its
ideas and politics; Protestant belief and practice; and seventeenth-century conflict. By
the end of the narrative, you should be able to draw some conclusions about how the
very distinctive religious culture of early modern Scotland developed, and how it
emerged not quite unscathed from a century of internecine conflict, invasion and
occupation, shifting monarchies, and finally union with England.

BEFORE THE REFORMATION

The religion of the Scottish people on the eve of the Reformation was an intensely
sensual experience that, in its many forms, encompassed nearly every aspect of their
lives. The sacraments defined life stages: from birth and puberty, with baptism and
confirmation; to marriage or ordination, with their rites of adulthood; to death, with
final anointing at the hands of the priest. The sacrament of penance antecedent to
communion served, at least in theory, as a sacrament of reconciliation within the
community as well as between individual and creator. Communion, on those rare
occasions when the laity received it (generally at Easter), was an incorporative ritual.
The sacraments as celebrated by the Roman church appealed to all the senses – taste in
communion, touch in the water and anointing of baptism, hearing in the liturgical
words and the music that often accompanied them, sight in the highly decorated
surroundings in which they occurred, replete with images in stone and wood, brightly
painted and illuminated with light from candles or filtered through coloured glass. For
the highest holidays, incense covered the odours of everyday life, transporting the
believer for a time to the realm of the holy (McKay 1962; Howard 1995, 168–74).

Formal worship was only part of it. Festivities and drama associated with the liturgical year and with the veneration of saints punctuated the agricultural calendar and offered respite from the drudgery of daily labour in fields and workshops. If the attendant activities and entertainments – the dancing, piping, singing, and sports – were not particularly religious, they served nonetheless to connect religion with pleasure. Prayers for the saints to intercede for petitioners, particularly during times of trouble, joined the mundane to the celestial and generated some hope in the midst of what was for most people a precarious existence. St Margaret watched over women in childbirth, St Peter over fishermen in tempestuous seas, and local saints such as Thenew of Lothian, Triduana of Restalrig, and Mungo in Glasgow offered healing. Every urban guild had its patron saint, its dedicated altar in the burgh church, a chaplain of its own appointment, and its annual procession and play on the saint's day to cement the guildsmen's relationships to each other and corporately to the larger community, as well as to God. For those anxious about the pains of the next world, collegiate churches offered prayers for the souls of the departed, on a sort of sliding scale: the wealthy endowed the buildings and stipends for their priests, but the prayers of the poor there brought spiritual value not only to the rich men for whose souls they prayed, but also to the devout poor themselves, who were often rewarded as well with food and drink for their petitionary services (Sanderson 1997, 11–22; Cowan 1982, 1–22, 60–71).

Lay patronage ensured that running of the church was not an entirely clerical affair. At least at the highest social levels, and in towns, laymen had a voice in appointing clergy to their benefices. And the lowest level of those clerics, both secular and regular, often hailed from the communities they served. Rural curates farmed their glebes just as their neighbours did, and friars not only preached in the towns, but also offered a range of practical services, from joinery to metalsmithing to notarial skills (Foggie 2003). Numerous and substantial bequests for chantries, images and altars abounded well into the sixteenth century, and roads were crowded with pilgrims venturing to holy sites, seeking the aid of the saints honoured there (Yeoman 1999). Scotland's three universities, all founded in the fifteenth century, likewise point to substantial support for the Catholic establishment; all were intellectually lively and expanding institutions at the turn of the sixteenth century, centres of humanist learning as well as theological teaching (Durkan 1962).

This is not to say, however, that all was well with the church at the beginning of the sixteenth century. Although historians of an earlier generation, often themselves Protestant partisans, have generally put far too much faith in complaint literature, its virulence cannot be entirely written off as polemical hyperbole. When in the 1530s Sir David Lindsay bemoaned the fact 'that ignorant warldly creaturis/Suld in the kirk haif ony curis', he knew what he was saying (Lindsay 1871, vol. 1, 70). Scotland's thousand parishes and roughly 800,000 people were served by about 3,000 clerics; however, these were concentrated not in parish churches, but in collegiate churches, the universities, and the cathedrals of the two archbishops and eleven bishops (Kirk 1989, vii). The teinds (tithes) that were to support priests had, in 90% of parishes, been appropriated by lay or monastic 'commendators', who spent as little as possible of their ecclesiastical revenues to hire ignorant, incompetent and often non-celibate men to provide cure of souls (McKay 1962, 86). The fifteenth-century feuing of church property – selling of hereditary leaseholds for ready cash, largely to meet the demands of increasing royal taxation – further impoverished the institution by reducing its real rental income as the result of inflation. Inadequate clerical stipends (10 merks, or just under £7 Scots, being the standard until the 1540s, at a time when other professionals made £80 Scots annually) naturally led priests to accumulate multiple benefices; pluralism in turn entailed non-residency (Donaldson 1973, 42). Rural and Highland parishes were especially under-served, so that portions of that population lacked even the sacraments. Appropriation of parochial revenues by laymen or by universities and chapels also reduced funds for building maintenance: for all the remarkable beauty and elaborate decoration of collegiate churches and cathedrals, parish churches were often reported as being in serious disrepair. Episcopal visitation of Berwickshire in the 1550s found many churches without windows, and with walls and roofs collapsed; the priest at Ayton had to suspend a canopy over the high altar during mass to keep the rain off the elements (Donaldson 1972, 45). The highest ranks of secular clergy were a venal crew, with lucrative cathedral prebends often inherited by clerical offspring. And for all their vows of poverty, the friars were a litigious lot when it came to collecting rents in arrears on their extensive properties. Clearly their rapacity generated ill will in the towns where they were resident (Foggie 2003).

Given the poor survival rate of pre-Reformation ecclesiastical documents, the full extent of the problem is impossible to gauge. What we do know is that, despite problems and complaints, the church continued to recruit clergy with no difficulty, and fervent lay piety funded frenzies of chapel-building and fuelled an extraordinary devotion to Mary, the saints and the particularly sixteenth-century cult of Corpus Christi. New shrines to the Virgin were erected at Musselburgh as late as 1534, and Corpus Christi processions persisted in the burghs long after they were made illegal by the Reformers. St John's church in Perth boasted seventy side altars, forty founded in the fifteenth and early sixteenth centuries. Of the twenty-four collegiate churches founded in Scotland after 1450, thirteen came into being between 1500 and the Reformation. The earl of Huntly was planning another in the 1550s (Cowan 1982, 8, 60; Todd 2002, 2). All of this activity – all the panoply of late medieval building, drama, art and festival – suggests popular acceptance of the constructs of purgatory and intercessory sainthood upon which they were built. However corrupt the church, then, Catholicism itself was by no means moribund on the eve of the Reformation. It was the religion of the people. To understand its demise, we must turn to two sixteenth-century developments: an alternative system of belief in Protestant teaching, and a changing political scene.

THE REFORMATION MOVEMENT: IDEAS AND POLITICS

Early Protestantism: Lutheran and Reformed

Martin Luther's notions of salvation by faith alone and the pre-eminent authority of the Scriptures had made their appearance in Scotland by at least 1525, when parliament was sufficiently unnerved to address the issue with a heresy act. The earliest Protestant inroads were in coastal towns, where continental trade introduced new ideas as well as goods, and in the universities. The Aberdeen council was typical in its worry in the 1520s that 'syndry strangearis and otheris . . . has bukis of that heretik Luthyr, and favoris his arrorys and fals opinionys' (*Aberdeen* 1844, vol. 1, 107–8). Scotland's first Protestant martyr, Patrick Hamilton, was roasted slowly in St Andrews in 1528 as a Lutheran, and a dozen more were burned by 1542 – including three friar-converts in 1539. There would never be very many religious martyrs in Scotland's Reformation – only twenty Protestants and a couple of Catholics, compared to England's 500 or more (nearly 300 Protestants) over the course of the sixteenth century. This striking contrast probably owes more to the comparative weakness of Scotland's central government – the force behind the English persecutions – than to the relative unpopularity of Protestantism or Scottish clerical tolerance. But in any case there is no evidence that at this stage Protestants were more than a tiny minority, concentrated in a few towns, notably St Andrews and Dundee, and in Ayrshire (Sanderson 1997, 48–55, 61–8; Cowan 1982, 89–97).

By the 1540s, Scots Protestants who had ventured to the Swiss Reformed cities were returning with a revised version of the Protestant message. The Reformed tradition of Zurich and Geneva added to Luther's theology an adamant condemnation of all images, ceremony, clerical vestments and religious festivity as dregs of 'popery' and superstition. In addition, Reformed theology – generally labelled 'Calvinism' – elaborated Luther's conclusion from Paul's Epistle to the Romans that God had predestined some for salvation, and (logically) others for damnation. This emphasis on divine election with no role for human will or works had disappeared from second-generation Lutheranism, but would be a hallmark of Reformed theology.

Reformed ideas were spread in the 1540s and 1550s not only by prohibited books, but also by itinerant clerics like George Wishart (martyred in 1546) and John Knox, both charismatic and fiery preachers shaped by experience in Swiss Reformed towns. The new theology was particularly warmly received in some Lowland towns, where it helped to inspire iconoclastic riots to destroy the 'monuments of idolatry' in mendicant houses, collegiate churches and, occasionally, parish churches. This early iconoclasm, however, cannot be attributed solely to the preachers' theological ideas. It was clearly fed also by resentment at clerical wealth and greed. Thus in the Perth riot of 1543 the mob, having sacked the Dominican house, then paraded through the town with the Blackfriars' stew pot – a monument to gluttony and wealth more than to popery and superstition. The precise extent to which their motivation was Protestantism, as opposed to economic grievance, is unclear at best (Cowan 1982, 100). The Protestant convictions of individuals in university towns are more certain, with St Leonard's College, St Andrews, proving a particular hotbed of new ideas in the 1540s.

By the 1550s, the growth of heresy was sufficiently worrisome to the authorities that they finally took steps to address their own clear need for reform. Archbishop John Hamilton held reforming councils in 1549, 1552 and 1559 in an effort to impose better discipline and higher educational standards on clergy. The 1552 council adopted a new catechism remarkable for its compromises with Lutheran ideas (omitting the term 'mass', for instance), and the 1559 council called for every bishop to preach in his diocese at least four times a year. And Hamilton doubled the standard for a parish priest's annual income to 20 merks – still paltry, though an improvement. But these efforts proved too little, too late. Evangelical preaching and the products of English and continental Protestant printing presses had by the 1550s won enough converts in the Lowlands – Ayrshire, Lothian, Fife, Angus and the Mearns – to establish numerous small 'privat conventiouns' meeting secretly 'in the feilds in sommer, in houses in winter', as Knox tells us, under the protection of converted lairds, lords and burgesses. These 'privy kirks' offered the two sacraments accepted by Protestants (baptism and communion) as well as vernacular Scripture reading, worship according to the English Book of Common Prayer, and sermons by the likes of Knox, John Willock, and Paul Methven (Kirk 1989). Still, their adherents were few, and their underground existence made proselytising difficult. It was only as political circumstance conspired with heretical ideas that the Reformers would triumph.

Politics, Foreign Policy and Reformation

The politics of the Scottish Reformation were rooted in a diplomatic revolution that shifted Scotland's traditional 'Auld Alliance' with France to a new friendship with England. It came about because of problems associated with the regency of Mary of Guise, widow of James V and mother of Queen Mary, who inherited the throne as an infant upon her father's death in 1542.

Mary was the great-niece of Henry VIII of England by the marriage of his sister Margaret to James IV. That matrimonial alliance had failed to prevent English aggression and the death at Flodden Field of James IV in 1513, and after Solway Moss of his son in 1542. Both English victories were read by some Scots nobles as signs of the failure of the French alliance and a signal that the time had come for a new approach to England. With Henry VIII's separation of his church from Rome in the 1530s, Protestantism (of a very conservative sort) became a second layer to the new, prospective alliance with a realm to whose throne, after all, Mary Stewart had a strong claim. An anglophile faction thus supported the efforts of its natural leader and Mary's first regent, James Hamilton, earl of Arran, to negotiate with England and move Scotland in a Protestant direction. By 1543, parliament had authorised a vernacular Bible (Tyndale's English translation) and Protestant preaching. It was soon after this that Knox and Wishart launched their preaching tour of 1545-6. Their efforts drummed up more support for the cause, but were cut short by Wishart's capture and Cardinal Beaton's order for his execution. Beaton paid the price the following year, when radical Protestants assassinated him and seized St Andrews Castle, with Knox spurring them on in their battle against French power and 'popery'. They controlled the castle for a year.

The infant queen's mother, however, was unwilling to go quietly. With French military aid, she re-established control in St Andrews, sent Knox to row in a French galley, and eventually took over as regent in 1554. Reform ground to a halt, though Mary of Guise did not follow the course taken by England's new queen, Mary Tudor, in actively persecuting Protestants. She told them instead to 'devise ye what ye please in matters of religion', even permitting the Protestant ministers who had fled to England in 1546 to return in 1553. (Knox, released from the galleys in 1549, came back in 1555.) Her principal interest lay in negotiating the marriage of her daughter in 1558 to the dauphin François, heir to Henri II of France. Her enemies still found fault, though. The price of her religious toleration was parliamentary agreement to the regnal rights of the dauphin in Scotland. While parliament acquiesced, fear of French domination persisted, aggravated by the rankling influence of French courtiers rather than native counsellors. Protestantism now served as the natural accompaniment to anti-French political sentiment. In 1557, a small group of powerful lords signed a 'common bond', swearing oaths of mutual obligation and defence of the gospel in the first of the covenants that would define Scottish politics and religion for the next century and more. The bond injected spiritual meaning into what was a longstanding and distinctively Scottish social institution. With this 'First Bond of the Lords of the Congregation', Scottish Protestantism moved out of the 'privy kirks' and onto the political and military stage (Wormald 1981).

The death in 1558 of Mary Tudor and accession to the English throne of her Protestant sister Elizabeth ensured the lords' ultimate success. Now, with the expectation of English military aid, and with Knox and Willock giving the movement religious legitimation by preaching resistance to the regent as a defence of the gospel, they added to their numbers and took up arms against her. They even managed to sign on a few Catholic lords, chief among them the very conservative earl of Huntly, willing to fight not for religion, but for 'the liberty of this your native country'. Among the Protestant nobles, Lord James Stewart, the earl of Glencairn (Knox's supporter in Renfrewshire) and Archibald, Lord Lorne (heir to the earl of Argyll) provided essential support. Under Arran's leadership, they suspended Mary of Guise from the regency and appointed a 'great council' to govern the realm. Eleven thousand English troops lent force to their actions. And, while most of those lower on the social scale just waited to see how things would turn out, some in Lowland burghs and the countryside where the preachers had been most active came to the lords' support. Perth's appeals to 'all brethren' to protect Reformed preachers brought an enthusiastic response from lairds and townsmen alike, while a series of sermons by Knox 'vehement against idolatry' provoked days of iconoclasm and the destruction of religious houses in Dundee and Perth in 1559. Ayr, Brechin, Montrose, St Andrews and Stirling, among others, likewise abolished their religious houses and committed themselves to the Reformed cause. The capital, however, was less enthusiastic, while Old Aberdeen (encompassing the university and cathedral) was downright hostile, and destruction of the friars' houses in New Aberdeen was wrought by a mob from the Mearns rather than by the townspeople (Cowan 1982,

108–17; Mason 1998). Local variety in popular responses to the new ideas characterised the Scots Reformation as much as that in England or in continental settings.

Mary of Guise, however, was not without her own resources. With the death of Henri II, she became mother-in-law to the new king of France and was able to draw on more French military aid. Providence, however, seemed to side with the Protestants. Winter storms prevented French troops from landing in 1559, while internal problems in France kept more aid from coming in the spring of 1560. The regent's own death in June of that year left her eighteen-year-old daughter, living in France, in charge of a realm where she had no desire to live, and a people of whom she had no understanding whatsoever (Wormald, 1988). By the treaty of Edinburgh, signed in July 1560, she brought French troops home and agreed to permit conciliar government and parliamentary settlement of religion.

Parliament, dominated by the lords of the Congregation, proceeded to abolish the mass and adopt a new, Reformed confession of faith. An assembly of Protestant clergymen in December 1560 settled on a new structure for the Reformed church in the *First Book of Discipline*, and their successors in the general assemblies of 1562 and 1564 accepted a Genevan structure for worship in the Book of Common Order, bound together with Calvin's catechism at each printing from 1562 to 1611, and in Knox's vernacular Scots *Confession* (Hazlett 1987).

The new queen, who returned to Scotland only in 1561, fourteen months after her mother's death, was thus greeted by a *fait accompli*. She sensibly agreed to permit Protestantism for the realm while retaining the mass for herself. This might have served, had Mary been better suited to govern. Despite efforts to rehabilitate her reputation, however, recent scholarship has portrayed her as both inept and given to destructive intrigue (Wormald, 1988; *cf* the more positive views of Cowan 1987, Lynch 1988, Donaldson 1983). Having lost the chance to be queen of France, she shifted her ambition to the English throne and, ignoring the interests of the Scottish nobility as well as the church, promoted foreign favourites and alienated whatever affections her subjects might have had for her. Her second marriage, to her dissolute cousin Henry Stewart, Lord Darnley, ended in his murder but at least produced an heir and sealed the boy's claim to the English crown at Elizabeth's death. Her third marriage, to the earl of Bothwell, widely condemned for his part in the Darnley murder, brought an already suspect queen into thoroughgoing disrepute. Once the child James had been born, though, Mary was dispensable. The Protestant nobility and their anti-French allies accordingly deposed her in 1567 (Wormald 1988). Six more years of civil wars followed, and not until Mary's execution in 1587 by Elizabeth's order would the threat of Catholic reconquest be eased. But the Reformation could at last proceed at the direction of the lords of the Congregation. A sequence of noble regents vied for control of young James, subjected him to a rigorous Protestant upbringing, and generally made his life a misery until he seized control for himself in the mid 1580s.

PROTESTANT BELIEF AND PRACTICE

Ecclesiastical Polity: Superintendents, Presbyteries and Bishops

The young king's regents were all avowedly Protestant, but none of them sought to extend reform of the church so far as to abolish the lay patronage system that had so eroded clerical incomes before the Reformation. Their vested interests, and the king's, were best served by retaining as much ecclesiastical revenue as possible for themselves and their clients. This obviously put them at odds with the new church, whose leaders saw clearly that, until a preaching ministry could be supplied for every parish, it would be an uphill battle to win the hearts and minds of people steeped in traditional Catholic beliefs. For the king and much of the nobility, rule of the church by bishops (on the English Protestant model) appeared to be the most efficient way to retain the control necessary to maintain their patronage. The Reformed clergy, however, inspired by the Genevan and French Protestant models, called for a church polity in which power was vested in a series of courts. These ranged from the parochial kirk session (the ministers and a large group of lay elders chosen by the congregation), to presbyteries (the ministers of a group of contiguous parishes), to regional synods (including the ministers of a number of presbyteries), to the general assembly (a national body of clerics with a smaller number of lay members to oversee the operations of the presbyteries and synods and to plant new churches where needed). The general assembly has been aptly described as a predominantly clerical body: 'if magnates and barons appeared occasionally as individuals, the primary element in its membership was ministerial together with a handful of lay commissioners drawn from the shires, burghs and universities' (Cowan 1982, 128).

The *First Book of Discipline* called for congregational election of ministers, rather than their appointment by local lay elites, and for church control of teinds and ecclesiastical property to provide clerical stipends. Ministers, elders and deacons were to be regularly vetted by the parishioners for their doctrine and behaviour. Ministers and elders comprised a session, charged with enforcing moral discipline on all parishioners; with providing for sermons, Bible-reading, catechism, schools, and sacraments; and, with the deacons, with maintaining the fabric of the church and administering relief to the poor of the parish. Kirk sessions, which generally included a dozen to twenty or so laymen – lairds, merchants and craftsmen – had been established in a few forward-looking 'privy kirks' even before the official Reformation; afterwards they multiplied, especially in urban parishes. They met weekly in most parishes, and would prove the most powerful weapon in the arsenal of the Reformers as they battled popery, 'superstition', theological ignorance and all sorts of behaviour defined as immoral.

Recognising a need for oversight, the authors of the *First Book* also called for the appointment by the general assembly of 'superintendents' (ministers, not old-style bishops), who would visit the parishes within their defined bounds and deal with questions of clerical appointment, doctrine and discipline. Five superintendents were in fact appointed in 1561, while three converted bishops carried out similar functions in their dioceses, and both old and new bishops continued to serve elsewhere. The Reformers of the 1560s were not actively anti-episcopal; their focus was more on the functions of the all-important parochial courts. An agreement signed at Leith in 1572 in fact affirmed episcopal nomination by the king, though it subordinated bishops to the authority of the general assembly.

Only after the *Second Book of Discipline* (1578) did presbyteries begin to enter the picture. This scheme, drafted by thirty ministers, defined the four categories of ministry found in Calvin's scheme (preaching ministers, elders, doctors [teachers] and deacons). It clarified the separation of magistracy and church, but made them mutually reinforcing – a recognition that, at the parochial level, civil magistrates were active both as elders on sessions, and as enforcers of sessions' rulings. It went on to call again for church control of ecclesiastical property, and now for the elimination of superintendents and bishops in favour of the Huguenot model of provincial and national assemblies – the former an oblique reference to presbyteries. The 1580 general assembly duly condemned episcopacy in favour of the parity of ministers. By 1581 plans were in place for thirteen presbyteries, charged with visitation of parishes, appointment and oversight of ministers, judicial responsibility for important disciplinary matters (including cases involving the nobility), and selection of representatives for future general assemblies. A full-blown presbyterian system would make the church virtually independent of secular governors. Naturally, the king and many of the nobility stood staunchly against it.

The opposition of James VI was sealed by his experience in 1582, when a group of presbyterians led by William Ruthven, earl of Gowrie, sought to control government by kidnapping the king. The 'Ruthven raiders' made their capture, but James soon escaped into the hands of an anti-presbyterian faction. The upshot of it all was the 1584 'Black Acts', which abolished presbyteries and asserted royal supremacy over the church, and the exile to England of a large group of presbyterian ministers who refused to accept this legislation. Often called 'Melvillians' after their radical spokesman, Andrew Melville, they would subject even the king himself to the demands of the church. Melville famously and tactlessly reminded the king that he was but 'God's silly [i.e. simple] vassal' (Wormald 1981).

Presbyteries, however, made good sense to the organisers of the new church – even to episcopalians. In fact, they continued to operate hand-in-glove with bishops, who often served as permanent moderators. Indeed, a bishop was involved in the establishment of Stirling presbytery. Revision of the Black Acts in 1586 simply recognised the *status quo* in its permission of presbytery meetings presided over by bishops. By the early 1590s there were forty-seven presbyteries operating in the Lowlands. A statute of 1592, the 'Golden Act', legitimated them, and conferred upon them most of the powers previously possessed by bishops, though the king retained the right to summon general assemblies. By the end of the 1590s, however, the king sought to reintroduce episcopacy and, for the next four decades, a system of presbytery within prelacy guided the church. While some historians still espouse the view of incessant struggle between presbyterians and royal episcopacy inherited from seventeenth-century presbyterian polemicists, at least for the post-1604 period, recent research in session and presbytery records suggests that bishops were in fact opposed only by a small but outspoken group of ministers. For people in the pew, ecclesiastical polity at this level was largely irrelevant. And, for most ministers, cooperation was the preferred option (Mullan 1986; Todd 2004; *cf* MacDonald 1998).

Parochial Protestantism: A Cultural Revolution in the Pews

Thus far our focus has been on politics and ecclesiastical polity at the highest levels. But what of belief? Until quite recently, the Reformation about which we have known the least, in Scotland as elsewhere, is the one that happened in the pew. In an era when the majority of people were illiterate, when the letters and diaries that allow us a glimpse into the minds of the elite simply do not exist for ordinary folk, it has been hard to assess the extent to which Protestant ideas and behaviour, however sternly mandated, were actually adopted by the people. New research based on the minutes of kirk sessions, however, has opened a window onto religion in the parishes.

At some point in their lives, nearly all parishioners would have appeared before the session. The elders did not just discipline those who misbehaved and correct the heterodox. They also entertained petitions from upstanding members of the congregation to erect family galleries in the church, or bury their dead under the church floor, or make special gifts to the poor box. Couples had to appear before the session to ask that their marriage banns be proclaimed, and for their children to be baptised. Individuals appeared to complain about their neighbours' mischief, or to offer depositions in support of a good neighbour's reputation. Through the session minutes, in other words, we get a glimpse of a broad cross-section of the Scottish population and the affairs of ordinary people.

The more punitive aspect of the sessions' operations – the discipline of misbehaviour – does dominate the records, and it confronts modern readers with a problem that is initially baffling. Parish elders were a remarkably intrusive group of men. They snooped into the most personal aspects of people's lives: arriving unannounced in bedrooms, peering into pub windows to find drunkards, making surprise visits on Sundays to find absentees from the sermon. They calculated the months between weddings and births, quizzed parishioners about whether their neighbours might be witches or warlocks, and punished bakers who made cakes on old festival days. They were enforcing a 'reformation of manners' more rigorous than that of any other Protestant movement, and arguably doing it more thoroughly than any of their continental Calvinist counterparts. Scotland alone among Reformed nations abolished not just saints' days, but all the celebrations of the liturgical calendar, including Christmas and Easter. In Scotland, even the sabbath could be declared a day of fasting for sin, and fasting seasons far outnumbered days of thanksgiving in the Protestant calendar. Wedding merriment was limited. Scottish couples intending to marry had to demonstrate a thorough understanding of Protestant doctrine in order to have their banns proclaimed; many were sent away, their weddings postponed until they had sorted out the finer points. Finally, only in Scotland was punishment by humiliation – the public 'performing' of repentance – carried out with a special piece of furniture installed in every parish church with the express intention of making offenders more visible, more humiliated before their neighbours. The penitents' seat, where sinners were assigned to sit one or two Sundays for a small offence, a year of Sundays for a major one, has no parallel in any other Reformed church (Todd 2002).

On the face of it, all of this appears calculated to make Protestantism distinctly unpopular. Festivals gave way to penitential fasting seasons; pageantry and procession disappeared in favour of godly sobriety; and the sensual aspects of the old worship faded away with the destruction of images and altars (monuments of idolatry), organs (the devil's box of whistles), and even harmonized music (distracting from the Word). Not surprisingly, initial support for the movement was lukewarm at best. In 1561, only about a fifth of the adult population of Edinburgh presented themselves for Protestant communion. Secret masses were tolerated in Aberdeen (where there were actually Catholics on the first kirk sessions) into the 1570s, and longer in the Highlands, where it took much longer to set up sessions. The shortage of preaching ministers hampered progress: there were fewer than 600 for Scotland's thousand parishes as late as 1597 (Kirk 1989).

Yet within a generation of the official Reformation, in the most populated crescent from Aberdeen and Fraserburgh in the north-east, to Ayrshire in the south-west, kirk sessions *were* established, readers in parishes without ministers made sure that people heard the vernacular Scriptures, sabbath breach became a rarity, parishioners paid to erect penitents' seats and fund the schools required by the books of discipline, and visitation returns by elders reported more often than not 'no disorder'. Lairds and sometimes even lords submitted themselves to the discipline of sessions and presbyteries (Graham 1993). Despite demanding examinations of doctrine and high standards for moral rectitude, nearly all parishioners managed to secure the tokens required for admission to communion. A new, unharmonised vernacular psalter, with its regular metre and simple tunes, had become so popular by the turn of the century that most could 'sing all or at least many of the psalms without the book' (Todd 2002, 70–3). Towns claimed a new, Protestant identity as 'Reformed burghs in which there is no slander' – a phrase oft-repeated in self-descriptions. Both women and men signed or put their marks on the sequence of covenants and confessions of faith promulgated against perceived threats of popery, from the definitive 'Negative Confession' of 1581 (virulently anti-Catholic) to the general bonds of the 1590s – covenants between people and God to defend true religion. And ministers, however much they complained about divine displeasure at pervasive sin and worldliness, nonetheless boasted of the superiority of their reform compared to England's 'half-way' version. At the most local level, the Reformation had succeeded beyond the wildest hopes of its founders, achieving in the lives of ordinary Scots what can best be described as a cultural revolution (Todd 2002).

What made this remarkable transformation possible was the work of fervent Calvinist preachers and kirk sessions. The elders' demand for the strictest sabbath observance and regular catechetical performance made serious ignorance of the

Protestant message nearly impossible. But, just as important, they combined their disciplinary efforts with provision of a range of social services designed to make society more orderly and less violent. They provided poor relief, schools (for girls as well as boys, at least in burghs), and the fostering of orphaned or abandoned children. They intervened in domestic conflict, requiring abusive spouses and parents to amend their behaviour, forcing absent fathers to support their children and adult children to sustain their elderly parents. They helped to bring an end to feud by offering binding arbitration of quarrels and public ceremonies of reconciliation. However distasteful modern people might find their prying and punishing, they served early modern communities much as modern police and welfare agencies do now.

Calvinist preaching introduced a new style of piety which is visible in sermon notes and the devotional writing of increasingly literate lay people, including women, right through the seventeenth century. These were characterised by obsessive introspection and persistent anxiety about election to salvation. Spiritual journals were records of incessant spiritual temperature-taking and lists of symptoms that might diagnose spiritual malaise. But both men and women also penned religious verse that suggested spiritual 'highs', and voluminous letters to ministers suggest real veneration of charismatic preachers, especially during their times of persecution (Mullan 2000, 2003).

Catholic Survival and Protestantism in the Gàidhealtachd

The most eloquent testimony to the success of the Reformation in Scotland, even in the Gaelic-speaking Highlands and Isles, is the complaint of Catholic missionaries. Missions were slow to get started, commencing their efforts only after the foundation of a college at Douai in 1576. A few Jesuits were reportedly active in the 1580s and 1590s. Their only hope for success lay in the sponsorship of noble Catholics. Earls like Huntly and Erroll, and entrenched Catholic families (Gordons, Leslies, Hays, and Cheynes) aided their efforts in Ross and Aberdeenshire. The Maxwells in Galloway and the Cunninghams in Ayrshire likewise sponsored and protected missionaries, while in East Lothian Lord Seton maintained a Catholic chaplain and encouraged recusancy. But, with a majority of Lowland parishes staffed with Reformed ministers by the 1570s, missionary delay had already spelled failure; moreover, the Jesuits, whose singular zeal might have had an effect, lacked both numbers and papal support for their efforts in Scotland (Kirk 1986, 285–6; Roberts 1998, 63–88).

As for the Highlands and Isles, the Franciscan mission commenced only in the 1620s, from a base in Antrim. The friars had the advantage of being Gaelic speakers, but what they encountered when they crossed the sea was a population largely won over by a half-century and more of fervent and unrelenting Protestant preaching and catechising. The only exceptions were isolated areas, notably the Hebrides, bereft of both priests and ministers (Giblin 1964; Kirk 1986a). Protestant bishops in the dioceses of Galloway and Orkney (Alexander Gordon and Adam Bothwell) had established preaching ministers in their parishes within the first decade of Reformation; Bishop Carswell, superintendent of Argyll, had translated the *Book of Common Order* into Gaelic in 1567, and with the fifth earl of Argyll had established the new religion firmly in Argyll (Meek 1998). While Protestantisation of the Highlands more generally had taken a generation or so more than that of the Lowlands, by 1574 as high a percentage of parishes in the *Gàidhealtachd* as in the Lowlands had Protestant ministers or at least readers. Many of them were drawn from the hereditary learned orders, able to draw on the Gaelic 'culture of oral literacy' to communicate Protestant ideas. For parishes without preachers, Gaelic-speaking readers translated the Bible in their weekly readings in the parish churches (Dawson 1994, 2003; Kirk 1986b).

The establishment of kirk sessions was slower in the Highlands, as in rural areas generally, though scarcity of surviving records from this predominantly oral culture should not be allowed to skew our judgment of the Reformation's progress there. Highland sessions often met fortnightly or monthly after the Sunday morning sermon rather than several times a week, as in Lowland burghs, and presbyteries seldom assembled more than monthly or quarterly rather than weekly, as they did in the Lowlands. The records do show commitment to instruction and discipline, and the same sorts of efforts to persuade parishioners still clinging to old traditions that had served in Lowland parishes, with ministers or pairs of elders being sent to the homes of the recalcitrant to 'deal with' them until their doubts were resolved and they could agree to the new confession of faith (Todd, 2002).

Reports of 'obstinate papists' anywhere in Scotland were rare by 1600, and organised recusancy was nearly non-existent. As little as 2% of the population professed Catholicism by 1600 (Sanderson 1970, 87–107; Macinnes 1992, 35). And criteria for counting Catholics may skew the numbers in favour of Catholicism: the St Andrews session, for instance, declared in 1595 that all those absent from communion 'salbe estemmit papists' (Fleming 1890, vol. 2, 808).

The seventeenth-century Catholic missionaries thus had their work cut out for them. Hampered as the earlier Jesuits had been by inadequate resources, papal neglect, and insufficient manpower, theirs proved a lost cause. Only when they were actively aided by the patronage of Catholic lords did they report a few converts, and even then there were too few priests to sustain recusancy. An Irish priest in 1685 reported of his efforts in the area around Knoydart: 'there were but two to serve all when we went there . . . We could not reach to christen the half of their children' (Roberts 1998, 72). Later, visiting Vincentians and Dominicans did find Catholic cells in the Highlands, either continuing in a pre-Reformation faith or restored by missionaries, but their numbers were small. Catholicism, especially in the north, was never obliterated, but by 1600 Catholics were 'an insignificant minority' (Cowan 1982, 181). Not until the second decade of the eighteenth century, when native priests began to serve the Highlands, was there a significant Catholic revival (Roberts 1998).

SEVENTEENTH-CENTURY CONTROVERSY

Conflict and Covenanters

The cooperation of presbytery and episcopacy established after 1600 continued through the rest of James VI's reign, despite his move to England in 1603. There he was, by all reports, delighted with royal supremacy over a church whose bishops were very much under the thumb of the monarch, and with a traditional liturgy whose gestures and accoutrements struck him as more reverential and therefore more supportive of hierarchy and deference than Scotland's simple service. Under no illusions that he could achieve such an order in his northern realm, he nonetheless determined to strengthen Scottish episcopacy and to decree some changes in worship along English lines. Had he been resident in Scotland and more inclined to enforcement, the results might have been more disruptive; as it was, he drew fire from presbyterian radicals and set a pattern which his less politically adept son would pursue to his violent demise, bringing all three of his kingdoms – England, Scotland, and Ireland – to disastrous civil war in the 1630s and 1640s.

James's most alarming attempts to anglicize the settlement were to press the Glasgow general assembly of 1610 to restore episcopal power, and in 1618 to force upon the Perth assembly (and in 1621 the parliament) five articles, which included orders to kneel rather than sit at communion and restored private baptism, private communion and episcopal confirmation (rare even before the Reformation). These innovations – coming from 'the midden of the corruption of the church of England', according to the presbyterian preacher John Row – were of the very visible sort that would arouse popular as well as clerical ire in a land where for generations the people had received the sacrament seated upon benches around the communion table and had heard their ministers condemn the 'popish superstition and idolatry' of kneeling, as if in veneration of the elements. However, communion was administered in this way only rarely, since even bishops declined to enforce the articles (Todd 2004).

Charles I was a different sort of king from his father. Exhibiting disdain for his Scottish throne by neglecting even to be crowned there until 1633, eight years after his father's death, he heaped affront upon insult by insisting on English trappings, bishops, and the Book of Common Prayer for the ceremony. He even attempted to install gilded images in St Giles – though foiled on this point by his more sensible Scottish bishops (Todd 2004). The king reproved these bishops, though, and began elevating to episcopacy in Scotland and England men sympathetic not only to ceremonies and vestments that smacked of popery but also to anti-Calvinist theology. In 1637 he finally did the unforgivable and imposed an English-style prayer book on the church. The opposition to what one critic called this 'vomit of Romisch superstition' showed no restraints: the congregation in St Giles' threw their stools at the dean reading the despised service, and the bishop of Brechin reportedly read it holding a pair of loaded pistols aimed at his angry people (Foster 1975).

Confronted with these clear threats to the Protestant gospel and the purity of the church, the Scots did what they had done so often before – they swore a covenant, binding themselves to defend the faith at all costs. The National Covenant of 1638, signed first by lords, then by lairds, ministers and burgesses, and eventually sworn publicly by men and women in every parish church, hands held heavenward, was a call to action. By the summer of 1638, the Covenanters were in arms. When the general assembly met at Glasgow in November (unusually well-attended by lay elders as well as ministers), the king ordered it to disband; instead, the assembly continued with its business: abolishing bishops, the service book, and the Perth Articles. The 'second Reformation' had begun.

Wars of Religion: Covenanters in Arms

The ensuing 'Bishops' Wars' would take Scots troops into England by 1640, forcing Charles to summon a parliament in Westminster to fund his military response. What that parliament did, however, was to side with the Scots; English puritans identified them as co-religionists with common grievances. The alliance was always an uneasy one, since the price of Scots aid for the English was the summoning in 1643 of an assembly of divines at Westminster that sought to impose presbyterianism, a Scottish style of worship, and a new Confession of Faith on a decidedly non-presbyterian English church. For their part, the Scots cheerfully adopted the Westminster Confession as their own creed, but they suffered no illusions that English acquiescence was more than a temporary expedient, and they worried with good reason about burgeoning sectarianism within the English army (Stevenson 1973). Many therefore abandoned the alliance and sought reconciliation with the king when he surrendered to them in 1646. The following year, the Scottish parliament approved an 'Engagement' with Charles on condition that he would implement presbyterianism in England. The Scots were divided, however, with old-style royalists and Engagers opposed by a more radical contingent that insisted that the king also sign the Covenant. Cromwell's victory at Preston and his army's 1648 purge of presbyterians from the English parliament thoroughly discredited the Engagers. In the 1648 Whiggamore Raid a band of Covenanters from the south-west seized Edinburgh, excluded the Engagers from government, abolished lay patronage in the church, purged the ministry, and heightened the level of church discipline with new laws against witchcraft, fornication and sabbath breach (Lynch 1991, 275–8).

With the execution of the king in 1649, and Cromwellian victories, the fundamentally royalist Scots parliament proclaimed the late king's son Charles II; early the next year, in dire need of Scots military support, the new king signed the Covenant. Much good it did him. Cromwell's defeat in 1650 of a rather over-purged Covenanter army at Dunbar again shifted the balance within Scottish politics. More moderate Covenanters (Resolutioners) now accepted into their ranks erstwhile Engagers and crowned Charles II at Scone. The more radical (Protesters) formed rival general assemblies in 1651 and 1652 and in some regions competing presbyteries (Coffey 1997). Schism in the church obviously weakened effective resistance to English invaders. Cromwell proceeded to impose military government on Scotland in 1652 and established for the next eight years the sort of inclusive, decentralised church that he had settled on England (Dow 1979; Lynch 1991, 278–86). Resolutioners, Protesters, and the rest now bided their time. With Cromwell's abolition of the privy council and imposition of English judges, even the witch hunts so vigorously pursued since the 1590s by ministers and the nobility were put on hold, only to erupt in a frenzy of 660 prosecutions in the sixteen months following the Restoration (Levack 1992).

The Church and the Restored Monarchy

It was no surprise to anyone that, after the king was restored to power in 1660, he immediately revived the hybrid of episcopal rule of a church with presbyteries which had worked so smoothly until his father had attempted to anglicise it, only without the general assembly to cramp the bishops' style. He did restore lay patronage, but he sensibly omitted the Perth Articles and the service book. Worship in the parishes returned to the *status quo ante*-1618, and the disciplinary courts carried on as always.

Decades of war and foreign occupation had taken their toll, however, and the disunity which had plagued the church was not abated by the settlement. More than a quarter of the ministry, the most radical Covenanters, refused to accept bishops and went their own way, organising secret conventicles and often meeting in open fields for want of church buildings (Lynch 1992, 290). Anxious to repress the sort of independency that was fostering active dissent in England as well, the crown initially determined to enforce the 1662 act against Covenants and Conventicles with a policy of ruthless repression. The Covenanters responded with equal violence in the Pentland Rising of 1666.

For the next two decades, the government alternated repression with indulgence. Conventiclers, never quite sure what to expect, held their open-air meetings protected by heavily armed guards. Despite – or perhaps because of – the persecution, their numbers multiplied. A field conventicle meeting near Dumfries in 1678 numbered in excess of 14,000 people (Cowan 1976, chs. 5–6). Nor did covenanting cease during these trying times. In 1680 followers of the radical minister Richard Cameron signed a covenant for defence of 'the true presbyterian church and covenanted nation of Scotland', only to have their leader killed by royal dragoons. In the 'killing times' of the 1680s, at least a hundred men and women were hanged, shot or drowned for covenanting.

Toleration

With the deposition of Charles' Catholic successor, James VII, in 1689, everything changed. William and Mary agreed to abolish episcopacy and to return to full-blown presbyterianism in Scotland, persuaded by the bishops' continued support for James VII. Authority over the church was duly returned to general assemblies, lay patronage was again abolished (until 1712), and the Westminster Confession was ratified. But presbyterianism after 1689 existed in a very different world – one where the state church was not the only show in town. The new monarchs had found by their experience in the Low Countries that religious pluralism could, after all, co-exist with political order, so in 1689 they implemented in Scotland (as more formally in England) a limited, *de facto* religious toleration (excluding Catholics). Because secular magistrates would no longer be expected to enforce the discipline of kirk sessions and presbyteries, people who disagreed with the established church (as long as they remained Protestant) need no longer fear financial or corporal reprisal. The upshot was that supporters of episcopacy, particularly in the north, where bishops were loyal to William and Mary, were able to settle their own church – tacitly permitted if not legal. Fully 165 episcopalians served as ministers of separate churches or 'meeting houses' after 1695. They organised their own synods, and after the 1712 Toleration Act many used the English Book of Common Prayer. With heightened English immigration after the union of 1707, their numbers grew (Cowan and Earle 1966).

Other dissenting groups also flourished, with obvious ramifications for the established church. If a hallmark of the church in the century following Reformation was its strict parochial discipline, the fact that people were no longer legally obliged to attend that church and submit to its oversight meant that sessions lost their clout. Excommunication had once meant banishment from one's community. Family and neighbours were forbidden even to break bread with an individual whose con-tumacy or recusancy had brought down the elders' wrath. Now, the church's weapons were blunt-edged, the sessions' hegemony ended. Episcopalians, conven-ticlers, even Catholics could worship as they would, and submit to or evade the old discipline as they chose (Donaldson 1973). If the Reformation was a cultural revolution, the Glorious Revolution ended it and ushered in a new era of religious options.

REFERENCES

Aberdeen Council Register: Extracts from the Council Register of the Burgh of Aberdeen, vol. 1 1844. Aberdeen.

*Cameron, J.K. 1972 *The First Book of Discipline*. Edinburgh.

Coffey, J. 1997 *Politics, Religion and the British Revolutions: The Mind of Samuel Ruther-ford*. Cambridge.

Cowan, I.B. 1976 *The Scottish Covenanters 1660–1688*. London.

*Cowan, I.B. 1982 *The Scottish Reformation: Church and Society in Sixteenth Century Scotland*. New York.

Cowan, I.B. 1987 *Mary Queen of Scots*. Edinburgh.

Cowan, I.B. and Earle, S. 1966 *The Scottish Episcopal Church*. Ambler.

Dawson, J. 1994 'Calvinism in the Gaidhealtachd in Scotland', in Pettegree, A., Duke, A. and Lewis, G. (eds), *Calvinism in Europe 1540–1620*, Cambridge, 231–53.

Dawson, J. 2002 *The Politics of Religion in the Age of Mary, Queen of Scots: The Earl of Argyll and the Struggle for Britain and Ireland*. Cambridge.

*Donaldson, G. 1970 *Scottish Historical Documents*. Edinburgh.

Donaldson, G. 1972 *Scotland: Church and Nation through Sixteen Centuries*. Edinburgh.

Donaldson, G. 1983 *All the Queen's Men: Power and Politics in Mary Stewart's Scotland.* London.

Donaldson, G. 1985 *Scottish Church History.* Edinburgh.

Dow, F. 1979 *Cromwellian Scotland, 1651–60.* Edinburgh.

Durkan, J. 1962 'Education in the Century of the Reformation', in McRoberts, D. (ed) *Essays on the Scottish Reformation 1513–1625,* Glasgow, 145–68.

*Fleming, D.H. 1889–90 *Register of the Ministers, Elders and Deacons of St Andrews 1559–1600,* 2 vols. Edinburgh.

Foggie, J.P. 2003 *Renaissance Religion in Urban Scotland: The Dominican Order, 1450–1560.* Leiden.

*Foster, W.R. 1975 *The Church before the Covenants: The Church of Scotland 1596–1638.* Edinburgh.

Giblin, C. (ed) 1964 *The Irish Franciscan Mission to Scotland, 1619–1646.* Dublin.

Graham, M. 1993 'Equality before the Kirk? Church Discipline and the Elite in Reformation-Era Scotland', *Archiv für Reformationsgeschichte,* 84, 289–309.

Hazlett, W.I.P. 1987 'The Scots Confession of 1560: Context, Complexion and Critique', *Archiv für Reformationsgeschichte,* 78, 287–320.

Howard, D. 1995 *Scottish Architecture: Reformation to Restoration 1560–1660.* Edinburgh.

*Kirk, J. (ed) 1980 *The Second Book of Discipline.* Edinburgh.

Kirk, J. 1986a *The Seventeenth Century in the Highlands.* Inverness.

Kirk, J. 1986b 'The Kirk and the Highlands at the Reformation', *Northern Scotland,* 7, 1–22.

*Kirk, J. 1989 *Patterns of Reform: Continuity and Change in the Reformation Kirk.* Edinburgh.

Levack, B. 1992 (ed) *Witchcraft in Scotland.* New York.

*Lindsay, D. 1871 *The Poetical Works of Sir David Lyndsay of the Mount,* 2 vols. Edinburgh.

Lynch, M. 1981 *Edinburgh and the Reformation.* Edinburgh.

*Lynch, M. 1986 'Calvinism in Scotland 1559–1638', in Prestwich, M. (ed) *International Calvinism 1541–1715,* Oxford, 225–55.

Lynch, M. (ed) 1988 *Mary Stewart: Queen in Three Kingdoms.* Oxford.

Lynch, M. 1992 *Scotland: A New History.* London.

MacDonald, A.R. 1998 *The Jacobean Kirk, 1567–1625: Sovereignty, Polity and Liturgy.* Aldershot.

Macinnes, A.I. 1991 *Charles I and the Making of the Covenanting Movement 1625–1641.* Edinburgh.

Macinnes, A.I. 1992 'Catholic Recusancy and the Penal Laws 1603–1707', *Records of the Scottish Church History Society,* 24, 27–63.

McKay, D. 1962 'Parish Life in Scotland 1500–1560', in McRoberts, D. (ed), *Essays on the Scottish Reformation 1513–1625,* Glasgow, 85–115.

Meek, D.E. 1998 'The Reformation and Gaelic culture: perspectives on patronage, language and literature in John Carswell's translation of "The Book of Common Order" ', in Kirk, J. (ed), *The Kirk in the Highlands,* Edinburgh, 37–62.

Mullan, D. 1986 *Episcopacy in Scotland: The History of an Idea 1560–1638.* Edinburgh.

*Mullan, D. 2000 *Scottish Puritanism 1590–1638.* Oxford.

*Mullan, D. 2003 (ed) *Women's Life Writing in Early Modern Scotland: Writing the Evangelical Self–c. 1670–c. 1730.* Burlington, Vermont.

*Roberts, A. 1998 'Roman Catholicism in the Highlands', in Kirk, J. (ed), *The Church in the Highlands,* 63–88. Edinburgh.

Sanderson, M.H.B. 1970 'Catholic Recusancy in Scotland in the Sixteenth Century', *Innes Review,* 21, 87–107.

*Sanderson, M.H.B. 1997 *Ayrshire and the Reformation: People and Change, 1490–1600*. East Linton.

Stevenson, D. 1973 *The Scottish Revolution 1637–1644: The Triumph of the Covenanters*. Newton Abbot.

*Todd, M. 2002 *The Culture of Protestantism in Early Modern Scotland*. New Haven.

Todd, M. 2004 'Bishops in the Kirk: William Cowper of Galloway and the Puritan Episcopacy of Scotland', *The Scottish Journal of Theology*, 57, 300–312.

*Wormald, J. 1981 *Court, Kirk and Community: Scotland 1470–1625*. London.

Wormald, J. 1988 *Mary Queen of Scots: Politics, Passion and a Kingdom Lost*. London.

Yeoman, P. 1999 *Pilgrimage in Medieval Scotland*. London.

FURTHER READING

The items above marked * are recommended for further reading along with the following.

Donaldson, G. 1960 *The Scottish Reformation*. Cambridge.

Henderson, G.D. 1937 *The Scots Confession, 1560*. Edinburgh.

Leneman, L. and Mitchison, R. 1989 *Sexuality and Social Control: Scotland 1660–1780*. Oxford.

CHAPTER EIGHT

Scotland and Europe
Steve Murdoch

[Scotland] adjoins the island of England and is a long peninsula to the north of the larger island. It is uninhabited and has neither town nor village. Its length is 150 miles.
>> Abu Aballah Muhammad al-Sharif al-Idrisi, 1154 (Lewis 1982, 147)

[Queen Anna] told the Venetian ambassador, Antonio Foscarini, that Scotland 'seemed to her like her native land'.
>> Anna, the Danish queen of James VI & I, on Scotland, 1613
>> (Murdoch 2003, 4; *CSPV*, vol. 13, 1613–1616, 36–37.
>> Relation by Antonio Foscarini, 2 September 1613).

I can say but little of Scotland. It is a large country full of steep mountains and barbarous people, and with the exception of various metal mines and an abundance of cattle, it produces little of any worth.
>> Piero Contarini, Venetian ambassador in London,
>> 1618 (*CSPV*, 1617–1619, 414–22)

Wild men such as those of Scotland and Ireland are also found throughout the islands of India, especially on Ceylon and many other islands within the territory of the Tarnatan King, namely on the coast of Batochina.
>> Anthonio van den Heuvel,
>> Dutch governor of Ambon, 1633 (Murdoch 2002, 63)

The Scottish nation has now for a long time, about sixty years, had a strong relationship and experience of us [Sweden], and a good portion of the Scottish nation has shown our previous kings and crown worthy services; for this reason their success and wellbeing has not been any less desired by us than the Scottish nation itself. Thus we unhappily hear [of] the misunderstanding and disunity that has arisen between His Majesty in England, your king, and the Scottish nation. Her Majesty our gracious queen and the royal government wishes nothing better than that they could come up with some means and advice to fix such disputes.
>> Chancellor Axel Oxenstierna responding on behalf of
>> Queen Christina of Sweden to the Scottish Covenanter
>> envoy John Cochrane, 1640 (*Riksråd* Debates, 1640).

These quotations paint very different pictures of Scotland and the Scottish people. For the twelfth-century Arab scholar, Scotland was on the periphery of the world.

Little had changed for a Venetian ambassador in seventeenth-century London. Piero Contarini's statement was based on second-hand reports filtered through the often hostile lens of jealous English courtiers, who felt snubbed by the number of Scots at the court of King James. Yet, crucially, neither the Arab nor the Venetian had first-hand experience of Scotland, or of many of the Scots whose native land they disparaged. To the Dutch official in Ambon, 'wild Scots' provided a common point of reference in describing indigenous Asian tribesmen to fellow Dutchmen – both sender and recipient must have had a knowledge of Gaels. The Danish princess who moved to Scotland as a young teenager longed for the country described as barbarous by an ambassador to her husband's court. Given the topographical and architectural differences between the two locations, her words actually suggest that she preferred Scotland to her own country of birth. The chancellor of Sweden noted something equally positive. A sixty-year connection with Scotland was sufficiently important to risk Swedish intervention on behalf of Scottish subjects rebelling against their anointed monarch (Grosjean 2003, 165–90).

The various opinions and descriptions reflect the different degrees of contact with Scotland experienced by the individuals quoted. Thus, depending on the sources consulted, one might conclude that Scotland was either a backward and remote country cut off from developments in the wider world, or, alternatively, a place of some influence and value among the European community of nations.

This chapter aims to help you to understand Scotland's connections with Europe in the early modern period. During this period the nation underwent a number of confessional realignments, moving, far from seamlessly, from being a Roman Catholic country at the start of the period to a Calvinist presbyterian one by the Treaty of Union in 1707. This confessional realignment was accompanied by a radical shift away from the traditional political axis of the Auld Alliance between Scotland and France. The rump Kalmar Union kingdoms of Denmark-Norway remained important, while England became a focus of Scottish diplomatic attention as the two converged through the Protestantism of both nations. Intermittently, Sweden and the Dutch Republic were also courted by those who held power in Scotland. At times the emissaries of Scottish governments and the agents of the opposition contested for the attention of foreign potentates. Their awareness of the importance of international support ensured that many European governments were kept abreast of Scottish affairs. Countless Scots involved themselves abroad in whichever trade or profession they could, regardless of official government policy. They were often to be found in the service of the expanding commercial empires of Spain, Portugal, the Dutch and the English. They corresponded with home and often returned to Scotland, where they informed their friends, families and communities of the world they encountered. Some put their experiences into print, most famously the soldier Robert Monro and the traveller William Lithgow (Monro 1637; Lithgow 1632). Such writings informed contemporary Scots about the wider world in which they lived, and also provide modern historians with valuable sources with which to try to make sense of Scotland's relations with Europe in the early modern period.

GEOGRAPHICAL AND POLITICAL ORIENTATION

Scotland entered the sixteenth century a Catholic country surrounded by Catholic neighbours in a Europe which was homogeneous in terms of religion. The relationship between Scotland and her neighbours was therefore shaped by other factors, such as shared histories of trade, commerce, war and politics. Such events left early modern Scots with a distinct view of Europe, in which their nation had frequently been at war with her closest neighbour: England. That fact, in turn, had necessitated strong alliances with other neighbours, not least France and the constituent countries of the Scandinavian Kalmar Union (Denmark, Norway and Sweden).

Margaret, daughter of Christian I of the Kalmar Union became the queen of James III in July 1469. Among other things, the marriage also saw the transfer of the Orkney and Shetland Islands to the Scottish crown from the kingdom of Norway, as a pledge for the four-fifths of Margaret's dowry that remained unpaid. The Scottish–Scandinavian pact that resulted from the marriage treaty of 1469 was eventually expanded thirty years later to include France, through the re-confirmation of the Treaty of Denmark (1499), which confirmed the 1469 arrangement and made provision for the re-confirmation of the Franco–Scottish Auld Alliance. After 1521, however, Scandinavia entered a period of domestic turmoil, ending with Gustav Vasa establishing himself as king of an independent Sweden and Frederik I ruling over the rump of the Kalmar Union, the united kingdom of Denmark-Norway. Subsequently, Scottish political connections with Denmark diminished. Perhaps surprisingly, Scottish involvement in the inter-Scandinavian crisis focused on supporting Sweden in its bid for independence. The result of this process has become known as 'The Unofficial Alliance', which endured from 1569 to 1654 (Grosjean 2003). A further reorientation of Scottish diplomacy followed the English invasion of Scotland in the 1540s: the 'Rough Wooing'. While the Auld Alliance with France was reasserted during the 1550s, many Scots began to fear annexation by France, under the guise of French support against England (Mason 1998, 160). The success of the Reformation in Scotland in 1560, combined with the reassertion of Protestantism in England under Elizabeth, drove Scotland and France apart. Protestant strongholds in Germany, Switzerland and the Low Countries also assumed a new importance for Scotland. The most significant shift in international relations resulting from these developments was the end to nearly three hundred years of hostility between Scotland and England, ushering in a period of peace which lasted for ninety years.

Between the Reformation and the beginning of the personal reign of James VI in 1585, those in power in Scotland tended to concentrate on internal affairs. In 1586 an 'amity' was agreed with England, while embassies continued to be exchanged between Scotland and Denmark-Norway in the hope of renewing the Northern Alliance and finding a Protestant bride for James. In 1589, Anna of Denmark married James VI by proxy and the young groom set off to collect his bride, arriving in Norway on 28 October 1589 and marrying Anna in person in Oslo soon after (Stevenson 1997, 34–40). The royal couple returned to Scotland on 1 May 1590 and an alliance was established that was to be of significance across Britain and Ireland after 1603; indeed it lasted as the principal British overseas alliance until 1645 (Murdoch 2003). The union of crowns saw Scotland's alliances dictating the foreign policy of the three Stewart kingdoms, with King James projecting himself abroad as James I of Great Britain and Ireland (Murdoch 2000, 93–107). The English war with Spain was brought to a close in 1604, a new 'British' treaty with France was drawn up in 1605, and the alliance with Denmark-Norway formed the centrepiece of British foreign policy throughout the reign of King James. Only the marriage of his daughter Elizabeth to Frederick V of the Palatinate in 1613 would add the dimension that ultimately altered the Stewart-Oldenburg alliance. When Frederick accepted the throne of Bohemia and made Elizabeth a queen, the whole of Europe became embroiled in what is known as the Thirty Years' War (1618–48).

The wars in Europe, often called the 'German Wars' or the 'War of Religion' by contemporary Scots, brought Scotland and the wider world into contact, alliance and conflict. The British civil wars did likewise. The Covenanters sought foreign support for their military campaign against Charles I. Through a broad network of agents and emissaries, the Covenanters managed to gain significant military and material support from Sweden and the Dutch Republic. The Swedish *Riksråd* debates provide a unique insight into the way in which the Scots portrayed their revolution to a foreign power and allow us a rare glimpse of a foreign perspective on Scotland: questions were asked abroad that would have seemed unnecessary to the indigenous Scottish audience (Grosjean 2000, 115–38). While Swedish support might have been anticipated, the fact that France, the native country of Queen Henrietta-Maria of England, remained neutral can be traced directly to the activities of Scottish Jesuits like Thomas Chambers and their ability to gain military resources from Scotland in return for the neutrality and good will of Cardinal Richelieu. More surprising is the correspondence from Christian IV of Denmark-Norway, which conceded that the Covenanters had a just cause, and his failure to support his own nephew, Charles I, against his rebellious subjects (Murdoch 2003, 92–110).

The Irish Rebellion of 1641 and the English civil war which broke out in 1642 also affected Scotland's international role. The Solemn League and Covenant of 1643, which imposed presbyterianism in England, was pressed on England by the Scots in return for Scottish military aid against Charles I. It also led to the formation of the Committee of Both Kingdoms, a body responsible for the foreign policy of Scotland and England (Murdoch 2003, 135). Not content with this, the Scots wanted to turn the good will shown to them by Sweden and the Dutch Republic during the 'Bishops' Wars' (1639–40) into something more tangible. The plan was to establish a confederal polity comprising Scotland, Sweden and the Dutch Republic, with the intention that England would also join (Young 2001, 87–103). This new 'super-state' was much debated but never realised, the English parliament in particular being suspicious of it. It is arguable that here, during these negotiations, Scotland lost its place as a significant European power. While the Scots understood the Solemn League and Covenant as a confederal alliance between the two British kingdoms, England saw it as a useful expedient to be removed at the first

opportunity. Thus, while Covenanters working towards the creation of the confederal super-state believed their English counterparts to be doing the same, the truth
was that Scotland was being marginalised as English diplomats pressed the agenda
of the English parliament rather than that of the Solemn League and Covenant
(Grosjean 2003, 200–10). The alliance was unilaterally dissolved by the southern
partner in 1647 and the reinvigorated English parliament took on the role of leading
British policy abroad for the first time since 1603.

The execution of Charles I saw Scotsmen trying once more to exert their influence
abroad. Most Scots held firmly to monarchy and the declaration of an English
republic in 1649 soon led to Anglo-Scottish war. The invasion, conquest and
occupation of Scotland by Cromwell's armies between 1650 and 1659 pushed
Scotland off the European political stage. However, with the restoration of Charles
II in 1660, Scotland's independence was restored. Through a series of acts passed in
1661–62, bishops were restored to the church and all ministers appointed since
1649 were ordered to resign and offer themselves for reinstatement by the lay
patrons of their churches. Not everyone was willing to conform and several hundred
ministers who continued to support the Covenants were deposed and began to hold
open air services called 'conventicles'. Royal dragoons violently dispersed these
conventicles, provoking armed rebellion, which was also severely dealt with (see
chapter 4). Fear of co-ordinated risings in Scotland by Covenanters in consort with
the Dutch in the various Anglo-Dutch wars of the 1660s and 1670s produced
attempts at limited reconciliation through various 'Acts of Indulgence'. These failed
to placate extreme Covenanters and something akin to a confessional civil war
broke out between legal ministers and 'field-preachers' operating within the same
parishes. The staunchest Covenanters, later known as Cameronians, produced
documents such as 'The Sanquhar Declaration', in which they set out their vision
of a covenanted state and eventually renounced their allegiance to the king. Many of
those who were not killed or captured went into exile and formed a community
based in the Dutch Republic, where they gained support from the government of
William of Orange (Gardner 2005, 277–99). Other presbyterian exiles moved out
from their Dutch base to numerous destinations, including the Lithuanian town of
Kėdainiai. From the 1660s onwards, Scottish Calvinists began to arrive there in such
numbers that they dominated the town's administration, attracting many Scottish
exiles to join them and forming a community that lasted into the middle of the
eighteenth century (Žirgulis 2005, 239–45). Another well-disposed city was the
North Sea port of Bremen. After moving there from Amsterdam in 1683, the English
exile Sir William Waller became governor of the city. He sought both Englishmen
and Scots to settle in the town, granting them the freedom of the city. The majority
who came were Calvinist exiles (Murdoch 2006, 111).

In the 'Glorious Revolution' of 1688–9, James VII & II was replaced by his own
daughter and son-in-law, Mary and William of Orange. William brought with him
many of the Scottish exiles in his entourage and the regiments of his Scots Brigade.
Episcopacy was once more overturned and the presbyterians were again in the
driving seat in Scotland. They ensured their status was secured through the 'Claim of

Right' and the 'Act Abolishing Prelacy' in 1689 and the 'Act Establishing Presbyterian Government' in the following year. Many presbyterian exiles returned home,
while a new exodus of episcopalian refugees occurred, firstly to England and then to
the Continent, where they formed the core of the European Jacobite community.

MILITARY MIGRATIONS

Throughout the sixteenth and seventeenth centuries, Scottish soldiers could be found
fighting in the armies of most European powers. They served both as individuals, in
small groups and in larger formations, including entire armies. The larger military
migrations of the early modern period occurred after 1560. Indeed it is no
coincidence that in the post-Reformation era the location of Scottish troops
frequently mirrored a desire to strike up a political alliance with a similarly reformed
state such as the Dutch Republic. Between 1573 and 1579 some 3,100 Scots were
levied for service in the Low Countries to assist in the fight against Catholic Spain,
known in the Netherlands as the Eighty Years' War (1568–1648). Within a few
years of the outbreak of war, a permanent Scots Brigade was formed in the Dutch
Republic and this remained in service until the end of the eighteenth century
(Ferguson 1899). The brigade of three regiments not only ensured improved
relations between the two states but also provided for a Scottish element in resisting
the counter-Reformation, without actually having to commit Scotland directly to
war against Spain or the Habsburg Empire. The military formations brought with
them chaplains to preach the Scottish interpretation of Calvinism in their own
languages: Scots and Gaelic. Thus the religious rationale for service and links with
home were maintained throughout the life of the regiment. Foreign service often
radicalised the soldiers, who returned to Scotland more confessionally aware than
when they had left.

At this time, Scots also became a more regular component of Scandinavian armies.
Though having served in small bands of mercenaries since the start of the century, a
new incentive drove many more to serve in the second half of the century. In the
1570s Archibald Ruthven received a royal licence to levy 1,600 Scots for Sweden
(Grosjean 2003, 14–24). This Scottish presence in Sweden was complicated by the
re-establishment of the Scottish–Danish alliance of 1589, for it entailed mutual
support in all wars. The presence of so many Scots in Swedish service led to the
likelihood of Scots facing each other in opposing armies – privately-enlisted soldiers
standing against an official allied force sent by their own sovereign. Clever
diplomacy by James VI averted conflict between these two groups in 1612, during
the intra-Scandinavian Kalmar War (1611–13), after his ambassador, Sir Robert
Anstruther, clarified the danger to him (Murdoch 2003, 40). Additional clauses
were then added to warrants for private military contractors which allowed them
only to recruit and serve in armies which were not hostile to the Stewarts or their
allies. With Scots soldiers now regularly engaged in France, the Dutch Republic and
the Scandinavian kingdoms, patterns of service and loyalty emerged which lasted
throughout the early modern period. These countries all participated in the Thirty

Years' War and in doing so brought Scotsmen into the heart of the Habsburg Empire.

When Frederick the Elector Palatine accepted the throne of Bohemia in 1619, in defiance of the soon-to-be Habsburg emperor, Ferdinand II, war ensued. Frederick's marriage to Elizabeth, daughter of James VI, led some 50,000 Scots and a similar number of Englishmen to volunteer for the war in support of Elizabeth and Frederick (Murdoch 2001, 14). A much smaller group – mostly officers – opted to serve within the Habsburg armies, from which vantage point some also claimed to be working for Elizabeth Stewart's cause (Worthington 2004, 235–41). The first Scot to join the Bohemian army was the Catholic Sir Andrew Gray, who recruited 1,500 Scots and 1,000 Englishmen in 1620. They fought alongside Colonel James Seaton's Scottish regiment of 1,000 men, which had been 'borrowed' from the Dutch Republic by James VI and had reached the conflict before Gray's 'Regiment of Brittons'. The Bohemian army collapsed under the Imperial offensive at White Mountain in November 1620. Nonetheless, Seaton held the Bohemian town of Trebon until 1622, nearly eighteen months after the rest of the army had disintegrated (Polisensky 2001, 111–14). Gray recruited in Scotland again in 1624 and eventually led 4,000 Scots in an army of 12,000 Britons to serve in Count Mansfeld's private army. Over 6,000 of these men died *en route*, and after the destruction of the remnants of Mansfeld's forces in 1626, the survivors joined the Scandinavian armies.

The devastation of this force, as much due to inept leadership as disease, dissuaded the Scottish nobility from participating in future private ventures. They even baulked at joint initiatives with the English (Murdoch 2003, 205–6). They therefore opted to levy and supply forces to serve under the leadership of Christian IV of Denmark–Norway, who entered the war against the Habsburgs in 1625. By March 1627, patents were issued to raise 9,000 Scots for Danish-Norwegian service. These were to be in three regiments of 3,000 under three Scottish colonels: Alexander Lindsay, Lord Spynie; James Sinclair, Baron Murckle; and the Catholic Robert Maxwell, earl of Nithsdale. They joined 2,000 Scots already in Danish service under Donald MacKay, who had left Mansfeld's service to fight for the Danish king. The impact of Scottish commanders in the Danish-Norwegian army was even more significant than the total number of Scots serving. Between 1625 and 1629, over three hundred Scottish officers joined the army of Christian IV, outnumbering indigenous officers by three to one. Twenty-five held the rank of major or above while two became generals: Robert Scott and the earl of Nithsdale (Murdoch 2003, 201–25). The efforts of the Danish-Norwegian army against Emperor Ferdinand came to nought and Christian IV retired from the war in 1629 through the Treaty of Lübeck. This treaty paved the way for Swedish intervention and many of the remaining Scots in Christian's service were cashiered and transferred to the Swedish army.

Along with those who had enlisted in anticipation of Gustav II Adolf's entry into the war, these new recruits brought the total of Scots in Swedish service by late 1630 to around 12,000. By the war's end in 1648, some 30,000 had fought in Germany on behalf of Sweden. Of the 3,262 officers at the disposal of Gustav II Adolf in 1632, over 410 (one in eight) were Scots. Between 1624 and 1660 the Scots produced eight field marshals and generals, over seventy colonels and fifty lieutenant-colonels, providing an officer corps that the Swedes themselves found hard to match (Grosjean 2003, 74–111). Recruiting for Sweden continued throughout the period and many reinforcements arrived from Scotland throughout the 1630s. The supply dried up in 1638, however, due to growing tensions in Scotland between the Stewart monarchy and the Covenanters, who began to build their own army to take on their king. Tens of thousands of Scots had fought against the armies of the Catholic Habsburgs and their allies for years. They did not want to see their endeavours on behalf of the Protestant cause abroad overturned at home by Charles I foisting what they viewed as crypto-Catholic Anglican uniformity upon the Scottish church.

It was not only Protestant states that opposed the Habsburg domination of Europe, however. Any Catholic state that joined the anti-Habsburg alliance, or that would not ally with the Habsburgs, could expect Scottish recruits. Thus Venice enlisted several thousand Scots throughout the 1630s and 1640s. When Franco-Habsburg relations deteriorated in the 1630s, it became clear that France would enter the war on the side of Sweden. Although France had continued to receive token military support from Scotland in the form of the king's personal Guarde Ecossais, larger migrations followed in anticipation of French entry into the war. The marquis of Huntly raised a regiment for France in 1632 and another entered French service in 1634 under Sir James Hepburn, with reinforcements arriving in 1637. The following year Lord Andrew Gray's regiment joined the other two. All three regiments were led by Catholics but, as Cardinal Richelieu noted, the majority of the troops were presbyterians and the anti-Habsburg motive highlighted in earlier Scottish participation remained relevant in French service (Glozier 2001, 118–21). The valued presence of these Scottish troops also helped to ensure that France did not intervene in the conflict developing in Scotland between Charles I and the Covenanters.

The Treaty of London in August 1641 formally concluded hostilities between the Covenanters and Charles I, allowing recruitment for the European theatre to resume. James Campbell, earl of Irvine, established a regiment of 4,500 men for the king of France. The regiment of Lord James Douglas, formerly Hepburn's, received new recruits in 1642, as did that commanded by Colonel James Fullerton. During the 1640s, warrants were issued to raise 10,320 Scots for French service. Soon after the Treaty of Westphalia, which brought the Thirty Years War to an end in 1648, the Scottish units in French service were merged as the Regiment de Douglas (Glozier 2004, 41–7). The Cromwellian conquest of Scotland in 1651 made it hard for many to return home and significant numbers of refugee Scottish soldiers remained abroad. Most followed traditional patterns of service in Scandinavia and the Low Countries, though some put themselves up for hire to whoever would pay them. Thus high-profile individuals like General Patrick Gordon, who served in Russia, or colonels John Mollison and Andrew Melville, serving under the duke of Lüneburg-Celle, became internationally famous for their military service (Ameer-Ali 1918).

After the failure of a royalist rising in the middle of the 1640s, individual officers travelled across Europe with commissions from Charles I. They sought enlistment in countries friendly to the Stewart monarchy, where they could await the better fortune of their king at home. This led to some regiments, such as the Bergenhus in Norway, being commanded by a Scottish royalist officer cadre overseeing Norwegian troops. By the 1650s, it was not just royalists who found themselves in this position. Scots of all persuasions looked to escape the 'Cromwellian usurpation'; indeed the option of foreign service over imprisonment was offered by the English authorities to those Scots still in arms as an enticement to end their uprising. So it was that another Scandinavian enlistment occurred in 1655–6, when Lord Cranstoun and William Vavasour each led regiments of 2,000 to Sweden (Grosjean 2002, 61–82). Other smaller groups went to France, Poland-Lithuania and Russia, while the Dutch Republic continued to absorb forces into the Scots Brigade. The private forces of the Dutch East India Company, the Dutch West India Company and various other colonial armies also absorbed Scottish volunteers (Murdoch 2002, 63–76; Mijers 2006, 243–54).

From the Stewart restoration of 1660 until the period following the defeat of the Jacobites in 1746, political changes in Scotland drove various waves of military refugees to the continent, usually to the Dutch Republic, but also to the traditional recipients of Scottish servicemen in France and Scandinavia. As the Stewarts returned to power in 1660, their enemies departed. This pattern repeated itself after William of Orange gained the 'vacant' Scottish throne in 1689, which led to an exodus of Stewart supporters (Jacobites) to the Continent. They enlisted in armies as far afield as Russia, Sweden, France and Spain (Murdoch 2006, 313–54). However, despite the presence in Europe of several hundred Jacobite officers after the failed Jacobite risings of the eighteenth century, the age of mass Scottish overseas enlistment had ceased. After 1707, the majority of Scottish servicemen fought across the globe as part of the British army. It was fitting that the last regular Scottish military force in continental Europe was one of the first established – the Scots Brigade – 'nationalised' as a Dutch regiment in 1782, with many of her officers and men disbanding and returning home (Migglebrink 2002, 83–103).

It is hard to ascertain whether those who left Scotland ever intended to return, or if they saw their military migration as temporary. In any case, many did not see their homeland again. Through a combination of disease, combat and shipwreck, rates of attrition could be extremely high, depending where they served during particular campaigns: William Lithgow's poem to Charles I in 1633 noted that some 12,000 out of 13,500 Scots in Danish service were killed between 1626 and 1629 alone:

> Thus look to Denmark where twelve thousand ly
> Serving thine Uncle, sharpest fortunes try.
> (Lithgow 1633, pp. 2–3)

Soldiers in the Scots Brigade fared much better, as did those stationed in garrisons rather than on field duty in countries like Norway, Sweden and Poland-Lithuania.

Many veterans did return to Scotland after protracted periods of military service abroad. For example, Field Marshal Alexander Leslie served in Sweden for some thirty years before leading several hundred Scots back to serve in the army of the Covenant in 1638. Their return on this occasion serves to highlight that lengthy foreign employment, even when rewarded by lands and titles, did not necessarily extinguish an interest in their homeland for many of the Scottish professional soldiers.

A continued concern for their native soil was not exclusive to the fighting men in a regiment. Military chaplains in Sweden, such as Robert Douglas, were also in constant contact with their homeland and delivered sermons abroad persuading the soldiers of the just cause of the Covenanters at home. Indeed, Douglas went on to become moderator of the General Assembly after his return with Alexander Leslie. A similar, though less successful, return migration was orchestrated from abroad by other Scottish veterans in 1649 under the marquis of Montrose, keen to dislodge the pro-presbyterian government secured by Leslie's efforts a decade previously (Grosjean 2003, 214–37). Thus these soldiers proved that not all Scots in foreign service sang from the same hymn sheet, even those of the same confessional orientation. Indeed, Montrose's chaplain, George Wishart, fled Scotland in the 1650s to join the Scots Brigade in the Dutch Republic as chaplain and to preach to the Scottish congregation at Schiedam. In something of a recurring cycle, two further attempts were launched on Scotland from abroad; one in 1685 by a Calvinist refugee army led by the marquis of Argyll spectacularly failed. However, the arrival in Britain of the Scots Brigade with William of Orange in 1688–90 at last saw the original rationale of the brigade – the protection of Protestantism in Europe – achieve its goal in Scotland (and England) as they swept aside the forces of the last Catholic Stewart monarch, James VII and II. In doing so, they completed the presbyterian settlement of Scotland which Leslie's army had sought to achieve in 1639.

COMMERCIAL MIGRATIONS

The service of Scottish soldiers, particularly in the Thirty Years' War, tends to dominate discussions of the movement of Scots abroad in the seventeenth century, and to overshadow the role of migrant Scots in commercial activities. The 'packman' (pedlar) was historically linked to the Scottish martial tradition: stories portraying packmen picking up weapons to fight at the first opportunity became common in Poland-Lithuania and Prussia (Frost 2001, 195–212). Packmen were only part of a much more complex mercantile hierarchy. They tended to work for travelling merchants, who in turn were employed by larger syndicates. These sent their merchant factors to a specific location, where they bought and sold their goods. They employed packmen, who stocked up from factories and warehouses in established towns, and also employed apprentices and servants.

Scottish packmen tended to work from private houses and did business on credit or in exchange for farm produce and raw materials. With fewer overheads and greater freedom of movement than native merchants, the Scots could sell the same goods as their competitors but at a cheaper rate. In December 1666, Hugh Acland noted that Scots pedlars in Cornwall could 'sell their wares 2d in a shilling cheaper than the shopkeepers in the area. Due to such practices, laws were passed in numerous locations to try to redress the balance in favour of local shopkeepers. Denmark was one of several places forbidding Scottish merchants from sending their servants into the countryside to hawk their wares and barring them from municipal rights unless they could prove they were residents (Riis 1998, vol. 1, 87). Duke Albrecht of Brandenburg issued a similar edict in Prussia in 1558. This was followed by a ban on Scots peddling their wares in the Polish countryside in 1566. In Norway in 1607, the bakers guild of Bergen sought and received guarantees that Scots sailors could sell bread only in the market. This was confirmed in the 1620s, with the addition that they were not allowed to become itinerant pedlars.

Poland-Lithuania also introduced legislation against the Scots at the end of the sixteenth century (Murdoch 2006, 131). The sheer quantity of immigrants placed tensions on the relations between the Scots and their host communities, eventually leading to action by Sigismund III in 1594 designed to curb the influx. His measures had little effect, so the Scottish factor in Poland, Patrick Gordon, drew up a strict code in 1616 to try to alleviate the problem. However, this and other Scottish requests also failed, compelling the Scottish community in Danzig to seek the intervention of James VI to prevent any more arrivals. In response, King James sent another Scottish agent, Hugh Mowatt, to Poland to try to resolve the problem, though again with little effect. Several estimates of 30,000 Scots were reported around 1620–1, with the number rising to 50,000 by the middle of the century. Regardless of the truth of such figures – and they are certainly worthy of healthy scepticism – belief in their accuracy caused uproar among indigenous traders (Kowalski 2005, 63–4). Was the resulting legislation designed to address this plague of Scots, or is it more likely that Thomas Fischer was correct when he wrote that it demonstrated an 'inability to withstand a sudden, keen competition of trade'? (Fischer 1902, 37) Whatever the case, packmen continued their trade and remained a common sight across northern Europe. Notable diarists like Patrick Gordon met them on their travels, recording 'that there were diverse Scottishmen who used this kind of trade in Prussia' (Gordon 1859, 10).

Although King James appears to have supported attempts to curb the flow of pedlars to Europe, he probably understood well the benefits to the Scottish economy of allowing them to go. It both rid him of the problem of a redundant population and allowed his subjects to accumulate mercantile expertise. Further, just as commercial opportunities were opened up in the larger English companies, such as the East India Company, the Muscovy Company and the Eastland Company, his accession to the English throne also opened up England and her colonies to increased attention from the Scots. This was facilitated by a growing demand abroad for Scottish wool, mutton and livestock, due to rising populations (Murdoch 2006, 132). While the stereotype of the Scottish pedlar remains strong, there is a growing understanding that the packmen themselves were only one cog in a much larger and more sophisticated machine of Scottish commercial activity on the Continent. One Polish scholar has observed:

In Polish historiography, there exists a stereotype of a Scottish merchant as a small pedlar going on foot from village to village, with a basket of goods on his back. In contrast to this picture, the Gdansk sources present us with an image of a rather well-to-do and even rich merchant engaging in long distance trade, taking an active part in the great Baltic commerce, especially in the exchange between the British Isles and Gdansk.

(Bogucka 2000, 41)

It was believed that the packmen maintained little contact with their native country or 'respectable' merchants residing with them abroad. Bogucka has suggested something rather more complex: that pedlars formed an important interface between Britain and the Baltic. They not only managed to bring the goods of Scottish peasants to market (often cloth products such as home-produced hats, gloves and linen), but they also served as intermediaries between those involved in cottage industries and the wealthier Scottish merchants both at home and abroad. Pedlars, in turn, were employed by the merchants to take more refined goods back into the countryside or wherever they could best be traded. With the profits gained, the merchants could build enough capital to move further afield (Murdoch 2006, 134–5). The choices of destination were not random. Scottish pedlars, apprentices and merchants were attracted to locations where their countrymen had already settled or had some knowledge of favourable conditions awaiting them. Once successfully located, they would repeat the process, inviting friends to join them and establishing migration chains (Grosjean & Murdoch 2005, 1–19). Over time, this process could be boosted as the number of well-heeled merchants, burgesses, councillors and other Scots of high station within the host societies grew. They were helped by governmental insistence on the plantation of thousands of Scots in Ulster after 1609, which many used simply as a gateway to richer pastures throughout Ireland (Fitzgerald 2005, 27–52). Another new destination was the American colonies, although far fewer went there than to Ireland or to the more traditional destinations in the Baltic region until the eighteenth century (Dobson 2005, 105–31).

    In the Baltic, the Scots did not establish a mercantile monopoly as did the English Eastland Company, or Muscovy Company, although the Elbing staple was initially something of a joint venture. The lack of formal companies proved to be to the advantage of the Scots in the long run, though several attempts were made to form companies to trade with Africa, the East Indies and the American colonies. Yet, with no company to restrict their exports to any one port, Scottish traders simply went wherever markets were best, often to the annoyance of their competitors. Irritating or not, the Scottish merchants in Elbing and Danzig have been singled out for their important role in facilitating Sweden's mercantile growth as well as that between Britain and the Baltic. Part of their success lay in their willingness both to exploit the networks that had brought them out of Scotland and to develop new ones through integration into host societies. This was not an option for those involved with mercantile monopolies (Murdoch 2006, 135–6). Thus, when the Eastland Company lost many of its trading privileges in Elbing in 1626, Scottish merchants unattached to the company were unaffected, in particular the family of Charles Ramsay, who had taken citizenship in the city in 1614. When the merchant Robert Jollie exported goods from Scotland to Hamburg in 1683, he was impeded from selling them because he was not a member of the *English* Company of Merchant Adventurers there. The Hamburg authorities argued that he was therefore in breach of an article between the city and the English company. As Jollie pointed out, that was an agreement between the city and the subjects of the king of England and thus did not apply to Scots, who were not bound by that contract (Zickermann 2005, 270). This argument was accepted and he continued to trade to and from the city with Scottish goods into the eighteenth century.

While Jollie opted to pursue his independent mercantile activities, Charles Ramsay was more typical of a merchant class happy to settle and take citizenship abroad. Many settled across the German-speaking Baltic coast from Pomerania to East Prussia, though trying to gauge numbers is fraught with problems. However, for the Polish-Lithuanian Commonwealth, specific figures are available: 5,969 settled Scottish merchants have been identified, some 500 of those in Danzig (Bogucka 2000, 40). Some of them were decommissioned soldiers: several merchants of Thorn in Prussia after 1659 were former soldiers of Lord Cranstoun's Scottish regiment, which had held the town for Sweden throughout the siege of 1657–8 – men like William and James Fraser (Fraser 1905, 424). Equally important were the large Scottish communities in Lithuania, particularly the sizeable Calvinist one established in the 'private' town of Kėdainiai (Žirgulis 2005, 225–45). Many of the Scots within the commonwealth formed themselves into brotherhoods and societies, which had seats in Danzig, Lublin and about a dozen locations throughout Poland. These were frequently used to conceal illegal Scottish immigrants who traded in the towns, and thus bolstered the Scottish population (Kowalski 2005, 80).

In many places there was less need for stealth. Under the terms of the Stewart-Oldenburg marriage alliance of 1589, Scots theoretically enjoyed the same status as Danes and Norwegians in their countries, while Danes and Norwegians would gain similar rights in Scotland. Norway sustained numerous Scottish communities engaged in the timber trade around Stavanger, Bergen and Trondheim. So important was the timber trade that in Norway it is still called *Skottehandelen* (the Scottish trade), while the sixteenth and seventeenth centuries are known as the *Skottetiden* (Scottish period) of Norwegian history (Pedersen 2005, 152). The importance of Norway to Scottish trade becomes apparent when one considers that some 150 Scots became burgesses in Bergen alone between 1600 and 1660. These burgesses were only one strand of the Norwegian settlement. For instance, some twenty Scottish families moved into Finnmark to take advantage of the patronage of the Scottish governor, John Cunningham (Hagen 2003, 35–7). Another group in the employ of the Dutch-based Scot, Sir William Davidson, operated the iron works at Mostadmark near Trondheim (Murdoch 2006, 195–202). While the majority of Scots settled in Norway, significant communities also evolved at Elsinore and Copenhagen, with a scattering of Scottish merchants throughout the rest of Denmark, mostly engaged in the 'carrier trade' in the Baltic Sea.

In Sweden, the situation regarding citizenship was less formalised. Despite the passing of the *Handelsordination* (Decree of Trade) in 1607, which limited non-burgess traders to an 8-week period of activity in Sweden per annum, in 1638 it was revealed that 70 merchants had undertaken trade for as long as twelve years without becoming burgesses (Ashton 2003, 9). Many of these retained strong links with their families in Scotland. Patrick Lyall sourced £3,000 sterling-worth of naval supplies in Sweden for the British Admiralty. There was a delay in receiving payment and an action was brought between him and the Royal Navy captain, John Strachan. Of great interest is Lyall's assertion that delay in payment had led to people drawing more from his uncle, Arthur Lyall, than he had cash to hand and that this would cost him future commissions from 'four other uncles in Stockholm' (Murdoch 2006, 140). Such men also provided contacts within Swedish society for transient Scottish merchants. A good example is provided by the appearance of the Edinburgh merchant John Weir (Hans Wijr) in a Stockholm court. He and his 'principal', a fellow Edinburgh merchant Thomas Inglis (Engelssch), had lent some iron to the Flensburg skipper Cornelius Jönsson in 1615. When Weir wished to recall the loan in the following year (in iron or cash) he could not do so as Jönsson had died. The arrangement was traced through the related paperwork, which proves most useful for historians, as does Jönsson's illiteracy: a small, cohesive Scottish network involving transient and embedded merchants is illuminated. Because he could not write, Jönsson asked the Scots Wellam Fernie (Fernij) and David Ramsay to draw up a document in Scots to which he would append his mark. This document was produced in court, and it shows that the two Edinburgh-based merchants (Weir and Inglis) were in contact with two other Scots in Sweden (Fernie and Ramsay). It also shows that Weir was a resident and burgess of Nyköpping and therefore an obvious partner for other Edinburgh merchants (Murdoch 2006, 140).

For the numerous Scots like John Weir who opted to become citizens of Swedish burghs, their choice proved advantageous. The best-known group are those in the fledgling city of Gothenburg: about fifty Scottish merchants and their families established themselves there between its foundation in 1621 and the end of the century. Among the Gothenburg Scots, John Maclean stood out both as an entrepreneur and allegedly as Sweden's second richest man after Louis de Geer. The Stockholm community was of longer standing and even more considerable than that at Gothenburg, with over a hundred identifiable Scottish merchants working from the city throughout the century (Grosjean & Murdoch 2005, 191–223). Norrköping supported a dozen or so Scottish merchant families, several of them branches of the Spaldings, but also merchants like James and Patrick Thomson, John Steel and David Kinloch. Importantly, these Scots did not confine themselves to trading, and many became involved in the production of goods such as cloth and iron *within* Sweden. In the later seventeenth century some twenty Scottish families owned no less than 45 Swedish foundries and forges, giving them a significant slice of the Swedish iron industry. They established networks to ensure their valuable commodity reached their countrymen and partners within Sweden, in Scotland and in third locations (Murdoch 2006, 170–205).

Influential Scottish entrepreneurs also resided at Riga, Narva and other place under Swedish control. Due to their integration they were not so badly affected as their competitors when the Swedish customs order of 1643 forbade 'foreigners' from having shares in cargoes. Citizenship for skippers and pilots carrying Swedish cargo was also enforced in 1667, while the wives of these men also had to live in Sweden (Murdoch 2006, 142). Those Scots who settled in the country thus had a significant advantage over their counterparts from England, who tended to remain for a short time before returning home 'to make their proper careers' (Müller 2003, 75). Though the examples selected here to illustrate the commercial network are chosen from the north of Europe, similar structures can be traced in numerous continental cities, including Rotterdam (Catterall 2005, 169–89) and Hamburg (Zickermann 2005, 249–73). Bruges, Paris, Bordeaux and the Mediterranean ports also supported Scottish merchants, companies and communities, though modern scholarship into the southern networks is yet in its infancy.

A final anchor in the mercantile network were the Scots resident in English cities, particularly London. Like their countrymen in southern Europe, Scottish migrants in England await serious scholarly attention for the early modern period. By 1610, Scots in England were already exploiting a legal loop-hole that allowed them to trade with the Low Countries without having to direct their goods to the Scottish staple port at Veere. The convention of royal burghs acted to close this back door and declared that any staple goods belonging to a Scottish merchant had to be delivered to Veere if destined for the Netherlands (Murdoch 2006, 142). Yet Andrew Russell's correspondence later in the century reveals the extent to which London-based Scots like James Foulis, John Robertson and William Jamieson were woven into the fabric of the northern European network. And they were not the only Scots based in England to be engaged in it. In Newcastle, the connection was through William Thomson, while Hull and Bristol were also tied in to the wider Scottish nation. Similarly, the Scots in Ulster and those smaller cohorts of Scots in the American colonies and the Dutch East Indies played their part. The importance of the commercial contacts built up between the merchant Scots in various locations simply cannot be underestimated, although the full extent of the global network awaits fuller investigation (Murdoch 2006, 127–69).

SCOTLAND AND EUROPE, SCOTLAND IN EUROPE

During the early modern period, long-standing foreign alliances, such as that with France, were eclipsed by the desire and need for firmer allies among the Protestant powers of Europe. This led to a strengthening of relations between the governments of Scotland and England, which in turn allowed for the Union of Crowns of 1603. The British alliance allowed the Scots to penetrate the English colonies in Ireland and the Americas, but, more importantly, England herself. Simultaneously, renewed Scottish alliances with Denmark-Norway and sympathetic relationships with Sweden and the Dutch Republic allowed for new rounds of chain migration, often bolstered by military participation in the continental wars. Indeed, the numbers and commitment of Scottish soldiery, and their rise to prominence in Russia, Sweden, France and Poland-Lithuania has diverted attention from the importance of civilian migration. To be sure, this often accompanied or resulted from military migrations, but as many civilians as soldiers probably left Scotland in the early modern period. The vast numbers going to Poland-Lithuania and Ulster alone are evidence for that. Their importance to the nation's development can too easily be forgotten, particularly when numerically smaller and usually disastrous migrations to the Americas, such as Nova Scotia (1629–33) or Darien (1698–1700), tend to dominate historical debate on early modern Scottish settlement abroad (Dobson 2005, 128–31). In truth, throughout the period it was Europe that drew the largest numbers of migrants and provided the greatest opportunities for Scottish soldiers and entrepreneurs; the Americas were of limited interest or importance.

The evidence available suggests that Scots who were prepared to integrate into foreign commercial and military empires (English, Dutch or Swedish) were more successful than those, such as the investors in the Company of Scotland, who tried to emulate English and Dutch mercantile monopolies and colonial ventures. The unobtrusiveness of integrated entrepreneurs abroad appears to have facilitated their success (Grosjean & Murdoch 2005, 19). For sure, their actions undoubtedly favoured the individual, the family or the specific consortium concerned, rather than the Scottish treasury directly. However, as Adam Smith reminded us:

[The entrepreneur] by directing that industry in such a manner as its produce may be of greatest value, he intends only his own gain, and he is in this, as in many other cases, led by an invisible hand to promote an end which was no part of his intention. Nor is it always the worse for the society that it was no part of it. By pursuing his own interest he frequently promotes that of the society more effectually than when he really intends to promote it.

(Smith 1863, 115–16)

This was as true for the commercially-minded Scots abroad as it was for their countrymen at home. Indeed, as one scholar has put it:

Instead of trying to separate Scotland from Scots communities overseas, it may be that for purposes such as calculating Scotland's economic and political impact it would make more sense to consider Scotland together with these communities.

(Catterall 2005, 188)

Given the unquestionable success of the overseas entrepreneurs, and their proven repatriation of both capital and commodity to Scotland, their contribution undoubtedly adds a significant and dynamic, if not yet fully-researched, dimension to Scotland's economic status on the eve of the 1707 British political union (Murdoch, 2006, 207–48). Of equal importance is the fact that the process of overseas integration within Europe did not end with or because of the 1707 union. There was no dramatic re-orientation in Scottish migratory patterns to the British colonies, or sudden abandonment of traditional European commercial partners. Those changes, when they did eventually happen, took decades to occur. Scrutiny of sources such as *The Letter-Book of Baillie John Steuart* (Mackay 1915) and numerous unpublished sources show that similar networks involving Scandinavia, the Baltic, the Dutch Republic and France continued long after 1707 and were not immediately replaced by Scots trying to grab a share of England's economic wealth or any dramatic shift west across the Atlantic. The establishment of the Swedish East India Company [SOIC] with the help of Colin Campbell and a host of other Scots confirms that infiltration continued as a useful economic device to Scots throughout the eighteenth century, allowing an additional route for Scots merchants to access the eastern trade (Murdoch 2006, 244). The formation of the SOIC in 1731 occurred in the same year as the formation of the first joint-stock company in Lithuania, Societatis Commerciorum – a project of nine Kėdainiai Scots, including the mayor of the town, Andrew Leith. They described themselves as British ('*Nationis Magna Britannia*'), established contacts with other Scottish concerns in Königsberg, Danzig and Riga, sought investment from Britain and thus established yet another commercial network similar to those operating throughout the previous century (Žirgulis 2005, 240–41).

Thus, consideration of Scotland and Europe, both before and after 1707, adds a fresh and exciting dimension to Scottish economic and social history. Set against, and in many ways aided by, the complex political and diplomatic background of early modern Europe, the entrepreneurial behaviour of the Scots anticipated a similar role for their countrymen within the British Empire by some considerable period of time. Understanding their activities offers challenges to the historian and provides a valuable addition to both Scottish and European history.

REFERENCES

Ameer-Ali, T. (ed) 1918 *Memoirs of Sir Andrew Melvill*. London.

Ashton, J.R. 2003 *Lives and Livelihoods in Little London*. Sävedalen.

Bogucka, M. 2000 'Scots in Gdańsk (Danzig) in the Seventeenth Century', in Macinnes, A.I., Riis, T. and Pedersen, F. (eds) *Ships, Guns and Bibles in the North Sea and Baltic States, c.1350–c.1700*, East Linton, 30–44.

Calder, A. 1981 *Revolutionary Empire: The Rise of the English Speaking Empires from the Fifteenth Century to the 1780s*. New York.

Catterall, D. 2005 'Scots along the Maas, c.1570–1750', in Grosjean A. and Murdoch, S. (eds) *Scottish Communities Abroad in the Early Modern Period*, Leiden, 169–89.

CSPV, Brown, R. *et al.* (eds) 1864–1947 *Calendar of State Papers and Manuscripts relating to English Affairs, existing in the Archives and Collections of Venice and in other Libraries of North Italy, 1206–[1674]*, 38 vols. London.

Dobson, D. 2005 'Seventeenth-Century Scottish Communities in the Americas', in Grosjean and Murdoch (eds) *Scottish Communities Abroad in the Early Modern Period*, 105–31.

Ferguson, J. (ed) 1899 *Papers Illustrating the History of The Scots Brigade in the service of the United Netherlands 1572–1782*, 3 vols. Edinburgh.

Fischer, T.A. 1902 *The Scots in Germany*. Edinburgh.

Fitzgerald, P. 2005 'Scottish Migration to Ireland in the Seventeenth Century', in Grosjean and Murdoch (eds) *Scottish Communities Abroad in the Early Modern Period*, 27–52.

Fraser, J. 1905 *Chronicles of the Frasers*, ed Mackay, W. Edinburgh.

Frost, R. 2001 'Scottish Soldiers, Poland-Lithuania and the Thirty Years' War', in Murdoch, S. (ed) 2001 *Scotland and the Thirty Years' War, 1618–1648*, Leiden, 191–213.

Gardner, G. 2005 'A Haven for Intrigue: the Scottish Exile Community in the Netherlands, 1660–1690', in Grosjean and Murdoch (eds) *Scottish Communities Abroad in the Early Modern Period*, 277–99.

Glozier, G. 2004 *Scottish Soldiers in France in the Reign of the Sun King: Nursery for Men of Honour*. Leiden.

Glozier, M. 2001 'Scots in the French and Dutch Armies during the Thirty Years' War', in Murdoch (ed) *Scotland and the Thirty Years' War, 1618–1648*, Leiden, 118–41.

Gordon, P. 1859 *Passages from the Diary of General Patrick Gordon of Auchleuchries, A.D. 1635–A.D. 1699*, ed Botfield, B. Aberdeen.

Grosjean, A. 2003 *An Unofficial Alliance: Scotland and Sweden, 1569–1654*. Leiden.

Grosjean, A. 2002 'Royalist Soldiers and Cromwellian Allies? The Cranstoun Regiment in Sweden, 1655–1658', in Murdoch, S. and Mackillop, A. (eds) *Fighting for Identity: Scottish Military Experience, c.1550–1900*, Leiden, 61–82.

Grosjean, A. 2000 'General Alexander Leslie, the Scottish Covenanters and the *Riksråd* Debates, 1638–1640', in Macinnes, Riis and Pedersen (eds) *Ships Guns and Bibles in the North Sea and the Baltic States, c.1350–1700*, 115–38.

Grosjean, A. and Murdoch, S. 2005 'The Scottish Community in Seventeenth-Century Gothenburg', in Grosjean and Murdoch (eds) 2005 *Scottish Communities Abroad in the Early Modern Period*, 191–223.

Hagen, R. 2003 'At the Edge of Civilisation: John Cunningham, Lensmann of Finmark, 1619–1651', in Mackillop, A. and Murdoch, S. (eds) *Military Governors and Imperial Frontiers, c.1600–1800: A Study of Scotland and Empires*, Leiden, 29–51.

Kowalski, W. 2005 'The Placement of Urbanised Scots in the Polish Crown during the Sixteenth and Seventeenth Centuries', in Grosjean and Murdoch (eds) *Scottish Communities Abroad in the Early Modern Period*, 53–103.

Lewis, B. 1982 *The Muslim Discovery of Europe*. London.

Lithgow, W. 1632 *The Totall Discourse of the Rare Adventures and painefull Perigrinations of Nineteene Yeares Travayles, from Scotland, to the most Famous Kingdomes in Europe, Asia, and Africa*. London.

Lithgow, W. 1633 *Scotland's Welcome to her Native Sonne, and Soveraigne Lord, King Charles*. Edinburgh.

Mackay, W. (ed) 1915 *The Letter-Book of Baillie John Steuart of Inverness, 1715–1752*. Edinburgh.

Mason, R. 1998 *Kingship and the Commonweal: Political Thought in Renaissance and Reformation Scotland*. East Linton.

Miggelbrink, J. 2002 'The End of the Scots-Dutch Brigade', in Murdoch and Mackillop (eds) *Fighting for Identity: Scottish Military Experience, c.1550–1900*, 83–103.

Mijers, E. 2006 'A Natural Partnership? Scotland and Zeeland in the early Seventeenth Century', in Macinnes, A.I. and Williamson, A.H. (eds) *Shaping the Stewart World 1603–1714: The Atlantic Connection*, Leiden, 233–60.

Monro, R. 1637 *His Expedition with the Worthy Scots Regiment called Mac-Keyes Regiment*. London.

Müller, L. 2003 'Britain and Sweden: the changing pattern of commodity exchange, 1650–1680', in Salmon, P. and Barrow, T. (eds) *Britain and the Baltic*, Sunderland, 21–46.

Murdoch, S. 2006 *Network North: Scottish Kin, Commercial and Covert Associations in Northern Europe, c.1603–1746.* Leiden.

Murdoch, S. 2003 *Britain, Denmark-Norway and the House of Stewart, 1603–1660: A Diplomatic and Military Analysis.* East Linton.

Murdoch, S. 2002 'The Good, the Bad and the Anonymous: A Preliminary Survey of the Scots in the Dutch East Indies 1612–1707', *Northern Scotland*, 22, 63–76.

Murdoch, S. (ed) 2001 *Scotland and the Thirty Years' War, 1618–1648.* Leiden.

Murdoch, S. 2000 'Diplomacy in Transition: Stewart-British Diplomacy in Northern Europe, 1603–1618', in Macinnes, Riis and Pedersen (eds) *Ships Guns and Bibles in the North Sea and the Baltic States, c.1350–1700*, East Linton, 93–114.

Pedersen, N.Ø. 2005 'Scottish Immigration to Bergen in the Sixteenth and Seventeenth Centuries', in Grosjean and Murdoch (eds) *Scottish Communities Abroad in the Early Modern Period*, 135–67.

Polisensky, J. 2001 'A Note on Scottish Soldiers in the Bohemian War, 1619–1622' and 'Scots in the French and Dutch Armies during the Thirty Years' War', in Murdoch (ed) *Scotland and the Thirty Years' War, 1618–1648*, Leiden, 109–16.

Riis, T 1988 *Should Auld Acquaintance Be Forgot . . . Scottish-Danish Relations c.1450–1707*, 2 vols. Odens.

Smith, A. 1863 edition *An Inquiry into the Nature and Causes of the Wealth of Nations*, Edinburgh, 115–16.

Smout, T.C. 1969 *A History of the Scottish People, 1560–1830.* London.

Stevenson, D. 1997 *Scotland's Last Royal Wedding: The Marriage of James VI and Anne of Denmark.* Edinburgh.

Terry, C.S. 1905 *The Pentland Rising and Rullion Green.* Glasgow.

Wodrow, R. 1835 *The History of the Sufferings of the Church of Scotland*, 4 vols. Glasgow.

Worthington, D. 2004 *Scots in Habsburg Service, 1618–1648.* Leiden.

Young, J.R. 2001 'The Scottish Parliament and European Diplomacy 1641–1647: The Palatine, The Dutch Republic and Sweden', in Murdoch (ed) *Scotland and the Thirty Years' War, 1618–1648*, 77–106.

Žirgulis, R. 2005 'The Scottish Community in Kėdainiai c.1630–1750', in Grosjean and Murdoch (eds) *Scottish Communities Abroad in the Early Modern Period*, 225–47.

Zickermann, K. 2005 '*Briteannia ist mein patria*: Scotsmen and the "British" Community in Hamburg', in Grosjean and Murdoch (eds) *Scottish Communities Abroad in the Early Modern Period*, Leiden, 249–73.

FURTHER READING

Mijers, E. 2005 'Scottish Students in the Netherlands, 1680–1730', in Grosjean and Murdoch (eds) *Scottish Communities Abroad in the Early Modern Period*, 301–31.

Worthington, D. 2001 'Alternative Diplomacy? Scottish exiles at the courts of the Habsburgs and their allies, 1618–1648', in Murdoch (ed) *Scotland and the Thirty Years' War, 1618–1648*, 51–75.

CHAPTER NINE

Urban Society and Economy
E. Patricia Dennison

Although it might sound paradoxical, the early modern period was a time of great change in urban Scotland; yet underneath these changes there was a surprising degree of continuity. Townspeople constituted as little as 5 to 10% of the population of Scotland at the beginning of this period. It was probably not more than 10% at the end, despite a steady rise in the overall population (Flinn 1977). And yet throughout many of the crises – political, economic and religious – that hit the country, towns held a tremendous sway on thinking in intellectual life, religion, the economy, and in aesthetic values: a distinct urban culture was emerging. So why were towns and townspeople important? This chapter aims to answer this question, and to explore a number of others, by looking at various aspects of life in Scottish towns between c.1500 and 1707.

Towns were both administrative and political centres, housing not only their own courts but also, in some cases, regality courts and sheriff courts, whose jurisdiction covered the surrounding countryside. Royal mints were always sited in towns; and parliament normally met in burgh tolbooths (municipal buildings), usually that of Edinburgh by this period. The king's household and entourage lodged in town houses, as well as palaces and castles. This close contact enabled privileged towns-people to serve the crown in many ways: as exchequer auditors, stewards in the royal household, deputies to the chamberlain, money-lenders to the crown and as part of diplomatic missions.

Most towns were also burghs. Burghs were created by a grant from the crown or, with royal permission, by nobles or senior churchmen; in this process a town obtained specific privileges, but also obligations. Burgh charters gave towns a near monopoly of markets. Only royal burghs and a few privileged ecclesiastical burghs (those with the right to send commissioners to parliament) were permitted to trade overseas in the Middle Ages. During this period, however, other burghs (called burghs of barony or burghs of regality) began to demand such rights for themselves, usually unsuccessfully before 1672.

The crown depended on parliamentary burghs for revenue to an extent which went considerably beyond their population. Ports brought in the great customs – duties levied on exports and, after 1597, imports as well. But parliamentary burghs also paid one sixth of national taxation and one of the key features of this period was the rising tax demands made by the crown. The share which each burgh paid was calculated by the convention of royal burghs, which met regularly and was by the early seventeenth century the most coordinated voice in politics, partly in response to what had by then become virtually annual taxation (Lynch 1992, 24). In order to meet their rising tax bills, burghs were forced into innovative devices: craftsmen were assessed individually rather than corporately; sons of merchants were taxed before they had become burgesses; lawyers, exempt from direct taxation, were charged for 'lent money', that is, the interest they made on loans; and *rentiers* were charged for their income (Lynch 1984, 10–11; Lynch 1987, 277–9). Burghs also began to use the novel device of the 'eke' (i.e. addition), by which sums for local purposes were grafted on to the regular demands for national taxation. Another new instrument in some towns was an annuity tax based on the value of one's property, to pay for the Protestant ministry. This was levied on all inhabitants, whether burgesses or not: in Edinburgh in 1635, 3,901 households and businesses were thus assessed (McNeill and MacQueen 1996, 456; Makey 1987, 206–9). Yet taxation did not bring new representation: urban populations grew and a higher proportion of townspeople paid tax in this period, but political power was exercised by an increasingly narrow group.

Burghs had a high level of self-determination: they had their own courts; they exercised close control over both the fabric of their churches and the services within them; they had responsibility, exercised through officers called liners, working as the agents of the guild merchant, for maintaining the alignment of burgage plots and streets and for the construction of new buildings and the repair of old. This power extended beyond burgh boundaries. Inhabitants of rural areas were obliged to attend only the market of a specified burgh. This came to mean that much of the piece-work for urban crafts was produced in this hinterland. The burgh's parish church often served a substantial rural area too (Haddington's parish stretched to 36 acres, Hamilton's to 25 and Dunfermline's to 20). The rural hinterland was thus drawn even more closely to the town. With the huge growth in burghs of barony and regality – approximately three hundred were founded in this period (Pryde 1965, 54–80) – the economic dominance of burghs over the surrounding countryside became stronger still. On the other hand, some royal burghs repeatedly complained of the growth of burghs of barony as harming their trade or industry. The self-determination of the burgh was mirrored in the status of some of its inhabitants. The burgesses, the merchants and craftsmen possessed the 'freedom' of the burgh. This enabled them to participate directly or indirectly in burgh administration and to pursue their own business affairs, while carrying out various services to the burgh, which included paying tax. The burgesses were in the minority, however, for the unfree made up at least 70% of the adult male population.

Circumstances, whether political, economic or constitutional, varied, of course, from town to town and from time to time, with changing values, economic pressures and social influences, although many changes were camouflaged by the apparent continuity of urban institutions. But, whatever the circumstances, towns always held an influence in Scotland that was quite disproportionate to their size.

THE TOWNSCAPE

Towns remained generally small, many being little more than villages by modern standards. Yet Timothy Pont's maps of Scotland, produced in the 1580s and 1590s, show us that towns were firmly distinguished from the countryside around them. They were set apart by their laws and jurisdictions as well as their appearance (Dennison 2001a, 125–38).

Walls, albeit small and insignificant in most places, provided physical and visual barriers, while ports (gates) controlled access. The early modern town retained many medieval features. Most larger towns had developed from a single street, with back lanes becoming thoroughfares, and the alignment of burgage plots, running back in herring-bone pattern from the front of the streets, was hard to alter. The market place was the focal point of the burgh. The parish church, tolbooth, market cross and tron (weigh-beam) were the most important civic structures, and the tolbooth and church would have been the dominant buildings in the town, being mainly built of stone.

Timber-framed housing was the norm across medieval European towns. By the sixteenth century in Scotland there was a move away from timber building, possibly because of a relative scarcity of suitable wood and an abundance of workable stone, although timber houses remained predominant. Seventeenth-century housing came to resemble Dutch or Flemish homes – usually of harled stone and often with crow-stepped gables. What was particularly significant in Scotland was that most of these dwellings were flatted and in multiple ownership (Stell 2001, 323). In many cases this led to the construction of a forestair, giving access to upper storeys, either with warehouses or another dwelling on the ground floor. Alongside this advance in the construction of houses there were concerted attempts to remove fire risks, as is evidenced throughout burgh records. The authorities encouraged the use of stone rather than wood, slated or tiled roofs rather than thatch, and the dispersal of dangerous industries, such as candle-making, to the outskirts of towns.

THE URBAN ECONOMY

Towns were essentially market places, where surplus rural produce, urban craft manufactures and imported goods were bought and sold by townspeople and those who came in from the rural hinterland. The pattern of the medieval economy, based on the export of the primary products of agriculture, fishing and mining, and the import of a wide range of manufactured goods, as well as raw materials such as timber and iron, can be still be traced throughout most of this period. The most prominent change lay in the increased concentration of overseas trade in a few larger burghs, leaving smaller and middling towns to concentrate on domestic and regional trade. The 'four great towns of Scotland' – Edinburgh, Aberdeen, Dundee and Perth – had paid 58% of customs revenue in the 1370s but by the 1590s the figure was 80% (Lynch 1988, 268–9). Edinburgh's domination of the export trade was more pronounced still: it paid almost 60% of all customs by 1500 and 72% by the 1590s; this domination was at its most pronounced in the areas of wool, hides, fells and cloth (McNeill and MacQueen 1996, 250–60).

In larger towns, the half century after c.1475 saw some radical changes in the urban economic structure. A growing number of crafts obtained the formal status of incorporated craft guilds, which brought a measure of independence from the dominant guild merchant. In Edinburgh, the skinners were the first to be incorporated (in 1474), although they had maintained their own altar in the burgh church since 1451. By 1523, Edinburgh had fourteen craft guilds, although some of them were conglomerate organisations: the hammermen, for example, were not merely a guild of smiths, but included seven different trades, including workers in leather, pewter, gold and tin. Dundee and Perth each had nine incorporated crafts and Aberdeen and Stirling seven by 1540. This pattern was followed by smaller burghs at a more modest rate (Lynch 2001, 624).

Craft guilds gave the craft masters greater control, not only over the quality of goods produced but also over their colleagues, their working practices and their journeymen and apprentices. Only those admitted to the guild by the masters were permitted to practise the craft, so the guilds also guarded against encroachment by unskilled workers. Through collective interest, mutual aid and fraternity the craft guilds were exclusive groups of tradesmen within the wider burgh community. In medieval times, production, wholesaling and retailing were not specialised operations but in the early modern period a distinction between these aspects of trade gradually arose. A close awareness of the relative importance of specific craft guilds also emerged. Large crafts, such as the hammermen and the baxters (bakers), in particular, had a strong sense of their own importance and would go to great lengths to project and defend it.

The manufacture of goods, however, could not be an exclusive, introspective activity. Towns might increasingly lay down rules to monitor production and quality, and to grant exclusive rights to the guilds, but craftsmen were often dependent on outsiders for their raw materials. This created the need for carters and carriers. In Aberdeen, porters (the forerunners of the Shore Porters) not only employed women as well as men, but even paid them the same wage – a sure comment on their strength and stamina! Burghs' rural hinterlands played a particularly pivotal role. It might even be argued that without its hinterland a town was incapable of functioning economically. Not only were the occupations of the town dependent on supplies of raw materials, but the surrounding areas also provided a workforce. Piece-work became more prevalent, a process that was intensified as the Scottish economy moved from concentration on wool to that on linen. Towns are often defined by the degree of specialisation in their occupational structures but, in practice, the close relationship between urban and rural industry varied from one trade or commodity to another. Most elements of the leather trade and of metalworking were located in towns (Lynch 1988, 134–47) but many stages of the textile trade were increasingly performed in the countryside, with the town acting only as a finishing centre.

Although the occupational profile of towns varied from place to place and over time, urban growth and increasing wealth brought about both economic diversification and stratification within urban occupations. As bodies formalised, internal dissensions might appear, and in the late fifteenth and early sixteenth centuries, there was in larger towns a hardening of roles and the emergence of elitism in both craft and merchant organisations. Moreover, at a national level, a jockeying between burghs for a share of the country's economy and the increasingly constricting stranglehold by Edinburgh played havoc with the occupational structures of many lesser towns. Allied to this, there was a proliferation of new burghs of barony in the sixteenth and seventeenth centuries. Some of them were quite substantial, such as Kilmarnock. The traditional occupational structure of the medieval burgh was challenged yet again (Whyte 1987, 219–44; Whyte 1995, 179–85).

Most townspeople were neither merchants nor members of a craft guild. In ports, various specialised occupations associated with the sea were established, albeit not as incorporated crafts. Rope-makers, net-menders, skippers, boatmen and fishermen plied their trade and were to be found in all coastal towns. Kirkcaldy and Dumbarton, along with other maritime burghs, were home to ship-builders. The admission of Irish sailors as burgesses in Stranraer in 1689 reflects that town's role in the trading networks of the Irish Sea.

Below the stratum of journeymen, apprentices and unincorporated crafts, there existed an under-class, rarely quantified in the records, who functioned as labourers, carters, servants, cleaners and beggars. A few acted as carriers of information and goods in overland communications. Large towns also served as a market for service skills, farming out the more menial tasks to the unfree, many of whom migrated from smaller towns or rural areas to the larger regional centres. There was a vast sub-culture of menial workers in the supply of food and drink and in agriculture. In fact the population of Perth is known to have doubled during the harvest in 1584, when this market centre became one enormous grain store for its hinterland. Such influxes of masterless men and women alarmed the authorities for they were a threat to order. In Perth in 1584 the dilemma was even more acute, for the town was also suffering from a plague outbreak, which had put enormous strain on provision for the burgh's own poor (Lynch 1988, 263).

When an analysis is made of the occupational structures of different towns at the end of the seventeenth century, Edinburgh stands out from other burghs because of the prominence of the professions. Lawyers accounted for around 60% of the capital's professionals, while those whose work related to medicine (surgeons, physicians and apothecaries) formed the next most numerous group. The church, education and the army constituted a significant proportion of the professions, and landowners, with their own urban households, were an economically important urban minority as well (Dingwall 1994, 215–40; Dingwall 1995, 25–30). This is not surprising in a capital city, nor is the vast array of support services that Edinburgh and its professions required. From domestic service, both male and female, to the production of luxury items, to prostitution, Edinburgh acted as a magnet for skilled and unskilled workers. The presence of goldsmiths, wig-makers, coachmen, printers, booksellers and clock-makers all reflect the culture of a capital city (Dingwall 1994, 135–6; 289–93).

The professions also featured prominently in regional centres, which were often heads of sheriffdoms, such as Aberdeen and Perth. Some relatively large burghs, however, such as Dalkeith, Musselburgh and Leith, had few professional occupations: proximity to Edinburgh negated the need for such facilities. Such burghs also had proportionately fewer merchants than most; Edinburgh's merchants dominated the trade of nearby towns. The impact of larger burghs on their smaller neighbours and the networking of satellite towns is also evident by the end of the seventeenth century. Musselburgh, a satellite of Edinburgh, took advantage of the market that the capital offered. Vegetables were grown, salt was manufactured and both were carried to the city by women with creels on their backs. On their return, they brought back washing, which boosted the sales of the several soap-boilers and starch-makers in the Musselburgh district. Dalkeith also had a high proportion of fleshers, which may well have resulted from the fact that the slaughtering of animals in Edinburgh was banned in 1695. Delkeith was clearly supplying meat to the capital, while Musselburgh's concentration of leather manufacturers suggests that Dalkeith's hides were being processed there.

The seventeenth century saw the rise of new manufactories in and around larger towns, with encouragement from parliament to establish specialised industries for domestic and overseas trade. Ventures in paper, glass, hardware, soap and sugar were new but much of the investment in wool, textiles and leather was an extension of established patterns of putting-out to rural industry. The famous cloth manufactory at Newmills near Haddington was a significant and important project. Most manufactories were small, but their concentration around Edinburgh, which had at least nine before 1650, at Dalry, and along the Water of Leith reflects the predominance of investment by the capital's burgesses and neighbouring lairds (McNeill and MacQueen 1996, 297).

Scottish settlements in New Jersey from 1682 and two years later in South Carolina provided a boost for overseas trade. The West Indies were also a vital trading partner. Commercial contacts to the west resulted in the development of soap works and sugar refining in Glasgow in particular. In 1688, a 'soaperie' was established, with permission for another five years later. The first sugar house, the Wester Sugar House, was established in 1667 and extended in 1675. Two years later it was again enlarged and a further process was added to sugar refining – rum was distilled from the waste molasses. In 1669 the Easter Sugar House was set up and by the turn of the century a further two had been established to boil sugar, to make candy and to distil spirits. The tobacco trade was another major area of growth in the west of Scotland and led to other economic developments: by 1668 a pipemaker was established in Glasgow and two years later the magistrates issued licences to dig for pipe clay. This trans-Atlantic trade remained minimal, however, compared with the traditional domination of the British–European interaction.

Although a home-based economy lasted into the late seventeenth and eighteenth centuries, small manufactories were set up in many smaller burghs, introducing a level of specialisation which had hitherto been unknown in most Scottish towns. By the end of the seventeenth century, Musselburgh had a broadcloth factory; Hamilton had a lace manufactory, to provide work and care for twelve poor girls, and a wool manufactory by 1705; linen weaving was introduced to Kirkcaldy in the

1670s; and Melrose and other Border towns became renowned for linen and wool manufacturing.

At the end of this period, throughout all towns, manufacturing was still the mainstay of burgh life, whether as a home-based industry or a manufactory, employing half the recorded male workforce in many cases. Food and drink production were still essential urban occupations, usually accounting for somewhere between 15 and 20% of the workforce. The rural characteristics of town life, which had been a feature of all medieval burghs, survived strongly in smaller burghs. Where the backlands of tofts had not been developed with outbuildings or dwellings, the traditional use of the land for growing food and keeping animals continued. In smaller towns, the medieval culture of self-sufficiency had not been totally eradicated and such towns' occupational structure in 1707 remained broadly similar to that of medieval times (Dennison forthcoming).

THE ROLE OF WOMEN IN THE TOWN

A large section of urban society barely features in the records but had a crucial role to play in the occupational and economic structure of the town – women. Women were rarely members of guilds merchant or craft guilds. In fact, they had little or no official role within the town hierarchy. Their presence, however, was keenly felt. Records suggest that much of the brewing within towns was the preserve of women. In Aberdeen, women are noted as brewers, bakers and shopkeepers, one woman even being described as a merchant in the 1690–91 customs book. Simpler crafts, such as baking, brewing and candle-making, might be undertaken by women at home, with the intention of supplying the family. Any surplus could then be sold at the market. Women also on occasion feature as ship-owners, custumars (tax collectors) and money-lenders. In the seventeenth century a few women were employed as bearers in coal mines and salt pans. Both of these required exceptional physical stamina with little financial reward: by 1700 a woman coal-bearer earned only fourpence a day and if her husband worked in a mine she was expected to assist him.

One role that fell to women was prostitution. Burgh records indicate that the profession was well-known. The authorities went to considerable lengths in regulating the activities of prostitutes, both in seeking to control the location of brothels and to prevent the spread of disease (Dennison, DesBrisay and Diack 2002, 82–3).

Before 1750 it was the custom throughout Europe for well-to-do women not to breast-feed their own children. Only the very wealthy could afford live-in wet nurses; the majority would hand over their children to a married woman in a rural village who took urban youngsters into her home. Those who did succeed in obtaining employment as a wet-nurse in the town itself might receive £20 Scots cash per year, double what a woman might earn as a domestic servant.

Women, particularly widows, played an important role in the economy, giving the lie to the notion that women as a whole were an under-class. Certainly, men dominated the more prestigious occupations, but many women were capable of running the family business during the absence of a husband overseas or after his death. Legally, however, women played a subservient role to their fathers, husbands and sons. As early as the twelfth century, in the *Leges Burgorum*, it was laid down that a man had the right to speak on behalf of his wife in a court of law; and, once married and away from the control of her father, a woman had technically no legal persona. Her movable property, including rentals of heritable property, annuities and interest on loans of money, passed to her husband. She retained only her 'paraphernalia': that is, dress, personal ornaments, jewellery and a repository in which to keep them, and *'peculium'* – a gown or gift to the wife if the husband sold lands in which she had interest as a 'tercer' (holder of a widow's right to a life-rent of one third of her deceased husband's heritage). The post-Reformation marriage service of the 1560s reinforced this position with the words that a wife 'is in subjection and under governance of her husband, so long as they both continue alive'.

One role for women was highlighted in large towns, where the demand for service within the homes of the wealthier townspeople led to an influx of young women from the countryside. This resulted in a skewing of the gender ratio. Women far outnumbered men, giving cause for concern amongst the burgh authorities. There was a fear that these 'masterless women' were not fully under control.

Women faced great hardship during their child-bearing years, perhaps as few as one third surviving. But, once past this crucial stage in their lives, women often lived longer than men. In 1550, for example, 18.7% of households in Stirling were headed by a woman. Widows and women living alone, however, might find themselves under suspicion and this group suffered badly in the witch-hunts of the late sixteenth and seventeenth centuries, although urban women suffered much less than their rural sisters.

Gradually, females began to receive formal education. A few fortunate girls were taught before the Reformation, but in the seventeenth century more girls received a rudimentary education, with a concentration on writing and sewing. This period witnessed the rise of schools for girls, usually taught by women, particularly after the Reformation. Dumbarton, Dundee, Haddington, Kirkcaldy, Leith South and North, Montrose and Paisley all had 'dame schools'. The first official regulated school for girls in Aberdeen came in 1642 and the rhyme in the commonplace book of the master of the music school in that town suggests that some at least felt that girls were as fit as boys to be educated:

> The weaknes of a womanis witt
> Is not to natures fault
> Bot laike of educationne fitt
> Makes nature quhylls to halt
> (Vance 2002, 319)

Although an increased provision for the education of girls potentially broadened educational provision for those from non-privileged backgrounds, few attended the schools which were provided, probably because their role in the domestic economy took priority (Dennison 2001b, 645–6).

LITERACY

The ability to sign one's name is usually considered by historians as a crude index of a minimum of literacy. In Perth in 1561 burgesses were required to sign their names. Two members of the town council, three deacons of crafts and a further 215 could not do so. Only forty-nine signed with their own hands. The remaining needed the assistance of the notary public to guide their hands. In 1588, sixty baxters in Dundee were required to perform this relatively simple task. Twenty-eight were able to do so. In Dunfermline in 1594, 50% of guild merchants could not sign their own names and five years later in Stirling this was true of ten of nineteen guild brothers. Twenty-five Dundee wrights were asked to sign their names and seventeen were able to do so, although in 1695 (in the same Dundee trade) of fourteen men nine had their signatures placed by the notary. Many of these men would have been quite adept at signing their merchant's mark, each of which would have been unique to themselves; some examples may be seen in the Dunfermline guild court book (Torrie 1986, p.ix). All merchants, particularly those travelling overseas, would have been numerate, even if they could not write.

Literacy in general probably improved during the seventeenth century. The godly society outlined by the Protestant church in 1560 was more interested in the ability to read rather than to write. In the seventeenth century, arithmetic and other practical schools were set up alongside the traditional 'Inglis' schools, which taught boys up to the age of eight, and the grammar schools, with their Latin curriculum, which catered for privileged boys up to the age of twelve or fourteen. But by 1707 universal literacy remained an aspiration (Torrie 1990, 91).

THE EFFECTS OF WAR AND MILITARY OCCUPATION

The ravages of Henry VIII's 'Rough Wooings' in the 1540s, mainly in the south of the country, were a foretaste of worse to come (Merriman 2000, 358–61). Towns had always prepared themselves for strife by regular 'wappinschaws' (weapon-shows) in the middle ages. By the 1590s military musters were extended to all inhabitants, not merely burgesses. This would come to a climax with the formation of burgh regiments in the 1640s.

The wars of the Covenant brought differing problems to Scotland's towns and some experienced an extreme level of ferocity. James Graham, first marquis of Montrose, took Aberdeen by force in 1639 but successfully restrained his men. He was less successful in 1644. Many of his battle-hardened Irish troops had participated in terrible atrocities in Germany and Ireland. At the Battle of Justice Mills in September 1644, the people of Aberdeen met these dreaded opponents. The battle lasted only two hours, but violence against the townspeople was systematically applied. For three days rape and slaughter continued, with Montrose adopting Irish dress in solidarity with his men, leaving 160 men and unknown numbers of women and children dead (DesBrisay 2002, 258–60).

This ruthlessness was unmatched until 1651, when Dundee fell to the English, in spite of the fact that, with its new town walls, it was considered one of the most defensible towns in Scotland. General Monck permitted his successful New Model Army a reward of twenty-four hours of looting. It was two weeks before the rampaging soldiers were brought under control. It has been estimated that, out of a population of approximately 8,000, one fifth were killed. In the following eight months, 159 babies were born, 25 of them to posthumous fathers, who would have been Dundonians; the fathers of many others would have been English men. Contemporary accounts agree on two matters: the vast numbers that lost their lives; and the destruction of not only the townscape but also the removal of so much of Dundee's wealth and archives, along with those of other towns which had sent their precious possessions for safekeeping to this supposedly impregnable town. The people of Dundee, it was said, were 'robbit evin to the sark' (Torrie 1990, 106–7).

During the seventeenth century, a military presence became increasingly common in towns, whether it was occupation by hostile forces or the billeting of friendly troops by the government. In 1639 Old Aberdeen became the first town in the Scottish wars to experience this and resident soldiers became a normal part of the life of many Scottish towns during the 1640s. Linlithgow, Dalkeith, Dumbarton, New Aberdeen and Ayr, amongst others, all played host to Cromwellian troops, billeted on them for quite extensive periods of time in the following decade. In some cases, the burgh became a garrison town: Stornoway, for example, virtually turned into one large military camp, as may be seen in a plan drawn by a soldier billeted there (Dennison and Coleman 1997, 26). Extortion was a fact of life under military occupation. The impact on the social and occupational balance of the town was profound. Demand for food, candles, blankets and bandages for the soldiers created a boom in certain sectors but led to dearth for the local people and tensions between those who profited from the military presence and those who were its victims. Retribution often followed on the departure of the troops.

One consequence of the destruction that towns sustained as a result of war was the need to rebuild civic institutions. The new building programme necessitated in Linlithgow gives a fair impression of the havoc that a visiting army could wreak. The *Register of the Privy Council* referred to 'the great loss sustained by the burgh, and the destruction of all their public works by the attack of the usurper, namely their church, hospital, school, market cross, tolbooth, well, four mills and store houses or granarie at Blackness' (the town's port, a few miles to the north on the Forth). The parish church was incorporated into the defensive structures round the palace, horses were stabled in the nave and troops occupied the triforium. On the departure of the military, it was estimated that £1,000 Scots was needed to repair the roof and windows alone. Other repair work was also required, so the town was granted a free fair for three days in order to raise revenue and was also permitted to double the normal rates of local taxation. The defences erected around the palace were all demolished and the tolbooth was reconstructed between 1668 and 1670 to a design of John Milne, the king's master mason. The council records show clearly that the 1660s and 1670s were a period of general building activity. Two clocks were made, one for the tolbooth steeple and one for the church's. The grammar school had to be rebuilt and the Cross Well, flesh and meal markets all had to be reconstructed. The homes of the people had likewise suffered and many had to be rebuilt (Dennison and Coleman 2000, 31–4).

LIVING IN TOWNS

Living conditions varied considerably across the social spectrum. For the more prosperous, luxuries such as bolsters and pillows, wall hangings – even rugs on the floor and tiled or slated roofs – reduced the miseries of draughts and dampness. On the other hand, wooden housing with thatched roofs, and beddings and floor coverings of straw attracted vermin and disease, and were more susceptible to fire, a constant hazard in pre-modern towns.

Exterior conditions also served to assist or prevent good health. Congestion in the backlands of the burgage plots, and the mixing of residential, agricultural and industrial premises added to the risk of illness. So did the placing of wells and midden pits in close proximity; the closeness of human beings to animals, such as pigs, which were free to roam the streets and root amongst the midden piles; and the continuing tendency to dump in the streets rubbish ranging from human excrement to the remnants of slaughtered animals and gutted fish on market day. Little of butchered animals, however, was intentionally abandoned – after the quality meat had been removed, intestines and stomachs could be used to hold offal and other waste parts of the carcass as a haggis- or sausage-type food; tripe, heads and feet are all documented in the records as being eaten; and spare fat could be rendered down for candles or soap.

Both archaeological and documentary evidence have shown that attempts were made to achieve a certain level of cleanliness. Cobbling made roads and alleys less likely to turn into quagmires. Wooden battening placed in soggy areas, such as latrines, and the raising of interior floor levels above that of the muddy exterior are also evidence of attempts at cleanliness. Moss was used as toilet paper, although the wealthier adopted more sophisticated modes of cleanliness.

The burgh authorities also had a role to play. Numerous burgh council enactments demonstrate that there were efforts to keep towns clean. The repetition of these rulings, however, would suggest that they were often ignored! In 1506 in New Aberdeen, for example, it was agreed that four men should be appointed to clean the four quarters of the town; the filth they collected was then to be taken to the common midden, for which each household was to pay one penny a year. And in 1512 the council decreed that fullers should not hang their cloth to dry over the churchyard walls or within the churchyard itself. Particularly serious attempts to clean up this town were made for the visit of Queen Margaret in 1511. All 'pynouris' (labourers or porters) who had horses were to clean the town of its accumulated middens; and no other work was to be undertaken until this was completed. All swine, normally free to roam the streets, were to be removed, on pain of slaughter of the offending pig and the banishment of its owner. Such measures were typical of many towns when the visit of royalty was imminent. They indicate that urban authorities were more concerned with appearances on special occasions than with the social benefits of cleanliness.

Medieval and early modern societies were inevitably susceptible to the vagaries of the weather: a poor harvest might bring with it famine or, at least, extreme hunger. The most usual meat eaten was cow, but sheep, goat, pig, deer, fish, chickens, geese and wild birds also featured on the table. Meat was not readily available in winter. Rather than feed animals over the colder months, only animals retained for breeding were allowed to over-winter. The rest were slaughtered. Any meat kept for winter eating had to be heavily salted, or spiced to disguise the rankness of flesh that was no longer fresh (Dennison, DesBrisay and Diack 2002, 70–1).

The availability of fish was dependent on the success of a catch, but the inhabitants of coastal towns also ate shellfish: shells of oysters, limpets, winkles, cockles, mussels and razor-fish have all been excavated at Aberdeen. Dairy produce and eggs came from the townspeople's own animals or were bought with other essential commodities at the weekly market. Vegetables were grown in the back-lands. Though more limited in variety than in more modern times, they ranged from kale to leeks, spring onions, fat hen (a nettle-type weed) and beans. Diets were also supplemented by gathering food in the wild: mushrooms and other fungi, raspberries, blaeberries, brambles, wild cherries and rowans were all picked in season. Cereals, however, remained the staple food, the main crops being oats, rye, wheat and barley (Gibson and Smout 1989, 60–6).

Water was essential for cooking and drinking. Most homes probably had water-butts to collect rainwater. Water from wells and from the lochs and streams was of little use for drinking by this time for it was becoming increasingly polluted with industrial waste and seepage from middens and cess-pits. Ale for the majority of people and wine for the wealthier sections of society were the normal drinks. On balance, the evidence does suggest that, as long as a sufficient supply of food and drink was available, although it may have lacked in variety, the diet was adequately balanced and not unhealthy. The poorer members of society, inevitably, were the most vulnerable in times of dearth and high prices.

The wealthier benefited from a luxury unavailable to the poorer members of society from the mid seventeenth century: sugar, and, associated with it, hot drinks. Hot chocolate, first recorded in 1667, was a favourite of upper-class ladies as a breakfast drink, a nightcap or a pre-dinner drink. Coffee also reached Scotland soon after 1650. Not only the wealthy in their homes but the middle-class professionals were able to partake of this beverage in coffee houses. Although tea was in circulation among the well-to-do from the 1670s, it was initially used for medicinal purposes and was not commonly drunk as a hot drink until after 1707 (Fenton 2001, 170).

For the vast majority, work predominated over leisure. The working day followed the medieval pattern of starting as early as 5 a.m. in summer (although the 'workman bell' could be heard at 4.30 a.m. in some towns) and 6 a.m. in winter. Although leisure time in the modern sense did not exist, documentary and archaeological evidence reveals a number of recreational activities. Social drinking, gossiping and story-telling were ubiquitous. Shooting at the 'buttis' (archery), encouraged by statute to enhance the kingdom's military preparedness, was a popular sport, as were football and handball, hawking (a type of bowls) and pennystanes (a sort of quoits). The survival of bone skates and sledge runners indicate that winter sports were also played. Bone and slate gaming-counters and references to playing cards show that board-games and gambling were enjoyed, while small clay animals suggest that children also had playthings.

The hardship of life was also alleviated by secular festivals and games, the most noted being the May revels. Traditionally the 'abbot of unreason' presided at this. In Aberdeen the abbot was called the 'abbot' or 'prior' of 'Bon Accord', in Peebles the 'abbot of unrest', and Edinburgh had an 'abbot of narent' and a 'lord of inobedience'. The whole point of these yearly May revels was to have a time of merriment when the conventional order and rule of society was upturned. The cult of Robin Hood was well known in Scotland from at least the early fifteenth century. He, too, in some towns could be found leading the unrest at the revels. These festivities died out at the Reformation, which also saw the end of the observance of holy days, celebrated because they were days free from work as well as for their spiritual significance. Processions on saints' days were days for veneration of the saints but also times for jollification with jesters, tumblers, minstrels and pipers.

In the seventeenth century, jollification at fairs and games remained popular. These were still days for drinking. To ale and beer were now added whisky and cheap West Indian rum. Tobacco, too, appeared on the scene, but it tended to be chewed rather than smoked in this period. To football matches and horse racing was added curling, introduced from the Low Countries in the seventeenth century. A very privileged few might enjoy a game of golf or enter a shooting competition (Dennison 2001c, 652). Life was hard, but it was not all work.

HEALTH IN TOWNS

Scotland experienced, as did many other parts of Europe, epidemic and endemic diseases as well as famine. When bad weather, and resultant poor harvests, occurred at the same time as disease the population was hit hardest. But dearth, and consequently high death rates, was not solely the result of bad harvests. The last great famine to hit Scotland came in the 1690s (see below). Population increase had a major part to play. In 1560, it has been estimated, about only 2.5% of Scots lived in towns with a population of over 2,500. By the 1690s, that figure would not have been appreciably greater. By 1750, in spite of stagnation or even decline in the second half of the seventeenth century, the figure had risen to 17.3% (Tyson 1986, 32–52; Tyson 2001, 488). Such an increase in mouths to feed, allied with economic swings, meant at times extreme hardship and high death rates.

Several diseases were prevalent in pre-modern towns, some being endemic and chronic, such as leprosy. Leprosy was common throughout western Europe and the need for isolation of victims was understood. Most towns had their leper house at a safe distance from their healthy inhabitants. Attached to the lepers' dwelling was normally a croft, where they could grow the absolute basics for their solitary existence, and probably also a graveyard. Lepers were buried near to the house in order to avoid contamination.

The records give little hint of the quality of life of these poor shunned souls. In most communities in western Europe a number of the leprous group were permitted into the town to beg for money or provisions, as long as no physical contact was made with the healthy and the leper stood down-wind; the leper was permitted to touch only with his stick and had always to carry a clapper or rattle to announce his arrival. Disfiguration, pain, the loss of toes and fingers and the twisting of limbs increased the sense of isolation and hopelessness. The forcible removal from family, home and normal companionship must have exacerbated the horror of the inevitable future for the leper. Death was the central theme of the pre-Reformation church service that removed the leper from the healthy society. From the moment of certification as a leper, the victim literally entered into a 'living death' (Richards 2000, 68).

Probably the most feared disease in medieval times, which persisted until the middle of the seventeenth century, was the plague or 'pest'. No other disease created such terror, partly because contemporaries, who knew only what could be deduced through observation and experience, were uncertain exactly how it was spread and how to stop it. Not until 1894, long after it had retreated from north-west Europe, was the plague bacillus identified and its deadly path traced from infected black rats to fleas to humans. Medieval and early modern people knew well, however, that plague was highly contagious and tended to move along trade routes from town to town. News of plague spread throughout towns in Scotland within days, and merchants and mariners helped spread the alarm whenever the disease struck English or Dutch ports.

'Plague' was really several diseases. Bubonic plague was best known to contemporaries simply as 'the plague' or 'the pestilence' or 'the pest'. Historians now believe that plague epidemics often involved other diseases as well, including typhus, which manifested itself when resistance was low, as it was after famine. Many infectious diseases shared symptoms and were difficult to tell apart – hence the frequent use in the records of the generic term 'fever' – but people knew the bubonic plague when they saw it. Symptoms were horrific and unmistakable. Pneumonic plague also hit in the Middle Ages. The cold and rain of Scotland offered ideal conditions for this form of the disease, which might strike either as a secondary infection of the bubonic variety or as a primary illness. Flugge droplets travelled six feet merely by speaking and as much as nine to twelve feet by coughing and sneezing (Dennison, DesBrisay and Diack 2002, 73).

Plague hit on a regular basis until the seventeenth century. Because there was no cure for bubonic plague, people in every town knew that their best hope lay in prevention. This required a collective response. The idea was to seal the town off from any people or goods that might be carrying the disease and, when that failed, to seal the sick off from the healthy. Beggars who were not local were banned and measures such as setting aside special areas for washing clothes during the time of plague were brought in. In 1644, when plague or possibly typhus hit Dumbarton, 'cleingers' (cleaners) were hired from Paisley to fumigate the house of a deceased woman, the body being handled as little as possible as it was dragged by ropes to the grave. Council registers show that the authorities were intent on keeping the towns free of plague if at all possible (Dennison and Coleman 1999, 31). In Dumbarton in 1604, when plague threatened, watchmen were placed on the town's bridge at the Knowle Burn and at the collegiate church to prevent strangers bringing disease into the town. In Aberdeen in 1514, goods suspected of being infected with plague were burned and cleansers were appointed to clean the houses and possessions of victims. When plague struck the town between May and December of 1647, 1,400 died – possibly a fifth of the population. Aberdeen town council estimated that this outbreak cost £30,000 Scots through loss of trade, hiring cleansers, burying the dead, building huts to house the infected and a gibbet to deal with those who disobeyed the plague rulings, and purchasing food for the poor.

Townspeople were susceptible to many other diseases and debilitating conditions. Syphilis had hit Scotland in epidemic proportions in the last years of the fifteenth century; it would continue to spread, along with other venereal diseases, throughout the following centuries. Smallpox, cholera, tuberculosis, leukaemia and amoebic dysentery might strike at any time. And, in an age before antibiotics, a minor chest infection could quickly turn into a fatal condition, or an open cut become infected, resulting in death from septicaemia (Stones 1987, 35).

Skeletal evidence has revealed arthritis and *spina bifida*. The condition of the teeth indicates that gingivitis was commonplace and caries was prevalent. Archaeological research into the samples taken from cess and midden pits shows clearly that townspeople suffered from internal parasites. Many people lived close to their animals, and parasites were passed from them to humans. Many suffered from the nauseous and debilitating effects of ring-worm as well as from parasitic worms, such as trichuris and ascaris, which might grow up to twenty inches in length. By travelling from the small intestine through the blood system to the liver, heart, lungs and trachea, worms produced obvious and immediate effects. Parasitic infection also reduced resistance to other diseases. The number of purgative powders purchased in the seventeenth century is sure evidence that parasitic infection was difficult to eradicate.

Hospitals did exist, but the reality was that these were not open to all and could accommodate only very few. Self-help was essential. Again, archaeological evidence has shown the types of medication taken. Figs were imported and it is possible that they were used as a purgative. Seeds of the opium poppy suggest its use as a sedative. Henbane (*hyoscyamus niger*), which induced sleep and caused hallucinations if taken in large quantities, and deadly nightshade (*atropa belladonna*), a muscle relaxant, were probably cultivated. Other species of plants would have been collected from the wild for their medicinal properties. Gradually, over time, improved knowledge and natural resistance alleviated some of the debilitating conditions townspeople suffered from. Yet many medieval diseases persisted into the seventeenth century and even later – some with devastating effects.

The chances of survival for new-born babies and toddlers were not high and an extra mouth to feed might prove disastrous for a family. Mothers may sometimes have sought remedies by their own hands. In 1690, parliament passed an act 'anent murdering of children', claiming that there had been 'frequent' such cases; the mother was automatically to be found guilty if she had concealed the pregnancy and her child was still-born. A virtual carbon copy of the English infanticide law of 1624, it is more likely that this act was part of the resurgent Protestant zeal after the restoration of presbyterianism in 1690 than a response to a real social problem. It is doubtful that infanticide was common, and there is an irony in such a measure, given the devastation that would hit much of Scotland and, in particular, the North-East in the form of famine and economic downturn five years later, with its resultant deaths and female infertilty. Four harsh years reduced the population of Aberdeenshire by 21% and recovery to pre-famine levels took more than fifty years (Dennison, DesBrisay and Diack 2002, 75–9, 90).

THE TOWN AS A COMMUNITY

It has been argued that the town, by setting itself apart from the countryside, formed a close, united society, exclusive and inclusive to itself. The alderman or provost (in Latin, *prepositus*) was the head of the town; he was supported by two or four bailies, depending on the size of the town; and these magistrates by lesser officers. The burgh council and assize conducted the routine business of the town and the burgh court dealt with judicial matters. These principal personages were reinforced in their roles by the burgesses, who were required to attend the three head courts, held at Michaelmas, Christmas and Easter. The 'best' ruled for the good of the whole community. And thus the town functioned as a corporate whole.

But, as we have seen, there were many of differing standing within the urban community. Was it possible to be a 'united whole'? Did the 'community' not, in fact, mean the minority of burgesses with their privileges? And how much power did even they have in reality? There is no evidence as to whether, even at head courts, the burgesses could amend or reject the magistrates' decisions. Might the burgesses' function and power have been merely one of approval – a show of consensus? This is a conclusion which can be reached in many towns for the period before the Reformation. After 1560, however, the distinction between those in power and those excluded from it sharpened rather than diminished.

A close look at the evidence seems to suggest that by the sixteenth century the medieval burgh community, whatever precisely that was, was increasingly under strain. In many towns, particularly the large ones, burgh life was experiencing a quiet but steady trend towards oligarchy. And this elitism was displayed in the trappings of power – burgh officials alone were entitled to wear furs and rich materials and colours. Their wives also were obliged to dress in a seemly manner, according to their elevated status. Garish garb was held to signal loose women or prostitutes. Such sumptuary laws or rulings, first issued in the late medieval period, were repeated time and time again in the sixteenth and seventeenth centuries. Disenchantment amongst the lower elements of society was inevitable. Public apathy was such that compulsory attendance at the head courts – only three times a year – was not obeyed. Canongate, a small burgh, listed scores of non-attenders in the 1590s. This disenchantment with communal living was reflected in other ways. In the defence of the burgh – one of the very basic obligations – servants began to stand in for their masters at musters. And in Stranraer, a new burgh founded at the end of the sixteenth century, burgesses failed to support their fellows on their journey into the afterlife, sending their servants to funerals in their place.

It could be argued, however, that some communal festivities served as a counter-balance to those in power. The May Games, with their abbots of unreason and Robin Hoods, permitted the lower members of society to enjoy a time of upturned rule, with the conventional order reversed, and their rule made law. But a closer look at the records gives a few hints which indicate that the traditional view of the May revels was not all it was made out to be. Most significantly, the occasion had the official blessing of the burgh authorities. In Aberdeen and Haddington, for example, the towns paid the abbots to fulfil their duties. In Edinburgh and Dunfermline the guilds merchant gave financial support to Robin Hood. And the choice of man to lead the common people in their time of unrest is revealing. It was decided in Aberdeen in 1445 that, due to 'diverss enormities in tyme bigane be the Abbits of this burgh callit Bone Acorde', there were to be no such abbots. Rather, in future, the abbot was to be either the alderman or one of the bailies. In Ayr, it became the custom that the treasurers should take the part of Robin Hood and Little John. In Dunfermline the role of Robin Hood was often filled by a member of the local gentry family, the Halketts. In Edinburgh, in 1518, the role of Little John was even offered to Mr Francis Bothwell, a university graduate and an associate of the earl of Arran – an invitation he stiffly refused.

The May revels may have served to release tension within burgh society, but they were monitored by the ruling group. The parliamentary ruling of 1555, that there should be no impersonations of Robin Hood, Little John, the abbot or the queen of May, may be proof of this. As so often in legislation dealing with social matters in the fifteenth and sixteenth centuries, this act was probably a response to a particular problem in a particular town: in Perth, the annual ritual of supposed disorder and power in the hands of the underdogs had perhaps begun to display precisely these features. And it had to be stopped. But Perth, predominantly a craft town, had the sharpest social tensions of any of the major towns – good reason for John Knox to choose it for his inflammatory sermon in May 1559, which triggered a riot of the 'raschall multitude'. In Edinburgh the association of Robin Hood and the lord of inobedience with civil disorder climaxed in 1561. John Knox (now minister of Edinburgh) declared that 'the raschall multitude war stirred up to mak a Robene Hude' by 'papistis and bishoppis' and a number of people were brought to trial for appointing these two men. Even in this most seemingly egalitarian of festivities there was no question that power would be devolved. The fear of the potential for public frivolity to release expressions of discontent continued into the seventeenth century. Although the church preached against traditional holy days such as Christmas, festivities associated with 'superstitious days' lingered obstinately. The gathering of greenery from the woods to herald in summer continued in many locations; Aberlady recorded at least seven guisers on 'hansall Monday' – the equivalent of the English 'Plough Monday' – in 1640, as did Prestonpans on Yule day; and in 1645 guising took place in Meikle Blackburn. Probably even more condemned by the authorities was the survival of pre-Reformation plays. In 1647, Haddington Presbytery railed against plays being performed by a number of its congregations and insisted that they be suppressed with 'diligence', most especially if they were performed on old saints' days (Williamson forthcoming).

THE CHANGING ROLE OF THE CHURCH

Medieval town life revolved around the church. From birth with baptism, through handfasting (a form of engagement to marry), to death, life was led through the church. The church calendar determined the phases of the year and the church bells called the start of the working day in the morning and tolled the curfew at night. The support of altars and care of the fabric of the church reflected a strong attachment to the church, which was typically vested in the dean of guild on behalf of the community.

A key feature of medieval urban Scotland was the single parish town, in which the community's sense of oneness and apartness was reinforced. This identity of parish and burgh, even though it might include a rural landward area, and although it would have become strained in larger towns by the sixteenth century, survived until the Reformation. The strains were to be seen, however, in the foundation of altars for individual crafts within the parish church. Parts of the community were using religious devotion to emphasise social divisions. The combination of unity and division was physically and powerfully expressed in the annual Corpus Christi procession. Underlying this spectacle was a dominant theme – the image of the body – oneness and wholeness. The focus of the procession was the body of Christ in the form of the host. This was accompanied by the town magistrates, the guild merchant and the crafts of the burgh in fiercely contested order of precedence, all of which was witnessed by other participants – the townspeople. The body politic was being portrayed as single community, yet one which was acutely conscious of stratification and exclusion, for the unfree majority had no part to play. Some have argued that their role in such public drama was as audience and that the onlookers therefore performed a crucial role. But were non-burgesses and frailer members of society genuinely involved in this display of the power-structure of the town? The ordinary men and women – the unfree – were also actively excluded from some of the burghs' religious observances. In Dundee, for example, in 1521 the burgh sergeants were instructed to keep 'the pur fowk out of the kirk' on holy days. Two years later the rule was extended to Sundays and festival days. Dundee was not alone in such exclusions. Without doubt, the common rabble could cause undue disturbance, but this is a telling comment on the powers of the ruling group and the lack of true unity in the burgh community.

The Reformation of 1560 changed much on the surface: altars were stripped and saints' day processions forbidden. Yet the solidarity and precedence of the crafts remained of paramount importance. These could be displayed by sitting together in church in assigned pews or lofts. Tension and rivalry between crafts may be exemplified in Dundee, where the baxters had written above their loft in the church 'Bread is the staff of life'. Their neighbours, the fleshers, countered with 'Man shall not live by bread alone'. In Aberdeen, where you sat in the church of St Nicholas had everything to do with power. Apportioning seats involved setting people not only in physical space but also in social – power – space. The wealthiest were at the front; in the central section were the burgesses with their wives and older children; servants, apprentices, the poor and children under eight – those with no power – sat at the back and sides. There then arose a problem over women, who were to be segregated because of their sex. A number of solutions were tried, one solution in 1640 being to allow prominent, powerful men to place low benches in front of their pews, where their wives might crouch. Inevitably, not all women were prepared to sit at their husbands' feet staring at the back of the pew in front and the scheme was dropped!

Perhaps the most significant change which followed the Reformation was as much to do with rising population as religious change and it dealt a further blow to the unity of the religious life of many burghs. Existing parish churches in larger burghs were subdivided to accommodate two, three or even four congregations. In a few towns, such as Forfar, Burntisland and Edinburgh, new churches were built either to accommodate a growing community under one roof or to provide an additional place of worship. In a number of towns, the worshipping community was thus fragmented, yet in the majority the single parish burgh remained a feature of urban life into the eighteenth century.

The loss of traditional forms of worship at the Reformation hurt many, although the new Protestant church was welcomed by others. The wealthiest remained the 'best', a view of urban life reinforced by the teachings of the church – all had their place in a divinely-ordained hierarchical society. The Reformation is usually said to have begun in towns, but they also imposed particular restrictions on its progress. It was the urban elite who dominated the new kirk sessions; ministers were forbidden to criticise 'notable or particular persons' – the great and the good; and the space inside the post-Reformation burgh church reflected the status of the powerful and the powerless (Lynch, DesBrisay and Pittock 2002, 294–5). Religion still underpinned social, economic and political inequality – and the balance of power.

CONCLUSION

By the sixteenth century, the medieval sense of a familiar, close-knit urban community was increasingly under strain and could not survive. Throughout the seventeenth century there was a growing divide between rich and poor, with power held by an increasingly narrow elite (Dennison 1998, 121). Its precise shape varied from one town to another. In Edinburgh, the elite was dominated by new professions from outwith the traditional burgh community; in many smaller towns the process of the consolidation of the mercantile elite came only in the seventeenth century, when a merchant guild was formed for the first time. What emerged in most cases, however, in the course of the seventeenth century was a more polarised version of the medieval urban community, an exclusive society, with the few and select in possession of more power than ever before.

REFERENCES

Dennison, E.P. and Coleman, R. 1997 *Historic Stornoway. The Archaeological Implications of Development*. Edinburgh.

Dennison, E.P. 1998 'Power to the People? The Myth of the Medieval Burgh Community in Foster, S., Macinnes, A. and MacInnes, R. (eds), *Scottish Power Centres*, 100–131 Glasgow.

Dennison, E.P. and Coleman, R. 1999 *Historic Dumbarton. The Archaeological Implications of Development*. Edinburgh.

Dennison, E.P. and Coleman, R. 2000 *Historic Linlithgow. The Archaeological Implications of Development*. Edinburgh.

Dennison, E.P. 2001a 'Timothy Pont's Portrayal of Towns', in Cunningham, I.C. (ed), *The Nation Survey'd*, 125–38, East Linton.

Dennison, E.P. 2001b 'Women to 1700', in Lynch, M. (ed), *The Oxford Companion to Scottish History*, 645–46, Oxford.

Dennison, E.P. 2001c 'Work and Leisure to 1770s', in Lynch, M. (ed), *The Oxford Companion to Scottish History*, 651–63. Oxford.

Dennison, E.P., DesBrisay, G., Diack, H.L. 2002 'Health in the Two Towns', in Dennison E.P., Ditchburn, D. and Lynch, M. (eds), *Aberdeen Before 1800. A New History*, 70–96, East Linton.

Dennison, E.P. (forthcoming) 'The Occupational Structure of Towns, 1100–1700', *Scottish Life and Society: A compendium of Scottish ethnology*, 7.

DesBrisay, G. 2002 '"The Civill Warrs Did Overrun All": Aberdeen, 1630–1690', in Dennison, Ditchburn and Lynch (eds), *Aberdeen Before 1800. A New History*, 238–66.

Dingwall, H.M. 1994 *Late Seventeenth Century Edinburgh: a Demographic Study*. Leicester.

Dingwall, H.M. 1995 *Physicians, Surgeons and Apothecaries; Medical Practice in Seventeenth-Century Scotland*. East Linton.

Fenton, A. 2001 'Diet', in Lynch (ed), *Oxford Companion to Scottish History*, 167–70.

Flinn, M. (ed) 1977 *Scottish Population History*. Cambridge.

Gibson, A. and Smout, T.C. 1989 'Scottish Food and Scottish History', in Houston, R.A. and Whyte, I.D. (eds), *Scottish Society, 1500–1800*, 85–117, Cambridge.

Lynch, M. 1984 'Whatever happened to the medieval burgh? Some Guidelines for Sixteenth and Seventeenth Century Historians', *Scottish Economic and Social History*, 4, 5–20.

Lynch, M. 1987 'The Crown and the Burghs, 1500–1625', in Lynch, M. (ed), *The Early Modern Town in Scotland*, 55–80, London.

Lynch, M. 1988 *The Scottish Medieval Town*. Edinburgh.

Lynch, M. 1989 'Continuity and Change in Urban Society, 1500–1700', in Houston, R.A. and Whyte, I.D. (eds), *Scottish Society, 1500–1800*, 85–117, Cambridge.

Lynch, M. 1992 'Urbanisation and Urban Networks in Seventeenth Century Scotland', *Scottish Economic and Social History*, 12, 24–41.

Lynch, M. 2001 'Urban Society, 1500–1700', in Lynch (ed), *Oxford Companion to Scottish History*, 624–5.

Lynch, M., DesBrisay, G. and Pittock, M.G.H. 2002 'The Faith of the People' in Dennison, Ditchburn and Lynch (eds), *Aberdeen Before 1800. A New History*, 289–308.

McNeill, P.G.B. and MacQueen, H.L. 1996 *Atlas of Scottish History*. Edinburgh.

Makey, W.H. 1987 'Edinburgh in Mid-Seventeenth Century', in Lynch, M. (ed), *The Early Modern Town in Scotland*, 192–218, London.

Merriman, M. 2000 *The Rough Wooings, Mary Queen of Scots, 1542–1551*. East Linton.

Pryde, G.S. 1965 *The Burghs of Scotland: A Critical List*. Glasgow.

Richards, P. 1977 *The Medieval Leper*. Cambridge.

Stell, G.P. 2001 'Urban Housing to c.1770', in Lynch (ed), *Oxford Companion to Scottish History*, 323–34.

Stones, J.A. 1987 *A Tale of Two Burghs: The Archaeology of Old and New Aberdeen*. Aberdeen.

Torrie, E.P.D. (ed) 1986 *The Gild Court Book of Dunfermline, c.1433–1597*. Scottish Record Society, New Series, 12.

Torrie, E.P.D. 1990 *Medieval Dundee. A Town and its People*. Dundee: Abertay Historical Society.

Tyson, R.E. 1986 'Famine in Aberdeenshire, 1696–1699' in Stevenson, D. (ed), *From Lairds to Louns*, 32–52, Aberdeen.

Tyson, R.E. 2001 'Population Patterns', in Lynch (ed), *Oxford Companion to Scottish History*, 487–91.

Vance, S. 2002 'Schooling the People', in Dennison, Ditchburn and Lynch (eds), *Aberdeen Before 1800. A New History*, 309–26.

Whyte, I.D. 1987 'The Occupational Structure of Scottish Burghs in the Late Seventeenth Century', in Lynch (ed), *The Early Modern Town in Scotland*, 219–44.

Whyte, I.D. 1989 'Urbanization in Early-Modern Scotland: a Preliminary Analysis', *Scottish Economic and Social History*, 9, 21–37.

Whyte, I.D. 1995 *Scotland Before the Industrial Revolution, An Economic and Social History, c.1050–c.1750*. London.

Williamson, E. and McGavin, J. (forthcoming) 'Crossing the Border: the Provincial Records of South-East Scotland'.

FURTHER READING

Pryde, G. (ed) 1963 *Court Book of the Burgh of Kirkintilloch*. Scottish History Society.

CHAPTER TEN

Rural Society and Economy
Margaret H. B. Sanderson

The majority of Scots in early modern times lived in the country, with about half of them living north of the River Tay. There is no information on nationwide population figures before the 1690s Poll Tax records but estimates suggest a steady rise from about 500,000 in *c.*1500 to 1,000,000, with the million mark being reached around the time of parliamentary union in 1707 (Whyte 1979, 8–9). Although country people had many urban contacts, their survival ultimately depended on the land, which was the source of their food, clothes and shelter, the resource from which they provided for their families, and the powerbase of those in authority over them. A clear idea of their rights in the land, or lack of such rights, is therefore essential if we are to understand their world.

It is comparatively straightforward to draw a picture of the structure of early modern rural society, from powerful lords to vulnerable peasants, but this can give too static a picture. Land-based socio-economic distinctions were not always clear-cut, and early modern Scottish society, like societies before and since, was subject to change, short-term and long-term, as we shall see. We shall begin in the sixteenth century when the social patterns, like the language in which they are documented, may be said to have been in their classic phase; always bearing in mind that the situation facing us had itself evolved and continued to change.

LAND AND PEOPLE

According to the feudal law of landholding, which applied to most of Scotland by our period, all land was said to be owned by the crown. The sovereign as 'superior' granted it out to 'vassals' – sometimes called 'tenants-in-chief' – by charters in which were set out the terms on which the land was to be held. These terms resolved themselves into certain dues and services: an annual money payment in place of the old military service, although there was still the duty to serve with the royal army in time of war; and services, which included responsibilities towards law and order by holding local courts. In addition to the annual payment and services there were periodic dues known as 'casualties', the most important and expensive of which related to the recognition and entry of an heir to the property. Ecclesiastical landholders, such as monasteries and other religious institutions, were also important tenants-in-chief, holding the land in 'free alms': that is, without payment other than divine service and intercessory prayers. Ecclesiastical landlords, however, also had a duty to hold local courts and the church was usually asked for a major contribution to royal taxations in pre-Reformation times.

Since only the crown was said to own land, these vassals were properly speaking landholders, not landowners. However, in the case of secular vassals their charters conveyed the land to them and their heirs in perpetuity (as long as the terms were honoured), so they could expect their descendants to possess the land generation after generation. Inheritance was by the law of primogeniture, which established a pecking order among the descendants: first to the eldest son, failing whom to the younger sons in order of seniority, then to an only daughter or to several daughters jointly. Land was often granted to a husband and wife jointly – in 'conjunct-fee' – giving the woman the right to the liferent of the property (the right to occupy it until death) should she be widowed.

Because of the varied means of acquisition (such as by marriage, exchange, a grant on another's forfeiture or outright purchase), the greater landholders, especially in the Lowlands, might hold land in different parts of the country. The earl of Morton, for example, held land in ten sheriffdoms at the end of the sixteenth century. In the Highlands, where a blend of feudal law and kinship ties characterised society, both these strands affected the way the land was held by the chiefs and occupied by the clansmen, although some chiefs tended to consolidate their holdings in certain areas (Dodgshon 1981, 106–14). In the Western Isles, after the forfeiture of the MacDonald Lords of the Isles in 1493, the land was held in fairly substantial units, sometimes whole islands, by leading families. In the Northern Isles of Orkney and Shetland, due to earlier Norse rule, landholding was not feudal but 'odal' or 'allodial'. The odaller held land outright, paying a land tax or 'scat' rather than the rents and dues paid to a feudal superior. Here, territory was divided between two major authorities: the crown and the bishopric of Orkney. The bishopric territories were spread through Orkney and Shetland and, due to political and religious changes during our period, changed hands several times (Shaw 1980, 22). Crown vassals might in turn grant parts of their land to others under them, with crown permission, either to sub-vassals by charter, or to tenants by lease, in Scots 'tack'. The majority of the rural population were tack-holding tenants who paid rent in money and/or grain and customary dues, known as 'maill', 'ferme' and 'cain' respectively. In areas where tacks for life were common the tenants were called 'rentallers'; their rights in the land were regarded as heritable in practice and their widows had the automatic right to liferent of the holding. It was also common for a husband and wife to be given a joint tack for a number of years, which entitled the widow to the liferent until the tack ran out.

The early-sixteenth-century philosopher and historian John Mair deplored the insecurity which he claimed resulted from the practice of the short tack. Contemporary records, however, suggest that this may not have been the inevitable effect. Even where land was set annually it was often re-let to the same families. Families can be found holding their land over several generations on the basis of renewable tacks. For example, the Porter family held the mill at Keithick (Angus) from Coupar Angus Abbey for almost a hundred years on renewable tacks of varying length. Estate rentals for the abbeys of Arbroath, Coupar Angus, Dunfermline and Holyrood in the decades before the Reformation show that 19-year tacks and those for life were common, and the tenants of the archbishops of Glasgow and the abbeys of Paisley and Kilwinning were largely rentallers, holding land by life-leases.

The backbone of the tenantry, the husbandmen, often held more than the husbandland (26 Scots acres) from which they took their name. They paid rent in a mixture of money and kind (mainly grain) and often created subtenants under them. There were three basic patterns of tenancy in relation to the occupancy of the ground and the way it was farmed. First, there were joint-tenancies, where the land was set to a group of tenants who were then jointly responsible for its cultivation and rent. The names of joint-tenants may not be given in estate rentals, but simply the name of the farmtoun concerned and the total rent due from it. Secondly, there were share-tenancies, where the land was granted in shares as set out in the tenants' individual tacks, with the amount of rent due from each tenant. Shares were commonly halves, thirds, quarters or eighths, but might be as small as sixteenths or even thirty-second parts. It might be left to the tenants themselves to divide the ground among them according to their shares or, as in the case of joint-tenants, the area to be cultivated by each: 'they shall divide the settings among themselves', as the Coupar Angus record puts it. Lastly, there were single tenancy farms, which could be quite large by contemporary standards, sometimes over 50 acres. While such farms became much more common in the later seventeenth century, they are also found in the sixteenth; the more prosperous husbandmen who farmed them resembled the English yeomen in status and substance.

The tenants discussed so far had clearly defined rights in the land and by the sixteenth century most husbandmen had written tacks. Even tacks of comparatively short duration would be written; many of them survive in the archives of landed families, having been returned to the landlord when they ran out or were renewed. Long tacks, of nineteen years or more, were regarded as alienations of the property requiring the authority of the superior's seal; Coupar Angus tenants spoke of getting 'a common seal' when they obtained or renewed a long tack (Sanderson 1982, 48).

It is difficult to judge the proportion of subtenants to tenants. The former are not often mentioned in rentals and accounts and, where their presence is referred to, they are rarely named. Yet they must have been numerous and, not surprisingly, their numbers were monitored by landlords. They may have been mainly tenants-at-will, holding land by verbal rather than written agreement, and were perhaps related to the main tenants from whom they held. Their immediate superiors in the rural pyramid were normally the husbandmen, but might be an absentee tacksman such as an urban merchant or lawyer.

Beneath the tenants and subtenants were the cottars, who provided a pool of agricultural labour. They generally occupied a cotland with a small dwelling and a kailyard on which to grow their food. Their labour for the tenants sufficed for rent. Any security they had depended on that of those above them; when tenants were evicted, cottars would often find themselves removed from the land with the stock. Landlords regulated their numbers; at Cupargrange, husbandmen who held a twelfth part were allowed two cottars, those with an eighth part, three. Cottars were warned not to employ labour but to undertake their own labouring tasks. At

Urie (Kincardineshire) they were fined eight pence a day for failure to labour for their masters. They might be used as an advance party in bringing new land under cultivation.

However, the circumstances of sixteenth-century cottars may have been somewhat different from those of their namesakes on the eve of the later agricultural improvements (Sanderson 1982, 43–4; 2002, 36–8). Some of them may even have found opportunities for advancement, occupying more than a cotland, or even a few acres as subtenants of husbandmen to whom they paid a rent. At Coupar Angus cottars who acquired holdings in the main ploughland were obliged to observe the same barony laws as husbandmen. In different parts of the country they are found holding directly from the landlord himself, paying rent to him, and thus merging with the small tenant class, although still designated as cottars in the records. Although cottars were forbidden to hire labour, some did, as their testaments make clear, including help with the harvesting of their own plots or the herding of their few animals. This might happen where the cottar also followed a rural craft which brought in additional income.

Cottouns, or cottartouns, many of whose names survive on the modern map, were settlements composed entirely of cottars, who were often answerable directly to the landlord's officers. The continued importance of the cottars at the time of the 1690s Poll Tax has been emphasised, when in the North-East (and probably elsewhere) they merged into smallholders and lesser tenants (Dodgshon 1981, 213–14, 285–7). A hundred years later, contributors to the first *Statistical Account of Scotland* (1790s) lamented their demise as a casualty of commercial agricultural 'improvement'. They appear to be a rural group who may have experienced a loss of status over the early modern period.

Last on the rural social ladder came the labourers, who had no rights in the land and were dependent on their employers for food and shelter. In addition, they received small money and grain payments for their work, which included harvesting, load-carrying, sheep-clipping, muck-spreading and dyke-building. They were not always locally recruited and their employment was often short-term and precarious. In 1574, 28-year-old David Findale, a married man from Perthshire, described himself when witnessing in a court case as 'having no dwelling place . . . not feed [i.e. regularly hired] with anybody, but works to any man that will give him meat [food] and fee, and his common labour is husband labour'. In 1580, 26-year-old John Caithness, an unmarried man from Angus, explained that he was 'a builder of dykes and worker of dargs [day-labour] through the country'. Labourers are usually simply called servants, making it difficult to distinguish them from domestic servants. Skilled workers such as ploughmen and shepherds were often retained for an annual fee and in many places a piece of land was allocated to them for their support.

THE BARONY

The local unit of rural life was the barony and the 'master of the ground', the baron, was in a sense a local government officer (Sanderson 1982, ch. 2). In terms of his charter he was responsible for both public law and order and the administration of the barony's internal affairs – responsibilities which were discharged through the barony court. The court's criminal jurisdiction included such acts as theft, assault and slaughter. The courts of those who had been granted rights of regality had power to try all criminal cases except treason, including the so-called 'four pleas of the crown': murder, arson, rape and robbery. The royal sheriff and justiciar were excluded from the regalities, making them little local kingdoms. All landholding men and women, the latter by proxy, had to attend the barony courts, many men taking their turn at serving on the jury or acting as court officials. The clerk who kept the court records was a professional, in pre-Reformation times often a cleric. The baron himself might preside over the court but was just as likely to delegate the job to his deputy, the baron-bailie, who was often a kinsman and who in turn might act through a bailie-depute. In the sixteenth century, the chief financial officer of the barony was known as the chamberlain. The baron's own legal business would be handled by an urban-based 'writer' (lawyer).

It is largely in the non-criminal business of the barony courts that we find the pattern of rural daily life reflected: disputes and investigations over the occupancy and cultivation of the land; damage to buildings, stock or crops; complaints by the lord against the tenants, tenants against 'the master' and neighbour against neighbour. The terms of agreements and contracts might be settled in court, as would the settings of the ground. People were accused or exonerated publicly before the court. The barony court existed before the kirk session and those who reported their neighbours' faults to the former had nothing to learn from the latter and its 'searchers'.

In many ways the barony was a closed community whose legal and physical boundaries were carefully guarded. No-one must hold land in their own and another barony, thus serving two masters; tenants could sue each other only in their own court in the first instance; only barony men might serve on the jury; subtenants must not be brought in from outside; widows must not remarry without the baron's consent and must not marry 'outtintoun' men. By the seventeenth century, the power of the barony court in criminal affairs was slipping away in the direction of the royal courts and its business was increasingly confined to internal, fairly minor matters (Dickinson 1937, Intro.).

Whatever the barony meant to the lawyers, to the inhabitants it was where they lived and worked. Scotland was not, on the whole, a land of nucleated villages but of scattered settlements referred to as farmtouns, or simply touns, which followed the arable land and good pasture, or stood about a mill, church, the baron's house, at a ferry, crossroads or other communication-point, near coal pits, salt pans or lime-kilns, or on the lands of a former monastic grange. Place names indicating such settlements pepper the modern map. Baronies contained a varying number of such settlements, all showing the characteristics of a self-supporting farming community: the loan or road through the settlement; the cultivated ground, infield more or less under constant cropping in a pattern of rigs, or runrig, and outfield, which was periodically allowed to lie fallow; the great outer or head-dyke, which acted as the boundary of the cultivated area, and beyond it the undrained moss and moor that yielded peat for fuel, turf for building and heather for thatching. On the commonty, pasture was allocated to the tenants in proportion to the extent of their holdings. Naturally-flooded meadowland was coveted for its hay and rich pasture. On the higher ground were the shielings or summer pastures. The nearest modern parallel to these farmtouns can probably be seen in crofting communities. The origins and development of traditional farming are still being investigated by historians (Whyte 1979, 1995, 1998, 25–9; Dodgshon 1975, 1980, 1981, 1983; Devine 1994, ch. 1).

People went about the tasks of the farming year and rural-based crafts and services under the laws which they called 'the lovable custom of the barony'. In common with mainland Europe, Scotland was at this period experiencing population increase, which contributed to the effects of inflation, especially in the second half of the sixteenth century. While population increase encouraged land intake and the establishment of new settlements, it could render existing townships crowded. A study of the settlements in the barony of Kilwinning (Ayrshire) between 1550 and 1570, using a series of rentals and lists of heads of households, compiled for the purpose of recovering arrears of teinds (English, tithes), yielded the names of seventy farmtouns and just over five hundred heads of households. Allowing for spouses, a conservative estimate of four children (some old enough to have families of their own), dependent relatives, servants and labourers to each household, there may have been between 3,500 and 4,000 inhabitants in Kilwinning barony in the middle of the sixteenth century; the barony, incidentally, was almost co-terminous with the parish of the same name. What is striking about the population of the barony is that the five hundred heads of households comprise only 126 surnames, an indication of how closely related the community was (Sanderson 1987, 312).

INHERITANCE

Of crucial concern to all families was their continued possession of the land. We can readily associate a preoccupation with inheritance with feudal lords, possessors by charter; but inheritance in the sense of continued possession was equally important to tenants. Those in Lincluden barony (stewartry of Kirkcudbright) were said in the 1550s to have been in possession 'sum 40 yeris, sum 50 and sum past memor of man'. Yet, while a charter granted land in perpetuity, a tack lasted at most for the grantee's lifetime and perhaps that of one heir. How was it then that tackholding families might remain in possession over generations? A concept lay behind the tenants' claim to inheritance: a customary law known as the 'kindness' or 'kindly tenancy' of the land. However the concept of kindness may have originated and become established, by the sixteenth century it was understood to be a claim to possession because one was nearest of kin (heir) to the previous possessor (Sanderson 1982, ch. 5; 2002, ch. 1). Historians have remarked that it is difficult to find an exact definition of kindly tenancy, but the many references to how it operated indicate that it was not *how* but *why* the tenant held the land. As long ago as 1908 John Arthur Brown, in looking at the kindly tenants of the archbishop of Glasgow, believed that the concept had originated in the benevolent or 'kindly' attitude of the church to its tenants, and that kindness tended to attach to those who were native inhabitants over many generations (Brown 1908, 114). Certainly, the clause 'native kindly tenants' was frequently used in claims to kindness. Brown noted that the written evidence of the Glasgow tenants' rights was a copy from the archbishop's register of the tenant's entry to his holding, usually for life, and that the Glasgow tenants were known as rentallers. He drew a parallel between rentallers and English copyholders, a parallel which has been generally accepted since. He also pointed out that, over time, kindly rights came to be exploited by the tenants themselves, being split, exchanged or sold, so that 'a free trade was done in land' at tenant level.

Dr Isobel Grant, who examined kindness at some length, again laid stress on the likelihood of benevolent origins, concluding that the kindly tenants may have had 'strong moral if not legal claims' (Grant 1930, 244). Recent research, however, has shown that the customary principle of kindness was upheld in both local and central courts. Dr Grant also equated kindly tenants with rentallers, a connection strengthened by the statement of the jurist Sir Thomas Hope that where a kindly tenant's written right put no limit of time on his tenancy it 'should be als sufficient to the tennent as ane rental for his lyfetyme' (Hope 1938, vol. 2, 232). The ongoing study of kindly tenancy in association with written rights was somewhat derailed by a study by A. Geddes in 1954 of the kindly tenants of Lochmaben, who had received possession of their land by the goodwill of Robert I, which tended to make some later writers assume that all kindly tenants were tenants-at-will (Geddes 1954). However, historians have since come to believe that kindly tenancy, however it may have originated, came to be regarded as an established principle of customary law. Ian D. Whyte, in summing up modern research, and suggesting that in the past too much emphasis may have been placed on tenant insecurity, again noted the analogy of Scottish rentallers and English copyholders, and described kindly tenants as those 'whose claim to occupy a piece of land was based on close kinship with the previous holders', also noting that the kindly right could be renounced or even sold. He was of the opinion that by the early seventeenth century the status of the kindly tenant was in decline (Whyte 1979, 30–1). R.A. Dodgshon, while remarking that the exact meaning of kindly tenancy remains elusive, having probably changed over the years, drew attention to the significant parallel between the Lowland principle and the Highland concept of *dùthchas*, which gave families the right to hereditary occupation (Dodgshon 1981, 110–1, 110–13).

It is in the concern with inheritance that we find most meaning in the term 'kindly tenancy', as it was understood and applied in sixteenth-century Scotland. Further research into public and private records, not all of which were accessible to earlier historians, has thrown light on the practice of this principle, and has linked it to customary inheritance practices in western Europe, even though questions remain as to its origins and development. The term derives from the words kin and kinship, and the right belonged to those 'native kindly tenants' who had occupied their holdings for generations, whether on the basis of life-leases (rentals) or shorter renewable tacks. Kindness descended in a family through both men and women. The principle was recognised by the courts. Disputes over who had 'the best kindness' might result in a formal enquiry, such as 'the trial of the kindness' held on the earl of Morton's lands of Preston (Kirkcudbright) in 1575 or that on the lands of Stobo and Eddleston (Peeblesshire) in 1580. Those who were judged 'unkyndlie' as a result of the investigation, having bought kindness without the landlord's permission, were fined, although allowed to keep their acquisitions. Even kindly tenants, however, had to keep the terms of their tacks or rentals. The landlord could withdraw their kindly rights for infringement of or failure to keep the barony laws. As with the land itself, the customary right to inherit it was ultimately at the will of the master of the ground.

PROVIDING FOR ALL THE FAMILY

The head of a household – freeholder or tenant – faced a dilemma when making provision for the family: how to provide for them all from the family's inheritance without overstretching its resources (Sanderson 2002, ch. 4). Of course, the law made some provision for them. The law of primogeniture and the customary law of kindness defined and protected heirs. The widow of a freeholder had the right to a third of the lands possessed by her husband at the time of their marriage: her *terce*. If she had been a conjunct-fear she would have the liferent of those lands contained in the charter of conjunct-fee. In marriage contracts of landed families, future provision might be made for the woman in widowhood, in the form of a *jointure* of designated property from the lands of her husband's family. Rentallers' widows and widows who had been joint tackholders also had the liferent of the land. A widow was entitled to one third of her husband's moveables (half if there were no children), after the best in each category had been set aside for the heir. The children shared a third of the parent's moveables (father's or mother's), although many a 'bairn's pairt', like many a 'tocher' (dowry), remained unpaid for years.

In the Northern Isles under odal law, the land was divided among the children on the odaller's death, a daughter's share being half that of a son. The only practice resembling feudal law was that the 'chief heir' inherited the dwelling house, with compensation to the other children. After the abolition of the Norse laws in the Isles in 1611, odal practices quickly declined and in fact many odallers had had their lands transferred to feudal law by charter before that date (Shaw 1980, 35–40).

There were ways in which the head of the household might try to improve on the legal provisions. In order to ensure the safe transfer of the land to the next generation, both freeholders and tenants might formally resign the land into the superior's hands in favour of the heir, retaining the liferent. By this means the transfer had already taken place, although the heirs did not receive the property until their mother's death. Many examples of this practice among freeholders are to be found in the crown's *Register of the Great Seal*. In the case of tenants, examples appear in landlords' rental books, where the record of the entry of tenants is accompanied by the clause: 'with consent of' the previous tenant, in many cases the father or other close relative. In the barony of Glasgow, for example, in the first half of the sixteenth century just over 45% of inherited holdings were transferred to the heir during the lifetime of the sitting rentaller. Family circumstances might dictate the move, as in 1545 when Thomas Drew was rentalled in a portion of Auchinloch with consent of his father Patrick, 'ane agit man beddrale [bedridden]'. The arrangement was also made by tenants who held by shorter tacks, as when (also in 1545) Steven Porter at Keithick (Angus) was granted renewal of a five-year tack of the mill at the request of his father Gilbert, who in his illness sent the request with a neighbour (Sanderson 1982, 48; 53–4).

These transfers of holdings to the younger generation of tenant families often followed or were accompanied by a 'retirement contract' (also paralleled in Europe) by which a parent (father or mother) made over their rights in the farm in return for a promise of food, clothes and lodging for their lifetimes. In Orkney and Shetland, where the practice was derived from odal customs, it included the Norse practice of *upgestry*, by which the odaller might dispose of land to someone outside the family in return for maintenance, if the family refused to provide it.

Strictly speaking, land could not be bequeathed in a will at this period – only moveable goods could. However, tenants got round this by bequeathing their right to the land, their kindness; and in many cases they divided the kindness among the children in order to provide several of them with holdings. In effect, this is partible inheritance, which was also practised in Europe, usually on good arable land which could sustain subdivision. Families might exchange, split or even sell their kindness to suit their circumstances. In 1551 at Over Smithston in Kilwinning barony (Ayrshire) John Watt paid his elder half-brother John White £6 for the latter's kindness of the holding, which appears to have come into the family through their mother. Such practices were permitted, provided that the superior gave consent, but were closely monitored by him through the barony court. Tenants at Crossmichael (stewartry of Kirkcudbright) were warned not to dispose of their kindness to anyone without the landlord's consent or their tacks would be terminated 'and their kindness to remain in my handis'.

When kindness was sold outwith the family, a new line of kindly tenants was created in the purchaser's family. Thus the sellers voluntarily cut across the traditional criteria for the claim to kindness: that is, the claim to be 'auld native kindly tenants'. Like the land to which it was a claim, kindness had become marketable: bought and sold, exchanged, bequeathed and compensated for. In resorting to this means of provision, families altered the line of succession and rendered the very basis of their possession of the land vulnerable. Some may have found that it was only a short step from disposing of one's inheritance to being bought out. Thus they themselves put their rights at risk, quite apart from the threat posed by the spread of feu-ferme tenure (see below), which generated so much protest by and on behalf of the kindly tenants.

Most forms of provision, even when they included money, involved land. Money bequeathed in wills was not intended to be spent but usually 'laid out upon land', whose rents meant income. A family member might be left a stated annual income from the holding: William Hoy, tenant at Gattonside (Roxburghshire), left to a younger son 'the crop of the orchard land yearly until the profit thereof mak him £120 [Scots]'. Marriage contracts of families great and small often reveal just how piecemeal provision was: for peasant farmers a few merks (a merk = 13s 4d Scots), some household goods and an animal or two; for landed families, often struggling with debt, some land already 'wadset' (mortgaged) might be given for a woman's jointure, and some borrowed money for her tocher. The marriage contracts of all classes were sometimes drawn up prior to marriageable age, with the maintenance of the future husband and wife becoming the responsibility of one family or the other until the marriage.

CHANGES IN THE PATTERN

In recent decades, historians have come to view the era before the agricultural revolution, especially the later seventeenth century, more positively than earlier writers, who tended to portray it as the dark days before the dawn of improved agricultural practice and commercially-orientated estate management. This brighter picture is the result of detailed research into surviving estate records and a reluctance to accept without question the picture drawn by the 'improvers' themselves and their admirers. However, change, even change for the better, came slowly, unevenly and with setbacks. The evidence of change as found in contemporary records is itself uneven and needs cautious interpretation. Nevertheless, changes there certainly were over the sixteenth and seventeenth centuries, some undoubtedly for the better, others not so good for sections of the rural population.

Historians of the seventeenth century who have detected increased tenant security have attributed this partly to the practice of giving tenants written tacks, although they warn us against mistaking the greater survival rate of such documents for increased usage of the practice itself. Detailed study of surviving tacks in the records of selected estates has suggested that the seventeenth century saw the expansion of better tenant security, with perhaps a set-back during the war years of the 1640s and 1650s, followed in turn by steady improvement later in the century (Whyte 1998, 22–5; Whyte and Whyte 1983; Dodgshon 1981, 253–4).

However, as we saw earlier, there is evidence of written tacks in the sixteenth century. Like freeholders, tenants were required to produce their written titles in court as proof of possession or as evidence that their tack had not yet run out. In 1578, the advocate for the tenants of the Kirkheuch at St Andrews produced five tacks in the court of session on behalf of his clients. Receipts for delivery of such evidence sometimes turn up among court papers, in one instance a receipt for no fewer than twelve tacks. Alexander Irvine in Strade (Moray) produced his tack in court in 1488 and in 1503 John Reid in Brintshiels (Ayrshire) produced a five-year tack, issued at Melrose Abbey on 7 November 1501. So, even though written tacks do not survive, it is clear that they were in use. Taken together with the operation of kindly tenancy and the possibility of improvement even for some cottars, it may suggest that the situation of the tenants had reached a kind of high-water mark by the middle of the sixteenth century, but that the later part of that century and the early seventeenth may have been a turning of the tide for many of them.

One of the most important changes in this period to affect the relationship of land and people was the spread of feu-ferme tenure, which peaked in the middle of the sixteenth century, on crown, other secular and church land, although probably most fully documented on the last (Sanderson 1982, chs 6, 7, 9–11; Sanderson 2002, ch. 2). Since church land represented much of the best farmland in Scotland, the change affected a very large portion of the rural population. Feuing offered tenants the opportunity to become owner-occupiers of their land, but at the same time threatened those who could not afford to take the opportunity, with the loss of their time-honoured rights of customary inheritance as others stepped in to feu the land over their heads.

Although Scotland had no dissolution of the monasteries, as in England, control of church land gradually passed from ecclesiastical into secular hands during the sixteenth century. The first step was the effect of the appointment of career clerics from politically influential families as heads of religious houses. Heavily taxed by the Scottish crown and acutely aware of the threat to church property by the more radical demands for church reform, these 'commendators', as they were called, saw feuing as a means of raising money in the short term from the land: a feu charter required a substantial down-payment and an immediate increase on the old rent as part of the feu-duty. For the grantees, however, the attractions were considerable: heritable possession once and for all, a fixed feu-duty and very often enhanced rights in the use of the land itself. Some noble families and many lairds did well for themselves out of the feuing of the church lands, adding substantially to their landed possessions. So too did many tenant families, as a study of nearly three thousand extant feu charters of church lands has shown.

Social status of feuars	*Percentage receiving charters*
Nobles and relatives	3
Lairds, other proprietors, and relatives	29
Burgesses and relatives	8
Tenants, others designated 'in', and relatives	44
Clergy, before and after 1560, and relatives; lawyers, crown servants and other officials	3
Those whose names only are given, with no designation; doubtful cases	13

These figures should be seen as a guide to the social background of the feuars rather than a final count. Additional charters examined since this study was first published (1982) have not significantly altered these proportions. Many tenants-turned-feuars undoubtedly prospered well into the seventeenth century, some of them merging with the lesser gentry, with whose families some of them intermarried. For example, the 'gentlemen' whom an observer saw taking part in the 'Mauchline Rising' of 1648 were descendants of the feuars of Melrose Abbey's Ayrshire barony of Kylesmure, whose ancestors had been rentallers for generations. Feuars who had previously been share-tenants became known as 'portioners', a designation borne with pride and even used on tombstones. A number of feuars of church lands became what were called 'bonnet lairds', one sign of their increased status being the number of tower houses built or enlarged on former church land. Also, commentators on the improved seventeenth-century landscape sometimes attributed this to earlier feuing.

Although tenants are found consolidating their scattered holdings into more manageable units before the flood of feu charters, there is no doubt that feuing did accelerate the process. Feuartouns, feued in existing portions to sitting tenants, were also a feature of the landscape in the late sixteenth and early seventeenth centuries, for example, in the valleys of the Rivers Tweed and Tay and in Strathisla in Banffshire. The crown feued extensively in the Border country and elsewhere. In the Western Isles the crown feuars included important clan chiefs, while in the Northern Isles incomers, including the Balfours, Bellendens and Cheynes, created large estates from both crown and bishopric lands, which helped to hasten the decline of odal landholding.

The fortunes of the feuars were mixed (Sanderson 2002, ch. 2). The records of the court of session contain many cases of complaint by those threatened with rack-renting or eviction by outsider-feuars. Other records reveal the activities of land-speculators, who feued church land and then resigned it to the sitting tenants for compensation that represented substantial profit. Some feuar families simply found that the initial outlay had been too much for them, so that within a generation or two they are found wadsetting or even disposing of their land. In 1592, for example, David Dunmure, who with his widowed mother had feued their half of Wester Gourdie (Angus) in 1564, sold the land, with plough oxen and sown wheat, to Alexander Wedderburn, town clerk of Dundee. It is difficult to discover what happened to people like Dunmure – whether they paid off their debts and whether they took another property or left for the town. In the barony of Strathisla (Banffshire), where feuartouns and small lairdships were created on Kinloss Abbey land in the mid-sixteenth century, Alexander Duff of Braco bought up the small proprietorships, vowing 'to make the smoke of these houses go through the one vent by and by'. The impression here and elsewhere is of the amalgamation of small properties into unified estates by the early seventeenth century.

Did the gradual removal of a layer of small proprietors expose a vulnerable population of tenants, subtenants, tenants-at-will and cottars, with nothing between them and landowners who had an increasingly profitmaking interest in the land? Was the turn of the seventeenth century one of the low points in the changing fortunes of Scottish rural society? When things improved later in the century, one of the signs of which is said to be the more frequent granting of written tacks to tenants, were those who benefited different people from those who had experienced a measure of security in the first half of the sixteenth century?

A second important change over our period was the increasing importance of money in the rural economy. For various reasons, more landowners began to find a cash income desirable and convenient. In the sixteenth century, the commutation of rents in kind and customary dues and services into money was on the increase, if geographically uneven. Part of the process of commutation was the selling of the grain rents to the tenants. In 1573, the chamberlain of Scone (Perthshire) sold almost half the grain rent to the tenants, while in 1591 the countess of Morton told her husband by letter from Auchterhouse (Angus) that no amount of haggling by her and the chamberlain could get a reasonable price from the tenants. The grain rents at Houston (West Lothian), whose landlord was a practising advocate in Edinburgh, were sold for £1,000 Scots in 1618. The commutation process was speeded up by the spread of feu-ferme, as feu-duty was very often paid in cash and labour services were commuted: of the 2,700 feu charters of church land initially examined in the study already referred to, 1,800 stipulated annual payments entirely in money (Sanderson 1982, 158).

The acceleration of commutation in the seventeenth century accompanied the growth of a recognisable market economy, with grain being regularly marketed by the landlords; this was encouraged by legislation (Smout and Fenton 1965, 73–93). While only the landlords could market on a large scale and on a regular basis, tenants and feuars can also be found selling surpluses in burgh markets. In 1593, for example, Patrick Air, a feuar of Scone Abbey who had originally acquired his feu on the resignation of a land-speculator, was sued by three Dundee burgesses to whom he had contracted to sell grain and who questioned the quantity delivered. In spite of the trend towards commutation, grain rent continued to be paid in many areas until the end of the seventeenth century; on the Panmure estates (Angus) tenants on pastoral farms paid in money, those on arable land in grain (Dodgshon 1981, 97–9; Whyte 1983, 39).

The fact that sixteenth-century tenants and others handled money suggests that, even then, farming in some places had risen above mere subsistence. Some Coupar Angus Abbey tenants handed over £20 Scots and more for the renewal of a tack and as much as £100 Scots for a feu charter, occasionally in instalments. One Inchaffray Abbey tenant was given a rebate on the down-payment for his feu because he had paid a 'large gressum [entry fee]' for the renewal of a tack only the previous year. By the seventeenth century, surplus resources have been detected among the rural population, 'with mechanisms for investment', and tenants have been found who made a practice of money-lending (Whyte and Whyte 1988; Dodgshon 1981, 241–2). Testaments show that rural communities operated a system, both formal and informal, of borrowing and lending. Bonds (legally binding promises to repay), taken for the repayment of loans and debts due for the hire of work animals and equipment or an emergency supply of victual or fodder, were common. Some tenants lent money to their landlords, who used land in security; debtors included landlords as substantial as the earl of Morton, Lord Ogilvy and the laird of Lochleven, the last as early as the 1520s. Failure to repay meant that the land was transferred by legal process to the tenant-creditor, which was one way of becoming a proprietor. The depositions of witnesses in court cases reveal money in the hands of a variety of country people, not only lairds, feuars and tenants but even servant men and women, craftsmen and labourers. Sometimes we learn that they had had it only because it had been stolen; Thomas Rolland in Abernethy (Perthshire) had £20 Scots and his precious tack stolen 'furth of ane pig [earthenware container] and . . . ane kist [chest]'. It is likely that most people in his condition had a rainy day rather than investment in mind.

WINNERS AND LOSERS

In spite of opportunities for advancement and improvement it is clear that hardship and poverty were the lot of many people. The reasons for poverty in any age are complex and historians are still trying to identify all the causes of destitution in the early modern period. There are some likely causes: inflation and price rises; population increase; intermittent warfare, with its destruction of the land and its produce; the smallish returns from agricultural effort; the inevitable effects of bad weather and poor harvests; and visitations of the plague. Shortage of food was probably common, depending on local conditions; it is now believed that some of the most severe famines may have been in the early seventeenth century, notably that of 1623, and not only in the 1690s. Recent research has suggested that, when available in reasonable quantity, the diet of early modern Scots was adequate and even nourishing (Gibson and Smout 1995, 226). One of the great difficulties in times of dearth was that of moving supplies around the country.

A problematic phenomenon of this period is that of vagrancy. It is difficult to identify all the reasons for movement of people around the country other than the normal reasons for everyday travel. Scattered, though illuminating, information on movement can be found in the circumstantial evidence supplied by witnesses in court cases. For example, information on the approximate ages and dwelling places of witnesses shows that many young men left their place of birth or upbringing to find work or a holding for themselves. Some said they had lived and worked in several places or had held land from a succession of 'masters'. While some improved their circumstances – moving up from labourer or household servant to cottar, or even tenant – others failed to make good (Sanderson 2002, 174–8). An examination of testimonials given by kirk sessions to parishioners changing parishes, usually for work, showed the number of such movements to be high, even if over short distances and chiefly around the servant hiring fairs at Whitsunday and Martinmas (Whyte 1989, 49).

Hardship certainly drove some people off the land for good. These circumstances may be revealed in a simple statement in a rental: 'the sixth rig of Aberdargie occupiit by Andrew Drone quha departit in povertie fra the samyn' in 1595. Or they may be reported by a court witness, as in the case of Donald Miller, whose laird pleaded with him in 1541 to stay on in his Ayrshire holding, 'quhilk he refusit because of povertie', or Thomas Jack, whose neighbour, in 1576, overheard the landlord offer to cancel Jack's arrears of rent if he would get the land back into good condition, which he refused for the same reason. These cases support the impression gained from other sixteenth-century records: that eviction for non-payment of rent was not always the first resort, but that the landlord's first concern was to keep the land in occupation and cultivation, hoping for better times. This attitude to land-management, which was both realistic and paternalistic, may help to explain why tenants who were in arrears of rent can be found in possession, rather than be seen as evidence that sixteenth-century management was necessarily slack. Enough references to lairds' account books and the survival of sufficient numbers of carefully-kept rentals and chamberlains' accounts show that landlords and their officials kept records (Sanderson 1982, ch. 3). It is a fact that the arrears, or 'rests', as they were called, tended to mount up over the years in contemporary government, ecclesiastical and burgh accounts. In any case, barony officials knew local circumstances and problems and would be forced to make allowances. The laird of Houston's clerk could tell his secretary: 'the lady herself knawis quha hes payit their dutie of the crop 1602'.

Many people who for one reason or another were unable to find support in their own locality did take to the roads, a situation highlighted by the legislation against vagrants, or 'sturdy beggars', whose predicament of being able-bodied but unable to find work or sustenance was to continue until almost modern times. In the early modern period, poor relief was strictly for the aged, infirm, widows and orphans, and those overtaken by an unforeseen calamity, and was handed out by kirk sessions who, on the whole, were doing their best with limited means (Mitchison 1989, 199–24). It has been calculated that in the parish of Monikie (Angus) between 1660 and 1710 20% of all poor relief payments were made to vagrants (Whyte 1989, 56). Yet, in spite of hardship and dislocation, it has been claimed that at the time of the Poll Tax in the 1690s 'a high proportion of the rural population still had a foothold in the land' (Whyte and Whyte 1983, 38).

CONCLUSION

At the end of our period, the land itself, with all its problems, still provided a degree of cohesion in society. The bulk of the population was still rural. The basic everyday needs of food, clothes and shelter were derived from the land and on the whole were locally produced and supplied. Lairds and other more prosperous proprietors, however, were likely to source some of their needs from outwith their home country, buying from urban merchants who imported the luxury items that enhanced their lifestyles. The peasant farmers' outside contacts reached as far as they themselves personally travelled.

Although money was in greater use and the commutation of rents and services in kind into money payments was on the increase in the sixteenth century, many rents were still paid in grain and custom payments in small farm produce. Money that came to hand was usually 'laid out on land', or annual rents from it. For most Scottish landed families the land itself was still the major source of their income, power and prestige. Not many of them had the capital to invest in the development of rural industry; the returns from any coal, salt or iron-workings on their land were still reckoned as simply part of the rents. It was common for those who followed a professional or political career to acquire landed estates as a more stable source of income.

For the majority of the rural population, their stake in the land, their substance and their prospects of improvement showed remarkable variation throughout these centuries, which could blur the edges of social and economic distinctions. Rural society showed elements of both stability and vulnerability. Within the limits of their customary rights, people were resourceful with regard to provision for their families and continued possession of the land. They were even prepared for their own purposes to exploit the very rights which safeguarded their possession. Customary rights, particularly that of inheritance, were also externally threatened by the most significant social change of the sixteenth century – the spread of heritable feu-ferm tenure, particularly, though not only, on church lands. At the same time, feuing created a group of new small proprietors – owner-occupiers – in rural society, some of whom undoubtedly prospered and threatened the continued possession of those who were unable to take advantage of it. It gradually reinforced the trend towards consolidation of holdings, apparent in the sixteenth century, by enabling those with the means to do so to swallow up the holdings of small feuars, creating larger estates as time went on.

There were undoubtedly ups and downs, advance and reversal, in the pattern of social change. The sixteenth century may have seen the high-water mark of stability and opportunity among the possessors of the soil, and at the same time the turning of the tide for those who lost out in these changes. Cottars and subtenants may have suffered most of all, becoming by the period of widespread agricultural 'improvement' a diminishing rural labour-force, very different from their predecessors two centuries earlier. Tenants towards the end of the seventeenth century may have benefited from a period of increased security of tenure and improved farming methods. Gradual changes in agricultural techniques and profitable land-management were to make the 'master of the ground' the main beneficiary in the long term.

REFERENCES

Brown, J.A. 1908 'The Kindly Tenants of the Archbishop of Glasgow', *Transactions of the Glasgow Archaeological Society*, new series, 5, 105–24.

Dodgshon, R.A. 1975 'Runrig and the Communal Origins of Property in Land', *Juridical Review*, new series, 20, 189–208.

Dodgshon, R.A. 1980 'The Origins of Traditional Field Systems', in Parry, M.L. and Slater, T.R. (eds), *The Making of the Scottish Countryside*, London, 69–92.

Dodgshon, R.A. 1983 'Agricultural change and its social consequences in the Southern Uplands of Scotland, 1660–1780', in Devine, T.M. and Dickson, D. (eds.), *Ireland and Scotland, 1600–1850: Parallels and Contrasts in Economic and Social Development*, Edinburgh, 46–59.

Geddes, A. 1954 'The Four Royal Towns of Lochmaben: A Study of Rural Stability', *Transactions of Dumfriesshire and Galloway Natural History and Antiquarian Society*, 39, 83–101.

Gibson, A.J.S. and Smout, T.C. 1995 *Prices Food and Wages in Scotland, 1550–1780*. Cambridge.

Hope, J. 1937–38 *Hope's Major Practicks*, ed Clyde, J.A. Edinburgh.

Mitchison, R.M. 1989 'North and South: the development of the gulf in Poor Law Practice', in Houston, R.A. and Whyte, I.D. (eds), *Scottish Society, 1500–1800*, Cambridge, 199–224.

Sanderson, M.H.B. 1987 *The People of Sixteenth Century Ayrshire*. Ayr.

Smout, T.C. and Fenton, A. 1965 'Scottish agriculture before the improvers – an Exploration', *Agricultural History Review*, 13, 73–93.

Whyte, I.D. 1989 'Population Mobility in Early Modern Scotland', in Houston and Whyte (eds), *Scottish Society, 1500–1800*, 37–58.

Whyte, I.D. 1995 'Before the Improvers: Agricultural and Landscape Change in Lowland Scotland, c.1660–c.1750', *Scottish Archives*, 1, 31–42.

Whyte, I.D. 1998 'Poverty or Prosperity? Rural Society in Lowland Scotland in the Late Sixteenth and Early Seventeenth Centuries', *Scottish Economic and Social History*, 18, 19–32.

Whyte I.D. and Whyte K.A. 1983 'Some Aspects of the Social Structure of Rural Society in Seventeenth Century Lowland Scotland' in Devine, TM and Dickson, D. (eds), *Scotland and Ireland,1600–1850: Parallels and Contrasts in Economic and Social Development*, Edinburgh, 32–45.

Whyte, I.D. and Whyte, K.A. 1988 'Debt and Credit, poverty and prosperity in a seventeenth-century Scottish rural community', in Mitchison, R.M. and Roebuck, P. (eds), *Economy and Society in Scotland and Ireland, 1500–1939*, Edinburgh, 70–80.

FURTHER READING

Devine, T.M. 1994 *The Transformation of Rural Scotland : Social Change and Agrarian Economy, 1660–1815*. Edinburgh.

Dodgshon, R.A. 1981 *Land and Society in Early Scotland*. Oxford.

Grant, I.F. 1930 *The Social and Economic Development of Scotland before 1603*. Edinburgh.

Sanderson, M.H.B. 1982 *Scottish Rural Society in the Sixteenth Century*. Edinburgh.

Sanderson, M.H.B. 2002 *A Kindly Place? Living in Sixteenth-Century Scotland*. East Linton.

Shaw, F.J. 1980 *The Northern and Western Islands of Scotland: Their Economy and Society in the Seventeenth Century*. Edinburgh.

Whyte, I.D. 1979 *Agriculture and Society in Seventeenth-century Scotland*. Edinburgh.

CHAPTER ELEVEN

Renaissance Architecture
Charles McKean

Between 1500 and 1700, the period for which we have the first reliable visual evidence of how most Scots lived in their country seats, towns and cities, much of what survives today of pre-modern Scotland took its current form. The Renaissance was a vivid and dynamic period in Scottish cultural history, when the country played a full role in European artistic movements (with the notable exception of Scotland's rejection of the reinvented classical architecture that permeated southern Europe). Social, political and cultural changes were expressed in buildings, decoration and art, with results entirely at variance with the perception of the country that has prevailed since the middle of the eighteenth century. Then – and this was deliberately fostered by the leaders of the Enlightenment – the perception of Stewart Scotland became, in contrast to that of England, one of an uncultured, backward nation perpetually at the mercy of religious or political strife (McKean 2006).

That this perception was profoundly imbalanced can be illustrated by a simple example. The minority of James VI (1568–5) has been portrayed as a period of impoverishment and bloody feuds, with the Scots nobility sheltering themselves in fortified castles when not indulging in raid, feud or assassination. This perception persists in much current historiography, but Hume Brown (1902) provides a good example of what was thought then and is still repeated today. Yet the largest construction boom of country houses during the early modern period took place during James VI's minority, with the erection of largely indefensible, lavishly-furnished buildings surrounded by fruitful yards, gardens, parks and enclosures.

Not only was most of Scotland at peace, but its elite was therefore sufficiently wealthy to build. Masons, wrights, plasterers, painters and gardeners were employed and domestic interiors were reorganised according to European fashions. Houses were furnished with libraries, Musselburgh hangings or 'Arras' tapestries from the Low Countries, countless brightly-coloured beds and soft furnishings, and a growing number of paintings. In this, Scotland was no different from any other European country. Indeed, it was in touch with the latest fashions: paintings, sculptures and plasterwork in the great houses display motifs which conveyed symbolic or moral messages derived from contemporary European publications.

Moreover, once James took full power in 1585, he appears to have set about the modernisation of his country. Exhaustive lists of landowners and their country seats were compiled by the privy council, and Timothy Pont began the process of mapping the country in such detail that his maps included minute but accurate elevations of country houses, for which he often provided the owner's name, and even the height of waves and the fish to be found in Loch Tay. The country's weights and measures were reviewed, and inspectors of mines appointed. This was the technocratic modernising culture, probably led by the future chancellor, the Catholic Alexander Seton, later earl of Dunfermline, that would eventually lead to Robert Pont's proposals to overhaul the calendar, and John Napier's discovery of logarithms.

The 'British' agenda of the Enlightenment in the eighteenth century, and the industrialisation of Scotland in the nineteenth, led to the annihilation of most of the pre-1700 built heritage and the discounting of its culture. As a result, far less evidence of our Renaissance survives than in other European countries: perhaps six out of every seven Renaissance country seats have been lost through adaptation or demolition. Although courtiers' houses were likely to be at the forefront of fashion, few survive to show us what they were like: Inveraray, seat of the earls of Argyll, the hereditary masters of the household, was demolished; Inverugie, Fetteresso and Dunottar, homes of the hereditary marshalls of Scotland, the Earls Marischal, were respectively blown up, wholly remodelled and abandoned to fall into ruin.

However, in its continued reluctance to adopt the rediscovered classical architectural language of the ancients, Scotland became architecturally unique in Europe. The treasures, rules and disciplines of the rediscovered classical world were propagated through books by Palladio, Vitruvius, Scamozzi and Serlio – books well known and circulating in Scotland. Pattern books, emblem books and illustrations from the classics or the Bible were widely used as sources for internal decoration and fittings. So, if they were European in so many other aspects of their lives, why did the Scots elite depart so strongly from the European norm in architectural expression? The rejection of the classical approach to architecture was probably a national cultural choice, reflecting the sense of intense national identity that was felt by the Scots, possibly as a consequence of their longstanding role as a pawn in the perennial battle between England and France. It is possible that some Scots felt that classicism was too closely associated with Catholicism. Moreover, after the 1590s, it seems that the Scottish fascination with constant national cultural reinvention had become so ingrained that the reinvention of the past of Renaissance architectural and cultural ideology had, in Scotland, become the reinvention not just of a Scottish past (Campbell 1995) but particularly of the 'Marian' architecture of the 1550s and 1560s.

The four principal expressions of architectural ambition were royal palaces, country seats, churches and civic buildings. However, architecture reflects, expresses and symbolises the principal political and cultural preoccupations of its era, and it evolved chronologically over this period, generally following the pattern of reigns: the early Renaissance (the reigns of James IV and James V); the 'Marian' period (under Mary of Guise and her daughter Mary, queen of Scots) 1542–1568; the minority of James VI to his wedding with Anna of Denmark (1568–1590); the later reign of James VI and that of Charles I (1590–1649); and, lastly, the later seventeenth century (1650–1700), with a particular focus upon the regency of James, duke of York. This chapter therefore examines the role of the four principal building types before examining each of these chronological phases in order to provide a rounded picture of architectural developments in early modern Scotland.

THE ROYAL PALACE

By 1500, kings of Scots had selected as their principal seat the palace that had been grafted onto Holyrood Abbey near Edinburgh. The palace in Edinburgh Castle, being cold and draughty, was reserved for times of emergency. Throughout the sixteenth century, however, the cultural focus of Scotland was the palace of Stirling ('fair Snawdoun', in the words of the court poet Sir David Lindsay), whereas the 'courtly' seat, if a distinction could be made, was probably Linlithgow Palace. Kings went on periodic and routine progresses, staying principally at the seats of greater subjects; the starting point of most of these progresses was the royal hunting seat of Falkland in Fife. There is no record of a monarch making a comparable trip to the royal castle at Dumbarton, on the Clyde estuary, and the only place they held in the west for such a purpose was Rothesay, which was visited but once. So the Scottish monarchy was tilted to the east, leaving the west largely in the hands of the 'westland lords', greatly under the influence of the Hamilton family, whose head, the earl of Arran, was heir to the throne for much of the period between 1495 and 1567.

Other palaces with royal connections included the great palace built on a sea-girt rock at Dunbar by the Regent Jehann Stuart, duke of Albany and duc de la Tour D'Auvergne, in c.1516. Protected by a militarily fashionable, enormously powerful blockhouse (octagonal artillery emplacement), this sumptuous palace was visited by a monarch seemingly only once – an ill-starred visit by Mary, queen of Scots in 1566 (McIvor 2003). Queen Anna's favoured seat was Dunfermline, where she had a new pavilion or belvedere erected for her in 1600 by the royal architect, her close friend and chamberlain, William Schaw: and that was where most of her children were born.

Royal palaces were theatres of monarchy, where the monarch would welcome ambassadors, hold birth, wedding and funeral celebrations, hear pleas and issue charters. The size of the Scottish court varied from about 350 to 500 courtiers during the sixteenth century; and great lords, who normally had a function at court, brought trains of dependents and servants. Palaces had to accommodate all of them, whilst observing gradations of rank. The accommodation had to distinguish between ceremony and business, and provide adequate privacy. Part of the royal palace had always been reserved for the monarch's own suite, as evidenced by the fourteenth-century David's Tower in Edinburgh Castle. Although the fashionable King's Tower, added to Holyrood in 1529, was inherited from this mediaeval tradition, a new form of twinned 'state apartment' emerged in the refashioning of Stirling and Linlithgow in the 1530s. Both king and queen had contiguous suites of ante-chamber (also called the hall or guard hall), chamber (throne room, presence chamber or chamber of dais) and bedchamber, which provided a formal sequence of increasing rank and intimacy. Those closest to the monarch might have an audience in the closet or privy.

THE COUNTRY SEAT

> Every man's proper Mansion House and Home, being the theatre of his
> hospitality, the seat of his Selfe-fruition, the comfortablest part of his owne life,
> the Noblest of his sonnes inheritance, a kinde of Private Princedome; nay to the
> possessors thereof, an epitome of the whole world.
>
> Sir Henry Wotton, 1624

Scottish country houses differed substantially according to when they were built,
and to some extent where they were built; and they were absolutely distinguished
one from the other by the rank and lineage of their builder. The country seat was the
centre of the local economy, the focus of local or regional power, the locus of justice,
and the expression of its owner's standing. Rank, degree, lineage and nobility all had
to be expressed appropriately and that was usually achieved in Scotland on the
skyline, sometimes by exaggerating height, and later by choreographing the way one
approached the building. The traditional warlike skyline of crenellations of the
mediaeval tower house was superseded by an equally impassioned creation, where
crenels and machicolations were used as decorative design motifs of a fundamentally
peaceable nature. Primary heraldic display now embraced rows of chimneystacks,
dormer windows (upper-storey windows which break the skyline), turrets as
gazebos, balconies and viewing platforms or belvederes. The frequency with which
a tall chimneystack rose proud above the principal entrance of a country house
implies deliberate design – it probably symbolised hospitality.

One of the most important roles of the country seat was, as Wotton put it, being
the 'theatre of hospitality'. The size of the household itself varied according to time
and to rank, but it was gradually reducing. In 1654, David, second earl of Wemyss,
had a chaplain, a lady and two gentlemen-in-waiting for his wife, two gentlemen to
ride with him, a porter and underporter, a coachman and (possibly) under-coach-
man, a groom, a falconer and man, a corn grieve, an officer, seven other unidentified
males (some responsible for others as well), three washers, and perhaps seventeen
other female servants – a staff of about forty-two (Fyfe 1927, 126–7). To that
number might be added visitors, whose retinues also depended on their rank.
Monarchs took an entourage of hundreds on their progresses, and James VI's
habitual summer progress took in Tullibardine, Kincardine (seat of the earls of
Montrose), Alloa (the earls of Mar), Hamilton (the earls of Arran), Kinneil (ditto),
Dalkeith (the earl of Morton), the palace of Seton (Seton family), and thence back to
Edinburgh. When Duncan Campbell of Glenorchy hosted the lairds of Tullibardine,
Inchbraikie and Abercairney, the tutor of Duncrub, the prior of Perth Charterhouse
and the bishop of Dunkeld in September 1590, visitors also included 'sundrie uther
comers and goers' amounting to thirty others at the very least. When he married his
second daughter to Robert Irvine of Fedderat in 1621, those coming to stay probably
numbered more than sixty. Guests had to be fed, entertained and provided with
places to sleep, even if the pages and personal servants slept on little cots or truckle
beds stored beneath the large beds. The emergence of guest wings, or guest towers,

or the conversion of the original tower for guest use once the laird had moved into his new lodging, was inevitable (McKean 2003).

Liberating themselves from the ordered constrictions and vertical rigidities of the mediaeval tower house after 1500, Scots designers gloried in the freedom to express the enormous changes that were taking place in social behaviour, and to reflect the variations in the wealth and standing of the occupiers. The rigidly geometric, opaque appearance of the tower was now replaced by an architectural flamboyance in which each new staircase, bedroom tower, study, turret, closet, chapel, laird's tower or great chamber could be identified from the exterior. While external decoration of the lower storeys would be restricted to the principal entrance and an armorial panel above it, the climax of the design was the elaborate superstructure, skyline and silhouette. In north-east Scotland, the transition between plinth and superstructure was signalled by an elaborate, swelling corbelled string-course (a continuous projecting line of stone built out from the wall on projecting stones [corbels]) that wound up and down across the facade and used, for decorative detail, echoes of the mediaeval military features of corbels, *machicolis*, turrets, and waterspouts disguised as gun barrels. Turrets were located on corners for compositional reasons (or for the view), and – particularly in the north-east – high oriel windows (projecting windows at the first storey or above) formed part of the composition. The roofscape would have been completed with dormer windows, brilliantly-painted finials, belvedere, and might have incorporated statues and weather cocks. So the silhouette of Scottish 'castle-wise' country houses, as one English observer of 1636 called them, was formed from a number of vertical elements in collision with each other, capped by crow-stepped gables (Hume Brown 1891, 148).

The country seat was the principal market for and focus of skilled trades – masons, plasterers, painters, joiners, glaziers, slaters and roofers, gardeners and nurserymen – in those large districts of the country beyond easy reach of the burghs. It was also the location of smiddies, foundries and kilns, sawmills and carpenters' workshops. The cultivation of orchards and tree-nurseries might be undertaken on a commercial scale. Taken together with its related fermtouns, kirktouns and cottouns, the country seat represented the principal community of rural Scotland, and comprised a population sometimes small and sometimes enormous. The study of these seats is not just that of the expensive architectural extravagances of the rich: it represents the focus of the life of the majority of Scots.

Most country seats were located on the sites of their ancestors. Thick stone walls and vaults provided a re-useable resource and, so long as that inherited fabric could be adapted to changing social and cultural patterns, it was. The structural material for most of Scotland was stone and, until the middle of the eighteenth century, the customary form of construction remained that of a stone vault, whose maximum span was rarely wider than twenty feet (Howard 1995, 68). That generated a vertical structure and a compact plan. The simplest way of adding more accommodation was to build a new module alongside. The original choice of site had been strongly influenced by access to drinking water, quarries of good building stone (Stell 1983, 15), and a sheltered, sunny and fertile spot. Long before it was reached, the Scottish country seat presented the visitor with a landscape of extensive walls – three to six metres tall or more (Reid 1988, 24) – which controlled the wind and created microclimates for cultivation. Once the wind was tamed, the climate proved surprisingly clement, as indicated by the 'home-produced artichokes, melons, asparagus, peaches and even fresh grapes', and the ubiquitous apricots (Stuart 1985).

In 1683, John Reid, the first gardener to publish in Scotland, advised: 'situate your House in a healthy Soyl, near to a fresh spring, defended from the Impetuous-west winds, northern colds and eastern blasts' (Reid 1998, 2). Most country houses eschewed a north-south alignment, preferring an angle that permitted the sun to reach all four facades during its daily run; and they were generally set on a slope downhill from the brow. They thus enjoyed protection from the wind and a good prospect in equal measure. As the English visitor Fynes Moryson observed, they were 'commonly compassed with little groves' of trees (Hume Brown 1891, 82). That was all the more striking because Scotland otherwise appeared to outsiders so very treeless.

Country seats dominated their maze of purposefully walled, interconnecting yards or courts ('closes' in Scots), of which the inner close was the most important ceremonial space – sometimes signified by a fountain or well of welcome. Other buildings would include the original tower (retained for reasons of filial piety, but often abandoned to guests or storage), a fashionable wing (known as the 'main house'), one or more galleries, guest chambers (sometimes in a separate tower) and offices. Galleries functioned as corridors, indoor exercise rooms or sometimes for the display of pictures. Occasionally, being the largest space, they became the principal reception room (with guest chambers on the floor below), as was the case at Dunnottar in Kincardineshire, and the Palace of Birsay in Orkney. The single court of a lower-rank house would juxtapose higher-status buildings (including the tower and main house) with operational ones (stables, a laundry and barns).

Although differing significantly in degree and wealth, country houses had certain common requirements: a brew house, a dairy or milk house, a bake house, a larder, byres (for beasts), stables, office houses, a doocot (dovecote) and girnels (barns) in which to store rents that were paid in kind. In Mugdock, Stirlingshire, the rents were paid in the outer court, where the barns were located. In larger establishments, there would be several courts or yards, customarily three sets of stables (court or riding stables, hunting stables and estate stables), a spicery, a gill house (where the house completed its brewing), a bottle house, a malt loft, a washing house, a candle house, a coal house, a woman-house (for the superior female servants and, sometimes, the family's children), a porter's lodge, a gardener's house, a glass house, a pine house, summer houses properly fitted up with marble tables and cane chairs, hen and apple houses, garden pavilions and a garden room.

Throughout the Renaissance, the whole of a greater country seat would not have been in constant use. If a family owned more than one estate, they would travel from one to another at different times of year, according to the season and the role of each house. For the earls of Strathmore, Castle Lyon (now Castle Huntly, west of

Dundee) was their summer house, whereas Glamis was their ancient paternal seat. Their principal seat of honour, the ancient paternal seat, represented their rank and lineage but for much of the Renaissance it was little used. Customarily, the family bought or built a more contemporary or fashionable residence. They would quite likely have a dower house, a summer house, and possibly a house for the heir; a seaside villa, a fishing lodge, a hunting lodge, a suburban villa near Edinburgh; town houses in appropriate principal towns and, perhaps, a travelling house: Melgund in Angus provided a convenient break for the marquis of Huntly between his main seat of Bog O' Gight and Edinburgh.

Generally, this chapter deals with houses built in the Lowlands, which followed court fashions. So far as can be ascertained, the elite of the *Gàidhealtachd* was already embracing Lowland ideas in the fifteenth century, by the addition of a fashionable tower with living accommodation to their curtain-walled strongholds. The rate of destruction in the Highlands has possibly been even higher than that in the Lowlands but, from what survives or is recorded, it seems that the Lowland fashion spread widely. Huntly's great house in Inverness was a magnificent villa on the model of Bog O' Gight; the McLeods added a guest tower and a fashionable gallery to Dunvegan Castle on Skye; and neither Inveraray nor Invergarry would have looked out of place anywhere in the Lowlands. These, however, were probably the exceptions. We know very little about how the architecture of the *Gàidhealtachd* evolved in any other way during these centuries.

THE CHURCH

Anglo-Scottish warfare and the Reformation had such destructive effects that it is difficult to establish whether the substantial reconstruction of cathedrals and abbeys that took place in other European countries in the first part of the sixteenth century occurred in Scotland. There are distant echoes of building and extension, rich libraries and substantial and colourful refurbishment with the employment, for example, of the painter Andrew Bairhum. Save in a few collegiate churches, any fashionable new work has long since vanished. After the Reformation, painted decoration was overpainted plainly with biblical text (Pitscottie 1778, 325), and the churches modified to provide auditoria for presbyterian worship, normally by subdividing them for separate congregations, as in St Mary's, Dundee. The interiors of smaller rectangular parish churches were reformatted toward a pulpit at the centre, with the principal heritors (the laird in rural parishes and the burgh councillors in towns) constructing projecting wings (called 'aisles') to contain their own pews, sometimes with a family vault beneath. The nave of St Giles in Edinburgh was converted into the burgh's tolbooth and the nation's parliament house above, with the Sheriff Court below. Few wholly new churches were built – or at any rate have survived (the 1572 steepled church in Fraserburgh, for example, has vanished without trace). The church of Burntisland (1592) remains the most prominent surviving example: a columned, virtually square auditorium, the pulpit against one of the columns, and the pews and galleries radiating around it. There was no spatial hierarchy, although social hierarchy was manifest through location, decoration and type of seat. It was much the same in John Mylne's 1634 Tron Kirk in Edinburgh: a virtually square auditorium, with the pulpit set behind the entrance porch in full view of the entire congregation.

The Chapel Royal in Stirling Castle, designed in 1594, probably by William Schaw with the participation of the king himself, was more traditional: a long rectangle, built to the proportions of the Temple of Solomon, with the minister at one end and the congregation at the other. Lit on the south facade by six full-height, double, round-headed windows framing a rare classical porch, it was essentially conservative in plan, but a striking departure from Scottish tradition in decoration. Surviving private chapels attached to a country house – for example Balcaskie (1606) or Dairsie (1621) – are rare. Generally they were small, rectangular and narrow, as suited the form of worship promoted by the five articles of Perth in a small household (see chapter 7). Dairsie was the most ambitious, as befitted its creator, John Spottiswoode, archbishop of St Andrews. By comparison with the Chapel Royal, its windows were retrograde gothic, but it also had a classical porch. The rectangular form persisted in the 1684 chapel at Glamis, where the painted decoration by Jacob de Wet survives in its entirety. The visuals, which would not have been allowed in a parish church, combined images taken from religious books that the earl of Strathmore provided, and those imagined by the painter. The chapel at Glamis is a rare survival of what other Protestant nobles might have possessed. Catholic nobles constructed chapels and oratories within their houses, imperceptible from the outside, favouring a reinvented late-fifteenth-century gothic vaulting – as in Towie Barclay or Careston – as their insignia.

TOWNS

Uniquely in Europe – as contemporaries such as George Buchanan boasted – Scottish towns were unfortified. It disconcerted visiting soldiers, such as the French-man Jean de Beaugué in 1548. He opined that St Andrews could not be fortified because it was too large, that Perth should demolish St John's church and construct a citadel in its place, and he produced a plan for how Aberdeen could be converted into a defensible city on the continental model (Hume Brown 1973, 66–8). Scottish town plans were linear and spacious rather than centrifugal, as in Europe, and were focused on a large single central space rather than a multiplicity of them. Their protection lay in their tightly-packed tenements and their gates (called ports), which were closed at night. These were primarily customs points, controlling trade and protecting against undesirables (such as beggars and lepers) and contagious disease. Their purpose being trade, towns required good communications, and were custo-marily located by a river or harbour, a frontier, or a major route. To permit conditions of comfort in the town's principal public space, the weather was always taken into consideration in the siting of the market place. The weather-protected market place was the focus of the principal business – 'the dealing floor' of the town. By contrast, the 'service' end of the town was located where wind was expected to blow away smells – as in Dundee's Fishmarket or Edinburgh's Grassmarket. Communication through the town otherwise was by closes, wynds, vennels and 'entries', often themselves kinked to block the wind.

Religious houses were customarily located outside urban boundaries and in a number of cases – notably Haddington, Dundee and Aberdeen – the parish church itself was originally located on the fringes. After many urban religious properties were gifted to the towns in the 1560s, their lands provided space and sometimes buildings for civic activity: Edinburgh's Dominican house was the site of the Grammar School, as was Glasgow's Franciscan house; Marischal College, Aberdeen, and Glasgow University also occupied former friars' properties, while Edinburgh's Toun's College (later its university) used the collegiate church of St Mary's in the Fields. In Perth, Dundee and Edinburgh, the yards of the Franciscans became municipal cemeteries.

The town council was responsible for only a limited number of buildings: the parish church, the school, the tolbooth, the mercat cross, customs house, weighhouse, shambles (slaughterhouse), possibly some charitable institutions, gates, bridges and harbours. The principal civic buildings were normally located in the market place, the weighhouse in a convenient location between market place and harbour, and the school either adjacent to the parish church or on former monastic land. The burgh authorities intervened in private building only where a structure or its materials were thought to be dangerous. In the early seventeenth century, Edinburgh's council banned thatch for roofing and discouraged timber-framed projecting galleries. After a grievous fire in 1652, Glasgow laid out strict regulations for the rebuilding and adornment of its principal streets: timber facades were to be replaced with ashlar stonework, four storeys tall, gable to the street, sitting upon arcades. The tenements in Edinburgh and Dundee were much taller, reflecting the pre-eminence of those towns, rising from six to twelve storeys. Glasgow's arcades were to be fixed, unusually in Europe, at the regular distance of eleven feet from the tenement behind, whereas it was variable in most other Scots towns (Dundee's arcades varied from 7 to 12 feet deep).

Civic pride would be expressed in architectural terms in the upgraded or rebuilt tolbooths, which in the larger towns virtually took the form of municipal castles, symbolising the town's independence. Dundee's, rebuilt c.1559, was four or five storeys tall, and capped by the town's clock tower and bell tower. Glasgow's, rebuilt in 1626 with fashionable 'buckle-quoins' (decorative features on the corner of a building), turrets and a soaring crowned steeple, was a 37-metre-high behemoth, with a battlemented viewing platform for a roof, and the great municipal chamber – the King's Room – occupying the entire fifth floor. There were also charitable hospitals (Hutchisons' Hospital in Glasgow, the Town's Hospital in Dundee, Heriot's Hospital and St Paul's Wark in Edinburgh), universities or colleges (Edinburgh, St Andrews, Aberdeen and Glasgow), and town gates.

The high point of Scottish Renaissance urbanism was probably the period from 1590 to 1639, when increasing prosperity led to the founding of several new towns, including the grid-iron Fraserburgh, with its (short-lived) university, in 1592, and the formalisation of a number of new royal burghs – the greatest number since the twelfth century. Edinburgh was by far the largest urban community, over twice the size of Dundee, the next largest, until the 1670s. By the end of the seventeenth century, however, most towns were petitioning parliament with pleas of such impoverishment that they were unable even to maintain their civic buildings, let alone build new ones.

THE EARLY RENAISSANCE, 1500–42

Architecture, wrote Sir Christopher Wren, 'has its Political Use; publick Buildings being the Ornament of a Country; it establishes a Nation, draws People and Commerce; makes the People love their native Country, which Passion is the Original of all great Actions in a Common-wealth'. That view from late-seventeenth-century England also applied to Scotland during the Renaissance. Indeed, beginning in the later fifteenth century, the architectural political agenda took a number of forms. Ian Campbell has pointed out that the curiously round-headed ('Romanesque') doorways of the great parish churches of the late fifteenth century were a deliberate invocation of the ancient glories of the reign of David I intended to celebrate the glorious new days of James IV (Campbell 1995). Even more striking was how the open 'imperial crown' spires capping the towers of some churches represented, as Roger Mason has suggested, the claims of both James IV and James V to *imperium* (authority which was free from interference from any earthly power) (Mason 1992, 60). The importance it held for these kings is underscored in one of the carved statues of 1538–40 on the palace at Stirling. Above the head of an almost life-sized statue of James V, a lion holds a cushion inscribed I5 [Jacobus V] between its paws. On that cushion sits an imperial crown.

Many landowners who were building or refashioning their country seats travelled, fought or studied abroad and returned with ideas, publications and engravings (Brown 2000). The country was awash with contemporary design information on symbols and motifs for interior painterwork (Bath 1995), and there is little reason to believe that there was not comparable information about contemporary architecture. So highly was European travel regarded as a sign of accomplishment and breeding that David Home of Godscroft felt obliged to exaggerate the virtues of Home of Wedderburn to offset the inconvenient fact that he had never been to Europe (Chambers vol. 1, 120). Not to have European experience was something to be ashamed of.

How the architecture of Scottish country houses was changing before the death of James V in 1542 is still imperfectly understood. Tower houses were lengthened to provide more than one chamber per floor, and their setting was becoming more elaborate. Courtyards were evolving into outer (service) courts and inner courts adorned with galleries and guest chambers. But, while royal architecture seemed to be French-influenced from 1529 – the new royal lodging at Holyrood, which might be compared to the donjon at Vincennes, and the towers grafted onto the entry tower at Falkland some years later are examples – the cultural leanings of the majority of the aristocracy are uncertain. Falkland's strikingly French aesthetic can be attributed to French masons brought by Mary of Guise, who added a gallery along the south wing, with a facade very similar to the garden pavilion at her own ancestral seat of Joinville. However, the royal architect (and king's cousin) Sir James Hamilton of Finnart was more inspired by Italian examples when he constructed his own four-towered retreat at Craignethan in the Clyde Valley in a manner unprecedented in Scotland, and then refashioned Linlithgow Palace into a similar four-towered form. Italian inspiration might also explain his design for the outstanding palace block in Stirling Castle, decorated on the outside with enormous vividly-carved statues of biblical or mythological provenance, such as Eve, Leda and the swan, and the Noonday Devil. The interior is decorated with a matching programme of paintings in the antique manner, tapestries, wainscoting and coffered ceilings ornamented with carved and painted heads (paralleled only in the Hall of Heads in the palace of the Wawel, in Kracow). Finnart's hand may also have been seen in several other towered country houses, but his influence did not survive his fall from grace and execution for treason in August 1540 (McKean 1999).

THE MARIAN PERIOD, 1542–68

In 1548, Queen Mary was betrothed to the heir to the French throne and her mother, Mary of Guise, became regent in 1554. Since Scotland was under the influence of two French-educated queens both called Mary until 1568, it seems appropriate to term the resulting French-influenced architecture 'Marian'. Mary of Guise confided to her family that she saw part of her role as bringing 'a young nation [Scotland] to a state of [presumably French] perfection' (Marshall 1977, 211). Before the Peace of Boulogne of 1550, Scotland was unsettled, with an infant monarch and English occupation, so there was little architectural activity. But, once calm and prosperity followed, Francophilia came to dominate Scotland. The blind poet, Sir Richard Maitland, mercilessly satirised the way in which Scottish dress aped the extravagant doublets, puffed-out breeches, frilly shirts, flat bonnets, high hats and perfumed gloves of the French: 'tout est à la mode de France'. The manners of the court, indeed, had changed. Sir James Melville of Halhill, ambassador to Queen Elizabeth, soon discovered that the protocols of the more relaxed French-influenced atmosphere of the Scottish court were poorly received when he practised them at Queen Elizabeth's (Melville 1683, 50).

Architectural shift emerged after the court returned from France, which Mary of Guise had visited in August 1550, accompanied by four earls, three lords and many others. She had visited her family seats of Joinville and Nancy, her own property of Longueville, and the seat of her widowhood at Châteaudun. Prominent at these châteaux was the tall, usually free-standing circular donjon or keep. Whereas this great round tower was the symbol of ancient lineage amongst the French aristocracy, the Scottish equivalent had been a rectangular tower house. Once the Guise party returned from France, some of the greater magnates proceeded to add a great round tower to their own seats. Too canny to go to the expense of constructing a circular tower merely for the purpose of symbolising lineage or status, they used it to accommodate the bedchamber – the final chamber of the horizontally-organised state apartment that had been introduced in Linlithgow and Stirling – in the major refashioning of their houses that followed.

First to innovate was Robert Reid, bishop of Orkney, who added a virtually self-contained, wide, circular tower to the west end of his palace at Kirkwall to contain his private chambers and, perhaps, his famous library. Next, in 1553, was the earl of Huntly, who had received permission to rename the Gordons' paternal seat of Strathbogie 'Castle Huntly' five years earlier. In order that his house could live up to its new status as a 'castle,' he added an enormous 38-foot diameter circular tower against the south-west corner of a fifteenth-century hall. This provided the space for the bedchamber and was balanced by a narrower round tower on the opposite corner, which contained the ceremonial staircase. The dominant expression of the new architecture was an asymmetrical turreted skyline of flamboyant romanticism that was clearly influenced by the Loire châteaux. Huntly's palace was ready to accommodate Mary of Guise on her justice ayre to the north in 1556. Her next stop was at the earl of Atholl's ancient castle of Balvenie, at the far end of the pass of the Cabrach. Atholl reconstructed Balvenie to rival Huntly by constructing a vivid palace-block graced with an array of delicate, semi-circular oriel windows and a 28-foot diameter circular tower at its north-east corner.

There does not appear to have been substantial work on royal palaces during the Marian period, nor is there much evidence of church construction. However, following damage caused by almost three years of English occupation, Dundee undertook substantial civic reconstruction by building a noble steepled and turreted tolbooth (to replace the burnt one) and a romantically Francophile, four-towered, arcaded customs house by the harbour. Edinburgh rebuilt its Netherbow Port, modelled, so it was said, on the Porte Ste Honoré in Paris.

The most notable survivors of the Marian fashion are country houses. There was some acceleration in the construction of lesser seats whilst Mary, queen of Scots ruled (1561–7); this demonstrates that there was no clear pre- and post-Reformation break to secular architectural history. Few of this second generation of 'Marian' houses were built for great lords or were as grandiose as Balvenie or Huntly. The circular tower with the bedchamber was brought into approximate balance with the staircase tower on the opposite corner, thus creating what so misleadingly became known as the 'Z-plan' house. Stair towers might be either circular or rectangular and sometimes contained what was presumably a guest chamber at their apex.

Sometimes (Claypotts in Dundee is a good example) the second tower was given entirely over to guest chambers, with the public staircase tucked into its armpit. Large courtyard houses or palaces, signalled by the gatehouse in the form of a mock miniature château or châtelet, as at Boyne, by Portsoy, expanded to embrace the entire courtyard, with round towers on each corner. It was, nonetheless, the skyline that carried the principal heraldic messages, for it was also probably at this time that the Scots imported the French 'tourelle' (the spiked-hat turret). In Scotland they were invariably called 'studies' and were often used as a 'cabinet for . . . books'.

Silhouettes were heightened by finials (decorative items at the apex) in the form of statues, emblems or the family's heraldic beast – the boar in the case of Huntly, the lion for Glamis. These wildly romantic and picturesque confections were what the French call 'châteaux des rêves' (dream castles). Over a third of them were built in Aberdeenshire and Kincardineshire, although there were striking examples further south and even in the central Highlands. Of around ninety country houses constructed in this period that survive, at least thirty took this form. There were probably many more.

THE MINORITY OF JAMES VI, 1568–c.1590

Mary, queen of Scots was exiled to England in 1568, and the country's architecture underwent a further major shift. The striking Francophilia of the Marian period ran the risk of being taken to imply disloyalty to the new regime. Between the conclusion of the civil war, with the victory of the king's men in 1572–3, and James VI's marriage to Anna of Denmark in 1590, the construction of Scottish Renaissance country houses reached peak numbers. The new country seats of James VI's minority are all distinguished by a rigid rectangular horizontality, with round towers replaced by chunky rectangular ones. Studies, corbelled from corners of the wallhead, were squatter by comparison with their slender, French-influenced predecessors. Menzies is an excellent example of how the entrance tower became rectangular, and the skyline lost its spiky fantasy in favour of sober crowsteps. The architecture, cleansed of its French affectations, had been 'Scotticised'.

These new houses evolved from the plan of their Marian predecessors. Whereas the staircase tower still projected into the courtyard, the public stair inside it now rose solely to the principal or public floor; and its upper storeys were given over to guest chambers. The principal chambers retained their position at the centre of the house; narrower turnpike stairs, usually at the back the building, led to the chambers above. The bedroom tower at the far end of the state apartment was changing into a family wing, located as far as possible away from the guest wing, buffered by the public rooms between.

Houses of this kind were rarely the 'ancient paternal seats' of the greatest nobility, but secondary houses of great families or the principal seats of minor landowners. They therefore had a lesser ceremonial function. An increasing number of the household no longer worked or slept in the main house itself, but in one of the service buildings of the inner court. While the radical change between these houses and their Marian predecessors could have had functional origins (an increasing desire for family privacy, or even a formalisation of providing adequately for guests), function alone could not justify such a dramatic change in their aesthetic. This second sudden break in Scotland's architectural evolution suggests a political rationale. It was in emulation of the French symbol of ancient lineage that land-owners had added a circular tower containing the significant bedchamber to their houses. Scotsmen of the succeeding generation were driven by an identical impulse, but the source of their inspiration was their own Scottish medieval architecture – the rectangular tower house. By subtle and largely marginal changes to proportion, height and expression, the French infection was eradicated. It was replaced by a massiveness that became the next identifying mark of Scottish Renaissance architecture.

Many of those flamboyantly Francophile round-towered houses were recast according to the new political correctness. Perhaps the first was the Regent Morton's own Drochil, near Peebles, whose round towers were decapitated and corbelled out at the third storey, to provide a rectangular, possibly two-storeyed superstructure above. Around 1587 the two round towers of Claypotts were likewise decapitated, to be recapped by well-proportioned, well-lit and warm rectangular caphouses or cabinets, of a different proportion and masonry. The fact that this might have been done for political reasons may explain why so little care was taken to conceal the dissonance between the new square cap and its old circular base: the replacement rectangular chambers were simply plonked on top. Perhaps it was an ostentatious gesture of allegiance to the new political reality: in short, the approved method of de-Frenchification.

THE UNION OF 1603 AND THE REIGN OF CHARLES I

By the 1590s, James VI was securely on the throne, married, and the likely heir to the throne of England. The need to disassociate oneself from France was waning. A strong Danish influence marked the court architecture of James VI's maturity but, once he had left Scotland for England in 1603, buildings were again used to convey strong political messages. The early seventeenth century was notable for three distinct architectural developments: the 'villa' of Queen Anna's court; the magisterial civic buildings of the court style; and the group of extraordinary tall houses in north-eastern Scotland attributed to the Bel family.

Queen Anna's court, under the patronage of Alexander Seton, future chancellor, and the architectural leadership of William Schaw and Sir James Murray, produced one of the most distinctive buildings in Scots history: the U-plan villa. Architecturally, it was a neat idea: in these buildings the family wing (set at the opposite corner from the entrance tower at Menzies) was brought round to project from the façade to balance the entrance wing, thus providing a house with public chambers at the centre, and a family and a guest wing facing each other on each side. There was usually a staircase in each corner so that one no longer needed to pass through one chamber to get to the next. An excellent, if miniature, example of this kind of structure was Murray's own house at Baberton. Seton's earlier villa at Pinkie, whilst not of this type, was embellished with an exceptional painted gallery, which, like his garden, was in imitation of the Ancients.

Royal works were rare, since the king returned only once. However, the north wing of Linlithgow Palace was rebuilt under Murray's guidance from 1617. He also recast the palace at Edinburgh Castle, and his George Heriot's Hospital was begun in 1634. These were all in a confident, large-windowed, Renaissance manner, capped by a disproportionately heraldic superstructure: the fashionable architecture of the Italian Sebastiano Serlio with a castle on top, as Konrad Ottenheym has characterised it. To some degree, this lead was followed in other buildings. The original Edinburgh University double courtyard vanished without being recorded, but Glasgow had two outstanding buildings, both designed by John Boyd: the most imposing tolbooth in Scotland of 1626, and the double-courtyard Glasgow University of 1630, whose glory was the street-front entrance wing, with its heraldry, balcony and, on the inside, its loggia and great flight of Lion and Unicorn steps up to the senate room.

The Scots nobility in the shires already felt remote from Edinburgh, and even more so from London. In the horizontally-proportioned U-planned villas of the court circle, this disenchantment was expressed in a Latin motto carved in stone or set in plaster: '106 kings have left us this [kingdom] unconquered'. The nobility in part of the north-east expressed their disenchantment differently. They constructed high into the sky – height being one of the signals of ancient nobility – by adding three or four storeys on top of existing towers; these contained chambers (like the gallery) that would line the inner court of more horizontal buildings (Davis 2005). Some twenty houses within a 20-mile radius of Inverurie follow this pattern, from Craigievar to Crathes; from a heraldic memorial on Castle Fraser, their design has been attributed to John Bel. The architecture, this time, was a display of a profound Scottish nationalism, a possible expression of the fear that, once having lost their king, they might lose their very identity.

THE LATER SEVENTEENTH CENTURY

It is generally held that the Restoration period can be characterised as the inevitable triumph of classical architecture. 'The stage had now been set where new classical houses almost free of references to castles could be built', under the architectural leadership of Sir William Bruce (Glendinning and MacKechnie 2003). However, in the thirty years to 1690, Bruce produced few such buildings and usually for 'new money': notably his own classically idiosyncratic house at Kinross. None of them adopted the full-blown Palladian classicism of England, but favoured instead contemporary Dutch models.

What dominated later-seventeenth-century country-house construction for the greater aristocrats was less the triumph of classicism than the flamboyant reinvention of Scottish 'Marian' architecture. When James, duke of York (later James VII) held court at Holyrood between 1679 and 1682, there was a strong injection of architectural adrenalin and the reconstruction drawing of Falkland Palace by John Slezer even suggests plans to repair and reoccupy it. Probably inspired by the remodelling of the royal palace at Holyrood, ancient paternal seats like Thirlestane, Melville, Methven, Hatton, Drumlanrig, Panmure and Alloa were transformed into proud, Scottish, and defiantly non-classical structures (save the rather botched interior court of Holyrood). The preferred architecture of those who were running the country was thus strongly Scottish Baroque: it emphasised balance rather than symmetry, a hierarchical order, and an extraordinarily expressive skyline, and used

stairs, round corner towers, studies and pavilions to resurrect, once more, metaphorical echoes of Scottish independence. Perhaps the most expressive was the earl
of Strathmore's 1684 refashioning of his seat of Glamis.

In churches, metaphors were mixed. James VII ordered the rebuilding of Holyrood
Abbey church as the chapel for the Knights of the Thistle, which required the
construction of a new church in the Canongate for the displaced congregation.
Despite its delicately-shaped Dutch gable and classical porch, James Smith's layout
within the cruciform Canongate Church was not so much that of a presbyterian but of
a potentially Catholic church. In the country, however, the centrality of the auditorium required by Protestant worship dominated, often achieved by adding a new
(usually the laird's) aisle half way along the church opposite the pulpit. In Sir William
Bruce's church at Lauder, it was taken almost to the degree of a miniature old Scots
cathedral. Instead of adopting classical architecture, which most suits a centrally-
focused form, he opted for four aisles branching out equally from the pulpit.

The wars of the Covenant caused considerable urban damage – particularly to
Aberdeen and Dundee – and in the period of prosperity after 1660 there was much
rebuilding. It became fashionable to rebuild tenements facing the street (rather than
gable-end on), sometimes amalgamating several closes into a single large property,
such as Gardyne's Land in Dundee's High Market Gait. Perhaps the most sophisticated examples of the new trend were the two enormous, ashlar-built courtyards of
mansion flats speculatively developed in Edinburgh by Robert Mylne: Mylne's
Court, and Milne's [sic] Square (now demolished). Even grander was the arcaded
Gibson's Land, on the corner of Glasgow's Trongate and Saltmarket, with its
striking multi-storeyed corner turret. After a second fire in 1677, Glasgow rebuilt its
Saltmarket, this time not in terraced arcades as earlier, but in unusual two-or-three-
storeyed houses above commercial premises, comparable to those in the Low
Countries. Late seventeenth-century urban leadership had moved distinctly west.

Although considerably fewer than in England, charitable institutions erected by
individuals or their trustees appear more frequently in later seventeenth-century
Scotland: the steepled Hutchison's Hospital in Glasgow's Trongate, for example,
Cowane's Hospital in Stirling, or Dundee's 1678 U-plan Town's Hospital at the
Nethergate Port. Of civic buildings, Glasgow's steepled Merchants Hall in the
Briggait was the only one of its type, but there was some rebuilding of tolbooths –
most strikingly Linlithgow's steepled tolbooth – where the buildings show great
confidence, combined with echoes of long-standing Scottish motifs. Occasionally –
as in Stirling (1703) and Dumfries (1705) – new tolbooth construction might have
been used to ward off the economic decline that was partly caused by the
considerable growth in burghs of barony.

CONCLUSION

Architecture is an excellent barometer of changing political, cultural and economic
fortunes. When prosperous, secure and confident, people build. Otherwise, they do
not, save in exceptional circumstances. Equally, architecture offers a measure of

national ambition, priority, culture, international contact and evolution. From the buildings erected during the Scottish Renaissance, it is clear that continuous social and cultural evolution reflected political circumstance and foreign links. These buildings offer us a much richer and more realistic impression of Renaissance Scotland than do the writings of post-Enlightenment historians, whose agenda was to promote post-Union Scotland at the expense of its earlier culture.

REFERENCES

Anderson, C. 1994 ' "Pallaces of the poets"; an idea of the Tudor and Jacobean Country House', in Airs, M. (ed) *The Tudor and Jacobean Great House*, Oxford, 19–28.

Bath, M. 1995 'Alexander Seton's Painted Gallery', in Gent, L. (ed) *Albion's Classicism*, New Haven, 79–108.

Brown, K. 2000 *Noble Society in Scotland*. Edinburgh.

Campbell, I. 1995 'A Romanesque Revival and the Early Renaissance in Scotland', *Journal of the Society of Architectural Historians*, 54, 302–25.

Campbell, I. 1994 'Linlithgow's princely palace and its influence in Europe', *Architectural Heritage*, 5, 1–20.

Cavers, K. 1993 *A Vision of Scotland*. Edinburgh.

Chambers, R. n.d. *Domestic Annals of Scotland*, 3 vols. Edinburgh.

Cunninghame, I.C. (ed) 2001 *The Nation Survey'd: Timothy Pont's Maps of Scotland*. East Linton.

Davis, M. 2005 'The Bel Family and their Renaissance Tall-houses', *Architectural Heritage*, 16, 14–30.

Fyfe, J.G. (ed) 1927 *Scottish Diaries and Memoirs*. Stirling.

Gifford, J. 1988 *William Adam*. Edinburgh.

Hume Brown, P. (ed) 1891 *Early Travellers in Scotland*. Edinburgh.

Hume Brown, P. 1909 *History of Scotland*, 3 vols. Cambridge.

Lindsay of Pitscottie, R. 1778 *The History of Scotland*. Edinburgh.

MacGibbon D. and Ross, T. 1887–92 *The Castellated and Domestic Architecture of Scotland*, 5 vols. Edinburgh.

MacIvor I., 1981 'Artillery and major places of strength in the Lothians', in Caldwell D.H. (ed), *Scottish Weapons and Fortifications 1100–1800*, New Jersey, 94–120.

McKean C.A., 2006 'A Scottish Problem with Castles', *Historical Research*, 79, 166–98.

McKean, C.A. 2003 'The Scottish Renaissance Country Seat in its setting', *Garden History*, 31, 141–62.

McKean, C.A. 1999 'Sir James Hamilton of Finnart – a Renaissance Courtier-Architect', *Architectural History*, 42, 141–72.

McKean, C.A. 1995 'Some castle-wise Country Houses of early Renaissance Scotland', in Gow, I. and Rowan, A. (eds) *The Scottish Country House 1600–1914*, Edinburgh, 1–14.

McKean, C.A. 2002 'The Laird and his Guests', *Architectural Heritage*, 13, 1–19.

Mackechnie, A. 2000 'James VI's Architects', in Goodare, J. and Lynch, M. (eds) *The Reign of James VI*, East Linton, 154–69.

Mackechnie, A. 1995 'Design in early Post Reformation Scots Houses', in Gow and Rowan (eds) *The Scottish Country House 1600–1914*, 15–34.

Marshall, R. 1977 *Mary of Guise*. London.

Mason, R. 1992 'Humanism and Political Culture,' in Mason, R. and Macdougall, N. (eds) *People and Power in Scotland*. Edinburgh.

Melville, Sir J. 1683 *The Memoires*. London.

Reid, J. 1988 *The Scots Gard'ner, published for the Climate of SCOTLAND* [1683], ed. Hope, A. Edinburgh.

Shire, H.M. 1988 'The King in his House', in Mapstone, S. and Wood, J. (eds) *The Rose and the Thistle*. East Linton.

Stell, G. 1983 'The Scottish Castle', *Royal Incorporation of Architects of Scotland Prospect*. Edinburgh.

Stuart, D. 1985 *Scottish Kitchen and Flower Gardens*. Edinburgh.

Tranter, N. 1962–8, *The Fortified House in Scotland*, 5 vols. Edinburgh.

Wemyss, C. 2003 'Paternal Seat or Classical Villa', *Architectural History*, 46, 109–26.

FURTHER READING

Glendinning, M., MacInnes, R. and MacKechnie, A. 1996 *A History of Scottish Architecture*. Edinburgh.

Fawcett, R. 1994 *Scottish Architecture from the Accession of the Stewarts to the Reformation 1371–1560*. Edinburgh.

Glendinning, M. and MacKechnie, A. 2003 *Scottish Architecture*. London.

Howard, D. 1995 *Scottish Architecture from the Reformation to the Restoration*. Edinburgh.

McKean, C.A. 2001 *The Scottish Château*. Stroud.

CHAPTER TWELVE

Early Modern Art

Duncan Macmillan

The Stewart kings, James III, James IV and James V were true Renaissance princes. They built great palaces, maintained artists of all kinds at their courts and also commissioned art from the best artists in France and Flanders. If that seems an unfamiliar idea – and traditionally we have not thought of the Renaissance as touching Scotland – that is because we have lost so much of what once existed. It is important to recognise this in order to understand the place of art in Scottish history. We were neither a deprived, nor an underprivileged nation and the art we once had was certainly no less significant than that in any other European country of similar size at the time. What survives also suggests that it was informed by a distinctive, national self-consciousness.

It is also true that modern scholarship has still not explored at all extensively the evidence that there is for the reflection of the Renaissance in Scotland. The exceptions to this in the general literature are the first four chapters of my own *Scottish Art 1460–2000* (2000); more briefly, Murdo Macdonald's *Scottish Art* (2000); and *A History of Scottish Architecture* by Miles Glendinning, Ranald McInnes and Aonghus Mckechnie (2004). The earlier histories of Scottish art do not include this period, with the exception of the very first: Robert Brydall's *History of Art in Scotland* (1889). It has no illustrations, but includes extensive quotations from primary textual sources. The art of the later part of this period is also discussed and extensively illustrated in *Patrons and Painters 1650–1700* by James Holloway (1989).

There are two reasons for the disappearance of so much of the art of the Middle Ages. The first is the Reformation. Under the Reformed church as it was established after 1560, art had no place in worship. Worshippers looked at the Ten Commandments, which they believed were the law of God; they saw there in the second commandment that religious art of any kind was specifically proscribed and so they ordered its destruction. Their iconoclasm was not barbarism, therefore, but the product of their deepest convictions. With the Reformation, too, the monasteries were closed and there was no longer any need for great churches designed to celebrate the elaborate rites of the Catholic church – churches such as St Andrews Cathedral, or Arbroath Abbey. Redundant, all the abbeys and most of the cathedrals fell into disrepair, eventually to collapse and become quarries for the towns that had grown up around them. The pier at St Andrews, for instance, is built with stones from the cathedral.

Much of the art of the Middle Ages was religious and almost all of it was destroyed. But iconoclasm was not the only reason for this loss. Although the

Reformers had no objection to secular art, it also suffered. After the union of the crowns in 1603, when the king of Scotland became king of England and moved south with all his courtiers, there was neither a king nor a court in Scotland to act as a source of patronage, or to preserve the secular monuments of kingship: the great palaces, the portraits and all the other trappings of royalty. This was especially critical in the upheavals of the succeeding century.

Nevertheless, the fact that these things do not exist now, or that if they do it is only in a much altered and often ruinous state, does not mean that they did not exist, nor that they were not once valued. Much of what does survive from the early period of Scottish history is of outstanding quality and in the later period, too, the visual arts were not extinguished by the Reformation. They went on to play an integral part in the Enlightenment, when art as much as the other branches of Scottish thought made a major contribution to the emergence of the modern western consciousness.

SCOTLAND AND THE RENAISSANCE, C.1460–C.1560

From the mid-fifteenth century Scotland shared fully in the Renaissance in northern Europe, and indeed had artistic links further afield to Italy and Spain. Between 1460 and the Reformation, the Stewart kings and their great courtiers regularly commissioned high quality work in the latest styles from France and Flanders. The beautiful academic mace of St Salvator's college, for instance, which is still carried in formal processions in St Andrews University, was made for Bishop Kennedy of St Andrews in 1460 by a Paris goldsmith, Jean Mayelle. As he signed the mace in Scots, it seems he was in fact a Scot who had settled in Paris. The mace is silver-gilt and has at its top the figure of Christ in a castellated Gothic shrine, flanked by angels, bishops and lions.

The Trinity College Altarpiece, painted in Bruges by the most advanced Flemish painter of the day, Hugo van der Goes, for James III in the 1470s represents a similar act of patronage and is the most important surviving painting from this period. Thompson and Campbell (1974) give a detailed discussion of this painting. The centre of the altarpiece was destroyed at the Reformation because of its religious imagery, but the wings survive, with their portraits of the king, the queen and the prince who was to become James IV. The king (James III) and the queen (Margaret of Denmark) are both presented by their patron saints to someone no longer visible on the missing centre panel. This arrangement suggests that this was a painting of the Madonna enthroned.

On the panels that would have been on the outside of the altarpiece when its wings were closed, there is a portrait of sir Edward Bonkil, provost of the Trinity Collegiate Church. He is kneeling in a church with an organ beside him and is presented by angels to a vision of the Holy Trinity in the adjacent panel. Christ is supported by his father, who is seated on a throne, and the dove of the Holy Spirit hovers above them. The painter has deliberately renounced a conventional perspective construction of the throne and the arrangement of the figures. If he were human, God could not support Christ's body in that position. The artist has also rendered the throne in gold leaf. At that time this was an archaic thing to do. It suggests he is being deliberately non-representational and so is making it clear that a different order of reality prevails in this part of the picture. It is a vision. Such details make this altogether a very modern painting for its time. They show that the Scots patrons were looking not just for the best, but also for the most up-to-date in contemporary art.

Bonkil had connections with Flanders, as did many merchant families at the time, and it seems that he sat in person to have his portrait painted. It is certainly among the most vivid portraits of any Scot from this early period. The royal portraits are timid beside it and it is clear that the royal personages could not go to Bruges to be painted, but were painted by a much lesser artist after the altarpiece was brought to Scotland. But Bonkil was not alone amongst non-royal Scots in leaving his portrait for us. Churchmen also travelled regularly and the archbishop of St Andrews, William Scheves, had a very fine portrait medal made for him in Flanders in 1495 by Quentin Matsys; and even a more modest churchman, Dean James Brown, commissioned in Bruges on his way to a mission to Rome a beautiful little book of hours, in which his portrait is included.

But art was not all imported. A groat (a type of coin) designed for James III by his 'sinkar', or master of the mint, with a convincing portrait of the king in three-quarter view is recognised as the first use of a true portrait on any coin outside Italy. The rood-screen painted with the crucifixion in the church of Foulis Easter near Dundee, the work of an unknown painter in the late fifteenth century, was painted on the spot (see the cover of volume 3 of this series). There are other fragmentary survivals of such paintings and they were clearly a normal part of church furnishing.

The altarpiece in the National Museum, Copenhagen, made for the Scottish community in Elsinore at the end of the fifteenth century, probably in northern Germany, is the only surviving work of this kind made for a Scottish community. It certainly reflects the kind of art that any wealthy Scottish congregation might expect to have in their church. The centre of the altarpiece is composed of sculptures of three saints: St Andrew, St Ninian and St James the Less. The double wings are painted with additional saints and eight scenes from the life of St Ninian, who was the most popular national saint. There is ample documentary evidence for the existence of similar altarpieces in churches in Scotland and also that the churches were decorated with wall paintings. Fragments of this kind of decoration survive in Dunkeld cathedral, for example. The existence of the St Ninian altarpiece also reflects the importance of Scottish merchant colonies overseas (see chapter 8). Similar links explain why Bergen Castle in Norway was built in the Scottish style by Scottish masons in the next century.

James IV, when he married Margaret Tudor in 1503, gave his new queen as a wedding present an exquisite illuminated manuscript from an artist in the circle of Simon Bening. The bulk of the numerous illuminations in this book, now in the Oesterreiches Staatsbibliothek, Vienna, are now attributed to a remarkable painter in Bening's circle known simply as the Master of the Hours of James IV. They include beautiful portraits of the king and queen at prayer and also a painting of the interior of a church with a royal funeral in progress. This is a reference to the violent death of James's father, James III, for which James himself always felt guilt, as he was involved in the insurrection that brought it about. The inclusion of this scene reveals what a deeply personal book this is, but the picture itself also gives us a glimpse of the solemn ceremonial that surrounded kingship and that was so much part of court life. Bruges was the great centre of manuscript illumination of the time. Simon Bening was the leading miniaturist in this group and his father, Alexander Bening, also a miniature painter, seems to have been a Scot. The work of the artists in this circle is discussed in the catalogue of the exhibition held in London in 2004, *Illuminating the Renaissance, the triumph of Flemish Manuscript Illumination in Europe.*

There was also manuscript illumination executed in Scotland. The Bothwell Psalter, for instance, may have been made in the abbey of Culross in Fife. Sir Thomas Galbraith, a clerk of the Chapel Royal at Stirling, is recorded as illuminating manuscripts for James IV. Galbraith also wrote and illuminated the treaty documents for James's marriage and so they are the earliest surviving work by a named Scottish artist. The king also patronised several other artists. Two fine portraits of him survive and were certainly the work of court artists. We also know of artists working outside court circles. A painter called Andrew Bairhum, for instance, worked at Kinloss Abbey. He also seems to have had an 'artistic' temperament, being notoriously cantankerous; the fact that his patron, Robert Reid, the learned abbot of Kinloss, put up with him in spite of his temper indicates the kind of esteem in which art and artists were already held.

There is simply not enough evidence left to judge if an artist like Bairhum represented a native style in painting, but, like the architecture of the period, contemporary sculpture is certainly very distinctive. The carved wooden heads made for James V's great hall of Stirling Castle, for instance, seem to be deliberately rugged and forceful and are typical of a style of woodcarving that flourished in Scotland in the sixteenth century. It was perhaps developed by a French woodcarver called Andrew Mansoun, but is quite distinctive and seems to reflect the same sentiment as Stirling Castle itself, combining rugged individualism with a sophisticated understanding of the modern style. This decoration is discussed by John Dunbar in his book *Scottish Royal Palaces* (1999) and also in his earlier pamphlet, *The Stirling Heads* (1975). As regent, Mary of Guise, James V's widow, continued to have artists at her court and her daughter, Mary, also understood very well the power of imagery. One of the earliest authentic portraits of her is on her coinage. The master of the mint, John Acheson, travelled to France to draw the portrait and was given facilities in the French Royal Mint to make the dies. That he should go to such lengths to secure a true likeness is a measure of how important the idea of the authentic portrait was. Mary's likeness is also recorded in a number of portraits from her life-time. Several of these, such as the lovely drawing of her by Clouet, were done while she was still in France, but others, such as *Mary Queen of Scots and Henry Darnley*, were certainly done in Scotland. Mary's image continued to be important after her abdication and indeed posthumously. One of the most interesting portraits of her is the full-length Blair College portrait, in which the inscriptions and subsidiary images of her execution and of her two faithful ladies, Joanna Keith and Elizabeth Curle, make it clear that it was painted after her death as propaganda in her cause.

THE IMPACT OF THE REFORMATION

It was during the reign of James V that the first incidents of iconoclasm are recorded, but after the establishment of the Reformed church in 1560, the destruction of images was undertaken systematically. Nevertheless, it was also from around 1560 that painted ceilings began to become fashionable and they continued to be so until the outbreak of the wars of the Covenant in the next century. This is a distinctive Scottish form of decoration, though it also has parallells in England and Scandinavia. It has recently been the subject of a major study by Michael Bath (Bath 2003).

Much of this kind of decoration is composed of grotesques, and animal and vegetable forms worked into chains of decorative detail; and emblems – pictorial riddles which present moral admonitions in symbolic form. This kind of imagery is combined to create colourful schemes of painting. Numerous examples survive, for instance, in the Palace at Culross, and in Crathes Castle in Aberdeenshire. Some are more elaborately pictorial, however, as at Pinkie House in East Lothian, where the central part of the ceiling has been painted to look as though we are looking up through an open domed structure to the sky above. These paintings were carried out by ordinary painters. We rarely know their names, though the elaborate decorations of the Skelmorlie Aisle in Largs are signed by J. Stalker. He seems to have been an Edinburgh artist, indicating that there was sufficient demand and sufficient specialisation involved in this kind of painting for an artist to travel across Scotland to carry it out.

These ceilings also occasionally include religious imagery, in spite of the ban placed upon it by the church. St Mary's Grandtully has a rich and complex scheme which includes religious scenes. Aberdeen was always a centre of episcopalian loyalty, which is perhaps why one of the most conspicuous examples of this kind of religious painting – a ceiling decorated with the crucifixion and other biblical scenes – is in Provost Skene's House, right in the centre of the city. Together with abundant evidence for the use of colour on the outside of buildings, the survival of so many ceilings in this style suggests that Reformation Scotland was by no means a drab place.

Painted ceilings are mostly the work of anonymous painters. So too are some of the finest portraits of the period, such as the brilliant painting of George, Lord Seton from c.1570. He is wearing a gorgeous costume of scarlet and gold and is holding the baton of his office as master of the queen's household. The Reformation was a movement that depended so much on individuals, indeed it had the idea of the individual at its heart – portraiture was very much its characteristic art form. Reflecting this, Theodore Beza, Calvin's successor in Geneva, published in 1580 a collection of the portraits of its leaders. The book is dedicated to James VI and includes as its frontispiece his portrait, taken from a gold coin of the period and drawn by the same master of the mint who had worked for Mary: John Acheson. It also contains the only authentic portrait of Knox himself. Though it was post-humous (Knox had died some years earlier) it certainly is authentic, for if Beza did not have an authentic likeness, he left a gap. Knox's portrait, together with a portrait of George Buchanan, James's tutor and another of the great men of the period, were both painted for Beza by an artist at James's court, though we cannot be sure who it was. In the end Beza did not use Buchanan's portrait, but a small circular painting of him by an unknown artist is one of the most striking to survive from the period.

It is in James's reign that it is possible for the first time to identify known artists with significant surviving works. Their work, along with that of their anonymous contemporaries, was the subject of an exhibition and catalogue by Duncan Thomson (1975). The fierce portrait of Regent Morton with a red beard and tall black hat, for instance, is attributed to Arnold Bronkhorst (fl.1565/6–1583). He was an artist of Dutch origin who worked briefly at the Scottish court between 1581 and 1583. A penetrating portrait of James himself, which is dated 1595, is certainly by Adrian Vanson (fl.1581–1602), the king's painter. (Its apparently off-centre composition indicates that it has been cut down at some time.) Adam de Cologne, who may have been Adrian Vanson's son, has also left several very refined and rather touching portraits. The painting of George Seton, earl of Winton, and his two sons, painted in 1625 is perhaps the finest. The way the artist captures the different expressions and thus the personalities and ages of the three sitters is very striking.

From the end of the sixteenth century, it also became increasingly common for painters to become heralds. James Workman, who was appointed Marchmont Herald in 1597, was the first to be honoured in this way. Painting coats of arms was a highly skilled and responsible business as it required a detailed knowledge of family history, etiquette and also of the elaborate pictorial conventions of heraldry: so this was a natural development for an artist. It was also a significant one as the herald's office conferred considerable status. Heralds had to organise great state and ceremonial occasions, where protocol was of real importance and often of great delicacy. Some of the grandest such events were the formal royal entries such as that of James and his queen, Anne of Denmark, into Edinburgh in 1590. An anonymous painted scroll of a grand funeral, c.1636, gives some indication of what this kind of occasion was like. Several armorials, or books of arms, painted by individual heralds survive. The Workman Armorial, for instance, was painted by James Workman himself. The finest of these armorials is, however, a little earlier in date. It is the Seton Armorial from c.1580, painted by an unknown artist for Robert, Lord Seton.

THE SEVENTEENTH CENTURY

The first native Scottish artist for whom we can establish a distinct personality was George Jamesone (1589/90–1644). He is the subject of a monograph and catalogue raisonné by Duncan Thomson (1974). Jamesone came from Aberdeen and spent most of his life there, but he trained with a decorative painter in Edinburgh: John Anderson. He may also have travelled to England or the Netherlands for his training, however, as he emerges as a more sophisticated artist at the very beginning of his career than he would have been if his only training had been as a decorative painter. His work has some similarity with that of Cornelius Johnson, a Dutch painter working in England at the time.

In Scotland Jamesone became a national figure. He was brought to Edinburgh to orchestrate the decoration of the city for King Charles I's entry in 1633. A detailed record of this colourful event survives, reprinted in part by Thomson (1974, 99–100). Twenty-six of the original one hundred and nine paintings of the ancestors of Charles I that Jamesone executed for the occasion also survive. All but the most recent ancestors were imaginary portraits. The paintings decorated an archway. In front of it an ode was addressed to the king. The paintings were also copied some fifty years later by Jacob de Wet and these copies, which hang in the Long Gallery, are one of the most striking features of the decoration of Holyrood Palace.

Jamesone's art is low-key, but it does not lack subtlety. It is seen at its best in a gentle, half-length portrait like that of Mary Erskine (1626). The full-length portrait of Anne Erskine, countess of Rothes, with her two daughters shows that he could also handle a grander style, and without losing anything in sensitivity. He also painted several self-portraits. His *Self-Portrait with an Easel* (c.1640), for instance, is particularly revealing. He presents himself very much as a professional artist. He is self-assured and dressed in a very respectable suit with a wide black hat. With one hand he indicates to us a wall covered with paintings that we are clearly meant to see as examples of his work, though he may have used some artistic license here. Some are recognisably in his style; others are not. He also includes a skull, an hour glass and parts of a suit of armour. One painting is larger and more prominent than the others; its subject is the Chastisement of Cupid, which represents the pleasures of the senses curbed. All these details are reminders of the deceptiveness of sensual beauty and of the transitoriness of worldly success. They constitute what is called a 'Vanitas', a symbolic invitation to reflect on such things. Such sentiments are typical of the period, but they also give the picture an introspective quality. They suggest both the artist's ambition for his art to deal with higher things, as poetry does, and also the complex self-awareness of the emerging Scottish professional class. The same metaphysical cast of mind combined with the self-assertion of a new urban bourgeoisie is also seen in the fine tombs and grave slabs from this period that are so numerous in Scottish churchyards.

Jamesone died in 1644 at the height of the wars of the Covenant. Civil unrest continued for many years after that and there was little opportunity for art to flourish. Nevertheless, a set of large canvases in Aberdeen appear to have been painted to mark the visit of the young Charles II to the city shortly before his hurried coronation at Scone in 1650.

In the seventeenth century Scotland's main trading link was with Holland and this is reflected in a variety of ways. One of the most striking portraits of the mid-century is, for instance, of the exiled earl of Ancram and it was painted in Holland by Rembrandt's associate, Jan Lievens. Rembrandt himself was represented in a Scottish collection remarkably early in his career. The merchant and dealer John

Clerk of Penicuik records a painting by him in an inventory of goods he had acquired during a trip to Holland and France in the late 1640s. And, in spite of the dislocation of the time, there were several great Scottish collectors.

With the insecurity of the mid-century many artists went overseas. Holland was a natural destination. William Gouw Fergusson (1632-3 – after 1695), for example, became well known as a still-life painter in the Netherlands. But there were still native artists working at home. David Scougall is the most distinguished and perhaps the most easily distinguishable of a family of artists of that name. His portrait of the cross-eyed marquis of Argyll is a forceful likeness and a memorable picture. Michael Wright was one of the most interesting painters of the period of the Civil War and Restoration. He was English, but he actually trained in Scotland with Jamesone. In his portrait of Lord Mungo Murray in full Highland dress he also left one of the most memorable Scottish images from the whole seventeenth century.

Foreign artists also continued to come to Scotland. Jacob de Wet (1640-97) was brought over from Holland to work on the refurbishment of Holyrood by William Bruce. He painted some rather stiff Baroque decorations there, but he also left a number of other much more interesting pictures, including a very fine still-life with a skull, candle, book and convex mirror – another Vanitas in fact – and *The Highland Wedding*. This is a picture of an earthy country wedding, with dancers dancing to a bagpiper in tartan trews and various scenes of drunken excess. It is in a tradition of wedding imagery that goes back to Teniers and Brueghel, but it in turn founded a tradition of wedding imagery in Scotland that starts with the poet Allan Ramsay's additions to the poem 'Christ's Kirk on the Green' and stretches down to David Wilkie's great *Penny Wedding*, 150 years later.

Sir John de Medina (1659-1710) was originally from Flanders. He came to Scotland from England in 1693 for a brief visit, but found a busy market and so stayed. He was a first-class portrait painter in a rather flamboyant, even Baroque style. He was invited to Scotland by the wives of the aristocracy – the political class who were spending more and more time in the south. Their wives either did not want to have to travel to London, or could not, but without a first class painter in Scotland they would have had to in order to have portraits painted of themselves and their families. Medina provided them with what they needed, but he also worked for people closer to his own social position. One of his outstanding achievements is the set of thirty-three oval portraits of the members of the Royal College of Surgeons, which he painted between 1697 and his death. It is a group to which he was invited to add his own likeness, thus confirming his status as a professional. Indeed his success and reputation were such that he was knighted. He was actually the last to be so honoured before the Union of 1707. Medina's informal portraiture is also lively and direct. We see it in the portrait of two of his children, one reading to the other, or in the delightful portrait of the butler of Wemyss Castle, with a flask of wine in his hand. Judging by the cheery expression on his face, the contents are about to be shared convivially with the artist.

Medina's success reflected the beginning of the change in status of artists from craft to profession. Native artists followed him, demonstrating a level of aspiration not really seen since the death of Jamesone. William Aikman (1682–1731) was actually a pupil of Medina, but he also travelled to Rome to study. On his return to Scotland he inherited Medina's position and produced some remarkable portraits, such as the austerely grand paintings of Hew Dalrymple, Lord North Berwick, or of Sir John Clerk of Penicuik, which have echoes more of Raphael than of the Baroque of Medina. This is a quality in Aikman's Scottish pictures which connects them with the classicism of his contemporaries: James Thomson, whose poem 'The Seasons' was begun in Edinburgh at just this time, and Colen Campbell, the architect who introduced Palladianism to England from Scotland.

John Smibert (1688–1751) was also their contemporary and he and Aikman were friends of the poet Allan Ramsay and members of a very interesting circle of Scots intellectuals gathered around him, including James Thomson. Both painters left portraits of Ramsay, Smibert's being the more robust and unexpected of the two. But the eclipse of Edinburgh as a political centre in consequence of the Union brought a disastrous decline in patronage. After 1707 the wives of the political classes, who had brought Medina to Scotland, moved south to join their husbands, who were now settled far more permanently in London. Both Aikman and Smibert moved south for lack of a market. Aikman enjoyed considerable success there, though he was never reconciled to his exile. Smibert on the other hand went even further afield. He was driven to leave London, according to George Vertue, who chronicled the art of the time, by what he saw as the 'selfish, gripping, over-reaching ways' of the city. He eventually settled in Boston, where he became the father of American painting. His journey to America was undertaken in the company of Bishop Berkeley and was part of an idealistic plan to set up a college in the West Indies. The plan came to nothing, but Smibert's painting of the group led by Berkeley – the so-called Bermuda Group – and including Smibert himself, is one of the icons of early American painting.

Richard Waitt was a more modest artist, but he is of special interest because he worked for the Grants of Rothiemurchus, virtually as clan painter, and he left a remarkable collection of portraits of some of the chief's retainers, including his champion, complete with sword and shield, and his humble henwife, Nic Chiarain. Portraits of such people are rare enough at any time and these are to be particularly valued as giving us a glimpse of Highland life. Richard Waitt's work is generally rather unsophisticated, but there is nothing unsophisticated about the brilliant treatment of still-life in his painting, *Still Life with a Leg of Lamb*.

Smibert and Aikman were not the only Scottish painters to travel to Rome in search of instruction. John Alexander was in Italy at the same time as them. He was in fact a Catholic and one of his most remarkable achievements was to paint the only fully Baroque ceiling painting in Scotland. It was for his Catholic patron, the duke of Gordon, and represented the rape of Proserpine. It was destroyed, sadly, and is now only known from his sketch. For Protestants, however, Rome had been the forbidden city for a century and more; but as religious strife gradually subsided, it became a place of pilgrimage for artists. It was to become for them what Paris was to be nearly two centuries later and throughout the eighteenth century Scottish artists played a prominent part in the artistic life of the city.

FOUNDATIONS OF ENLIGHTENMENT ART

Medina's achievement in securing recognition for painting as a profession was an important step for artists in the next century and demonstrates the continuities between seventeenth-century art and the art of the Enlightenment period. It is mirrored in the attempts by the painters within the Trades Guild in Edinburgh in the early eighteenth century to secure a special status for themselves as masters of an art, rather than of a craft. Two artists in particular were involved in this: James Norie and Roderick Chalmers. Norie was a decorative painter who introduced a style of freely painted landscape decoration that proved very popular and can still be seen in houses on the east coast such as Caroline Park or Newhailes. He also founded a family firm, which provided training for a number of important painters in the mid century. Chalmers was a decorative painter likewise, but he was also a herald painter. The two men were involved in an incident within the Incorporated Trades when Norie proposed to repaint the chimney piece of the meeting room, which showed all the trades together. He did this, but altered the order of precedence, evidently to favour the painters at the expense of the masons. A row broke out which was only resolved by Chalmers repainting the picture in the original order, while Norie's replacement was cut in half and given, half each, to the two contending parties among the trades. Chalmers' replacement survives. It shows the mason at the centre, but the painter still registers his claim, for he paints himself in a velvet coat and full-bottomed wig, painting at an easel. All the others are in work clothes. He is claiming his status as an artist and professional. He is no longer merely a tradesman and that was indeed the way of the future.

The collapse of patronage for painters in Scotland after 1707 might have been a more severe setback if it had not been for the initiatives taken by men like these to remedy the situation. Norie, Chalmers and Allan Ramsay senior were all signatories to a document that set up St Luke's Academy in 1729: an art school and the first art institution in Scotland. It may not have flourished for long, but while it did last it counted among its pupils both Allan Ramsay junior and Robert Adam. They went on to become, respectively, the greatest portrait painter and the greatest architect of the eighteenth century.

REFERENCES

Bath, M. 2003 *Renaissance Painting in Scotland*. Edinburgh.
Brydall, R. 1889 *History of Art in Scotland*. London.
Dunbar, J.G. 1999 *Scottish Royal Palaces: the Architecture of the Royal Residences during the Late Medieval and Early Renaissance Periods*. East Linton.
Dunbar, J.G. 1975 *The Stirling Heads*. Edinburgh.
Glendinning, M., MacInnes, R. and MacKechnie, A. 1996 *A History of Scottish Architecture*. Edinburgh.
Holloway, J. 1989 *Patrons and Painters 1650–1700*. Edinburgh.
Macdonald, M. 2000 *Scottish Art*. London.

MacMillan, D. 2000 *Scottish Art 1460–2000*. Edinburgh.

Thompson, C. and Campbell, L. 1974 *Hugo van der Goes and the Trinity Panels*. Edinburgh.

Thomson, D. 1975 *Painting in Scotland 1570–1650*. Edinburgh.

Thomson, D. 1974 *The Life and Art of George Jamesone*. Oxford.

Royal Academy 2004 *Illuminating the Renaissance, the triumph of Flemish Manuscript Illumination in Europe*. London.

CHAPTER THIRTEEN

Early Modern Music

John Purser

During the early modern period, two fundamental changes in the nature of music-making in Scotland took place. The first was the cessation of composition and performance of all complex polyphonic (many-voiced) church music. The second was a gradual shift from vocal to instrumental music. The decline of polyphonic music is directly attributable to the aims and achievements of the Reformation. The growth in instrumental music is a reflection of a trend throughout Europe, and occurred despite the Reformed church's suspicion of dance music and its refusal to allow the use of instruments in church, including the organ. In parallel with these changes a major decline took place in the provision of musical education in the main centres of population, counterbalanced by the flourishing of instrumental and vocal forms in the Gaelic-speaking areas of Scotland, where the oral tradition was, and remains, paramount. The period also includes the compositions of some of the leading Scottish composers, whose work is of international stature: in particular, the masses and motets of Robert Carver (c.1484–post 1568), the keyboard music of William Kinloch (fl. 1580s), the viol music of Tobias Hume (c.1569–1645) and the cantatas of John Clerk of Penicuik (1676–1755).

The chapter is divided into two sections: pre- and post-Reformation, followed by an overview. It should be stressed that research into the music discussed here is still largely in its infancy. Little has been published, and few alternative views are available. Readers are encouraged to go to the modern editions of primary sources, where available, or to the originals themselves, including recordings, on which the liner notes sometimes provide the most recent as well as comprehensive treatment.

MUSIC IN SCOTLAND BEFORE THE REFORMATION

Surviving Scottish music manuscripts are few in number. The most significant sources for pre-Reformation music are 'The Sprouston Breviary' (c.1300), 'The Inchcolm Antiphoner' (post–1264), 'The St Andrews Music Book (W1)' (c.1240) and 'The Carver Choirbook' (c.1500–c.1550). The first two consist of monophonic (single voice or line) chants, and contain texts and music in honour of St Kentigern and St Columba respectively. The second two contain outstanding examples of polyphony both in its first medieval forms and its highest Renaissance manifestations.

While each of these manuscript's contents demonstrate that Scottish musicians were learning from, and performing the work of their continental and English counterparts, efforts were made to retain Scottish practices, as opposed to the prevailing liturgical orthodoxies according to the practice of Salisbury:

> And als it is divisit and thocht expedient be us and our counsall that in tyme cuming mess bukis, manualis, matyne bukis and portuus bukis [portable breviaries] efter our awin Scottis use and with legendis of Scottis sanctis as is now gaderit and ekit be ane reverend fader in God and our traist counsalour Williame, bischop of Abirdene, and utheris, be usit generaly within al our realme als sone as the sammyn may be imprentit and providit; and that na maner of sic bukis of Salusbery use be brocht to be sauld within our realme in tym cuming . . . under pane of escheting [confiscation] of the bukis and punising of thair persons, bringaris thairof within our realme in contrar this our statut, with al rigour as efferis [as appropriate].
>
> (Livingstone 1908, 223–4)

What was 'our awin Scottis use' as far as music was concerned? The evidence is scanty. We know from a reference in David Lyndsay's 'The Testament of the Papyngo' (*c.*1530) that 'Sanct Mongois matynis' was still being sung at that time (Hamer 1931, ll. 703–5). Chants for First Vespers and Matins in the form of readings and responses survive in the 'Sprouston Breviary'. Their texts are unique, but some of the chants, such as the *Prosa* (an early form of sung verse) '*Gens Cambrina*', (People of Cambria) undoubtedly share a repertoire in common with the rest of Europe, while others, including the expressive Response '*Jubente Petrus*' (Peter, at the Lord's command) (Linn CKD 008, tr 2, disc 1), which describes the miracle of the fish and the ring, appear to be particular to the manuscript. However, these chants have yet to be properly analysed.

The chants for St Columba of Iona use unique texts closely based upon St Adomanan's *Life of St Columba* (Linn CKD 008, trs 3, 4, disc 1). Salisbury influence is already evident in the music for a number of them, but the music for one or two appears to be unique to the manuscript and may date back to the ninth century. In some of these chants, the intimate marriage between the vocal line and the formalised verse forms suggests a Gaelic provenance. The manuscript itself was compiled after 1264 for it contains chants for the feast of Corpus Christi, instituted in that year. In the light of the evidence, it seems likely that both manuscripts were in use over long periods, especially considering the importance of St Mungo or Kentigern as patron saint of Glasgow, and St Columba as patron saint of Dunkeld and Inchcolm, as well as the still-revered Iona.

'The St Andrews Music Book', on the other hand, has been closely analysed but its provenance and dating are disputed. What is not in dispute is that it is not only Scotland's earliest source of polyphonic music, with chants in two and three parts, but one of the earliest substantial collections of such music in the world. It is heavily influenced by the earlier Parisian repertoire, which supplies the bulk of the contents, but has unique and possibly locally-composed chants, some requiring considerable virtuosity (Linn CKD 008, trs 8–10, disc 1). The manuscript was still in St Andrews in the early sixteenth century, but how much of it was in use at that time is not known.

'The Carver Choirbook' was compiled by the Scottish composer, Robert Carver, and contains music by the famous Flemish composer Dufay (d.1474) and composers of the Eton school; but its primary importance lies in the works by Carver himself – five masses and two motets. Technically, these works are extremely demanding and argue a high standard of performance, most likely available from the Chapel Royal choir based at Stirling, and at other major centres such as Dunkeld, Glasgow, Aberdeen and Edinburgh. Perhaps the most famous of Carver's works is the nineteen-part motet 'O Bone Jesu' (O good Jesus) (Linn CKD 008, tr 16, disc 1), composed for the Feast of the Holy Name and probably commissioned as a penitential offering on behalf of James IV, who had been implicated in his father's murder. Nineteen was regarded as a perfect number, representing an ideal balance between male and female (the difference between three cubed and two cubed), and was used symbolically by Carver's contemporary, Robert Henryson, in his poem describing Orpheus' search for the music of the spheres. It stands for Jesus as perfect man, and on each occasion when the name 'Jesu' is sung by all nineteen voices, the music is surmounted by a pause mark or 'corona', thus crowning him as true king. This extraordinary work is composed with great care to detail in the balancing of the voices, as well as making use of an almost improvisational device for shifting between parallel chords, known as 'cant organe', and which appears to have been a particular feature of Scottish practice (Woods Preece 2000, 169–93).

Gavin Douglas's description of the court of Venus in his 'Palace of Honour', written around 1501, gives some idea of the technical and instrumental variety available.

> In modulatioun hard I play and sing
> Faburdoun, pricksang, discant, countering,
> Cant organe, figuratioun, and gemell,
> On croud, lute, harp, with monie gudlie spring,
> Schalmes, clariounis, portatives, hard I ring,
> Monycord, organe, tympane, and cymbell.
> Sytholl, psalterie, and voices sweit as bell,
> Soft releschingis in dulce delivering,
> Fractionis divide, at rest, or clois compell.

The technique of 'cant organe' is also found in Carver's ten-part Mass for the Feast of St Michael, the ten parts representing the nine orders of angels with mankind providing the tenth, joining in the heavenly chorus, as referred to in the Proper for the Feast of St Michael. It is possible that the six-part mass was composed for the launching of the Great Michael, then Europe's biggest warship and intended to lead a crusade (Ross 1993, 27–8). Carver also composed a mass based on the ribald song, whose title 'L'Homme Armée' (The Armed Man) has a double meaning. This was commonly used in mainland Europe, but Carver's is the only instance from the

British Isles. The melody is not used merely as a *cantus firmus* (a fixed pre-existing melody used as the basis for a polyphonic composition) but is integrated into the part-writing. The vocal writing is ornate and virtuosic, and makes use of imitative entries, a technique developing on the Continent at that time.

Carver was far from being alone. There were composers such as Fethy, who brought a new style of organ fingering to Scotland; the martyr Patrick Hamilton, possible composer of the virtuosic '*Ave Gloriosa*' (Hail Glorious [Queen Among Virgins]) in praise of the Virgin Mary; and Robert Johnston, who fled to England and whose refined style shows the increasing influence of the move towards simplicity and directness of communication in its use of English as well as Latin texts, and note-for-syllable settings. Carver's last mass also betrays the increasing demand for simpler textures that was emanating from the reformists, amongst whom was Carver's fellow-Scot and Augustinian canon, Robert Richardson, who complained of:

> those who introduce new masses of their own, formed after their own fancies. It is so prevalent that some would wish a different mass to be sung: and so confusions and arguments arise in the service of the Lord, when one reviles the work of another, always finding fault either with the mass, or the sound, the voices or the notes . . . Good God! how much valuable time is inanely wasted in sung masses in England and Scotland!
>
> (Coulton 1935, 80, 87)

Such sentiments were translated into action. Books were burnt, statues pulled down, windows smashed. The artistic expression of Catholic devotion was systematically destroyed, and with it went the major source of artistic patronage outside the court. There is every likelihood that a great deal of music was lost in this process though, at the time, the repression of such kinds of worship seems to have been accepted as of relatively minor consequence:

> Her grace's devout chaplains would, by the good device of Arthur Erskine, have sung a high mass: The Earl of Argyle, and the Lord James, so disturbed the quire, that some both priests and clerks, left their places, with broken heads, and bloody ears: it was a sport alone, for some that were there to behold it; others there were that shed a tear or two, and made no more of the matter.
>
> (Chalmers 1818, 54)

Secular music from this period is scarcely represented in music manuscripts until after 1560 (see below), and examples such as 'The Pleugh Sang' (Linn CKD 008, tr 13, disc 1) – a fascinating canon (self-imitating melody) on a ground bass (repeated bass line) extolling the virtues of a plough-team – are dated to the early sixteenth century on internal evidence only. Many popular tunes and songs are referred to in literary sources, and a great deal of these were parodied by the Wedderburn brothers in their publication of *The Good and Godlie Ballads*, turning secular preoccupations into songs of religious fervour. Occasionally an original can be reconstructed but, in a *fricasee* (literally a 'stew', meaning a medley) such as 'Trip and Go, Hey!' the tantalising fragments of songs which are included along with the titles of many others are all that are left to us.

POST-REFORMATION MUSIC IN SCOTLAND, 1560–*c*.1700

The number of Scottish music manuscripts from the period after 1560 is consider-ably greater than the few pre-Reformation survivals. Some examples of the more significant works will be discussed below and are as follows: 'The Art Of Music' (*c*.1580); 'Duncan Burnett's Music Book' (*c*.1610); 'Thomas Wode Partbooks' (1562–*c*.1592); Tobias Hume's 'The First Part Of Airs' (1605), and 'Captaine Hume's Poeticall Musicke' (1607); 'Robert Gordon of Straloch's Lute Book' (*c*.1620); 'Skene Lute Book' (*c*.1625); 'Robert Edward's Commonplace Book' (*c*.1630–1665); Edward Millar's 'The Psalms of David in Prose and Meeter' (1635): 'Lady Margaret Wemyss Manuscript' (1643–8) and 'Companion to Lady Margaret Wemyss Manuscript' (*c*.1660); John Forbes's 'Cantus, Songs and Fancies' (1662, 1666 and 1682); 'Robert Taitt's Music Book' (*c*.1680); John Leyden's 'Lyra-Viol Manuscript' (*c*.1690); 'Balcarres Lute Book' (*c*.1690); 'Blaikie Manuscript' (1692); 'The Clerk Papers' (*c*.1690–*c*.1720).

'The Art of Music' is a Scottish treatise with several unique music examples, influenced by the Reformation but with older styles represented. It was probably produced for the Edinburgh song school. A number of burghs had song schools before the Reformation but most of them fell into disuse as the Glasgow Burgh records show:

> [the council] seeing that the musik school is altogether dekayit within this burgh
> to the great discredit of this citie . . . and that Duncan Birnett, who sumtyme of
> befoir teatchit musik within this burgh is desyrous to tak up the said school
> againe and teitche musik thairin, has granted licence to the said Duncane Birnett
> to tak up ane musik school within this burgh.

The date of compilation of the 'Duncan Burnett Music Book' is not known, but it is not likely to be any later than 1610, and much of the music in it probably dates from the 1580s. The main composer represented is William Kinloch, whose history is obscure but who may well be the William Kinloch referred to by his fellow virginalist and composer James Lauder (Linn CKD 008, tr 19, disc 1), in connection with secret missions to the imprisoned Mary, queen of Scots. Internal evidence suggests that some of the music itself carried secret meanings. In any event, Kinloch's '*Passme-sour*' and '*Quadran Pavan*' (both Renaissance dance forms) and their accompanying galliards are outstanding achievements, bearing comparison with some of the great English composer Byrd's keyboard works, one of which is represented in the manuscript. Kinloch was clearly a virtuoso player, but his extended works show mastery of form, not least the politically significant 'Battel of Pavie', which makes a much more coherent whole than Byrd's more famous 'Battel'. Kinloch's 'Battel of Pavie' celebrates the victory, in 1520, of a Spanish-Papal alliance over the French. In the context of the later sixteenth century the piece would have been construed as resolutely pro-Catholic. The 'Duncan Burnett Music Book' is our only substantial source for Scottish keyboard music of the period. Likewise, the 'Thomas Wode Partbooks' are responsible for saving a body of Scottish music which would otherwise have been lost to us. Wode, a monk from Lindores Abbey in Fife, was conscious of the importance of his work: 'To ane great man that has bot ane resonable gripe of musike; thir fyve bukis wer worthy thair wayght of gould.' The music exists only in part books, but they are neat, and almost all of the double set he made are preserved, so the music can be readily reconstructed. They contain many of Wode's own marginal comments, such as his description of the composer, David Peebles, and his setting of 'Si Quis Diliget Me' (If Any Man Loves Me).

> David Pables sumtyme ane channone in the abbay of Sanctandrous – ane of the principall musitians in all this land in his tyme. This sang was set about the yeir of God 1530 and presentit to Kyng Iamis the fyft . . . and being a musitian, he did lyke It verray weill . . . the King had ane singular guid eir and culd sing that he had never seine before, bot his voyce wes rawky and harske. Ane lytill before pinky Francy Heagy sumtyme ane nouice in the abbay of Sanctandrous a trim playar upon the organs and also ane dissciple to David Pables, maid this fyft pairt to this, si quis diliget me.

But Wode's was a despairing rescue attempt, and if what he saved is a clue to the quality of what was lost, then his pessimism, when he penned the following, should not be harshly judged: 'I cannot understand bot musike sall pereische in this land alutterlye.'

As for singing in church, with the gradual removal of organs and choirs, standards fell. Psalms were sung in metrical versions set to tunes from European, English and Scottish sources. Attempts to introduce variety into congregational psalm-singing were of limited success. Some psalms were set 'in reports' (using vestigial imitation in the parts) but, in the absence of adequate music teaching, the number of tunes used was reduced to little more than a handful, and congregational singing appears to have adopted a style of free heterophony (the varied presentation of a single line by several people simultaneously, later regarded by many as chaotic), which became increasingly altered and embellished in the Gaelic-speaking tradition, the latter surviving to this day, having evolved, or perhaps reverted to a style closer to Middle-eastern singing than anything now to be heard in Western Europe.

In addition to the metrical psalms, there was a repertoire of secular and sacred part-songs popular at the Scottish court, which can be reconstructed using Wode's parts in conjunction with 'Robert Edward's Commonplace Book', John Forbes's 'Cantus, Songs and Fancies', and 'Robert Taitt's Music Book'. These songs, some of which would have been danced to, are sophisticated expressions of courtly love, often showing French influence, but setting some of the finest Scots poetry of the period, as in the works of the poet-composer Alexander Scott. But the removal of the Scottish court to London in 1603 was undoubtedly a watershed.

While some musicians such as the Ramsay family of trumpeters, travelled south with the court, others, no doubt, were simply left without employment. Amongst those who arrived unofficially in London, seeking support for their poetry and music, was the notable eccentric Tobias Hume, described as 'a Scottish Musicion' in Queen Anne's papers. Hume's music for voices and viols, but chiefly for the bass viol, represents a quantum leap in writing for a solo stringed instrument and includes some of the earliest expression marks and the first known use of techniques such as *col legno* (with the wood of the bow rather than the hair on the strings), now commonly employed.

It was shortly after the publication of Hume's music that the earliest surviving manuscripts of lute music in Scotland were written. While they contain music from England and the Continent, their chief glories lie in the uniquely Scottish material. This includes such treasures as the theme for the epic late mediaeval Scottish romance 'Greysteil' and a substantial number of tunes, often with the title '*Port*' (Gaelic for 'tune'), which are generally accepted as being closely related to the clarsach (Celtic harp) repertoire. The tradition of clarsach playing in Scotland was broken by 1800, but it was revived in the late nineteenth century. Research in the twentieth century, making use of the lute manuscripts, amongst others, and publications such as Oswald's *Caledonian Pocket Companion* (1740s–50s) Daniel Dow's *Collection of Ancient Scots Music* (1776) and (from Irish sources), Bunting's *Ancient Irish Music* (1840) restored something of what was lost. These drew their material largely from the oral/aural tradition, and the accuracy of transmission can be judged by comparing the famous '*Da Mihi Manum*' in the 'Lady Margaret Wemyss Manuscript' of 1644 with its subsequent taking down by Bunting from an Irish harpist in the late eighteenth century. The differences are relatively minor and no more than might have been heard within the tradition shortly after Ruairidh Dall O'Cahan composed the piece, probably in Glasgow in 1617.

O'Cahan is not to be confused with Roderick Morrison, also known as Ruaidhri Dall MacMhuirich, nicknamed *An Clàrsair Dall* (The Blind Harper) (*c*.1656–*c*.1713), one of the last of the traditional harpers in Scotland to compose his own poetry and perform it in a traditional clan context. There is no clear evidence that he composed his own music, but he will certainly have arranged it, and the theme for his extended and brilliantly bawdy poem '*Féill nan Crann*' (Harp-key Fair) may be by him. Its simple beauty makes the search for the lost harp key (a sexual metaphor) all the more hilarious. Though he adopts standard bardic practices, a strong personal note is present in his verse, revealing a complex personality coming to terms with personal – difficulties which, he was aware, reflected the change coming over the whole world of which he was such a distinguished part, including, in 1688, his retiral to Totamor in Glenelg, probably following a difference of opinion with his chieftain with respect to the Revolution of that year, the harper being a Jacobite. This separation is bitingly referred to in his poem '*A' Cheud Di-luain de'n Ràithe*' (The First Monday of the Quarter) and his

Jacobite sympathies are evident in every stanza of '*Oran mu Oifigich Araid*' (A Song About Certain Officers), which is the only surviving poem written down during the poet's lifetime.

But there remains a gap in our knowledge with respect to the harp's function as an accompaniment to recitation and song, as well as its possible role in the development of *piobaireachd*. The word literally means 'pipe music', but it is now exclusively applied to *ceol mòr* (great music), a form of theme and variations which generally become increasingly elaborate, with returns to the theme at intervals, though these returns are nowadays confined to a partial repeat of the theme (*ùrlar*, or ground) at the end. It has, however, often been suggested that the clarsach also made use of, if not actually initiated this form. Support for this comes not only from some of the variations to be found in Oswald and Bunting, but from a Welsh source known as the '*Ap Hyw Manuscript*', where the formal procedures underlying the music have parallells with those found in *ceol mòr*. Research continues in this area, with fascinating attempts at reconstruction of *ceol mòr* for clarsach, which have included reconstruction of instruments and re-stringing the bass strings with gold, as early sources have suggested was done, with excellent acoustic results.

We are on slightly surer ground with respect to Highland bagpipe music. We know that it was used for the main genres of laments, gatherings and marches; and music survives from the three main dynasties of pipers. They were: the MacCrimmon family (fl. 1600–1772), hereditary pipers to the MacLeods of Dunvegan on Skye; the MacArthurs (fl. 1600–1750), hereditary pipers to the MacDonalds of Sleat, also on Skye; and the Mackays of Gairloch (fl. 1600–1772), hereditary pipers to the Mackenzies. The most famous of the MacKays was Roderick MacKay's son, Iain Dall (1656–1754), also known as *Am Piobaire Dall* (The Blind Piper). He is credited with the composition of a number of outstanding *piobaireachd*, including 'The Lament for Patrick Og MacCrimmon', 'The Blind Piper's Obstinacy', and 'Corrienessan's Salute'. He was also renowned as a poet, in particular for his superb nature poem '*Cumha Choire an Easa*' (A Lament for *Coire an Easa*), composed in 1696.

The first authenticated mention of the MacArthur pipers is in an early-seventeenth-century satirical poem '*Seanchas na Pìob o Thùs*' (History of the Pipes since the Beginning), ascribed to the famous bard Niall Mór MacMhuirich, though some would ascribe it to his son Niall Òg. The pipers referred to were Iain and Dòmhnall MacArtuir, and the poem's dislike of the pipes reflects their increasing dominance over the clarsach, which was the traditional bardic instrument.

The MacCrimmons are undoubtedly the most famous of all piping families and their superiority received early acknowledgment in 1651 when 'John M'gyurmen' was declared by his fellow pipers to be 'the prince of Pipers'. Charles II called him forward and permitted him to kiss the royal hand, upon which he composed the *piobaireachd* '*Thug mi pòg do làimh an Righ*' (I Got a Kiss of The King's Hand). It is a reasonable conjecture that 'M'gyurmen' (a name otherwise unknown) is a rendering of 'MacCrimmon'. As piper to the 'Earle of Sutherland', the player in question would not have been employed by the MacLeods, but evidence of the family's employment and status can be found in the records of the MacLeod estates, where they probably held their lands rent-free, as did Roderick Morison. That they were formally recognised as teachers is reflected in an entry for 1698 referring to the 'Prentisep of McIntyre the pyper with McCrooman'. Their musical prowess is mentioned in the Gaelic poems of Mary MacLeod – notably '*Crònan an Taibh*' (The Ocean-croon), composed shortly after 1666, which refers to *Pàdraig Mòr* and his '*pìob nuallanach mhòr*' (great shrill-voiced pipe) (Carmichael Watson 1934, 44–5).

The main names in the family in the seventeenth century are Donald Mòr (fl. 1600), Patrick Mòr (fl. 1640–1670), and Patrick Òg (*c*.1645–*c*.1730); to them are attributed a number of *piobaireachd*, often on legendary rather than historical grounds, their skills having been originally acquired from the fairies – a common motif in Gaelic mythology. However, there is historical as well as stylistic support for some of the attributions. Donald Mòr is credited with the composition of 'MacLeod's Salute' and this tune shares a characteristic fingering feature with others attributed to him. A remission issued by the crown under the great seal on 13 January 1614 refers to a piper called 'Donald MacCruimien' and it is assumed that this is the same man. Patrick Mòr is said to have composed 'The Lament for the Children' – one of the most famous and extended of *piobaireachd*. Others attributed to him also tend to be extended, though '*Cumha Dhomhnaill an Lagain*' (The Lament for MacDonald of Laggan) is an exception. It was said that this lament was played nightly at Dunvegan because Donald's daughter, wife to The MacLeod, could not sleep without hearing it. Patrick Òg is particularly remembered for the 'Lament for Iain Garve of Raasay' and the beautiful and gentle 'Lament for Mary MacLeod', unofficial bardess as well as nurse to the MacLeods, who died in 1707.

Outwith the sphere of Gaelic and traditional music, however, music-making in Scotland was at a low ebb. The appearance of the singing-teacher, Louis de France, would have been of little note in any other European country. In late seventeenth-century Scotland, he was a rarity, although the evidence from his manuscript of teaching material would suggest a level of competence amongst his pupils that would scarcely be acceptable to a talented amateur.

Only with John Abell and John Clerk of Penicuik do we have any signs of high levels of musicianship being developed, and both these men probably acquired their best skills in London or, in Clerk's case, in Holland and Italy. Clerk's cantatas are amongst the finest contributions to Baroque music from these islands and they come from a man of great cultural significance. John Clerk of Penicuik was born in 1676 and died in 1755. The range of his interests and abilities was enormous and he takes a crucial place in the history of Scottish culture. He was a lawyer, judge, amateur architect, artist and poet, landscape gardener and musician. He was also a signatory to the 1707 Treaty of Union between the parliaments of Scotland and England, though his tract '*Leo Scotiae Irritatus*' (The Lion of Scotland Angered) demonstrates unequivocally that he started off life with no love for such an idea.

Despite pressure from his father, who told him in a letter that 'You were sent by me to Holland to studie not architecture, nor policie nor fidling nor to see curiosities for that is no dutie, but to studie law', Clerk continued his musical studies in Rome under Corelli and Pasquini. This was an act of cultural self-assertion in another sense. Rome was the home of Roman Catholicism and had a bad reputation in Protestant circles such as Clerk's. But for the young Clerk it was a vital and formative experience, and all his musical works seem to have been composed during or shortly after his European tour in the late 1690s. A fascinating element in Clerk's compositions is his use of number symbolism. However, this need not surprise us in a man who became a Freemason, who restored the fifteenth-century Rosslyn Chapel with its complex symbolism, and who was the great-great-grandfather of one of the greatest scientific minds of all time: James Clerk Maxwell.

He had a natural melodic gift and his vocal writing is magnificent: intense, sensuous, varied. He enhanced his texts with subtle illustrative touches, from a ground bass to represent Fortune's wheel, to delicate trills on the violins to depict hovering cupids. This variety of presentation and mood was a part of Corelli's technique which was particularly admired, and which Clerk made his own. At a deeper level, Clerk's cantatas offer a remarkable insight into Baroque attitudes to structure. Clerk was in Rome partly to study architecture. He became an amateur architect and drew parallels between music and architecture which he realized in both fields. '*Dic Mihi Saeve Puer*' (Tell Me, Savage Boy) (Linn CKD 008, tr 1, disc 2), a cantata protesting at the cruelty of Cupid, is derived from a single motif which in various forms determines the melodic outline of each section. Allied to this is Clerk's use of symbolic numerology to motivate the structures: in the '*Miserere Mei Deus*' (Have mercy upon me, O Lord) he uses Hebrew numerological values to determine the length of sections in a setting of Vulgate Psalm 50: in another work he makes an indelicate sexual pun out of the number values for the names of Bedford and Howland, whose nuptials he celebrates in '*Odo di mesto intomo*' (Around Me I Hear).

These works also provide an insight into the social and political attitudes of their time. '*Odo di mesto intomo*' tells us much about the dynastic marriage system in England – the duke of Bedford being possibly the richest man in Europe, and his wife being from a similarly wealthy background; but it is the cantata which reveals that they were married so young that the bedding of the bride was only about to take place two years later. '*Leo Scotiae Irritatus*' shows us a Dutch writer collaborating with a Scot to claim for Scotland the right to set up a colony on the Panama isthmus without interference from the English and Spanish. '*Dic Mihi Saeve Puer*' confesses to a somewhat ambivalent sexuality, and the '*Miserere*' sets a penitential psalm which seeks forgiveness for adultery. At its very centre is a highly personal recitative, suggesting that Clerk himself was the penitent – though whether his adultery was carnal or a spiritual adultery with Roman Catholicism is a moot point.

There are undoubted contradictions between his music and his later career, which led to his abandonment of composition as unbecoming in a judge; for he was a gentleman amateur in a world where to be a professional musician was to be little more than a servant. It is worthy of notice that, during the seventeenth century, music flourished at least as well in the remoter parts of the country, where there remained a degree of aristocratic patronage among Highland chieftains and Lowland lairds, as it did in the main centres which had been abandoned by the court and where even the larger churches showed no interest in anything but the simplest music making.

CONCLUSION

The church in Scotland has yet to recover anything approaching the magnificence of worship of the pre-Reformation days, and probably never will. Performances of music from this repertoire are largely undertaken by professional musicians outwith any liturgical context. On the other hand, secular music by Scottish composers writing between 1500 and 1700 has yet to take its full and proper place in the national consciousness, whether for its own artistic qualities, or for its potential significance for historians and ethnologists. But it is worth holding in mind that, unlike much other historical evidence, music, when performed in an appropriate style, presents its evidence in living form. It is not an account of what happened. It is what happened.

REFERENCES

Carmichael Watson, J. (ed) 1934 *Gaelic Songs of Mary MacLeod*. Edinburgh.
Chalmers, G. 1818 *The Life Of Mary, Queen Of Scots*, vol. 1. London.
Coulton, G. (ed) 1935 *Robertus Richardinus, Commentary On The Rule Of St Augustine*. Edinburgh.
Hamer, D. (ed) 1931 *The Works of Sir David Lindsay of the Mount, 1490–1555*, vol. 1. Edinburgh.
Livingstone, M. (ed) 1908 *Register of the Privy Seal of Scotland*. Edinburgh.
Ross, D.J. 1993 *Musick Fyne*. Edinburgh.
Woods Preece, I. 2000 ' "Cant Organe": A Lost technique?', in Woods Preece, I. *Music in the Scottish Church up to 1603*, Glasgow, 169–93.

FURTHER READING

Collinson, F.J. 1966 *The Traditional and National Music of Scotland*. London.
Elliott, K. and Shire, H.M. 1957 *Music of Scotland* (vol. 15 of *Musica Britannica*). London.
Elliott, K. 1958 *Early Scottish Keyboard Music*. London.
Elliott, K. 1960 *Fourteen Psalm Settings*. Oxford.
Elliott, K. (ed) 1996 *The Complete Works of Robert Carver & Two anonymous Masses*. Glasgow.
Elliott, K. (ed) 1996 *Sixteenth-century Scots songs for voice & lute*. Glasgow.
Elliott, K. 2003 *Now fayre, fayrest off every fayre*. Glasgow.
Purser, J. 1992 *Scotland's Music*. Edinburgh.
Purser, J. 1998 'On the Trail of the Spies', *Scotlands*, 5, 23–44.
Purser, J. 2001 'Greysteil', in Williams, J.H. (ed) *Stewart Style 1513–1–1542: Essays on the Court of James V*, East Linton, 142–52.

Ross, D.J. n.d. 'New Roots for a Renaissance Scottish Master', *Cencrastus*, 64, 18–22.
Shire, H.M. 1969 *Song, Dance and Poetry of the Court of Scotland Under King James VI.* Cambridge.
Woods Preece, I. 2000 *Our Awin Scottis Use: Music in the Scottish Church up to 1603.* Glasgow.

RECORDINGS CITED IN THE TEXT

Scotland's Music. Linn CKD 008 (two discs).

FURTHER LISTENING

The following selected citations are arranged by title, followed by the publisher's name and number for the CD.

Notes of Noy Notes of Joy. Dorian DOR COMD 2058

Carver

Complete works of Robert Carver. ASV Gaudeamus CD GAU 125,126,127
An Eternal Harmony. CORO COR 16010

Johnson

Robert Johnson. ASV Gaudeamus CD GAU 154

Music of the Scottish Court

Mary's Music. Chandos CHAN 0529
Mary Queen of Scots. ASV Gaudeamus CD GAU 136

William Kinloch

Kinloche his Fantassie. ASV Gaudeamus CD GAU 134
The Songs of Alexander Montgomerie. ASV CD GAU 249
Psalms for the Regents of Scotland. Edinburgh University Music Dept EURS 003 1600–1700

Tobias Hume

Captaine Tobias Hume Musicall Humors. ASTREE E 7723.
A Souldiers Resolution. Move MD 3232.
Play This Passionate. VIRGIN CLASSICS VC7 91451–2, 5
Tobias Hume. HARMONIA MUNDI RD77165. *The Spirit of Gambo Tobias Hume.* GLOSSA GCD 920402.
Dramatic Laments Elegies and Lullabies. ADDA 581033 CD.
My mind to me a Kingdom is. Hyperion. CDA66307.

Lute music.

The Scottish Lute. Dorian DOR 90129.
Scottish Lute Music. BIS CD–201.

Robert Ramsay

An Eternal Harmony. CORO COR 16010

John Clerk of Penicuik

Leo Scotiae Irritatus. Hyperion CDA 67007

CHAPTER FOURTEEN

Early Modern Literature
Theo van Heijnsbergen

After Flodden, the future could be perceived only apprehensively. In contrast, the commanding achievements of the immediate past provided powerful frameworks of cultural reference for a nation in search of a new footing in history. Consequently, Scotland tried to renew itself by continuing past cultural paradigms. This paradoxical inclination was reinforced by long royal minorities, which meant sixteenth-century Scotland benefitted only intermittently from the kind of patronage through which international influences passed into national cultures. Concurrently, the aristocracy no longer considered literary patronage a main priority, while the post-Reformation church actively discouraged most kinds of imaginative writing. When Scotland under James VI did enjoy a long personal rule, he encouraged his courtiers to write. James understood that literature could play a key part in a sovereign's art of rule, propagating the language of peace and the rewards for serving a divinely-appointed ruler. His departure in 1603 allowed the unopposed policing of cultural expression by the church, yet this did leave room for non-courtly textual initiatives, such as ballads, sermons, autobiographies and diaries, and nurtured the capacity for 'strenuous thought [and] egalitarianism' (Scott 1993, 12).

By counterbalancing ecclesiastical authority, the restoration of royal power after 1660 advanced the return of a more urbane literary voice. The laicised community encouraged different cultural practices and, particularly in Edinburgh, literary energies circulated that recovered Scotland's connection with international literary developments as well as with its own literary past. Out of this grew not only the Vernacular Revival of the eighteenth century but also the conditions that allowed Scotland to contribute to later European cultural developments such as the Enlightenment and Romanticism.

This chapter investigates the ways in which literature both shaped and reflected Scottish cultural experience in the sixteenth and seventeenth centuries, and selects particular avenues of inquiry that align literature with history to combine survey with analytical argument. (It is difficult to chronicle developments within the relatively homogeneous genre of folk ballad, but individual specimens are referred to when appropriate.) The chapter is divided into broadly chronological sections. Its principal aim is to show how appreciation of the literary texts of this period and of modern ways of studying them can interact positively with historical scholarship.

CRITICAL CONTEXTS, INTERDISCIPLINARY THEMES AND LITERARY DEVELOPMENTS BEFORE 1513

Cultures with a more 'courtly-metropolitan' emphasis than Scotland have tended to prioritise aesthetic criteria to determine which texts reproduce meanings that are worth preserving. They thus distinguished 'literature' from 'letters' and institutionalised the former, narrower definition as the norm for 'literary culture'. The additional dimensions of early modern Scottish texts – particularly theological and popular discourses – represent powerful challenges to this previously dominant model, the critical foundations of which, nevertheless, still hinder a historicised appraisal of Scottish texts. The nineteenth century conceptualised 'medieval' and 'Renaissance' as mutually exclusive rather than consecutive concepts. This notion found its most enduring formulation in cultural studies inspired by Jacob Burckhardt's *The Civilization of the Renaissance in Italy* (1860). It proposed that medieval people were conscious of themselves only as members of a group, whereas 'Renaissance' people became aware of themselves as individuals. This posited a clean break with the 'medieval' and allowed the representation of the 'Renaissance' author as a strong individual who fashioned his authentic, secular self in idiosyncratic, self-referential writing. Thus, 'modern man' gave retrospective birth to his – though not her – articulate self.

Such hypotheses became the presuppositions that underpinned the cultural worldview of modern Western thinking, substituting 'artistic' for 'historical' reference points. This served English early modern literature well, but questioned the profitability or even validity of the study of its Scottish equivalent, which accommodates this distinction between medieval and modern less easily. Moreover, Tudor culture was increasingly secular and pursued close connections to Italian, courtly and 'Renaissance' writing, while the principal influences in contemporary Scottish letters were French, with a predominantly middling audience pursuing godly citizenship rather than 'Renaissance' individuality. Scottish writing continued to give prominence to relations between self and society rather than to the autonomous individual. The challenge for modern readers is to read the resultant language of virtue not just as an ethical but also as a psychological and self-expressive analytical language.

The challenge arises from the Christian-medieval notion that there is no difference between the inner and the moral self; experience outside the latter is not part of the self but is potentially destructive of self. Individual experience could be profitably judged only by collective morality rather than vice versa, which prompted a reliance on universal ideas, such as good and evil, rather than on individuality. This allowed the continuation of the literature of ideas rather than character, and of writing that looks for moral designs and creates literary protagonists as 'exemplary types of virtue and vice' (Reid 1982, 187). This continues narrative practices shared by late-medieval literature and historiography. In a Burckhardtian model, however, this does not constitute literary activity but nullifies it.

In neighbouring cultures, when medieval approaches could no longer articulate new social realities, international influences and interplay between sacred and profane discourses allowed literature to adapt accordingly. In Scotland, however, especially after 1603, the church's preoccupation with controlling people's behaviour led to an identification of church with society. This helps to explain why powerful ideological forces within Scottish historical criticism 'had no wish to recognise the richness of the material and literary culture which the Reformation destroyed – or to admit the extent of the reformers' collusion in its destruction' (Mason 1998, 2). While implicitly rejecting the Burckhardtian prioritisation of the artistic, such ideological forces exploited its most fundamental assumption: that cultural value arises from a break with late-medieval culture.

The study of early modern Scottish culture thus involves complex relations between metropolitan bias, historiographical practice and literary evidence. Scrutinising critical preconceptions will produce more nuanced balances between these. Thus, using the period's own, wider definition of 'literature' as 'letters' (i.e. writing) allows for a more integrative cultural history, which includes family and national histories, diaries, (auto)biographies, travel-writing, translations, women's writing, dedications, letters, scientific, practical, didactic or legal material as well as a wide range of religious writing. However, students are often still guided towards literary evidence with a preconceived distinction between 'literature' and 'letters'. An awareness of recent literary theory may remedy this. Examining its own critical practice, it has exposed the fact that what is found in literary texts is often a matter of what is imposed by the reader. Consequently, literary scholars now prefer to seek the most plausible interpretations of available data rather than to superimpose cultural models. This provides a promising template for re-evaluating early modern Scottish culture.

By focusing on the shared features of literature, letters and history, the argument below tries to facilitate interdisciplinary dialogue in a mutually intelligible language. For the early modern period, a key point of comparison may be attained by recognising that both literary text and historical action were preoccupied with situating the individual in the socio-political order. Investigating relations between self and society therefore provides the points of comparison by which contemporary cultural expression and historical events can be discussed within the same frame of reference. It enables us to map the contemporary search for inwardness as a way to achieve happiness or salvation amidst unprecedented change. It also allows interdisciplinary discussion of key issues that link the medieval to the modern period, such as the humanist belief in the autonomy of the individual, expressed through the ethical exercise of free will. The tension between freedom and moral responsibility towards self and community highlighted one specific protagonist in both literature and history: the monarch. Adapting the prominent fifteenth-century literary genre of 'advice to princes', sixteenth-century texts increasingly depicted the sovereign as, paradoxically, the most unique and least individual (because most representative) of all people. The monarch thus increasingly became a psychological as well as moral exemplar, onto whom many anxieties of the early modern (male) self were projected.

Focusing on how literature negotiated the relationship between self and community also highlights the contemporary appreciation of what it meant to read and write. The understanding gradually forced itself upon society that human identity was contingent, not predetermined by Scripture, and that the act of story-telling to investigate that contingency was in itself a moral choice. Late-medieval Scottish authors therefore made the act of writing itself the subject of their narratives, often by using a narrator-figure who himself becomes a protagonist in the text (e.g. James I's *Kingis Quair*, Henryson's *Testament of Cresseid*, Douglas's *Palace of Honour*). This dramatisation of story-tellers highlighted the capacity of texts to communicate different levels of meaning, e.g. by differentiating between author and narrator. It also augmented the illusion of spoken address, which encouraged an interest in the personal and its enactment. Our constant point of attention, therefore, is how these texts continually evaluate the nature and function of fiction itself.

Such a profound engagement with literature as a dialectical tool was fully in accord with developments abroad. In the late fifteenth century, it allowed Robert Henryson to marry complex allegory to a vernacular narrative style and add Christian emphases to classical stories. William Dunbar used it to make Scots a flexible medium not just for narratives but also for lyrical expression, developing a vernacular language in which one could express one's self but also evaluate that expression. Gavin Douglas's *Palace of Honour* sought to heighten the status of authors by suggesting that poetry as metaphysical inquiry helps to define virtue and thus leads to honour. Such a complex synthesis of medieval and humanist ideas points towards new socio-cultural values, secular but grounded in Scripture, in which it is not birth but the practice of virtue in the public arena (which includes writing fiction) that leads to honour.

The next step was a logical one. Translating the classics was a key tool in turning vernacular literature into more flexible tools of expression and cultural inquiry, and in July 1513 Douglas completed the *Eneados*, his translation of Virgil's *Aeneid*. As the exemplary leader of his people, who learns that peace is preferable to war, Virgil's Aeneas was the perfect hero for Douglas's purpose in the politically darkening reality of Scotland in 1513. As significant as the act of translation itself – the *Eneados* was only the second complete translation of Virgil's classic into any European vernacular – were the prologues which Douglas added to each of Virgil's twelve books. Cast in as many different genres as possible, they affirmed the ability of the vernacular to articulate many distinct voices. They also explicitly instructed readers to investigate discontinuities in the logic of narratives in order to make reading fiction instrumental in developing their moral and intellectual faculties and, thus, their self-governance. This reliance on the reader allowed writers to jettison the explicit moralising which was a feature of many contemporary texts; the text becomes an autonomous whole, exercising its own judgement. Literature, authors and readers can thus formulate their own truths.

THE AFTERMATH OF FLODDEN

After the defeat at Flodden, we hear no more of Dunbar, while Douglas turned to politics. However, the late fifteenth-century push for education had created Scottish men of letters of European standing and an educated lay audience. Through such cultural intermediaries, continental writing and thoughts found their way to Scotland and ensured continued literary activity during the minority of James V (1513–28). Thus, John Mair or Major (c.1467–1550) of Haddington was a celebrated philosopher, theologian and friend of the great humanist scholar Erasmus in Paris, where he lectured for several decades before returning to Scotland in 1518. Mair taught many who were 'responsible for the religious and humanist changes of the earlier part of the sixteenth century' (Broadie 1990, 21), both in Scotland and abroad, among them John Knox and George Buchanan. Mair's *Historia Maioris Britanniae* (Paris, 1521) advocated greater friendship between Scotland and England and may have triggered another national history in Latin, the *Scotorum Historia* (Paris, 1527) by Hector Boece (c.1465–1536). Boece had been a colleague of Mair in Paris before he, too, was tempted back to Scotland to become principal of the University of Aberdeen. Boece's techniques were literary rather than historical, preferring the persuasive style of humanist eloquence to Mair's analytical logic. To Boece, the quality of a work of historiography was determined not by its accuracy but by how effectively it made the protagonists perform virtuous acts that encouraged imitation by readers. He accordingly dramatised rather than documented history, in order to communicate its essence. (It should be borne in mind that modern literary theory would argue that *all* historiography does that, albeit unwittingly and to different patterns and extents.) Such a humanist blend of historiography and literature evolved from medieval practices that understood both disciplines as means of presenting moral philosophy through examples of virtue. Literature, historiography and morality make common cause here, each with the writer as the centre for moral reflection.

James V's personal reign brought together such scholarly writing and vernacular literature, notably through John Bellenden (c.1495–c.1547). Bellenden, too, studied in Paris before returning to Scotland, where he became archdeacon of Moray. James V paid him to translate historiographical works into Scots, notably Boece's *Scotorum Historia* (1531) and Livy's history of Rome (1533). These translations indicate the prevailing state-sponsored interest in worldly history and in the history of nations and cities in particular, suggesting a patriotic dimension to the new learning and a widening of its audience. Both Bellenden and his contemporary David Lyndsay (c.1486–1555) continued Douglas's search for a 'knychtlyke [i.e. knightly] style', but sought to adapt its chivalric ethos to the concept of the commonweal (the common good), which became a prominent concept as a result of humanist inquiries into classical statecraft. But, where Lyndsay was preoccupied with turning chivalry into a viable template for *social* action, Bellenden gave civic responsibility and the pursuit of virtue a more patriotic emphasis, defining as the noblest man he who dies in defence of his native country. In this upgrading of older cultural and political values Bellenden consciously imitated the earlier makars. Apart from his 'heroicall' style, this appears from his aureate diction (his ornamental use of vocabulary), difficult stanza-forms, astrological openings, and his use of dream-vision and classical gods. Likewise, Bellenden endorsed the notion, derived from the Roman author Horace, that poetry should be a mixture of teaching and entertainment, which lay behind Henryson's fables as well. Bellenden's humanism thus appears to be progressive within socio-politically and culturally conservative intentions.

The dominant poet of James V's reign was David Lyndsay, whose literary models, like Bellenden's, were past makars, native and classical. He had been a trusted caretaker of the infant James, which in later years allowed him to practise the Scottish tradition of literary advice to princes with considerable authority. Lyndsay urged James to govern himself well, not just for James's own spiritual sake but also because the moral well-being of a head of state corresponded to that of the nation as a whole. This concept of the 'body politic' underlies Part One of Lyndsay's play *Ane Satyre of the Thrie Estaitis* (performed 1552 and 1554), in which King Humanitie, besieged by personified vices and virtues, learns to govern himself. Consequently, he can regenerate his country in Part Two, in which the allegorical world of Part One is grounded in contemporary reality. In doing so, Lyndsay directs medieval ideas regarding the head of state as the dominant part of the 'body politic' towards the concept of the 'commonweal', in which the monarch acts more in service of the community. The folk ballad of Johnny Armstrong, mentioned in Lyndsay's play, is a memorable reminder of such views. Its dignified tune lends force to the song's paradoxical argument that Johnny, a powerful Borders raider, has behaved as an exemplary caretaker of his community, in deliberate contrast to the treacherous king, James V, whose graceless command to execute Johnny is disloyal to the interests of the local commonweal. The clash between the interests of regional and national communities here leads to folk literature generating its own ideal image of the 'sovereign', in response to the imposition of a more distant monarch, who is represented as acting exclusively in his own interests.

Lyndsay's later verse reveals a similar interest in the regenerative role of monarchy, combined with the adaptation of chivalric to civic consciousness. Chivalric romance dominates the opening of *The Historie of Squyer Meldrum* (*c.*1550), but gradually Lyndsay turns Meldrum from a romance hero into an experienced magistrate. Chivalry is stripped to its core concepts – justice and public service – which are relocated within a civic vision of the commonweal. The knight, like the king, is changed from a chivalric role model into an exemplary figure, with 'nobility' now defined as an inward virtue rather than a matter of birth or martial achievement.

Lyndsay's emphasis on the commonweal was linked to his increasing alienation from the ecclesiastical establishment. Poems such as *The Testament of the Papyngo* (1530) and *The Tragedie of the Cardinall* (1547) illustrate that Lyndsay thought those appointed to exercise pastoral care had failed to do so and were the major culprits for the decaying moral state of the nation. This has often made critics label Lyndsay a Protestant, but recent studies have stressed Lyndsay's instinctive conservatism: a reformer rather than a Reformer, he was preoccupied with social stability rather than theology, preferring reform from within to any radical break-up of the existing order. As such, Lyndsay was part of a mid-century movement for compromise that tried to open up orthodox Catholicism to reform-minded ideas. Its desire to adapt existing formats – of government as well as literature – to new realities manifests a dynamic view of the world that drew on the creative potential of individuals to adapt to their environment on their own authority rather than refering everything back to prescribed categories. Thus, literature allowed people to re-interpret the relations between individuals and society 'in terms of the causal forces actually operating within [society]' (Ferguson 1997, 127). That such political concepts found confident literary expression indicates that Scotland was abreast of developments in humanist Europe. However, the Catholic church failed to provide the necessary reforms, and Lyndsay would probably have become a Protestant if he had lived beyond 1555. But it is even more likely that he would have stayed loyal to the Stewart monarchs. Loyalty to the monarchic commonweal often transcended – by absorbing – individual or confessional loyalties.

In Lyndsay's *Satyre*, too, writing shows an awareness of its own potential. The play is orchestrated by Diligence, who functions as master of ceremonies both within the play and to the audience. As such, Diligence is another 'narrator-protagonist' who blurs the boundaries between fiction and reality. Moreover, his role as royal messenger in the play mimics Lyndsay's official identity as the Lord Lyon, the king's chief herald, a position that itself complemented Lyndsay's literary capacity: as chief herald he communicated the monarch's narrative to the people; as a writer he presented the community's message to the king. The play thus connected its general injunction to observe moral integrity with a specific example of how writers can propagate this by using the pen to serve the commonweal. Reading and writing are virtuous undertakings on both the private and public level, with readers and audiences playing a vital role. Lyndsay frequently combined several contrasting genres within one work to create gaps in interpretation, which forces readers to ask themselves questions of what is read and of how they read, and to become aware of their own creative activity and underlying assumptions when reading. In other words, it questions their moral vigilance, with a humanist emphasis on observing the self and monitoring the relationship between its basic instincts and its own ability to reflect upon them.

Writers' interest in the individual and society (and relations between the two) thus interacted with their understanding of the nature and role of literature. But, while writers elsewhere were increasingly seen as uniquely gifted visionaries pursuing their own truths, Scottish culture continued to emphasise their socio-political dimensions as educators of both king and country. Thus, in James Wedderburn's prose *Complaynt of Scotland* (1549/50), Dame Scotia calls on her three sons (the three estates) to remedy the country's moral laxity and divisions, because these make Scotland defenceless against the scourge of the English. This dream-vision is framed by a lively description of Scottish shepherds engaged in music, dance and learned conversation in the archetypal setting of Renaissance pastoral verse. This sets a target for contemporary Scotland: the leisured life of 'new learning' – now called 'humanism' – in an ordered society. A work that similarly seeks private and public moral balances is the Latin prose dialogue *De animi tranquillitate* (1543) by Florence Wilson ('Volusenus') from Elgin. Written in France, its Renaissance-style dialogue frames yet another dream-vision, in which the dreamer embeds the classical injunction to 'know yourself' in its Christian counterpart, 'know your God'. This combination procures an inner assurance that underlies the self's happiness in the public domain, and thus the harmony of that public domain itself.

This humanist quest for personal and national peace counterbalanced contemporary forces of polarisation that have traditionally gained more attention. At Lyndsay's death, Scotland's new regent, Mary of Guise, held the centre ground between Protestants and Catholics, but Catholic reform was unable to stave off the Protestant Reformation. John Knox's voice comes into its own here, not looking for a humanist *via media* but seeking to impose an absolute alignment between private and public conscience along exclusively Scriptural lines. This challenged the contemporary literary dramatisation of individual consciences, in which private and public feelings did not necessarily run parallel. Yet Knox's writing betrays considerable literary skill. His preaching experience shows in his engaging narrative style and observant irony. Most crucially, in his *History of the Reformation* he represented himself in the third person. This self-fictionalisation separated his writing self from his historical self, thus skilfully manipulating readers' responses: Knox appears as a detached observer, but conveys his opinion through style and the orchestration of monologues and dialogues. Representing personal points of view as impersonal reportage, he effectively blurs the boundaries between propaganda, autobiography and historiography.

THE RISE OF THE LYRIC

The lyric, here defined as a short poem, often set to music, and expressing the feelings of a first-person speaker, accommodates both introspection and expression with reference to that speaker's inward thought. James V's personal reign coincided with the period in which Sir Thomas Wyatt introduced the sonnet and other forms of Italian Renaissance lyric at the English court; in these forms, increasingly, the first-person speaker is the author's thinly-veiled alter ego. This type of lyric made a lasting impact on the English – and thus British – cultural memory: in order to command service from her courtiers, Elizabeth I astutely used the way in which these lyrics propagated obedience to an unattainable, objectified female figure. In Scotland, however, the literary preoccupation with religious and ethical choices and the commonweal led to the prioritisation of narrative literature and historiography. Nevertheless, James V's two French marriages encouraged Scottish poets to take their cue from contemporary French lyricists. These did not embrace to the same extent the sublimation of sexual love and the abandonment of the male self to the female beloved – even if only in word and posture – that characterised Italian Renaissance writing. Another consequence of this different cultural emphasis was that Scottish lyrics tended to seek viewpoints on human passion outwith that passion itself in order to find stability and personal integrity. They are therefore less inclined to explore the fragmentation of self that passion can bring about. Away from comic genres, many Scottish lyrics, framed by the Christian ethos of northern humanism, cannot conceive of any distinction between morality and self that such a fragmentation might imply. Consequently, instead of sublimating love, a comparatively large number of these lyrics represent love as a physical phenomenon – either rejecting or embracing it as such – and frequently discredit love that requires surrender of the male self. This reflects an age of anxiety, in which the search for ethical coherence and tranquillity of the soul was as compelling an imperative as erotic fulfilment. However, because of scholars' Burckhardtian, dehistoricised readings of Elizabethan lyric, these extra dimensions of Scottish lyrical writing have been insufficiently acknowledged.

By 1550 there was a sufficiently sizeable audience to sustain the cultivation of a vernacular lyrical tradition even in the absence of a monarch. It consisted of urban circles of merchants, lawyers, crown servants, university graduates and secular churchmen, interacting with local lairds and a small number of aristocratic families close to the royal household. These networks, centred on Edinburgh but with connections across the country, were able to absorb and sustain literary impulses, bringing together court, church, town and gown. The Bannatyne Manuscript (1565–1568) reflects this audience. This substantial compilation is divided into separate sections of religious, moral, merry, and amatory poems, concluding with narrative tales. The poems of John Bellenden (a relative of the compiler, George Bannatyne) and Gavin Douglas frame the manuscript, and demonstrate its intention to present predominantly late-medieval material within a vernacular-humanist framework. Only the amatory section has a substantial selection of work by contemporary Scottish poets, which indicates Bannatyne's awareness of the conceptual importance of amatory lyric. However, many of the poems see love as a matter of self-governance: protection of the self's moral integrity frequently takes priority over erotic abandonment and sanctions the inclusion of misogynist verse.

The work of Alexander Scott, the poet whose work dominates Bannatyne's amatory section, exemplifies such lyrical practice. His lyrics frequently consider love either in physical terms or as a spiritual theme in the self's search for practical and ethical self-sufficiency. Scott developed Dunbar's ability to dissipate identity over a wide range of voices; Scott's works included, but went well beyond, the erotic. Thus, in keeping with his professional status as a musician in the Chapel Royal, Scott practised another introspective genre that characterises the spiritual anxiety of the age: metrical translations of the psalms. Devotional poetry showed the same desire for inwardness and coherence in the face of fragmentation as amatory verse; both helped to create a vernacular in which to express and discuss the self.

The Bannatyne Manuscript and the audience of *literati* associated with it emphasise responsible citizenship, serving the commonweal through virtue, self-governance and piety. Humanist and classical influences appear side-by-side with medieval vernacular narrative, devotional verse and love poetry. Their different responses to a rapidly changing world register a shift from a spiritual to a strategic interiority, i.e. to a private morality increasingly fashioned according to the worldly advantage gained by one's actions rather than their spiritual quality. The consequent ambiguities in public morality led to a fascination with masks and with personae who, in order to balance a range of contradictory identities and loyalties, develop a lateral resourcefulness, the ability to move around obstructions in unorthodox ways and not necessarily according to established morality. A fascinating example is the sonnet sequence in French attributed to Mary, queen of Scots, allegedly expressing her adulterous love for the earl of Bothwell. Whether the sequence was indeed hers is less important than noting that lyrical writing could be politically charged. It also indicates the stigmatisation of the female as the voice of illicit and irresponsible behaviour, discredited on account of its association with the lyrical mode and sexual passion. Mary's sonnets thus 'proved' Knox's *First Blast of the Trumpet against the Monstrous Regiment* [i.e. unnatural rule] *of Women*, which argued that women could not rule themselves, so should not be allowed to rule a godly society.

Due to such censure and to the civil war that followed the forced abdication of Mary in 1567, court lyric gave way to polemical street ballads, whose party-political and confessional shrillness only serves to offset the more impersonal, timeless quality of contemporary folk ballads. Away from politics, literature tended to hark back to a previous, more stable era: there were many reprints of late-medieval favourites, while new work, such as that of John Rolland, was written in the tradition of Bellenden and Lyndsay.

TOWARDS THE SEVENTEENTH CENTURY: DIVERSITY AT AND BEYOND THE COURT

The adult rule of James VI provided a national focus for literature again. To reconnect Scottish literature to international cultural developments, James in 1584 published his *Reulis and Cautelis* [Rules and warnings] *to be observit and eschewit in Scottis Poesie* (included in his *Essayes of a Prentise* [apprentice] *in the Divine Art of Poesie*), which encouraged courtiers to achieve prominence by writing poetry according to James's guidelines. These titles signal James's prescriptive impulse and his ambition to attain divine status as a king. The relationships between king, commonweal, subjects and advisers again impinge upon the world of letters here: James's ideas of kingship and the relations between the crown and its subjects collided head-on with those of his tutor, George Buchanan, whose *De iure regni apud Scotos* [Concerning the law of government among the Scots] (1579) asserted the right of the people to depose an inept or tyrannical ruler.

In this context, James's *Reulis* served both aesthetic and political purposes. It not only advanced James's cultural status both at home and abroad but also his hold on political life: by providing the blueprint for cultural expression, he was seeking to control who was allowed to participate in it and on what terms. He thus also sought to determine how his subjects represented their king and themselves metaphorically, so that they might sing from the royal hymn sheet rather than their own. Textual (self-)representation thus played a crucial role in the production of identity, and politics and literature purposefully come together in this linking of the art of poetry to the art of rule, fuelled by James's humanist conception of poetry as a form of rhetoric – a primarily intellectual rather than emotional medium. Thus, in contrast to Elizabeth's cultural politics, love poetry should describe an irrational state of mind rather than celebrate a woman's beauty or heterosexual desire in general. Similarly, James discussed, rather than promoted, the development of poetry from moral eloquence to divine, all-transcending inspiration that speculated about experience rather than just ordering it. In his courtier-poets such a style might trigger undesirable levels of self-authorisation. Instead, reason and self-government were the implied watchwords, inculcating a model of behaviour that would make a disparate body of subjects easier to control.

Although the *Reulis* specifically advocates art poetry, with learned Latin rhetoric informing several of its ideas, it emphasises the home-grown qualities of Scots verse. James's patronage attracted a new generation of poets who, encouraged by the *Reulis*, combined a tightly-woven plain style with metaphorical references drawn from classical as well as medieval, popular as well as courtly traditions, and exploited the poetic terseness of Scots to maximum effect by the use of alliteration and proverbs. Nevertheless, James realised the need for an invigorating injection of foreign influences and, apart from producing their own verse, James and his so-called 'Castalian' group of poets – a modern label – translated key Renaissance texts. Thus, William Fowler translated Machiavelli's *Il Principe*, and John Stewart of Baldynneis a French version of Ariosto's *Orlando Furioso*. In addition, Italian Renaissance influence grew in Scottish lyrics, notably via the sonnet. The whole Castalian output therefore reveals ethical and theological as well as aesthetic interests, illustrating how James's court, especially in the 1580s, provided a remarkably diverse cultural melange which articulated medieval and modern, native and foreign, Catholic and Protestant influences. Within this diversity, relationships between sovereign, subject and nation, and between different political and religious convictions, were negotiated.

James's 'maister poet', Alexander Montgomerie, embodies this rich variety of sixteenth-century post-Reformation Scottish literature. He was a Catholic convert from Ayrshire at the Protestant court in Edinburgh, where his king, taught by Europe's foremost humanist, George Buchanan (himself a prolific writer and translator), published a poetical manifesto. Montgomerie himself successfully combined highly stylised courtly poems with flytings (poetic contests) full of folklore motifs and scatological images. His political involvement, reflected in his verse, saw him fight on the Continent and spend several years in an English prison. His sharp tongue did not spare even the king, yet James publicly mourned his death, and Montgomerie's allegorical *The Cherrie and the Slae*, despite its author's well-known involvement in Catholic plots, was frequently reprinted in seventeenth-century Protestant Scotland. Most significantly, his best lyrics combine musicality with wit and substance of thought. They are unquestionably of international quality.

An important feature of the diversity of early modern Scottish literature is the increasing evidence of women as readers, dedicatees, bookowners or booksellers, revealing women's increasingly sustained involvement in literature. The key manuscript collections of lyrical verse in this period were compiled by women in lairdly circles. Out of such coteries the first women poets writing in Scots appear, notably Elizabeth Melville from Culross. The spiritual journey of her *Ane Godlie Dreame* (1603) became a seventeenth-century bestseller. Its allegorical dream-vision suggests an awareness of this format's previous use in Scottish literature for spiritual autobiography (as in *The Kingis Quair* and *The Palace of Honour*), while its prioritisation of sacred over worldly perspectives set the tone for many seventeenth-century texts.

Another important aspect of this literary diversity is its widening geographical spread. There is increasing evidence of smaller-scale literary coteries across the country, feeding off the main urban and royal centres (notably at Edinburgh and Stirling) to develop an urban-lairdly dynamic of their own. Culture in towns benefited greatly from churches, which often had song schools attached to them, some of which survived the Reformation. Thus, John Fethy and Alexander Kyd, churchmen whose verse features in the Bannatyne Manuscript, were musicians in the Chapel Royal and acted as song-school masters in Aberdeen and Edinburgh. Scholarly interaction with the Continent centred on the east-coast universities and towns that also acted as conduits for texts with Lutheran sympathies from the 1520s onwards. This helps to explain the role played by the Wedderburn brothers from Dundee in compiling the Protestant collection of *Gude and Godlie Ballatis* (1565). Aberdeenshire is also – together with the Borders – one of the areas where many folk ballads survived.

Drama played its part in this diversity, but again only if we apply contemporary, inclusive definitions of this literary genre. George Buchanan's mid-century Latin dramas, written whilst teaching in France, pointed the way forward in their adaptation of medieval theatrical practice and Christian themes to their classical equivalents. Moreover, they dramatise religious persecution and conflicts of conscience, stressing the importance of good counsel when one is forced to choose between heavenly and earthly authority – all core issues in humanist and Reformation Europe. The anonymous *Philotus* (not printed until 1603) is an attractive comedy following continental Renaissance examples. Its dramatisation of the transition of power from one generation to the next is particularly appropriate for a period of great change. Emily, its female protagonist, tries to make her own choices in an urban context in which love is subservient to sanctioned marital union. She is allowed to choose whom, not whether, to marry. Yet her choices, at least purportedly, come from within rather than solely from an exterior moral scheme. *Philotus* thus begins to use psychological motivation instead of 'extreme moral contrasts at the level of characterisation [to] produce clarity of moral guidance' (Jack 2001, 125), allowing the audience to engage directly with the characters. Finally, *The Monarchick Tragedies* (1604) of William Alexander, earl of Stirling, although ostensibly plays, were never meant to be performed. Their versified dramatisation of inward states of mind combined a moralising Protestant ethic with the vogue for Senecan closet drama. This fashion was short-lived, and this has alienated modern audiences from these texts.

THE IMPACT OF THE UNION OF THE CROWNS

The court's departure in 1603 and the subsequent scarcity of international influences left fledgling urban or aristocratic cultural initiatives largely defenceless against attempts by the church to impose its own conscience on cultural expression. The literary investigation of human existence based on worldly experience as well as literature written largely for aesthetic pleasure were considerably affected by contemporary religious sensibilities. Drama, dependent on patronage, audience and resources, was virtually non-existent; literary prose fared little better. Oral ballads continued to be enjoyed, though in popular literature religious energy left its mark, too. The church objected to the representation of identity as fissile, and therefore argued strongly against any *performative* relationship between the self and its cultural expression. That is, it rejected the notion that texts are a matter of role-play, advocating instead forms of writing that anchored the self or indeed any narrative firmly in the textual authority of Scripture. Humanism and divinity consequently became mutually exclusive. Scotland thus largely operated outside the main contemporary European literary paradigm, in which interaction between the sacred and profane allowed classical metaphor and humanist thought to be integrated with a Christian ethics that accommodated the pursuit of individual happiness. In other words, it did not evolve a literary culture that integrated difference by generating (whilst containing) a multiplicity of voices.

William Drummond (1585–1649) is this era's main poet. Unlike most men with courtly and literary aspirations, he did not follow James south but settled on the family estate at Hawthornden. His ability to absorb many influences yet to produce from them something manifestly his own endorses pre-modern notions of creativity. A key example is his adaptation of Europe's most prominent sixteenth-century lyrical genre: the amatory sonnet sequence. English writers turned this genre's originally quite philosophical investigation of male desire into practical erotic pursuit, but Drummond and other Scottish sonnetteers stuck closer to its original sensibilities by forcing their personas to confront the self-absorbed nature of their love. Contemplation of the female figure thus triggered an understanding of a much higher form of love – that of God. In other words, Scottish writers gave sensuous experience its place, too, but always within spiritual parameters. But the dominant religious spirit opposed this dynamic relationship between sacred and profane knowledge; only a small group of poets at isolated country seats pursued such modes of inquiry. Only Robert Ayton (1570–1638), who did move south, completely exchanged his native literature's religious emphasis for the urbane, witty 'Cavalier' style that became fashionable in the England of Charles I.

Literary writing thus contributed to Scottish culture from its margins, accentuating the stagnation at its centre. Nevertheless, in these margins women continued to increase their literary presence. A notable achievement was the verse translation of Petrarch's *Trionfi* in 1644 by Anna Hume. Her ingenious concision and witty glossing of the original text mark her own achievement as well as that of the Protestant plain style. Apart from writing themselves, women played a vital role in the preservation of oral ballads and were important cultural intermediaries as bookbuyers and 'patrons' of literary coteries or as students of music who compiled poetic anthologies.

Historiography now reflected religious affiliations. The two key contemporary national histories, by John Spottiswoode and David Calderwood, were both called *History of the Church of Scotland* (published posthumously in 1655 and 1678 respectively), one with an episcopalian bias, the other a presbyterian one. In (auto)biography the lively prose *Memoirs* of Sir James Melville of Hallhill (*c*.1535–1617) outline a sixteenth-century international courtly career, contrasting with the more sober but moving *Autobiography and Diary* of James Melville (1556–1614), one of the earliest examples of religious self-writing in prose. A new historiographical genre was family history: Richard Maitland's manuscript history of the Setons and David Hume of Godscroft's *History of the House of Douglas and Angus* (1644) were self-advertisements of noble families, who asserted their past prominence as loyal counsellors to the sovereign in order to secure their contemporary status and future role in society. Thomas Urquhart's translation of Rabelais's *Gargantua and Pantagruel* (1653) may still be the best available, but the linguistic exuberance that also characterises Urquhart's self-authored writing was too eccentric to spark many imitations. Readers instead appreciated its stylistic opposite: collections of proverbs. As compact cultural-didactic narratives, proverbs – like oral ballads – combined the vernacular's quality of expressive compression with the ability to pass on deep-rooted cultural values.

It was in sermons that pre-Restoration prose contributed most to the vernacular language of introspection and expression. The church was suspicious of literary effects, but in sermons the spoken vernacular was allowed to utilise the metaphorical resources of Biblical language. The best sermons strike a forceful balance between practical theology and plain-style Protestant rhetoric, their everyday diction and imagery mediating between individual experience and the deity. From the pulpit and through the medium of print they instilled a contemplative piety as well as a particular kind of literary vocabulary into the national psyche. However, their emphasis on the sinfulness of sensuous life limited their capacity to communicate the experiences of this world to their audience.

The lack of a language that integrated profane and spiritual experience within a centred self also affected William Lithgow's colourful travel writing and his lyrical reflection on his travels. Both convey the desire to have a home again and to confront the foreign. This echoed the sixteenth-century search for happiness and investigation of the unexplored, now operating within a divided Christianity and without a clearly defined political centre to hold extremities together. Moreover, Lithgow's persona travels to confirm a pre-disposed self, not to shape a new one through new experiences or observe ideas or himself through language. Like John Knox in his *History*, Lithgow's traveller already knows what he will discover (God's plan). What redeems both in literary terms is a narrative flair, maximising the vernacular ability to equate firmness of resolve with the truth.

Nevertheless, the marginalisation of 'creative' writing in the seventeenth century highlights a crisis in vernacular literature, which was losing its previous coherence of range, in which the popular, religious, learned and courtly had interacted within one continuum. Even the diversity of Drummond of Hawthornden feels like the testimony of a fading world. Significantly, some of the most up-to-date verse by Scots was written in Latin and published abroad (such as Ayton's, and the collection of *Delitiae Poetarum Scotorum*, Amsterdam, 1637). Scottish writing of this period lacked the interaction between different discourses that elsewhere made literary style the imprint of a thinking, assimilating mind. Its performance of voices was restricted to very particular areas of experience, which upset the earlier intimacy between author and audience as well as between the author and his art. Readers are often allowed only a passive or prescribed role, with explicit didacticism and verbosity frequently ousting any reliance on the imagination. Therefore, although there was more to seventeenth-century pre-Restoration Scottish letters than modern definitions of 'literature' have traditionally acknowledged, its diversity cannot prevent questions about its quality. Nonetheless, later cultural and intellectual currents drew some of their most distinctive characteristics from its internal tensions between civic humanism and Calvinism.

RESTORATION TO UNION

The increase in spiritual autobiographies and diaries which this period witnessed again indicates that the relationship between individual and community, often expressed through the relations of both of these to God, was central to early modern culture. This evangelical confessional mode of writing rejected absolutist royal authority because human claims to such authority were by definition idolatrous. However, the very act of autobiographical writing contradicts these texts' own professed losing of the self in God. Moreover, a conscience that derived its identity from a privately conceived deity represented an individuality that could exist only within itself, an intense rather than complex response to worldly experience. If one's relationship with God was intensely personal, how could one's writing about it be anything else? Nevertheless, the liberating and subversive edge to such thinking, among other things, allowed women to participate freely in such religious self-writing.

More generally, Scottish post-Restoration culture gradually returned to literary writing again, often looking back to the period before 1603. Drama – albeit intermittently – returned to Edinburgh. Even though there were few plays by Scots, plays provided a point of contact with international culture as well as an outlet for public performances of works which projected a secular selfhood. William Clerke's *Marciano* (1663) has effective comedy and individualised characters, but it fails to unite its tragic and comic plots and retains some of the less successful qualities of sixteenth-century rhetorical drama, due to the lack of a popular theatrical tradition. Similar defects apply to *The Assembly* (1692; no performances known), Archibald Pitcairne's inflammatory satire on presbyterianism. It dramatises worldly and religious individuals dealing with the same moral dilemmas, its linguistic wit providing moments of memorable comedy. However, rather than individualising protagonists or analysing the central conflict between religious and libertarian perspectives, the text represents worldly perspectives as by definition more valid than religious ones. It avoids rather than answers questions, exhibiting the characteristics of the very thing it parodies (the presbyterians' preference for dogma over inquiry) and thus undermines what it propagates (the concept of the gentleman, whose worldliness indicates experience and, thus, disinterested moral authority).

Sixteenth-century influences dominated contemporary lyrics because, in the absence of new material, these featured a felicitous combination of vernacular rhythms with their particular subjects. However, across such a time-gap this attempt to regain breadth of lyrical expression implied distance and loss rather than participation in a living tradition. Scots verse was becoming a matter of nostalgia. Thus, many sixteenth-century lyrics had survived in manuscripts preserved in country houses, and were for the first time printed with music (*Songs and Fancies*, 1662). However, the different prefaces and lyrical selections of subsequent editions (1666, 1682) indicate the fate of such older indigenous lyric: it was gradually being replaced by more recent English and continental material.

The work of George Mackenzie of Rosehaugh (1636–91) exemplified how Scottish writing could regain a more literary, international dimension again. His *Caelia's Country House and Closet* (1667) unapologetically propagated refined cultural expression, while his romance *Aretina* (Edinburgh, 1660) allegorised contemporary Scottish politics as well as echoing sixteenth-century civic concerns. Romance as a genre proposes that we consent, through our own free will, to be coerced, which Mackenzie parallels to relationships between the sovereign and the subject – a 'marriage' in which kingship, like love, should always be controlled by reason and avoid extremes. This is what Aretina (i.e. 'the virtuous one') represents, and what prompts the subject's obedience. Moreover, Mackenzie challenged readers to decode the underlying meaning *exactly* as Henryson and Douglas had done: 'albeit [romances] seem but fables, yet who would unkernel them, would finde . . . in them reall truthes . . . these kernels are best where the shells are hardest'. Such overlap in themes and textual practice underlines how Mackenzie, as a well-educated lawyer and a man of worldly affairs as well as of letters, was closer to the sixteenth than to the earlier seventeenth century. The leading part he played in establishing the Advocates' Library in Edinburgh in 1689 (now the National Library of Scotland) also demonstrates such a coming together of legal, literary and political discourses. The Library was initially meant as a resource for law students, but almost immediately upon its foundation expanded into other areas of knowledge.

Post-Restoration literature thus frequently picked up sixteenth-century issues, widening its resources through study of classical and foreign models together with Scripture. But the Glorious Revolution, the Union, and the Jacobite defeat in 1715 mark the gradual disappearance of pre-Restoration vernacular writing from active cultural memory. Once a flexible vernacular capable of expressing complex issues in any literary mode, Scots became perceived by the social elite as substandard. Yet this very decline triggered attempts at conservation, such as James Watson's *Choice*

Collection (1706–11) or Thomas Ruddiman's editions of Drummond, Buchanan, and Douglas's *Eneados*. To some critics such preservation reveals a confused cultural identity; others claim that it provided a cultural dynamic in which the continued identification of 'literature' with 'letters' more generally (a distinction explained at the beginning of this chapter) preserved a social engagement that is missing from 'literature' in the more exclusively aesthetic sense. At its best, the practice of seeing literature as both practical and aesthetic discourse, as both analysis and catharsis, allowed Scottish writers to speak with a particular authority.

This authority was partly derived from the fact that the Scottish monarchy was frequently in crisis in the very period when the sovereign provided the most important secular template for both individual and public identity, and for virtue, through which individuality could be absorbed into the community. Such identities were, moreover, disseminated particularly through textual representation. The collective image that elsewhere neutralised divisions within the nation and the individual (the monarch as both political body and model for an integrated self) in Scotland instead generated faultlines between past and present, Catholics and Protestants, male and female, and Scotland and Britain. Both individual and collective identities were thus left in a decentred condition of displaced or deferred identity, which has appealed to other cultures, especially in times when certainties were challenged. Taking account of this radical condition within an integrative study of history and literature improves our understanding of early modern Scottish culture.

REFERENCES

Broadie, A. 1990 *The Tradition of Scottish Philosophy*. Edinburgh.

Ferguson, A.B. 1997 ' "By little and little": The Early Tudor Humanists on the Development of Man', in Rowe J.G. and Stockdale W.H. (eds), *Florilegium Historiale. Essays Presented to Wallace K. Ferguson*, Toronto and Buffalo, 125–50.

Jack, R.D.S. 2001 'Renaissance and Reformation (1560–1660): Language and Literature', in Michael Lynch (ed), *The Oxford Companion to Scottish History*, Oxford, 124–7.

Reid, D. 1988 'Prose after Knox', in Jack, R.D.S. (ed), *The History of Scottish Literature. Vol. I: Origins to 1660*, Aberdeen, 183–97.

Scott, P.H. (ed) 1993 *Scotland. A Concise Cultural History*. Edinburgh and London.

FURTHER READING

Chambers, R.W. *et al.* (eds) 1938–41 *The Chronicles of Scotland Compiled by Hector Boece. Translated into Scots by John Bellenden 1531*, 3 vols. Edinburgh and London.

Coldwell, D.F.C. (ed) 1957–64 *Virgil's Aeneid. Translated into Scottish Verse by Gavin Douglas, Bishop of Dunkeld*, 4 vols. Edinburgh and London.

Cowan, E.J. (ed) 2000 *The Ballad in Scottish History*. East Linton.

Craig, C. (ed) 1987–88 *The History of Scottish Literature*, 4 vols. Aberdeen.

Dunnigan, S.M. 1997 'Scottish Women Writers c.1560–c.1650', in Gifford, D. and Macmillan, D. (eds) *History of Scottish Women's Writing*, Edinburgh, 15–43.

Dunnigan, S.M. *et al.* (eds) 2004 *Woman and the Feminine in Medieval and Early Modern Scottish Writing*. Basingstoke and New York.

Durkan, J. 1959 'The Cultural Background in Sixteenth-Century Scotland', *Innes Review*, 10, 382–439.

Edington, C. 1994 *Court and Culture in Renaissance Scotland: Sir David Lindsay of the Mount (1486–1555)*. Amherst, MA.

Findlay, B. (ed) 1997 *A History of Scottish Theatre*. Edinburgh.

van Heijnsbergen, T. 2004 'Paradigms Lost: Sixteenth-Century Scotland', in Macdonald, A.A. and Twomey, M.W. (eds), *Schooling and Scholarship: The Ordering and Reordering of Knowledge in the Western Middle Ages*, Leuven and Paris, 197–211.

van Heijnsbergen, T., and Royan, N. 2002 'Introduction', in van Heijnsbergen, T., and Royan, N. (eds), *Literature, Letters and the Canonical in Early Modern Scotland*, East Linton, vii–xxx.

Jack, R.D.S. (ed) 1978 *A Choice of Scottish Verse, 1560–1660*. London.

Jack, R.D.S. 1985 *Alexander Montgomerie*. Edinburgh.

Lyall, R. (ed) 1989 *Sir David Lindsay of the Mount. Ane Satyre of the Thrie Estaitis*. Edinburgh.

Lyall, R.J. 1993 'The Literature of Lowland Scotland, 1350–1700', in Scott, P.H. (ed), *Scotland: A Concise Cultural History*, Edinburgh and London, 77–98.

Lyle, E. 1994 (ed) *Scottish Ballads*. Edinburgh.

MacDonald, A.A. 1998 'Early Modern Scottish Literature and the Parameters of Culture', in Mapstone, S. and Wood, J. (eds), *The Rose and the Thistle. Essays on the Culture of Late Medieval and Renaissance Scotland*, East Linton, 77–100.

MacDonald, A.A. *et al.* (eds) 1994 *The Renaissance in Scotland. Studies in Literature, Religion, History and Culture*. Leiden.

MacDonald, R.H. (ed) 1976 *William Drummond of Hawthornden. Poems and Prose*. Edinburgh and London.

MacQueen, J. (ed) 1970 *Ballattis of Luve. The Scottish Courtly Love Lyric 1400–1570*. Edinburgh.

MacQueen, J. (ed) 1990 *Humanism in Renaissance Scotland*. Edinburgh.

McRoberts, D. 1962 *Essays on the Scottish Reformation*. Glasgow.

Mason, R.A. 1998 *Kingship and the Commonweal. Political Thought in Renaissance and Reformation Scotland*. East Linton.

Parkinson, D.J. (ed) 2000 *Alexander Montgomerie. Poems*. 2 vols. Edinburgh.

Reid, D. (ed) 1982 *The Party-Coloured Mind. Prose relating to the Conflict of Church and State in Seventeenth Century Scotland*. Edinburgh.

Shire, H.M. 1969 *Song, Dance and Poetry of the Court of Scotland under King James VI*. Cambridge.

Various authors 2001 'Culture', in Lynch, M. (ed), *The Oxford Companion to Scottish History*, Oxford, 116–33.

Williams, J.H. (ed) 2000 *Sir David Lyndsay. Selected Poems*. Glasgow.

Index